EVERY DAY WITH

A DAILY DEVOTION
FOR PERSONAL REVIVAL

WAVERLEY
ABBEY

ANCIENT SPARK NEW FIRES

Contents

Foreword

Every Day With Jesus has been helping people around the world to encounter God in a simple, accessible way every single day for more than fifty years.

Its author Selwyn Hughes – a son of the Welsh Revival – was a humble coal-miner who became a pastor and began writing these notes on postcards for the members of his church. Word spread, demand grew, printing became necessary, and before long *Every Day With Jesus* had become one of the very first daily devotions of its kind, reaching more than a million people each day.

The impact was astounding. Somehow these simple reflections, quietly composed in leafy Surrey at Waverley Abbey, and printed for many years as hard copy, reached the very ends of the earth. For example, in Nigeria so many people used *Every Day With Jesus* that, when Selwyn landed at Lagos airport, the president met him with a marching band! But the most moving stories are the testimonies from prisons where this resource is used to this day.

It's remarkable that Selwyn Hughes continued writing these notes every day for the rest of his life, even when his wife tragically died, followed by both of their sons. This is hard-won wisdom compiled for the first time in a single volume containing many of Selwyn's best, most insightful reflections.

If you're looking for something cool and contemporary, this book may not be for you (there are plenty of trendier devotionals out there on the market today). But if you're looking for accessible, seasoned wisdom from a humble, faithful friend of God, here in this book you are holding a time-tested guide to personal, daily revival.

Pete Greig
24-7 Prayer International, Waverley Abbey

JAN
— & —
FEB

Divine Discipleship

FOR READING & MEDITATION – 2 CORINTHIANS 3:1–18

'And we, who... all reflect the Lord's glory, are being transformed into his likeness with ever-increasing glory...' (v18)

As we begin this new year we shall think together about the nature of the spiritual journey we are making, and explore what is involved in our movement towards God. If I had been asked to consider this subject in the early days of my ministry, I would have said that the spiritual journey is different for everyone. I would even have argued that the Holy Spirit leads each individual in the way best suited to his or her personality, and concluded that there is no one method or strategy which the Holy Spirit uses in His dealings with people. However, after walking with Christ for over 60 years – much of which time I have been a minister and a counsellor – I have come to view things in a very different light.

Though we do not all travel along the road of discipleship at the same rate, I believe there is a divine pattern at work. In other words, while the Holy Spirit respects our individuality since every person is different, there are certain stages and experiences through which we must all go for spiritual formation to take place. The phrase 'spiritual formation' simply means God's creation of the image of Christ within us.

The apostle Paul, in Romans 8, says, 'For from the very beginning God decided that those who came to him... should become like his Son, so that his Son would be the firstborn, with many brothers' (Rom. 8:29, TLB). God is so excited about Jesus that He wants to make everyone like Him. It is the way God goes about the task of producing the image of Christ in us, and the stages we have to go through – stages which are common to us all – that we shall seek to discover as we start another year.

Father God, on this first day of a new year I ask that You will help me to journey with You. As I commit myself to You again, please provide all the strength and grace that I need to become more like Your Son. Amen.

FURTHER STUDY
Eph. 4:20–24; 1 John 3:1–3
1. What does Paul mean by being 'made new'?
2. As the children of God, what is our hope?

Are You Saved?

FOR READING & MEDITATION – LUKE 24:1–35

'Were not our hearts burning within us while he talked with us on the road and opened the Scriptures to us?' (v32)

We need to begin by considering the Christian life as a journey. One of the things some Christians fail to understand is that when we become followers of Jesus Christ we are just starting out on a journey. We are saved when, by faith, we receive the salvation God offers to those who believe that Jesus was sacrificed to take the punishment due to us. But saying we are saved may make it sound as if all the work has been done (and in a sense that is true, of course). Some people, therefore, think there is nothing more to do.

A group of Christians from a church which regarded clerical attire as inappropriate and a sign of liberalism were giving out gospel tracts. As they were doing so, they saw a minister wearing a clerical collar coming towards them. So one of them went up to him and said, 'Excuse me, sir, but are you saved?' With a twinkle in his eye the minister responded, 'Yes and no. If you mean am I saved from the penalty of sin, then the answer is yes. If you mean am I saved from the power of sin, then the answer is yes and no. The power of sin has been largely broken in my life, but there is still some way to go. If you mean am I saved from the presence of sin, the answer is most definitely no. That is something I wait for with eager anticipation. Now does that answer your question?' The young man felt duly humbled.

There is the tendency for some believers to view the Christian life in terms of making a one-off commitment and then observing certain obligations, such as praying regularly, reading the Bible, and being involved in a church. It is much more than that. We are on a transformational journey that will lead us to a deeper understanding of the Lord.

Lord Jesus, thank You that as I begin this year I know I am not alone because You are with me. As we journey together, open up the Scriptures to me, reveal Your glory and make Yourself known to me. In Jesus' name I pray. Amen.

FURTHER STUDY
Ps. 119:33–40; 2 Tim. 3:14–17
1. How does the psalmist link following God to His Word?
2. In what way is Timothy to be 'thoroughly equipped'?

A Gospel of Sin Management

FOR READING & MEDITATION – ROMANS 12:1–21

'Do not conform any longer to the pattern of this world, but
be transformed by the renewing of your mind.' (v2)

In his book *The Divine Conspiracy*, the Christian writer and professor Dallas Willard comments that for many Christians, 'The current gospel becomes a gospel of sin management'. In other words, Christians become preoccupied with the problem of sin that keeps occurring in their lives. This is an important issue, of course, but there is much more to the Christian life than that. He observes that, 'Transformation of life and character is no part of the redemptive message'.

Professor John H. Westerhoff says, 'No aspect of thinking on conversion is more foreign to… evangelical experience than this stress on conversion as a process. Evangelicals emphasise emotion and an initial movement… But… conversion is a continuous and lifelong process. Conversions proceed layer by layer… until the whole personality, intellect, feeling and will have been recreated by God.'

I have a little difficulty with Westerhoff's use of the word 'conversion'. As I see it, conversion is the entrance into the Christian life, and the continuation is sanctification. Of course, it could be argued that sanctification is really a continuous conversion, but let's not miss the point this writer is making, that as Christians we have embarked on a transformational journey during which we should be passing from one degree of glory to another. As Paul puts it in 2 Corinthians 3:18: 'But all of us who are Christians have no veils on our faces, but reflect like mirrors the glory of the Lord. We are transfigured, and the transformation comes from the Lord who is the Spirit in ever-increasing splendour into his own image' (Phillips).

Gracious and loving heavenly Father, thank You that You love me so much, and that by Your Spirit You seek to transform me into the image of Your own dear Son. Help me this day to receive Your transformational power. Amen.

FURTHER STUDY
John 17:13–19; 2 Thess. 2:13–15
1. How are the disciples to be sanctified?
2. How does Paul describe what it means to be saved?

The Long Walk

FOR READING & MEDITATION – JOHN 1:1–18

'From the fulness of his grace we have all received
one blessing after another' (v16)

Our Christian walk, we are saying, should be viewed as a transformational journey. As a young Christian I was told that having been regenerated by the Spirit I now needed empowering by the Spirit. Following the advice of my elders, I sought God for this empowering. The encounter with the Holy Spirit that followed completely transformed me. I asked the elders, 'What's next?' 'That's it!' they said. 'Now that you have the Spirit's power, go out and win souls.'

Thinking back to my youth, I recall how we would talk repeatedly about our conversion experience. Focusing on what Westerhoff calls 'an initial movement', we would try to recapture the emotion that went with it. The emphasis was on full-blown newness. We were led to believe that we had arrived as Christians in the time it takes to walk the length of the aisle following a call to accept Jesus as Lord and Saviour. Having walked to the front of the church as a sign of your commitment you are converted. What then? Do you just wait to go to heaven or do you fill the time as best you can? I set about keeping busy and almost became a workaholic.

Walking to the front of the church as a sign of your decision to follow Jesus can be a wonderful thing. Not so long ago I went back to the church where I was converted and stood on the spot where I found Christ. When the Spirit of God gripped me and I walked to the front of the church, what I didn't know, and no one told me, was that the walk didn't end there but would continue through the whole of my life. Have we been too focused on exuberant beginnings and victorious endings, forgetting the slow unravelling of God's grace that takes place along our journey?

O God, may I not forget the moment when You so wonderfully stepped into my life, but may I not forget either that You're not finished with me yet! Please work the wonder of Your grace in my life today and every day. Amen.

FURTHER STUDY
Ps. 138:1–8; Phil. 1:3–6
1. What is God's purpose for the psalmist's life?
2. Of what is Paul confident?

Microwave Christianity

FOR READING & MEDITATION – LUKE 15:11–32

'So he got up and went to his father.' (v20)

The idea that I was on a journey became clear to me when I was reading a book on spiritual direction. The writer said that there are three phases through which God takes us: the purgative phase (cleansing of sin), the illuminative phase (the revelation of God's Word), and the unitive phase (a closer communion with God). The realisation that I was on a journey – a transformational journey – revolutionised my whole way of thinking.

A story is told of someone who was quietly meditating. A visitor approached and asked, 'Why are you sitting here?' 'I am not sitting,' the person replied, 'I am on a journey.' And that is true of us also. So before we move on I would like to stress that the concept of being on a journey is key. Life is, to use the imagery of today's reading, about moving from the pigsty of self-rule to the outstretched arms of a loving Father.

It is interesting that the term used to describe Christianity in Acts is 'the Way' (Acts 9:2). This suggests movement. And the fact that we are on a journey indicates that our life is one of 'becoming', not simply 'doing'. It is a process of transformation.

There are different definitions of maturity, but to me it is a matter of whether a person is making good progress, to what extent they focus on the hope of the gospel and avoid being distracted by the attractions of the world, and how well established they are in the things of God. The trouble with many Christians these days is that they are in too much of a hurry when it comes to spiritual formation. Someone has called them 'microwave Christians'. They want everything to happen in a few minutes rather than being willing to take the slow, sure approach to transformation.

O God, help me this day to be totally focused on You and not distracted by the things of the world. May I be caught up with You in wonder, adoration, and praise. In the precious name of our Saviour I ask this. Amen.

FURTHER STUDY
Acts 8:26–35; 9:1–5
1. How was the Ethiopian changed on his journey?
2. How was Paul changed on his journey?

The Journey of Life

FOR READING & MEDITATION – DEUTERONOMY 10:12–22

'What does the Lord your God ask of you but to fear
the Lord your God...' (v12)

So what form does movement towards God take? Is it possible to gain a clear idea? Although every Christian is unique, there are some things that every believer has in common. Almost all the great saints of the past recognised that life is a journey, and that on the journey there are steps which every Christian must take. I have identified eight of these steps. That isn't to say there aren't more, but certainly not less. These are what might be described as the essential ingredients of soul-making which we must all experience to some degree if we are to move towards maturity.

The first of these is acceptance of the fact that we need to develop biblical holiness. While considering this subject, my mind went back to a very godly man who, during the early years of my Christian life, sat me down and said, 'Selwyn, do you realise God's primary goal for you is not to make you happy but to make you holy? It's not a matter of happiness first and holiness if possible. Holiness must come first and happiness will then be a consequence.'

I remember feeling somewhat intimidated by this statement. Holiness to me, in those early days of my conversion, meant dressing in dark colours, carrying a big black Bible, and having a grim, serious expression. Sadly, my attitude was something like that of the person who prayed, 'Dear God, so far today I've done all right. I haven't gossiped, I haven't lost my temper, I haven't been greedy, grumpy, nasty, selfish, or over-indulgent. I'm very thankful to You for that, but in a few minutes, God, I'm going to get out of bed, and from then on I'm probably going to need a lot more help! Amen.' How much I needed to learn!

O Father, I see that holiness is something I cannot have too much of – I cannot be too much like You or have too much of Your holiness. Lead me, guide me, empower me, for I long to draw as close to You as I can. Amen.

FURTHER STUDY
Isa. 35:8–10; 1 Pet. 1:13–16
1. Who will journey on the way of holiness?
2. Why does Peter urge his readers to be holy?

Ambassadors for Christ

FOR READING & MEDITATION – ISAIAH 6:1–13

'With it he touched my mouth and said, "See, this has touched your lips; your guilt is taken away and your sin atoned for."' (v7)

Throughout Church history all the saints have been of one mind on this issue: *because God is holy we must be holy too*. Holiness is, I believe, the first thing the Holy Spirit wants to impart to us as we set out on our personal spiritual journey, which brings us closer to God.

When we become Christians, God implants in each one of us a yearning to know Him better and more deeply. But much depends on whether we cultivate this yearning or simply ignore it. The prophet Isaiah speaks of this most powerfully. In the cry of the seraphim in today's reading, Isaiah learns the truth about God. The blinding glimpse of God's holiness creates in him the longing for holiness. He is held by this one desire – that the burning holiness of God would sear his soul and remove sin from his innermost being. Symbolically it is done. A live coal touches his lips and he is cleansed of his sin.

This same deep desire to be rid of sin, and the eagerness to pursue holiness, is, I say again, characteristic of all who long for a close relationship with God. It was there in the heart of the ancients and it is there also in the heart of the moderns, such as John Stott. In one of his writings Stott says, 'One of the God-appointed functions of the Holy Spirit is to make us know, feel, mourn, loath and forsake our sins.' It is evident that we are walking in holiness when we are no longer comfortable with sin. Sin becomes less attractive as we grow more attracted to God's ways, which are far higher than ours. Holiness is a sign that we have been set apart by God for His purpose. If we are to be Christ's ambassadors then our lives must be holy, otherwise we are misrepresenting Him.

Lord God, help me and teach me how to make holiness a way of life, as I, too, want to join with the seraphs declaring, 'Holy, holy, holy is the Lord Almighty.' Amen.

FURTHER STUDY
1 Pet. 1:17–21; Rev. 4:6–11
1. How does Peter say we are rid of sin?
2. Meditate on the songs sung in heaven.

Growing by Gazing

FOR READING & MEDITATION – PSALM 99:1–9

'Exalt the Lord our God and worship at his footstool; he is holy.' (v5)

As we journey together we spend another day considering what form movement towards God takes, and the fact that the very first step of our journey is the need to understand that God wants us to be holy. In the Bible the word 'holy' means 'separate' or 'set apart' – in other words, separated from sin and consecrated to God. God Himself is holy because He is distinct from His creatures and exalted above them, and also because He is pure and perfect and cannot have any communion with sin (see Hab. 1:13).

In the soul of every Christian there is something that responds to what is holy. Experience has shown me that the best way to understand holiness is to gaze steadily at Jesus Christ and consult one's heart and mind at the reaction one feels. Never did a human form hold One so pure, so adorable, so holy. Whatever degree of holiness is present in my life – and God knows how I lament the fact that I am not as holy as I ought to be or even long to be – it has come about not solely by poring over the Bible (though that has helped, of course), but through prayer and meditation and just gazing at Jesus.

This adoring contemplation of the Saviour has been called 'the secret of the saints'. Their biographies show them to be people who did not devote themselves to constant probing or asking endless questions. Instead they looked in love and longing at Jesus. And their holiness was a by-product of this contemplation. They grew in holiness as they grew in the steadiness and fixity of their gazing.

If ever the message of holiness was needed in the Church it is now. Have you been too busy in service, I wonder, to stop and enjoy the secret of the saints? Time spent with Jesus is never time wasted.

Father, I must search my heart this day and ask myself: Do I know what it is to serve a holy God? Have I received a vision of the moral majesty and purity of the One who is divine? Deepen my understanding of all this, I pray. In Jesus' name. Amen.

FURTHER STUDY
John 12:20–26; Rev. 1:12–18
1. What was Jesus' reply to those who wanted to see Him?
2. What did John see and what did he hear?

Boiled Alive

FOR READING & MEDITATION – EXODUS 3:1–22

*"'Do not come any closer," God said. "Take off your sandals,
for the place where you are standing is holy ground.'" (v5)*

In recent decades statistics show there has been a sharp decline in church attendance. Several possible explanations for this have been given, and one that strikes a chord with me is this: the Church has lost its prophetic edge due to a lack of teaching on the nature of God's holiness and the implications this has for our lives.

Research shows this emphasis has been missing from the Church now for many years, having been replaced by the one-sided proclamation that God is loving – and nothing more than that. A report concluded that many who used to attend church are filled with apathy; they no longer see any point in attending because the message they have been given is that 'God loves me regardless of whether or not I go to church or change my life' – so why bother? The report also pointed out that the low standard of Christian living is a consequence of the church community's failure to defend the faith and teach biblical truth, especially the truth that God is holy and said, 'Be holy, because I am holy' (Lev. 11:44). Yes, God is love, but He is *holy* love. It is important for us to remember that even though we are not saved by our works, we are saved to do good works and to live in a way that honours Him.

The Church in the UK is going through a phase that is best called 'gradualism'. Let me illustrate what I mean by telling you about a frog. When the frog was put into boiling water it understandably jumped out. But when it was put in cold water, and the heat was increased gradually, it adapted to the temperature until it was boiled alive! We are in danger of being brainwashed by the world – not only by its post-Christian ideas but also by its lifestyle.

O Father, if ever Your Church needed a fresh vision of Your holiness it is today. Fill our pulpits with prophets and teachers who have a knowledge of the holy, loving God. This we ask in Christ's precious name. Amen.

FURTHER STUDY
Exod. 15:11–13; Ps. 77:10–15; Phil. 2:12–16
1. Meditate on the holiness of God.
2. How are the Philippians to work out their salvation?

Almost Innocent

FOR READING & MEDITATION – JOSHUA 24:14–28

'Then choose for yourselves this day whom you will serve...' (v15)

In his book *The Great Divorce,* C.S. Lewis describes a young man who is tormented by a red lizard that sits on his shoulder and mocks him. The lizard represents indwelling sin, with which we all struggle. An angel promises to get rid of the red lizard and, for a moment, the man is joyful about this. However, as the angel begins to glow with a fiery heat, the man realises the lizard is going to be killed. He begins to have doubts and says, 'Maybe you don't have to kill it, maybe you don't have to get rid of it entirely.' He continues to prevaricate and wonders, 'Can't we do this another time?' The angel's response is to say, 'In this moment are all moments. Either you want the red lizard to live or you do not.'

Seeing the hesitation, the lizard begins to both mock and plead at the same time. He warns the man to be careful and tells him that the angel really can kill him, as he threatens to do. 'One... word from you and he will,' he says. 'Then you'll be without me forever.' In an attempt to persuade the man not to destroy him he promises, 'I'll be so good... I'll give you nothing but really nice dreams, all sweet and fresh and almost innocent.'

For Lewis, these words typify the tendency we all have to compromise and allow indwelling sin in our lives. 'It's almost innocent,' we say to ourselves as we try to justify holding on to the things we know are wrong but are reluctant to part with. And with such words we allow the lizards that torment us to live. Yet what seems almost innocent is, in fact, deadly. We are living in a day when holiness is a word that is missing in the Church's vocabulary. The situation is serious.

O God, may Your holiness reveal the insidious disease of sin that is deep within me. By the light of Your Holy Spirit please search me, know me, and help me surrender to Your great love today. Amen.

FURTHER STUDY

Ps. 139:23–24; Prov. 16:16–24; Rom. 6:19–23
1. What choices does Proverbs encourage us to make?
2. How does Paul describe being set free from sin?

Hardened Hearts

FOR READING & MEDITATION – EPHESIANS 4:1–19

'They are... separated from the life of God because of...
the hardening of their hearts.' (v18)

While we are thinking about holiness you might like to ask yourself what you consider to be the most significant text in the Bible. You might decide it is John 3:16, but many young adults will say Matthew 7:1: 'Do not judge, or you too will be judged'. There is, perhaps, an unrecognised tolerance of sin today. Youth workers and ministers have commented on the fact that young people can give themselves to mission and service but continue sleeping with their girlfriend or boyfriend. We are living in an age in which sin, as C.S. Lewis said, is regarded as 'almost innocent'.

In today's reading Paul says to the Ephesians, 'I tell you this, and insist on it in the Lord, that you must no longer live as the Gentiles do, in the futility of their thinking' (v17). The word 'insist', which can also be translated 'testify' or 'bear witness', shows how seriously Paul wanted them to take the warning not to follow the old way of life. We are walking along a different path, he tells them. You must not live like everybody else. What is more, he is insisting on this as one who lives in the Lord and has the authority of Christ.

The Gentiles were living in the futility of their thinking; they thought there was fulfilment in the way they were going, but there was not. What appeared 'almost innocent' would prove to be deadly. This darkened understanding was caused by their stubbornness and resistance to the things of God. They were given opportunities to change, but they would not change. The choices they made may have seemed almost innocent, but they resulted in hearts that were hardened. And hardened hearts alienate us from the life of God and bring about spiritual death.

Father God, may Your Holy Spirit keep my heart soft and my eyes always turned towards You so that the 'almost innocent' things will not enter my life and separate me from You. In Jesus' wonderful name I ask this. Amen.

FURTHER STUDY
2 Cor. 6:14–7:1; Heb. 3:12–14; 4:14–16
1. How can we perfect holiness?
2. How does the writer of Hebrews warn and encourage his readers?

Epidemic Numbness

FOR READING & MEDITATION – EPHESIANS 4:17–32

'They have given themselves over to sensuality so as to indulge
in every kind of impurity, with a continual lust for more.' (v19)

Our reading today warns us what will happen to those with hardened
hearts.

There's almost a biology lesson in these verses. When the heart ceases
to pump the spiritual blood in the way that it should because it has been
hardened by the wrong choices made, the mind becomes cloudy. It does
not function properly and the senses become numb. But we cannot live
that way, so the senses begin to call out for more and more because we
can't live in numbness. Since sin numbs us we try to get more of the things
we think will help, but in fact do not.

In our society today there are issues that are almost epidemic amongst
us. Thousands are hooked on pornography, gambling and other addictions.
We are living in an age when the inducements to sin are many, and they
crowd in on us from all directions. I remember hearing the story of a man
who, in the days of horse-drawn transport, advertised for a coachman for
his coach and horses. 'How close could you go to the edge of the cliff?' he
asked the coachmen. 'I could go within a foot,' said one. Another said, 'Six
inches,' while a third said, 'One inch.' A final applicant said, 'You wouldn't
find me trying to do anything of the sort. I would keep as far away from it
as possible.' Needless to say, the last man got the job.

The deadened soul requires a greater level of stimulation to arouse it.
This is the downward spiral of any addiction. Can this be proved? Consider
television dramas over the years. Programmes that were considered
shocking to an earlier audience are now regarded as relatively harmless.
What can seem almost innocent is, in reality, creating an addiction for
greater and greater forms of depravity.

**O God, help me to hide Your Word in my heart so that I might not sin
against You. Guard my spirit, soul and body so that I might be wonderfully
transformed into the image of Your dear Son. Amen.**

FURTHER STUDY

Gal. 5:16–23; 1 John 2:15–17

1. What transformation does life in the Spirit bring?
2. How does John describe life in the world?

Riding with Horses

FOR READING & MEDITATION – DEUTERONOMY 30:1–20

'I call heaven and earth as witnesses... I have set before you life
and death, blessings and curses. Now choose life...' (v19)

The writer John Eldredge says that holiness is sensitivity as opposed to numbness. It is being attuned to the godly desires that the Almighty puts within us as we receive Christ into our lives. Our problem, he says, is that we have grown accustomed to seeking life in all kinds of worldly pursuits and not in God Himself.

When we don't look to God as *the One who loves us perfectly*, we seek perfection in human relationships and are distraught when those close to us let us down. When we don't look to God for *our ultimate security*, we seek safety in power and possessions, and then we find that we continually worry about them. When we don't look to God for *our self-worth* then we try to seek it from others, and we end up manipulating people or withdrawing from them altogether.

Returning to C.S. Lewis's story of the red lizard, the man finally agrees to allow the angel to help, and the angel throws the lizard to the ground, dead. But when it hits the ground, an amazing thing happens; it turns into a stallion, and the young man rides away with great joy. What has been the ruler now becomes the ruled. What has ridden him, he now rides. It is C.S. Lewis's way of saying that when we deal with the sin in the way it should be dealt with – by killing it – then we know a joy and freedom that no amount of sinning could give us.

What does it mean to ride with the horses? We need to make the right decisions and we need to examine our lives for the presence of sin. If we are not asking 'Lord, what are the things in my life that are hardening my heart and so denying my mind the light of Your life?' then we are allowing ourselves to become terribly vulnerable to sin's deadly effects.

Heavenly Father, I know that Your eyes range throughout the earth to strengthen those whose hearts are fully committed to You. Give me the courage and strength to choose You this day. Amen.

FURTHER STUDY
Ps. 27:4–8; Rom. 6:1–7
1. For what does the psalmist seek?
2. What kind of freedom does Paul outline?

Don't Drink the Water

FOR READING & MEDITATION – MATTHEW 13:1–23

'For this people's heart has become calloused; they hardly hear with their ears, and they have closed their eyes.' (v15)

In my years of ministry I have noticed several types of people who are more likely to fall into moral error, including those who allow things that are 'almost innocent' into their lives. Slowly they widen the forms of entertainment they find acceptable and the degree of language they will tolerate, but this hardens the senses and creates a longing for more. We need men and women who are sufficiently courageous to say, 'I am going a different way'.

I once read about the sinking of the battle cruiser USS Indianapolis at the end of World War II. It was returning to the States following a mission to deliver enriched uranium to Allied forces in the Pacific. But it never made it home. A Japanese torpedo hit the cruiser and it sank within minutes. Of the 1,200 men aboard, 300 died. The other 900 went into the sea. After four days and five nights without fresh water only 316 of these men survived. Those who perished died because they drank the seawater despite medical officers, who knew the danger of this, remonstrating with them and telling them not to do so.

In Ephesians 4:17–19 – some verses we considered recently – the apostle Paul is trying to warn us of the danger of this world's waters. In effect he is saying, 'Don't drink the waters of this world. They might look inviting, and for a moment they will seem to slake your thirst, but in the end they will destroy you. Your minds will be deadened and you will have a lust for more.' Have you tried to slake your thirst by drinking the waters of the world? Don't close your eyes and heart to God. Listen to Jesus, who says this day, 'If anyone is thirsty, let him come to me and drink' (John 7:37).

Thank You, Lord Jesus, that You have given us the promise that streams of living water will flow from within anyone who believes in You. From this day forward help me to draw on Your streams of life. Amen.

FURTHER STUDY

Isa. 55:1–3, 6–7; 1 Pet. 2:1–6
1. For what should we thirst, according to Isaiah?
2. For what should we crave, according to Peter?

No Power Failure

FOR READING & MEDITATION – EPHESIANS 1:1–23

'I pray... that you may know... his incomparably great
power for us who believe.' (vv18–19)

Another stage on our spiritual journey, and the second aspect of our movement towards God, is developing an understanding of suffering. When we start to consider this matter we enter an arena that is strewn with the scalps of many a theological gladiator.

Over the centuries the problem of suffering has been debated endlessly. People struggle to reconcile the fact of a loving God with the existence of suffering. Studdert Kennedy, a chaplain in World War I, used to say that anyone who is not disturbed by the problem of suffering had either a hard heart or a soft brain. Kennedy was right. Everyone who believes in a God of love must wrestle with this difficult issue. It is, perhaps, one of the greatest problems in the universe. The difficulty of reconciling the issue of suffering with the teaching that God is love is said to have produced more atheists and agnostics than any other matter.

A book by Rabbi Kushner called *Why bad things happen to good people*, which I have mentioned in previous publications, argues that sin has so disrupted God's universe that although God is still love, His power has been diminished. He is no longer able to control things in the way He did before sin entered the universe. He would like to, He wants to – indeed, says the rabbi, His love yearns to do so. But because His power is limited, He is unable to do what He longs to do. Theologically, the rabbi is a million miles off the right track. God never experiences a power failure. Today's text is just one of countless verses in the Bible which show that God's power has not in any way been diminished by sin's presence.

Father, I realise that I am looking into the heart of one of the deepest mysteries of the universe – suffering and pain. Help me to believe that when You don't deliver me from suffering it is because You plan something better. In Jesus' name. Amen.

FURTHER STUDY
Ps. 66:1–4,8–12; 2 Cor. 4:7–12
1. How does the psalmist celebrate the power of God?
2. How is God's power undiminished by suffering?

Jesus – Our Overcomer

FOR READING & MEDITATION – REVELATION 19:1–10

'Hallelujah! Salvation and glory and power belong to our God...' (v1)

Yesterday we refuted the claim of Rabbi Kushner that sin has diminished God's power. Yet even though that power is undiminished there are times when He refrains from using it to deliver His people from difficult and distressing circumstances. And at such times He longs for us to trust Him. He has promised to give us the inner strength to go through whatever He permits. But this demands faith.

When Dr W.E. Sangster, the famous Methodist preacher, was a boy, he went to a camp. Soon he had spent all his money. So he sent a telegram to his father urgently requesting more. But he did not receive a reply. His friends teased him saying, 'Your father doesn't love you.' Sangster, however, knew that his father loved him. He said to his friends, 'I know I'm loved and I don't know why my father didn't reply. I'll simply have to wait until I get home and then he will tell me himself.' When he returned home his father explained that he was tempted to send some money. He thought, though, that maybe his son was not treating money with sufficient care and needed to learn its value. It was out of love, therefore, that he decided not to respond to his son's request. Later Sangster said the answer he gave to his friends was the answer he gave to everyone who asked him for light on the subject of suffering: 'I will wait until I get home and He will tell me Himself.'

Although we cannot explain fully why a loving God allows suffering, we know without any doubt that suffering plays a vital part in the development of the soul. Jesus promised us that we would suffer for our testimony to Him. 'In this world you will have trouble,' He warned (John 16:33). But remember, Jesus has overcome the world.

Lord God, may I never forget that Jesus has overcome the world. As I face this day let the truth settle in my spirit that whatever problems lie ahead, they are not as great as the power behind me. Amen.

FURTHER STUDY
John 15:26–16:4; Acts 4:27–31; 5:41–42
1. How did Jesus prepare His disciples for suffering?
2. How did the apostles react to suffering?

The Inevitability of Suffering

FOR READING & MEDITATION – JOB 5:1–18

'Yet man is born to trouble as surely as sparks fly upward.' (v7)

A surprising number of people believe God should spare those who are good-living from troubles. As I have said many times before, Oswald Chambers observed that 'Life is more tragic than orderly'. Chambers knew that unless Christians are willing to accept this truth, they will be plagued by 'oughts' and 'shoulds' that lead them down the road of illusion. They will find themselves saying, 'It ought not to be like this' or 'Things should be different' – and the only thing this kind of demanding attitude produces is frustration and anger.

The Fall has spoilt this world, and though much about it is still beautiful, accidents, calamities and suffering prevail. And these will continue to occur until the time when God brings all things to a conclusion. Though prayer does move God to work supernaturally in some situations, life will go on being more 'tragic than orderly' until Christ returns and finalises His plans for this fallen planet.

I do not question that God can and sometimes does intervene to save His children in particular situations, for one thing is sure: God is not restricted in the universe He Himself has made. The laws He has designed for the running of the universe are His habitual way of maintaining it, but He is perfectly capable of suspending those laws when He sees fit. Such an event we call a miracle. But miracles, by definition, cannot be the norm.

When Jesus hung upon the cross, the crowd cried, 'He trusts in God. Let God rescue him now' (Matt. 27:43). God did not deliver Him; *He did something better.* And it is along this line of 'something better' that we must search in order to find the Christian solution to the problem of suffering.

Lord Jesus, I am so thankful for the cross. What is my suffering compared to that? And even if I have to bear similar suffering, I know that out of it will come to me what came to You – a resurrection. Blessed be Your name for ever. Amen.

FURTHER STUDY

Acts 7:51–60; 12:11–18
1. What happened to Stephen?
2. What happened to Peter?

FOR READING & MEDITATION – PSALM 119:49–56

'My comfort in my suffering is this:
Your promise preserves my life.' (v50)

Suffering can be spiritual, emotional or physical. Let us consider emotional and spiritual suffering. What events in your life, I wonder, have taught you the most? What moments have made you who you are today – have flexed your courage and stretched your soul? What moments have taken you to the depths of yourself? Not the moments, I suspect, of ease and pleasure, but the things that have happened to you in the cold harsh winds of life. There is something about suffering that, even though we dislike it and try to avoid it, has the power to transform us.

Dr G. Campbell Morgan, a great British preacher of a past generation, was once asked what he thought of an up-and-coming young preacher. 'At the moment,' he said, 'he is a *good* preacher. When he has suffered he will be a *great* preacher.' History records countless testimonies of those who have plumbed the depths of emotional and spiritual suffering and yet claimed that they would not have missed the experience for the world.

In *A Twentieth Century Testimony* the writer and broadcaster Malcolm Muggeridge records how, surprisingly, he gained particular satisfaction from looking back on experiences which, when they occurred, seemed painful and distressing. Perhaps even more surprising is the fact that he claims that everything he had learned in life which had been of benefit had been through anguish and not through happiness. 'If it were ever possible to eliminate the cold hard winds of life,' he writes, 'the result would not make life delectable but make it too banal and too trivial to be endurable. Every happening... is a parable whereby God speaks to us, and the art of life is to get the message.'

My gracious Father, set me free today from the tyranny of trying to fathom the unfathomable. As I acknowledge Your sovereignty, please breathe Your calm and peace into my being. No longer will I struggle to understand – I shall just stand. Amen.

FURTHER STUDY

Ps. 3:1–8; Rom. 5:1–5

1. How does the psalmist react to his 'foes'?
2. How does the gospel make suffering productive?

A Wounded Healer

FOR READING & MEDITATION – HEBREWS 2:1–18

'It was fitting that God... should make the author of their
salvation perfect through suffering.' (v10)

Yesterday we said that even though we try to avoid suffering,
nevertheless it has the power to transform us. And it is often in those
moments of suffering that we learn most about ourselves and our faithful
God.

The first half of my Christian life was comparatively free from suffering.
Then my wife was struck with cancer. I remember sitting by her hospital
bed before she underwent major surgery and reading this: 'Try to exclude
the possibility of suffering which the order of nature and existence of free
wills involve, and you will find that you have excluded life itself. However,
perceiving a suffering world, we can be assured on different grounds that
God is good.' I sat and cried as I read these words. 'How could anything
this bad produce good?' I wondered. After several years my wife died.
Three weeks later my father also died. Some years later, I myself was
diagnosed with cancer and 'maturity onset diabetes'. And then, within the
space of just ten months, I lost my two sons – my only children.

Yet, as a result of all the emotional and physical suffering I have
experienced, I have gained a deeper compassion for those in need and
an increasing awareness that just as Christ was made perfect through
suffering – in other words, brought to the glory that God intended – so I
too, through suffering and submission to God, am being brought closer
to perfection and the fulfilment of God's plans for my life. What has that
done to me? It has transformed my life, deepened my message, given
me a sensitivity to others and a new note in my ministry. I am a wounded
healer. From experience I can say that though I have hated the pain, the
rewards of suffering are of infinite value.

**Lord Jesus, my suffering seems so insignificant when compared with what
You suffered for me. You turned Your pain to good account; help me to
strengthen myself in You to do the same. Amen.**

FURTHER STUDY
Phil. 4:10–14; Heb. 5:7–10
1. What secret did Paul learn?
2. What did Jesus learn from what He suffered?

FOR READING & MEDITATION – JOB 1:13–22

'At this, Job got up and tore his robe and shaved his head.
Then he fell to the ground in worship...' (v20)

Both teaching and personal experience show us that God uses suffering to bring us to holiness and spiritual maturity. If you study the Scriptures you will find that time and time again those who experienced suffering and difficult circumstances developed a far closer relationship with God and a much greater trust in Him. From experience I know that whatever character has been built up in me, whatever of Christ's love and compassion flows through my life, it has largely come about through suffering.

In the early days of my ministry I was wonderfully delivered from sickness by a miracle. While I was a pastor in Sheffield I was given just a few days to live. However, I was healed, and subsequently I became a healing evangelist and held crusades at which wonderful miracles took place. I was determined to combat sickness, attacking it with force and fury. But the years have given me a different perspective, and some might say a loss of faith. God can and does heal, and indeed it is right to pray for this, but not everyone experiences healing and I have developed a deep concern for people who don't.

Often I have asked myself: what should be my attitude to suffering? After much thought on the matter I have become convinced that it should be one of worship. I am always challenged when I read the opening chapter of the book of Job. After receiving the tragic news of the death of his servants, sons and daughters, and the loss of all his possessions, today's text tells us that Job fell on his knees and worshipped. Have you noticed that there is often an indefinable something about people who have suffered? They have a fragrance that reminds one of the meekness and gentleness of Christ.

O Father, is it really possible that You give us grace at such a moment? It is written in Your Word – and so I must believe it. May I, like Job, accept all suffering with grace and not a grudge. In Jesus' name I ask this. Amen.

FURTHER STUDY
Ps. 4:1–8; 2 Cor. 1:3–7
1. How does the psalmist respond to distress?
2. How does Paul worship in a time of trouble?

Bitter or Better

FOR READING & MEDITATION – 1 PETER 4:1–19

'Therefore, since Christ suffered in his body, arm yourselves
also with the same attitude...' (v1)

Over the years I have spent a great deal of time studying the Psalms, and what is remarkable is that even if the psalmist begins by venting his anger on God for allowing bad things to happen to good people, he almost always concludes with worship.

I wish I could tell you that this was my reaction when I lost the four close members of my family in death. Even though I cried out in prayer, I am afraid it was a long time after each event before I could kneel down and worship. Yet I am much more blessed than Job. He knew only the God of the crocodile (Job 41:1); I know the God of the cross. I have to admit that despite fully accepting the idea that there is meaning behind suffering, I still have some way to go in the matter of responding correctly to it.

John Stott says, 'I sometimes wonder if the real test of our hunger for holiness is our willingness to experience any degree of suffering if only thereby God will make us holy.' I wonder too! Being a Christian does not exempt us from suffering. Have you ever noticed how the same thing can happen to two different people yet have an entirely different effect upon them? Sorrow and suffering will make some bitter while it makes others better. A similar situation but with opposite effects. The difference is our attitude.

There were three crosses set up on a hill outside Jerusalem 2,000 years ago. The same sentence had been passed on three different people. One thief was contemptuous because Jesus didn't save Himself and them. Another thief was contrite and saw his tragedy as a result of his own behaviour. The third, of course, was Jesus, from whom flowed compassion. And in the midst of His pain He saved a dying thief (see Luke 23:39–43).

O God, how I long to respond to the problems in my world in the way that Job responded to his. May I never forget that You are my refuge and strength, an ever-present help in trouble, and may I live in the light of that truth today. Amen.

FURTHER STUDY
Mark 14:32–36; Jas 1:2–7
1. How did Jesus face His time of trial?
2. How does James counsel those who face trials?

Soul-Making

FOR READING & MEDITATION – PSALM 103:8–18

'For as high as the heavens are above the earth, so great
is his love for those who fear him...' (v11)

Our theme is the nature of the spiritual journey. Even though we don't travel the path at the same speed, there is, as we have said, a divine pattern at work to bring about an experience of spiritual transformation, and one aspect of this pattern is suffering. Does God heal and free us from our physical suffering? Yes He does, but sometimes He does not, for reasons known only to Himself. As I mentioned two days ago, I was once healed when I had just days to live. But in more recent years I have also suffered sufficiently severely to make me doubt God's previous intervention.

When nobody suffers, nobody cares. Lighthouses are built out of drowned sailors; maimed motorists widen roads. C.S. Lewis used the wonderful term 'soul-making' in connection with this observation: 'I have seen men for the most part grow better, not worse, with advancing years.' Suffering is not good in itself, but can contribute to our good when used by God.

Suffering helps cure us of the illusion of independence. There are limits to the understanding of the human mind. We may investigate the nature of disease, its causes, incidence, symptoms, and cure, but no laboratory will ever witness the discovering of its meaning and purpose. In my opinion, one of the reasons why God has not revealed to us the mystery of suffering is to keep us proud mortals humble. Our broad horizons are so narrow in God's eyes, our vast knowledge so small to Him. Even the wisest human mind is so limited in His sight. Like Job, our attitude to suffering should be one of worship and humble self-surrender – not a grovelling obsequiousness, but a sober humility.

Heavenly Father, I can allow the disappointments of life to either move me towards You or away from You. Help me to commit myself and all that I have into Your hands – holding nothing back. In Jesus' name. Amen.

FURTHER STUDY

Acts 3:11–16; 1 Pet. 5:1–7

1. What is Peter's reaction to the healing of the lame man?
2. Meditate on Peter's teaching on sober 'humility'.

God is Good

FOR READING & MEDITATION – 2 CORINTHIANS 11:16–32

'Five times I received from the Jews the forty lashes minus one.
Three times I was beaten with rods, once I was stoned...' (vv24–25)

When we are struggling to understand why God permits suffering we should climb the hill called Calvary and from that vantage point survey all life's tragedies. The cross does not solve the problem of suffering, but it helps us to put it into the right perspective.

Perhaps few of us realise there is biblical evidence that God not only suffered in Christ, but that God, in Christ, suffers with His people still. Is it not written that during the days of Israel's bitter bondage in Egypt God saw their oppression, heard their groaning, and was concerned about His people (Exod. 2:24; Acts 7:34)? Did not Jesus ask Saul of Tarsus, 'Saul, Saul, why do you persecute me?' (Acts 9:4), thus disclosing His solidarity with His Church? Jesus shares in our suffering. We may say that suffering is unjust. But life is not just. At the heart of the Christian faith there is a cross, and that is the world's supreme injustice. We live in a sin-stained world.

In today's reading Paul highlights some of the injustices he experienced. However, he allowed those hardships to make him more dependent on God. 'In all things God works for the good of those who love him,' he said (Rom. 8:28). The happening itself may not be good, but God works in it to bring about our eternal good. Like two cog wheels that work together, God actually uses evil for the destruction of evil. He uses devil-inspired evil for the making of God-inspired men. He turns defeats into victories. That is the power of the cross. In the Lord's presence, I have learned that even in suffering God is good. We are able, as C.S. Lewis says, to look at suffering and God's goodness and see them as being without contradiction.

Lord Jesus, bring me to that wonderful place at the foot of Your cross where I see Your suffering, and by Your Spirit please provide the power to turn injustice into something of spiritual benefit. Amen.

FURTHER STUDY

1 Pet. 1:3–9; 2:21–25

1. From what vantage point does Peter view suffering?
2. How is Jesus our example in suffering?

Blessings or Blisters?

FOR READING & MEDITATION – PSALM 41:1–13

'Even my close friend, whom I trusted, he who shared my bread,
has lifted up his heel against me.' (v9)

So far on our journey together we have considered holiness and the issue of suffering. Now we move on to the issue of interpersonal relationships.

The spiritual journey is not one that we are meant to walk alone. God intends us to travel in the company of other people. For some this is a wonderful arrangement; for others it is not so wonderful. People can be helpful or they can be hurtful; they can bless us or they can blister us.

Over the years I have met many people who have been hurt by other Christians. Sadly, in recent years we have frequently heard the term 'friendly fire'. Have you ever been hit by a form of 'friendly fire'? It is the flak we take from our own side. It is the misguided missile that lands right in our own hearts. People have admitted to me that they have been more hurt by the Church than they have ever been by the world. As we see from the psalm we have read today, King David knew this pain, and Jesus quoted this verse when He said, 'He who shares my bread has lifted up his heel against me' (John 13:18).

The question we must start to think about is how do we deal with relationships, because the way we deal with difficult relationships will determine whether we advance or retreat on the journey of life. Some people live by the words of Ernest Hemingway, who said, 'We have to distrust each other; it is our only defence against betrayal.' God does not call us to live in distrust, but to live by faith in Jesus Christ. We are disciples of the One who knows what it is to be betrayed. And through His grace we can be victors, and not victims.

Father, may I grasp this truth that I cannot act in isolation, for I am bound up with my redeemed brothers and sisters. Help me experience an ever-growing consciousness of this important fact. In Jesus' name. Amen.

FURTHER STUDY
Gen. 45:1–8; Matt. 18:15–22
1. What helped Joseph to be a victor rather than a victim?
2. What did Peter learn about forgiving his brother?

We Are Not Alone

FOR READING & MEDITATION – GENESIS 45:1–25

'Then he threw his arms around his brother Benjamin and wept,
and Benjamin embraced him, weeping.' (v14)

When I first became a Christian this chorus was popular: 'On the Jericho road./There's room for just two,/No more and no less./Than Jesus and You./Each burden He'll bear,/Each sorrow He'll share./There's never a care/When Jesus is there.'

The impression this gave me was that the Christian walk was with Jesus alone. So I had a great surprise when I discovered that by receiving Jesus into my life I inherited His family also, and that I was to relate to the members of His family in the same way that I was to relate to Him. The difficulty was that some of them were awkward, some irritating, and some downright obnoxious. However, the interesting thing was that the more I related to them, the more real God became to me. How does that work?

A well-known missionary named Norman Grubb explained it like this. Imagine, he said, that you have been brought up in a house with walls but no doors or windows, and you have lived this way for 30 years. There is, however, a hole in the roof through which you relate to God. Then one day you hear voices beyond the walls, and you wonder if there is anyone like you out there. Inspired by the voices, you push on the walls. They fall over, and you stand there now with no walls and no hole in the roof. Instead everything is as wide as the horizon.

Norman Grubb's point is that as you make the effort to relate to others you discover that your relationship with God is widened. You see that God is bigger and grander and greater than you had previously realised. You gain a clearer understanding of God.

O God, in this delicate, difficult, but delightful business of getting along with other people, help me to gain the skill, insight, and patience I need. May I relate to others in the way that You relate to me. In Christ's name I ask it. Amen.

FURTHER STUDY
Rom. 14:5–12; Phil. 4:2–7
1. How does Paul say we should handle our differences?
2. Meditate on what it means to 'agree in the Lord'.

FOR READING & MEDITATION – 1 THESSALONIANS 3:1–13

'May the Lord make your love increase and overflow
for each other...' (v12)

Yesterday we finished by saying that as we make the effort to relate to others we discover our relationship with God is widened. Let us think a little more about how this works.

It is my belief that God has so arranged our lives that as we relate to one another in our horizontal relationships, our experience of Him deepens. I have found that the better I relate to others in the Church, the better I relate to God. Human relationships have brought God closer to me.

This is something I discovered in my marriage also. I once came across this statement made by the great Reformer, Martin Luther: 'Marriage is God's best way of explaining Himself.' That intrigued me. I thought, What does he mean? Then it came to me. And the understanding of what he was saying transformed my marriage, and the marriages of others with whom I have shared my discovery in different parts of the world. There are certain facts we know about God. One of them is that God is love. Nothing can change that. But God is intangible, invisible and inaudible. We can't reach out and put our arms around Him, or feel Him hug us, or hear His voice audibly in the same way that we hear a human voice. So is that all we are left with – a statement that God is love?

No. The greatest way, of course, in which God has demonstrated His love for us was by sending His Son to die for us, as verses such as John 3:16 and Romans 5:8 make plain. But 1 John 4:12 tells us that God's love is also seen in our love for others – in fact, it is perfected in us. God intends our relationships to be the means by which we give each other a much clearer picture of His own love for us.

Lord God, thank You that You are love – not distant and detached but pure and passionate. May I experience that love today, and love others with Your love. Amen.

FURTHER STUDY
John 15:9–17; Eph. 5:22–32
1. How did Jesus define our love for each other?
2. How does marital love 'explain' God?

Making God More Real to Others

FOR READING & MEDITATION – 1 JOHN 4:1–12

'No-one has ever seen God; but if we love one another, God lives
in us and his love is made complete in us.' (v12)

At present we are focusing on the fact that when we relate to others
in the way that God intends, we enable them to have a clearer
understanding of God's own love. Every Christian can know that he or
she is wonderfully loved by God at all times. This is an incontrovertible
fact – nothing can be added to it and nothing can be taken away from it.
There is, however, a lot we can do for one another to add to the *feelings*
associated with that fact.

Look at it like this: as we said yesterday, God is intangible and invisible.
We, however, are tangible and visible. We are able to see, touch and hear
each other. As physical beings we relate to one another in a way we do
not relate to God, and in a way that God does not relate to us. When you
are feeling spiritually low or disconsolate and I move towards you with
genuine care and concern, when I talk with you, smile with you or cry with
you, when my entire body language demonstrates to you that I care, then,
although these things cannot add to the fact that God loves you, they can
add greatly to the *feelings* that go with that fact. God doesn't come to you
and talk to you in an audible voice or put a warm hand on yours when you
are in need of support – but I can.

God has made me as a physical being, and He has made you in the
same way too. And when I need support, you can give it to me. Together
we can make the invisible God more real to each other, and bring about in
each other's lives an experiential awareness of what it means to be deeply
loved by Him. Seeing this clearly and entering into it fully makes the task
of rightly relating to others not a mere duty but a delight.

**O God, the realisation that I can bring to my brothers and sisters a deeper
understanding of what it means to be loved by You utterly overwhelms me.
But I see that it is true. Help me to make You more real to someone today.
In Christ's name. Amen.**

FURTHER STUDY

1 Cor. 13:1–7; Eph. 4:29–5:2

1. What does love look like?
2. What does imitating God involve?

Sandpaper People

FOR READING & MEDITATION – PHILIPPIANS 2:1–18

'Each of you should look not only to your own interests,
but also to the interests of others.' (v4)

Today we hear many stories of disunity and disagreement within churches.

Francis Schaeffer made the comment that God has given the world the opportunity to see His face. How sad it is when this does not happen. There are in life what might be termed 'sandpaper people'. Their sole ministry, it has been said, is to develop patience in others! We have to admit there are those who are better loved from a distance! Some people are downright difficult. Yet God tells us that we are to love them because this is the way in which He intends us to relate to one another. This old rhyme speaks clearly on the matter: 'To dwell above with saints in love,/ My, that will be glory./To dwell below with saints we know,/Now that's a different story.'

There is no doubt that interpersonal relationships are fraught with difficulties. The miserable minor jealousies which afflict local churches are so familiar to those who have any contact with them. Pettiness can be found in nearly all walks of life. It astonished a mentor of mine, when training for the ministry, 'that scholars, nigh to being "world authorities" on their subject, belittle each other in private with the spleen of chorus girls'!

If I were to go to my bookshelves and pick up, at random, one of the many biographies I possess of the saints of the past, I can almost guarantee that somewhere in the pages I would come across paragraphs recounting their difficulties with relationships and how they sought to overcome them. Many of these notable Christians tell how, even though they inherited a difficult and passionate temperament, they allowed God's grace to work in their lives until they overcame such hindrances to their spiritual growth as pettiness, temper, and lack of consideration towards others. And we can too.

O Jesus, I long with all my soul to learn the art of loving relationships. I want to think love, feel love, and act love. Indeed, I want to become love, for I see that it is as I do so that I live. Help me, dear Father. In Jesus' name. Amen.

FURTHER STUDY

Rom. 12:3–8; Gal. 5:24–6:5
1. How should we show consideration for each other?
2. How are we to 'fulfil the law of Christ'?

The Essence of Reality

FOR READING & MEDITATION – JAMES 2:5–26

'If you really keep the royal law found in Scripture, "Love your neighbour as yourself," you are doing right.' (v8)

What, then, is the divine purpose behind relationships? It is, I believe, to enable us to understand the essence of reality. Let me explain. Some years ago I heard Larry Crabb make reference to a quotation from a book entitled *The Everlasting God*, written by D. Broughton Knox, in which the author says, 'The Father loves the Son and gives Him everything. The Son always does that which pleases the Father. The Spirit takes of the things of the Son and shows them to us... We learn from the Trinity that relationship is of the essence of reality and therefore of the essence of our existence, and we also learn that the way this relationship should be expressed is by concern for others.'

That statement made by Knox, especially the phrase *relationship is of the essence of reality*, brought about one of the greatest paradigm shifts in my thinking I have ever experienced. Before I read what Knox said about the Trinity I used to believe that truth is of the essence of reality, but here a reputable theologian was saying something quite different. The more I considered it, the more right it seemed. For days I reflected on it and, looking back, I can see how that one insight changed my approach to God, to people, and to the whole of my work for the Master.

As I pondered this new truth I came to see that the energy which pulses at the heart of the Trinity is other-centred. Each member of the Trinity is more concerned about the others than He is about Himself. Movement towards God, I am convinced, involves learning to relate to others in the way the Persons of the Trinity relate to one another – in true other-centredness.

Loving heavenly Father, may I live according to Your design and be more concerned about others than I am about myself. And by doing so may I witness to You. In Jesus' name. Amen.

FURTHER STUDY
Rom. 12:9–13; 1 Cor. 12:4–7; Gal. 5:13–15
1. How should we express our love for each other?
2. How does the 'energy' of the Trinity relate to our 'common good'?

The Art of Loving

FOR READING & MEDITATION – ROMANS 13:1–10

'Let no debt remain outstanding, except the continuing
debt to love one another...' (v8)

Relationships, as we well know, are more easily talked about than entered into. In my early years on the Christian pathway I regarded other people as the cause of many of my problems. But then I realised that relationships do not so much cause problems as reveal problems. The problems in my relationships were caused not so much by the way others treated me but by the way I reacted to them. The major problem was not other people, but myself. One of the greatest challenges of my life has been to consider others as more important than myself. Nowhere do I have a greater opportunity to demonstrate other-centredness than in my relationships, in moving in love to those I might even dislike.

Dr E. Stanley Jones defined Christianity as 'the science of relating well to others in the spirit of Jesus Christ'. He also said that 'we are as mature as our relationships'. Unless we learn to relate to others in the way the members of the Trinity relate to each other – in other-centredness – we may well find our union with God somewhat blocked.

C.S. Lewis described the Church as a laboratory in which we have the opportunity to fine-tune our relationships. There we learn to love as we have been loved. As we come in contact with people we have an opportunity to practise the art of loving which, we said yesterday, is of the essence of reality. We are to relate to people, not on the basis of how they relate to us, but on how Christ relates to us. 'Love one another. As I have loved you, so you must love one another,' Jesus instructed (John 13:34). That's the third element of our spiritual journey. We are to love others as we love ourselves. And, as we do so, we will find we are moving closer to God.

Gracious Lord, if it is true that I am as mature as my relationships then help me to make my relationship with You the strongest relationship in my life. For then I know that everything good will follow. Amen.

FURTHER STUDY
Eph. 4:11–16; Col. 3:12–17
1. What contributes to our unity and to our maturity?
2. Describe the lifestyle of God's chosen people.

Living in the Light of Eternity

FOR READING & MEDITATION – COLOSSIANS 1:1–7

'... the faith and love that spring from the hope that is
stored up for you in heaven...' (v5)

The fourth aspect of the spiritual journey that we shall consider, and again one that was recognised by all the great saints of the past, is *learning to live life in the light of eternity.* I once heard it said that a journey is only as good as its ending. Without a happy ending that draws us on in eager anticipation our journey can seem futile. We may find ourselves saying, 'Is this all there is? Is this as good as it gets?'

Followers of New Age teaching believe that life is a never-ending cycle of birth and death. What a dismal prospect. If I believed that I would be most disconsolate. The apostle Paul felt the same. 'If the dead are not raised, "Let us eat and drink, for tomorrow we die,"' he said (1 Cor. 15:32). Our hearts cannot live without hope. Gabriel Marcel says that 'hope is for the soul what breathing is for the living organism'. God's Word declares, 'These three remain: faith, hope and love. But the greatest of these is love' (1 Cor. 13:13). That may be so, but faith and love depend on hope; it plays a vital role.

Our courage for the journey so often falters because we have lost our hope of heaven – our journey's destination. Take away the hope of arrival in heaven at the end of our journey and our journey becomes no more than a death march. A.J. Conyers sums up the current situation when he says, 'We live in a world no longer under heaven.' Most of the emotional problems we struggle with, he claims, arise from that fact. Much of the rage and deadness that simmers just beneath the surface of our Christian façade has a common root: we live in this world and have no expectation of the world to come.

Gracious Father, wonderful though this world may appear, help me to keep heaven clearly in view. May the prospect of heaven influence all my living here on earth. In Christ's name I pray. Amen.

FURTHER STUDY
Matt. 6:19–21; Heb. 11:5–10
1. What does Jesus teach us about true investment?
2. What motivated the heroes of faith?

A Life Without Hope?

FOR READING & MEDITATION – ECCLESIASTES 3:9–22

'He has also set eternity in the hearts of men...' (v11)

C.S. Lewis once said, 'If I find in myself desires which nothing in this world can satisfy, the only logical explanation is that I was made for another world.' Shouldn't we therefore devote ourselves to gaining a vision of the end of our journey and picture our destination as vividly as we can? After all, 'If only for this life we have hope in Christ,' Paul told us, 'we are to be pitied more than all men' (1 Cor. 15:19).

During a service a pastor asked the children how many wanted to go to heaven. All but one of them raised their hands. 'Don't you want to go to heaven when you die?' the pastor asked. 'Oh, when I die,' the young boy said. 'I thought you meant right now.' Perhaps we don't think enough about the end of our journey because the images we have of heaven are shaped by pictures of strange, sickly-fat babies fluttering with tiny wings, or bored saints lazing on shapeless clouds, strumming harps and wondering what's happening back on earth.

The philosopher Peter Kreeft believes the crisis of hope that afflicts the Church today is a crisis of imagination. Our images of heaven, he says, are dull, platitudinous and syrupy, therefore so is our faith, our hope, and our love of heaven. Dullness, not doubt, he claims, is the strongest enemy of our faith, just as indifference, not hate, is the strongest enemy of love. There are so many things that excite me about going to heaven: intimacy, adventure, beauty, joy. In fact heaven is so wonderful that, as Paul writes, 'No mind has conceived what God has prepared for those who love him' (1 Cor. 2:9). And we too will be perfect, in other words, our souls will be what God wanted all along.

Heavenly Father, I am thankful that I have not been left to my own subjective feelings when it comes to this matter of heaven. The Word of Your Son has settled it for ever. And though I may lose faith in my feelings, I can never lose faith in Him. Amen.

FURTHER STUDY

John 6:25–35; Phil. 3:12–16

1. According to Jesus, what contrasts with the 'food that spoils'?
2. How does Paul describe his future hope?

Upwards Towards Heaven

FOR READING & MEDITATION – HEBREWS 12:1–12

'Let us fix our eyes on Jesus, the author and
perfecter of our faith...' (v2)

On the matter of living in the light of eternity, the eighteenth-century American theologian Jonathan Edwards said, 'This life ought to be spent by us only as a journey towards heaven.' And that journey will end in unutterable joy. That's the only story worth living in now. The road stretches ahead of us and our destination awaits us. In the imagery of Hebrews, a race is set before us, and we must run it for all we are worth.

To get the sense of what the writer to the Hebrews is saying it is helpful to read Eugene Peterson's paraphrase of verses 2 and 3 in *The Message*: 'Keep your eyes on *Jesus*, who both began and finished this race we're in. Study how he did it. Because he never lost sight of where he was headed... he could put up with anything along the way... When you find yourselves flagging in your faith, go over that story again... that long litany of hostility he plowed through. *That* will shoot adrenaline into your souls!' Jesus remembered where He was heading and with all His heart He wanted to get there. Without a sense of where we are heading we will not run well.

Most of us are fortunate in that we have family and friends who love us, but even they may let us down. When they do we have several options. We can retreat into cynicism and deaden the pain through self-pity, saying to ourselves, 'That's the way life is. I guess I'll just have to put up with it.' Or we can become demanding and manipulate them into giving us more attention. Or we can remember that the day is coming when we will all live in perfect love. We can let the ache lead us to think more deeply and turn our eyes upwards towards heaven.

Lord Jesus, thank You for making clear to me where my real home is and how I can get there. Help me to keep my eyes fixed on You, the Author of life – a life that will last for ever. Amen.

FURTHER STUDY
Matt. 7:7–14; John 16:25–33
1. How does the direction of our lives determine our destiny?
2. How does Jesus describe His departure?

Forgetting to Remember

FOR READING & MEDITATION – DEUTERONOMY 4:1–14

'... watch yourselves closely so that you do not forget the things
your eyes have seen or let them slip from your heart...' (v9)

One of the greatest challenges that we face on our journey towards heaven is forgetfulness. The human heart is crippled by forgetfulness. If you are a long-time reader of *Every Day with Jesus,* you may remember that in other editions I have written on this matter of keeping eternity in view. How often do your thoughts turn to heaven? God has doubtless spoken to you many times; how many of those occasions do you remember? Over the years I have had several encounters with God – enough to provide a lifetime of conviction. So why don't I live more faithfully? Because I forget.

When I read the story of the golden calf recorded in Exodus 32 I am humbled. The Israelites had seen so many astonishing things happen. They had witnessed the ten plagues, the deliverance from Egypt, the provision of manna. They drank water from a rock (Exod. 17:1–7). And, at Mount Sinai, they gazed in awe at the terrifying spectacle of lightning and heard loud claps of thunder and a loud trumpet blast – signs of the presence of the Lord which made them tremble in their sandals (Exod. 19:16). Yet, despite all this, when Moses disappears into the mists that mantled the mountain top to receive God's laws, they blow the whole thing in a wild bacchanalian party. How could they be so foolish? How could they forget everything they had received from the hand of God?

Our memories are short, and we easily forget what we should remember. Dr Martyn Lloyd-Jones commented that we would even forget the Lord's death if it weren't for the reminder provided by the Communion Service. Spiritual amnesia is so likely that, from Genesis to Revelation, the Bible is full of calls to remember.

My Father and my God, help me to remember at all times that this world in which I live is just my temporary home because my real home is in heaven. How I praise You that a place has been secured for me there by the blood of the Lamb. Amen.

FURTHER STUDY
Deut. 4:23–31; Heb. 4:1–11
1. What does God remember and what do we forget?
2. What are the lessons of the Israelites' wilderness journey?

Going Somewhere?

FOR READING & MEDITATION – JOHN 13:1–17

'Jesus knew that the time had come for him to leave
this world and go to the Father.' (v1)

If, as we were saying yesterday, we are so prone to forget things, how do we reclaim the memories we should be treasuring for our life's journey? The writer to the Hebrews answers that question in the verse we looked at two days ago: 'Fix [your] eyes on Jesus' (Heb. 12:2). Rehearse the story of Jesus, go over it bit by bit. The story of Jesus Christ is at the heart of the Bible. We should ensure that we become familiar with the Gospels which tell us what Jesus did and what He said, and not get sidetracked by studies on the management techniques of Jesus or the marketing methods of Jesus or some other topic of current interest. And just what is it the writer to the Hebrews wants us to remember? What does he want us to concentrate on in order to follow our Master in the race ahead? How did Jesus sustain His heart in the face of brutal opposition? *He never lost sight of where He was heading.* Jesus had a vision of the future that was grounded in the past.

At the beginning of the story of the washing of the disciples' feet we are told that Jesus knew He had come from God and that He was returning to God. He remembered where He had come from and where He was going (v3). And so must we. We too have come from God – though not in the same sense as Jesus, of course. But as Charles Wesley expresses it in this verse: 'Away with our fears!/The glad morning appears/When an heir of salvation was born!/From Jehovah I came,/For His glory I am,/And to Him I with singing return.'

It is only as we realise that our time on earth is a journey, and keep our destination in view, that we will truly capture a sense of what this life is all about. You see, my friend, there is an end to this journey, and the end for those who have committed their life to Jesus Christ is both wonderful and glorious.

O Father, how exciting it is to be reminded that though I am a loyal member of the country and community in which I live, my real citizenship is in heaven. May heaven's laws govern everything I do. In Christ's name I pray. Amen.

FURTHER STUDY
Luke 13:31–35; 1 Pet. 5:1–11
1. What did Jesus' prophetic vocation mean to Him?
2. How does Peter describe the rewards?

This World is Not My Home

FOR READING & MEDITATION – 1 CORINTHIANS 2:1–16

'As it is written: "No eye has seen, no ear has heard...
what God has prepared for those who love him..."' (v9)

Jesus is the Author and Finisher of our faith (Heb. 12:2, KJV). He enables us to finish what He made it possible for us to begin. He will not forget us even though we forget Him, and He will give us reminders on the way. 'The world is fairly strewn', wrote Annie Dillard, 'with unwrapped gifts and free surprises... cast aside from a generous hand'. What gifts has He dropped your way?

When our eyes are focused on our future in heaven then one of the consequences is that the material things which so many crave have little appeal for us. The seventeenth-century Puritan Thomas Watson said, 'The world is but a great inn, where we are to stay a night or two, and be gone; what madness is it to set our heart upon our inn as to forget our home.' Those who keep heaven in view regard material possessions as no more than the furnishing of an inn. After all, we are only staying for the night.

With a mind set on God and a heart aflame with supernatural love, those who move close to God can sing:

This world is not my home, I'm just a-passing through,
My treasures are laid up somewhere beyond the blue.
The angels beckon me from heaven's open door,
And I can't feel at home in this world any more*.

Malcolm Muggeridge once said that from the time he was a boy he had a sense of being a stranger in this world, and that there was a world beyond this to which he felt he was moving. He wrote, 'The only ultimate disaster that can befall us, I have come to realise, is to feel ourselves to be at home here on earth. As long as we are aliens we cannot forget our true homeland.'

Gracious and loving heavenly Father, may I grasp the fact that this world is just an inn at which I am staying for a short while. Please help me to keep my eyes fixed on the home You have prepared for me in heaven. Amen.

* Jim Reeves, *This World Is Not My Home*. Lyrics © Sony/atv Tree Publishing.

FURTHER STUDY
Luke 12:13–21; 2 Cor. 5:1–5
1. What makes rich men foolish?
2. How does Paul view his death?

Eyes Focused on Heaven

FOR READING & MEDITATION – HEBREWS 9:11–28

'For Christ did not enter a man-made sanctuary...
he entered heaven itself...' (v24)

Heaven is our home; it's where we *belong*. That truth is something we should keep in mind all the time. Now I know that some will disagree with this statement and say a preoccupation with heaven will lead us to become so heavenly minded that we are no longer any earthly good. However, some of the greatest social reformers of the past – John Wesley, Lord Shaftesbury, William Booth, for example – were God-intoxicated men who always had heaven in view. They worked better down here on earth because, by faith, they always had a vision of the perfect end. To talk and think and look forward to heaven is not a sign of an escapist mentality – providing that is not *all* we think about.

I cannot claim to have kept heaven before me during all the days of my Christian life. There was a time when I would read the apostle Paul's words in Philippians 1:22–24 in which he tells his readers that as far as heaven was concerned he was *eager* to go but, for their sake, *willing* to stay, and I would say to myself, 'I am *willing* to go but *eager* to stay.' For the past third of my life, however, my thinking has been different. I am now willing to stay but *eager* to go. And the anticipation of what awaits me thrills me as I begin each new day.

'The happiest people on earth,' someone has said, 'are those who keep their eyes focused on heaven.' The psalmist wrote, 'You have made known to me the path of life; you will fill me with joy in your presence, with eternal pleasures at your right hand' (Ps. 16:11). Joy will be found when we get to heaven through realisation, but it can also be found now by anticipation.

O Father, when I think of all the God-intoxicated people who, down the ages, worked so effectively on earth because they were sure of heaven, I know that I want to be found among their ranks. May I serve You with all my heart. Amen.

FURTHER STUDY
Acts 2:22–33; 2 Pet. 1:10–15
1. Reflect on how Jesus fulfils the psalmist's aspirations.
2. How does Peter live in the light of eternity?

Inconsolable Longings

FOR READING & MEDITATION – ISAIAH 55:1–13

'Why spend money on what is not bread, and your
labour on what does not satisfy?' (v2)

Clearly, as we have been seeing over the past few days, most people, if they only allow themselves to feel it, experience the sensation of not being quite at home in this world because something very important awaits them elsewhere. The writer Aldous Huxley said, 'Sooner or later one asks even of Beethoven, even of Shakespeare... "Is this all?"' This has been described as 'the inconsolable longing... news from a country we have never visited.'

You don't need to be a Christian to experience what I am talking about. Augustine, the Christian philosopher and writer of the fourth and fifth centuries, spoke about having this perception long before his conversion. C.S. Lewis struggled hard and fought against the idea that the source of his 'inconsolable longing' and the God of traditional religion might be one and the same. Of his search for God, Lewis said, 'They might as well talk about the mouse's search for the cat.'

This prompts a question which we now turn to and must pursue over the next few days: If it is true that a longing for heaven has been built into the human heart, how does the great mass of humanity go about dealing with it? One way is to pretend this mysterious aspect of our existence does not exist. It is a strange fact of life that this aspect of human nature – the soul's deep sense of homelessness – is not studied more intently. I wonder why. Perhaps it's because it fits none of the usual categories of thought. It can't be labelled, sorted, explained or matched, so men and women make a detour to avoid it and treat it as if it wasn't there. But this detour is really a denial.

My Father and my God, though it seems strange to me now that people should want to make a detour to avoid this fact, I am aware that prior to meeting You I did the same. How glad I am that I have found what my soul truly longs for. Amen.

FURTHER STUDY

Ps. 63:1–8; Heb. 11:13–16

1. What characterises the psalmist's desire?
2. In what ways were the faithful forward-looking?

Sit Quietly Before Mystery

FOR READING & MEDITATION – PSALM 46:1–11

'Be still, and know that I am God...' (v10)

We continue with the question we started to consider yesterday: If it is true that a longing for heaven has been built into the human heart, how does the great mass of humanity go about dealing with it? One way, as we saw, is to make a detour to avoid it – to avoid it and go in some other direction. Another way, however, is to face the fact that there is an inconsolable longing in the heart but to reduce it to something classifiable and explainable. When human beings are unable to find an explanation for some matter they have a tendency to fit it into a category for which they do have an explanation. This brings it into the sphere of manageability.

Dr Larry Crabb, a Christian and a psychologist, frequently stresses this point in his writings. 'Instead of sitting quietly before mystery,' he says, 'we try to bring it into the area of manageability. What fools we are.' When we do this then it should not surprise us that the phenomenon we are talking about gets a little damaged in the process. William Kirk Kilpatrick, another psychologist, says of such an attempt, 'It is like trying to fit a size twelve shoe into a size four shoebox, or trying to stuff a bird of paradise into a canary cage. Once you cram it in there it won't look like a bird of paradise any more.'

This passion to explain matters is our way of bringing them under our control. We feel less helpless and vulnerable when we are able to manage things than when we have to sit quietly before mystery. But the affairs of the soul cannot always be managed; they are best handled by coming quietly before God in private prayer.

O God, much that is within me is a mystery. But help me to be more concerned with knowing You than knowing myself, for in knowing You I shall better know myself. In Christ's peerless and precious name I pray. Amen.

FURTHER STUDY

2 Sam. 7:18–29; Ps. 131:1–3

1. How does David respond to God's word to him?
2. Reflect on the analogy the psalmist uses.

Crisis of Confusion

FOR READING & MEDITATION – PSALM 28:1–9

'The Lord is the strength of his people, a fortress of
salvation for his anointed one.' (v8)

Today we continue on our journey of faith and movement towards God. We are looking at the things that I want to suggest to you are non-negotiable issues – those that are vital in soul-making. In order to have a soul that is continually being transformed into the image of Jesus Christ, these steps and stages that I am sharing with you are, I believe, essential.

This brings us to another topic. Everyone who walks the path of faith will sooner or later come face to face with this issue of *mystery*, which we touched on yesterday. People have often asked me, 'Why can't God make His purposes clear to us and relieve us of a great deal of uncertainty and anxiety?' The path we are called to walk is often shrouded in mystery and confusion. So why doesn't God explain in advance and in detail what is going to happen in our lives? Now if God did this for us it would save us considerable anxiety, but it would also deprive us of one of the greatest contributions to soul-making – the development of faith and trust. This is what brings our Master joy: when we trust Him implicitly even though we have no answers. Some of the answers might not come until the next generation. But be assured – God is at work.

Confusion and mystery, I found as a pastor, are the issues that create such great problems for the people of God. Often people would come to me and say, 'Selwyn, I am so confused by what God is allowing to happen in my life.' They would then tell me all about it, embarking on a story of circumstances that were so perplexing I could see no answer to them. And all I could do was to sympathise.

Father, I see how crucial this issue is. Help me to deal with any doubts that may be circulating in my mind. May nothing create distance between You and me because I long for closeness. I am listening, dear Father. Continue leading me on. Amen.

FURTHER STUDY
Ps. 37:1–9; Rom. 15:7–13
1. How does this psalm help us confront perplexing events?
2. What sustains Paul's trust?

Exercising Muscles of Faith

FOR READING & MEDITATION – PSALM 55:1–23

'Listen to my prayer, O God... hear me and answer me.' (vv1–2)

Have you ever asked yourself, 'Why doesn't God speak to me?' The difficulty is that silence can cause us to panic and we demand a response. Yesterday I mentioned those who have shared with me the confusion they felt over events in their lives. Often, a little while later, these same people would put forward some far-fetched answers and attempted explanations. This happened many times. After much thought and prayer I was given what I believe is an understanding of this predicament.

Living comfortably with confusion and mystery is not easy. It erodes our sense of competence. We like to feel we are in control. We feel better when we know what is going on and we know what to expect. We like to have answers for everything mysterious because walking in the dark is disturbing. So *any* answer is better than none. Many people will accept glib explanations because it provides them with a way out of confusion; it provides something to hold on to. Since we don't like to be in the dark, we seek to replace confusion and mystery with understanding. Let's face it: few of us handle ambiguity well. This desperate desire to be in control makes us cling to the illusion that if we search hard enough we will find answers. We are unwilling to brave the fog of confusion, and fail to see that it is often in the midst of massive confusion that we have the opportunity to build the muscles of faith and trust.

The truth is that God has not chosen to answer every question we ask, but He has promised, 'Never will I leave you; never will I forsake you' (Heb. 13:5). Whatever your situation or circumstance, strengthen yourself in God today for He is with you.

O God my Father, help me to have an unshakable confidence in Your character. Even when I am perplexed, may I cling to Your promise to be with me at all times. In Jesus' name. Amen.

FURTHER STUDY

Hab. 1:13–2:4; 2 Cor. 12:7–10

1. What answer does Habakkuk find to his complaint?
2. What answer does Paul receive?

My Life in God's Hands

FOR READING & MEDITATION – JOB 13:6–24

'Though he slay me, yet will I hope in him; I will surely
defend my ways to his face.' (v15)

As we were saying yesterday, when we are disturbed by confusion we embark upon a search to try to reduce the sense of mystery. Will the answer be in the next sermon or book? Will we settle for superficial explanations? I repeat: the truth is that God has not chosen to answer every question we ask. It all revolves around this important issue of trust.

But trust is not easy. Perhaps one of the greatest evidences of our ability to trust is our willingness to walk on in the darkness. Can we trust God? One measure of trust is how deeply we relate to God and are prepared to live without answers. Answers are not essential; trust is. In this world in which we live there are many voices similar to those of Job's so-called friends offering supposed answers and explanations. Though we find it hard to trust God, it is vital that we do so.

How deeply do you trust God? A little or a lot? In today's text Job declares, 'Though he slay me, yet will I hope in him.' He had come to that place of deep reliance on God, which was powerful. That's the place we, too, can come to. In the midst of mystery and confusion we can say, 'I see no sense in this, but I know that God, the Architect of this universe, has my life and times in His hands.'

Did Jesus, in His earthly ministry, ever have to battle with such thoughts? We may never know. But if He did, His faith in His Father's purposes would have overwhelmed any doubts and despair. It can be that way for us also as we place our lives into the care of the One who has promised, 'I will not forget you! See, I have engraved you on the palms of my hands' (Isa. 49:15–16). God can be trusted. Take that step of trust today.

Gracious and loving Father, help me to focus on the things that You want me to be concerned about and leave all other matters to You. Bring me to that place of calm, confident trust that Job rested in. In Jesus' name. Amen.

FURTHER STUDY
Ps. 31:1–8; Luke 23:39–49
1. What fortifies the psalmist?
2. How does Jesus echo the psalmist?

The Word Within

FOR READING & MEDITATION – JEREMIAH 20:7–13

'O LORD, you deceived me, and I was deceived... I am ridiculed
all day long; everyone mocks me.' (v7)

If all 150 of the psalms included in the spiritual songbook we know as the book of Psalms were songs of joy then the book would not be true to life. A close examination shows that the psalms of complaint, confusion, doubt and heartache significantly outnumber the psalms of joy. The book of Psalms invites us to feel the emotion of uncertainty and confusion that has no resolution. To experience that puts steel into our souls.

Reading through the psalms we see the psalmists constantly being overwhelmed by what they cannot control or change. Yet their cry of desperation opens them to the development of a faith and a trust that holds them fast in the midst of everything. And though they do not have answers, they have God.

Notice this: God allows us to express our feelings. In the passage we have read today we find Jeremiah expressing his thoughts and feelings of confusion without being rebuked. He accuses God of deceiving him, failing him and of bullying him. His words sound blasphemous. Will the Almighty let him get away with it? God does not respond.

As Jeremiah reflects on the clear call that came to him in his youth and the word that God gave him to speak, something begins to burn within him. It is the message that God gave him. His hurt and confused feelings scream out within him, but God's Word screams louder. He had allowed God's Word to penetrate his being to such an extent that in the moment of overwhelming test it was the divine Word that cried out the loudest. Similarly, if we allow God's Word to live and take root within us, when our hurts and frustrations scream within, God's Word will burn in us, and we, too, will hear His message above the tumult.

My Father and my God, let Your Word so penetrate and permeate my being that when my emotions scream within me Your voice will be heard above the tumult. This, I ask, in our Lord's precious name. Amen.

FURTHER STUDY
Ps. 119:25–32; 2 Cor. 4:13–18
1. What is the effect of God's Word?
2. What is the source of Paul's faith?

God Questions

FOR READING & MEDITATION – JOB 38:1–20

'Where were you when I laid the earth's foundation?
Tell me, if you understand.' (v4)

For one more day we deal with this unsettling issue of mystery. Now that Job has taken his confusion to God, we find God giving him an audience. And God has questions of His own which He puts to Job.

In the closing chapters of the book of Job you can see these questions coming one after the other. The interesting thing is that God never does answer any of Job's questions. Instead He reminds Job of His incomparable power, seen in the world He has created. When God has finished speaking to him Job says, 'My ears had heard of you but now my eyes have seen you' (42:5). Something happened to Job in this dramatic encounter with God. It was as if God had said, 'I will not give you answers, but I will give you something infinitely greater – I will give you *Myself.*' Job experienced a new revelation of God; he gained an understanding of the Deity that enabled him to continue living despite his questions going unanswered.

Job's longing for answers to his questions ceased when he discovered God drawing near to him. And once he had entered into a personal relationship with God he found that knowing God closely and powerfully meant that his mind was at peace. What is more, we too, by God's grace, can walk in the dark knowing that God is good. Mystery and confusion are part of our spiritual journey, and their purpose is to increase our trust in God. Though we are big enough to ask the questions, God knows that we are not necessarily big enough to understand the answers. And so, as our confidence in Him increases, we learn to trust Him even when we cannot trace Him. Our faith grows stronger and more powerful.

Father, thank You that in the presence of mystery You do not necessarily give answers, but You do give Yourself. That is better than any answer. I would far rather have You, and no answers, than to have answers, but not You. Amen.

FURTHER STUDY

Isa. 40:25–31; Jonah 4:1–11

1. In Isaiah, what aspects of God's character do His questions reveal?
2. What aspects of His character does God reveal to Jonah?

A Change of Mind

FOR READING & MEDITATION – ACTS 2:29–41

'Repent and be baptised, every one of you, in the name of
Jesus Christ for the forgiveness of your sins.' (v38)

Another important step on the journey of faith is *to come to a clear understanding of repentance*. When asked what they understand by the word 'repentance', the vast majority of people will answer that repentance is what is required in order to become a Christian – that it is the way *into* the Christian life. Now that is entirely true, but not true entirely because repentance is much more than that. One of the first things written in Martin Luther's *95 Theses*, which he nailed to the door of the castle church in Wittenburg in 1517, sparking off the Reformation, is this: 'When our Lord and Master Jesus Christ said "Repent" He willed that the entire life of the believer be one of repentance.'

What did Luther mean? As many of you will know, the Greek word for repentance is *metanoia*, which signifies a change of mind. When we become a Christian we repent and change our mind about running our life on our own terms, deciding instead to surrender it to Jesus Christ. That is the initial act of repentance. Now this is where many stop. They believe that they have made a once-and-for-all decision. But is that initial act of repentance the beginning and the end?

The church at Ephesus, we read in the book of Revelation, had left their first love (Rev. 2:1–7). Jesus said in effect, 'You don't love Me like you used to.' How were they to recover their lost love for Christ? We might have suggested they start doing the things they hadn't been doing, such as works of love or service. It is so easy to get involved in works of reparation. But, as we shall see tomorrow, this wasn't the way that Jesus, the Wonderful Counsellor, dealt with them.

Father God, thank You that You have made a way for me to enter into Your presence. How I rejoice that because of the death of Your dear Son, Jesus, I can have a relationship with You both in this life and in eternity. To You be the glory. Amen.

FURTHER STUDY

Mark 1:1–8; Acts 3:17–26

1. How does John prepare the way for Jesus?
2. What is the outcome of repentance, according to Peter?

Finding Our Way Back

FOR READING & MEDITATION – REVELATION 2:1–7

'Remember the height from which you have fallen! Repent and
do the things you did at first.' (v5)

Today let's consider how Jesus, the Wonderful Counsellor, deals with the church at Ephesus. In today's text we find that He told the Ephesians to remember, repent, and *then* return to doing the things they did at first. And we should follow this pattern. We first remember from where we have fallen. Then we repent and return to doing works of love. There needs to be the admission that we have moved away from Christ and that we are now going to move back. That has to be a conscious decision. And it is the making of that conscious decision that is so often missing. Whenever we move away from our relationship with the Lord, or whenever we find that something has come between Him and us, then the way back is through the door of repentance.

Where do we find our life? It's so easy to echo Paul's words in Philippians 1:21 and say, 'For to me, to live is Christ.' But do we mean it? Often we forget what sin really is. Sin is pushing God out of the place He has reserved for Himself. We tend to think of sin as overt forms of behaviour, such as cheating, lying, stealing, swearing, and rudeness. But sin can be subtle as well as obvious. It's easy to move from dependency on Christ to something else, and when we move away from dependence on our Lord then in order to restore our relationship with Him we must repent.

This, I believe, is something so many forget on the journey of faith. Many believe repentance is a one-off act. But repentance is a change of mind about where life is found, and sometimes we seek life in something other than God. The entire life of the believer is to be one of repentance, as Martin Luther so rightly said.

Lord Jesus Christ, please help me to remember how things once were and, if I have done so, to repent of relegating You and finding my life in something other than You. May I return to the close relationship I once had with You. Amen.

FURTHER STUDY
Ezek. 18:30–32; Mark 1:14–20
1. How does Ezekiel exhort the people?
2. How do the disciples demonstrate their dependence on Christ?

The First Steps of Repentance

FOR READING & MEDITATION – HOSEA 14:1–3

'Return... to the Lord your God. Your sins
have been your downfall!' (v1)

The verses we have read today are some of the most enlightening when it comes to this matter of repentance. As we have been saying, there is no way we can return to a right relationship with God without repentance. The teaching on repentance we find in Hosea helps us to move from independence to reliance upon God, and these verses show us a divine pattern we can follow.

'*Return... to the Lord your God.*' We have chosen to look elsewhere for the energy to make our lives work; now we must make another choice – to transfer our dependence to God.

'*Take words with you*' (v2). When we come to God we should not stutter and stammer, wondering why we are there. We must have a clear idea of what we are repenting of, and the clearer our understanding, the deeper our repentance. The prodigal son, you will remember, carefully rehearsed what he would say to his father when he returned home: 'I will set out and go back to my father and say to him: Father, I have sinned against heaven and against you. I am no longer worthy to be called your son' (Luke 15:18–19).

'*Forgive all our sins*' (v2). What is sin? It is the ego in the place God reserved for Himself. We cannot rid ourselves of sin; it has to be forgiven.

'*Receive us graciously, that we may offer the fruit of our lips*' (v2). Repentance involves throwing ourselves on the mercy of God so that we may learn how to approach Him in true worship. The thought here is: 'Receive us so that we may rightly worship.' True worship flows from an understanding that the power to make our lives work is to be found in God through Christ – and nowhere else.

Gracious Father, Your Word has such clarity and gives me all the directions I need for life. Help me to see the path I should take – and follow it. In Christ's name. Amen.

FURTHER STUDY

Ps. 51:1–6; Lam. 3:22–26, 40–42; 2 Pet. 3:8–9

1. For what did David pray?
2. What words were to be used in the lament over sin?

Further Steps of Repentance

FOR READING & MEDITATION – HOSEA 14:1–3

'Assyria cannot save us; we will not mount war-horses.' (v3)

We continue looking at these verses from Hosea which spell out in detail the steps that are necessary for true repentance.

'*Assyria cannot save us; we will not mount war-horses.*' Assyria was a nation with horses and chariots. Politically, a pact with Assyria looked like a wise move. Do you have an 'Assyria' – something you are trusting to save you? If Israel turned to Assyria for support, the nation's dependence would not be fully on God. And in reality Assyria was powerless to save Israel. Without God's intervention Israel would be destroyed.

'*We will never again say "Our gods" to what our own hands have made*' (v3). Only when we accept that the real issue underlying sin is idolatry (that is, choosing to devote ourselves to something other than the Creator God) will we see how our self-sufficiency violates the divine scheme of things. Even our foolish attempts to rely on our own strategies as we relate to others must be seen for what they are – idolatry.

'*In you the fatherless find compassion*' (v3). Fatherless children are unprotected children, defenceless and vulnerable to the point of helplessness. Repentance involves us accepting disappointments from which our souls would naturally shrink. The willingness to acknowledge our helplessness enables us to see how desperately we need God's love and mercy, and this causes us to turn to Him and become dependent upon Him. When we do, we find He is indeed a compassionate Father.

Repentance is the path that leads to life. It is not only the entrance into the Christian life but also the means by which we make progress in our movement towards God.

O God my Father, solemnly and sincerely I take these steps of repentance. Let them be the means by which I return to the love I had for You at first. I want to love with Your love, for then, and only then, can I kindle Your love in others. Amen.

FURTHER STUDY

Ps. 51:7–12; Acts 17:25–31

1. What further steps of repentance did David take?
2. How did Paul confront idolatry in Athens?

The Benefits of Repentance

FOR READING & MEDITATION – HOSEA 14:4–9

'Who is wise? He will realise these things. Who is discerning?
He will understand them.' (v9)

Today we ask ourselves: what happens to those who repent deeply? Our repentance enables God to move into our lives with might and power.

The first thing that happens is that our waywardness is healed (v4). The compulsive desire we have to go astray and do our own thing is checked and brought under His control. The second effect is that our lives become spiritually refreshed. 'I will be like the dew to Israel' God promises (v5). Our roots go down further into the soil of God's love, giving us a deeper foundation and greater stability (v5). The third result is that our lives gain an attractiveness that was not there before (v6). People sense we love them for their own sake, not for what they can do for us. The fourth consequence of repentance is that our new way of living encourages people to want to 'dwell in our shade' (v7). They like to be near us for they become aware that in our company they are being ministered to – not manipulated. And finally, we learn that idolatry is futile and that the only fruitfulness that matters is the fruitfulness that comes from submission to God (v8).

'Who is wise?' asks Hosea. The answer is: the one who realises these things (v9). When we repent in the way Hosea describes in the first half of this chapter we will experience the benefits he describes in the second half.

The challenge I have put before you over these past few days has been strong. I have walked this way myself and I know how disturbing it can be. But if repentance is to be sufficiently deep to bring about changes at the core of our being, we must be willing to accept the challenge. Without pain there is no gain.

Father, let the steps I have taken over these past few days be ones that I am reminded of whenever I find myself moving in a direction away from You, so that I know how to return. Please grant it. In Jesus' name. Amen.

FURTHER STUDY
2 Cor. 7:8–11; Heb. 10:19–25
1. What does godly sorrow produce?
2. On what basis can we draw near to God?

Theology Leads to Doxology

FOR READING & MEDITATION – ROMANS 11:11–36

'For from him and through him and to him are all things.
To him be the glory for ever! Amen.' (v36)

The seventh issue that we must tackle on our transformational journey is the development of a rich devotional life. This is something I have encouraged people to do ever since my conversion. A rich devotional life involves communing with God in a relationship that is more than cerebral, it is passionate. Many Christians have a good mind and they think a lot; they read the Bible, understand it, believe it, appreciate it, but they lack that heart relationship with the Lord that involves the emotions and the feelings.

One of the saddest things, in my opinion, is a Christian who remains content with practising the duties of the Christian life, and relying on them to bring satisfaction, rather than entering into a dynamic and passionate relationship with God. The soul is capable of immense passion. We see this in great music and great art. The apostle Paul was a passionate man. Look at how he reacts in his letter to the Romans. He was an outstanding expositor of the Word of God and had a brilliant mind. But his love for Jesus breaks out in several places. At the end of Romans 11, after several chapters in which he has been dealing with the most taxing theology, he is unable to contain himself any longer, and bursts out in passionate praise, as we see from today's reading.

Our theology should lead to doxology or else its purpose is not being fulfilled. Students of theology frequently become immersed in deep theological discussion, but do not always allow it to set their hearts on fire in wonder, love, and praise. What our Lord seeks to lead us into is a passionate relationship with Himself. God does not want robotic obedience, but passionate engagement.

My loving heavenly Father, help me come to You now with expectancy – expecting that my weakness shall become strength, my doubt become faith. And as I respond to Your great love, may my passion become stronger. In Jesus' name. Amen.

FURTHER STUDY
Deut. 6:4–9; Mark 12:28–34
1. How passionate towards God is Israel called to be?
2. How does Jesus reinforce the greatest commandment?

FOR READING & MEDITATION – HOSEA 11:1–12

'My heart is changed within me; all my compassion is aroused.' (v8)

Yesterday we finished by saying that God seeks to lead us into a wonderful, passionate relationship with Himself. The book of Hosea presents us with a picture of a God whose heart burns for His rebellious people. Though the Israelites rejected Him, God was unwilling either to discard them or to back off. He persists in His desire to be their God. Despite their rebellion, this passage describes His incredible love for them.

Hosea, by his love for his wife who was unfaithful to him, models God's own commitment to His people, and His unfailing love despite their waywardness. God pours out His heart to Israel, promising to take His people back, to heal them and cause them to flourish. Speaking of Israel God says, 'Therefore I am now going to allure her; I will lead her into the desert and speak tenderly to her' (Hos. 2:14). God holds that same love for each one of us. He is a passionate Being and He wants to engage with us passionately also.

Have you noticed how the apostles talked in romantic terms about their relationship with Jesus Christ? 'Though you have not seen him, you love him...' (1 Pet. 1:8). 'We love because he first loved us...' (1 John 4:19). 'To him who loves us and has freed us from our sins by his blood...' (Rev. 1:5). The language of love is used a great deal in the New Testament. It is so easy for us to be more taken up with the cause of Christ than with Christ Himself, to be preoccupied with the work of God rather than with the God whose work we are called to do. What God longs for more than anything as we travel on this journey is that we have a passionate relationship with Him, and this He desires with all His heart.

O Father, I am grateful for the way in which I have come to know You, but I long to know You still more. You open Yourself fully to me; may I open myself fully to You. In Christ's name I pray. Amen.

FURTHER STUDY

John 21:15–19; Rom. 8:37–39; Gal. 2:20–21

1. How is Peter's love for Jesus linked to his journey of faith?
2. Of what is Paul convinced?

Where Does it Begin?

FOR READING & MEDITATION – 1 JOHN 4:7–21

'We love because he first loved us.' (v19)

As I said two days ago, a rich devotional life leads to a loving relationship with God that touches the emotions, not just the intellect. Are you aware, I wonder, that we are not the instigators of this relationship? When we pray, we are simply responding to God's call to our heart. God is longing to engage with the passions of your heart. He is always seeking to instigate a relationship with you.

Consider this. Perhaps you feel burdened by a situation and so you go to God in prayer. Could it be that God was behind the circumstances that led you to feeling loaded down, and ultimately brought you to your knees? He is constantly seeking to bring us to Himself so that we will respond to His love. Today's text tells us that 'We love because he first loved us'. That's how it all began.

Many years ago I told God that I felt that He did not love me enough. In His great kindness He took me to the cross and He gave me a vision which was so wonderful that the scales fell from my eyes and my own love flamed in response. And for the first time I realised what real love for God is. It's not something we can manufacture or generate by telling ourselves, 'Oh, I must love God more.' Focus on how much He loves you and the Holy Spirit will bring this alive for you. You will begin to grasp what His Son – the Man of Calvary – has done for you. As a consequence, the machinery of your soul will start to turn, and you will begin to love Him back. We cannot develop this love ourselves – our love for God is a response to His love for us. He is a passionate God, continually instigating a relationship with His people.

O Father, my heart is almost bursting with gratitude as I think about how You sent Jesus, Your Son, to this earth to die for us. May the wonder of this amazing love kindle love in me. Amen.

FURTHER STUDY

Rom. 5:1–8; 1 John 5:1–5

1. How does God demonstrate His love for us?
2. What does loving God involve?

FOR READING & MEDITATION – MATTHEW 26:1–13

'Wherever this gospel is preached throughout the world, what she has done will also be told, in memory of her.' (v13)

Do you know who has taught me most what intimacy with the Lord means? It is Mary of Bethany (Mary is named in John 12:3 in what appears to be an account of the same incident). I have spent much time studying the Bible and subjects such as systematic theology, and hermeneutics – the interpretation of the Bible. Through my studies I have learned a lot of important things, but it is Mary of Bethany, in her special moment with the Saviour, who has taught me what is most important.

The most important matter is our love relationship with our Lord Jesus Christ. That's what was of significance to Jesus. That's what He called beautiful. That's what He said would be remembered for all time. It is no surprise to me that many commentators have called Mary's anointing of Jesus the loveliest deed of all in the Gospels. It was without doubt a most beautiful act and it brought from the lips of Jesus an unusual and extraordinary commendation.

Jesus had been invited to a house in Bethany. It was while the meal was in progress that Mary came in and opened up a costly alabaster jar of ointment, and in one great extravagant act poured it over the head of the Lord Jesus. We read that when some of the disciples saw this they were quite frankly incredulous and murmured that it was a waste. But Jesus defends Mary and praises her for what she did.

Now I don't know about you, but I long to be commended by Jesus. Many of my ambitions have been unworthy of me, but this one is absolutely right. How wonderful to be commended by Jesus. Can we fully understand what elicited this great commendation? Then maybe we can put ourselves in the way of receiving one too.

Lord Jesus, may my relationship with You be one of selfless love. By my actions may I show others just how much I love You. For Your own dear name's sake. Amen.

FURTHER STUDY

John 13:31–35; 1 John 3:16–24

1. How are Jesus' disciples to be known?
2. How do we know what love is?

Worship First - Work Second

FOR READING & MEDITATION – LUKE 10:38–42

'Martha, Martha... Mary has chosen what is better,
and it will not be taken away from her.' (v41)

A few days ago we commented that sadly some Christians are more taken up with the cause of Christ than with Christ, whose cause they represent. I have known Christians who have defended the Church so savagely that it has undermined their whole purpose. People become so zealous for the truth that they forget the One who is the Truth.

The Bible college where I trained for the ministry had this motto: 'Let me never lose the important truth that I must love Thyself more than Thy service'. And yet I left college more enamoured with preaching and delivering a sermon with scholarly points to impress my listeners. At that time I was more interested in eloquence and the artistry of preaching than the One I was preaching about. We can work for God, and He will use our abilities, but more than anything He wants our love. It is a great tragedy that people think of the quiet time, of Bible study and prayer as being solely about spiritual growth – *our* growth. Our times of devotion are primarily not about us but about God. Activity and intimacy are not mutually exclusive. The point is that our activity for our heavenly Father should grow out of intimacy with Him. Worship first, work second. That is the most effective way to serve Him. We are likely to earn His commendation when everything we do is out of love for Him.

Years ago I stayed with a family whose daughter was asked to say grace. 'Lord Jesus,' she said, 'I love You more than anything else in the whole world.' Could anything be more delightful to the heart of our Lord than that? That's what is beautiful.

My Father and my Friend, in my times of communion with You may I not act as if I am a petitioner talking to a Supplier. Instead may I express my love for You. In Christ's name I ask it. Amen.

FURTHER STUDY
Ps. 116:1–7; Eph. 6:23–24; Phil. 1:8–11
1. Compose a psalm beginning, 'I love the Lord because...'
2. What does love help us discern?

An Act of Beauty

FOR READING & MEDITATION – MATTHEW 11:20–30

'Come to me... and I will give you rest.' (v28)

Again we consider Mary's anointing of Jesus recorded in Matthew 26:1–13 – an act of beauty that Jesus defended and commended to His disciples. Why does Jesus say this story will be told wherever the gospel is preached? It is my belief that He wants to draw our attention to the fact that the most important thing in our lives is not our grasp of doctrine – though that is essential – but how passionate we are in our love for Him.

The Pharisees and teachers of the law were the most biblically-educated people in the world at the time of Jesus. They believed the Scriptures, taught them zealously, prided themselves on their keeping of the law, and yet Jesus said, 'These people honour me with their lips, but their hearts are far from me' (Matt. 15:8). The picture dear to Jesus, the one He held close to His heart, the one that quite possibly brought a tear to His eye as He moved towards the cross, was that of Mary anointing Him with precious perfume. The Pharisees and teachers of the law were fighting over theology, but Mary was at His feet – and to Him that was beautiful. As far as we know she never cast out devils and never worked miracles, as the disciples did. All she did was love the Saviour. It was the way she loved Him that made the difference – passionately, extravagantly, lavishly.

Try to imagine with me the aroma of extravagant love flowing not only from the translucent alabaster jar in Mary's hands but also from her heart – a heart broken by the hard reality of the Saviour's imminent death. The perfume has lingered on throughout the centuries and is still with us now. The scent lingers to this very day.

Thank You, my Father, that in You I have found a love that satisfies my heart and quenches the deepest thirst of my soul. I rest in that love today. May my worship be received as the aroma of an extravagant love flowing from my heart. Amen.

FURTHER STUDY
Ps. 150:1–6; Eph. 3:14–21
1. How extravagant should our worship be?
2. How extravagant is Paul's prayer?

Not Personal But Intimate

FOR READING & MEDITATION – JOHN 4:1–26

'True worshippers will worship the Father in spirit and truth, for they are the kind of worshippers the Father seeks.' (v23)

Often when I am interviewed people ask, 'How did you come to place such an emphasis upon reading the Bible devotionally? What are the most important lessons the Lord has taught you during your years of ministry?' I simply tell them, 'The realisation that Jesus is not simply seeking a personal relationship with me but an intimate one.'

When Mary poured that jar of costly perfume over Jesus, the fragrance would have been absorbed by His garment, and would have accompanied Him through the humiliation of His trials, and remained despite the heavy smell of sweat and blood as He made His way to Golgotha. A hint of the fragrance must have clung to His garment until shamefully it was stripped from Him and gambled away. And then Christ made His own infinitely greater sacrifice as He 'gave himself up for us as a fragrant offering and sacrifice to God' (Eph. 5:2).

As Mary walked away from the cross that same scent probably still lingered in her hair – the hair that she used to dry the Saviour's feet (see John 12:3). It was a reminder of the love that spilled from His broken body on the cross, the perfume of His sacrifice that rose to heaven and brought pleasure to the nostrils of God. So pure, so lovely... so truly extravagant. It was a sacrifice motivated by love which He never regretted making, just as I'm sure Mary never regretted making her own sacrifice prompted by love. And now, today, as the perfume of our Lord's sacrifice still fills the air, and your heart, like mine, longs to be commended by Him, will you seek to enter into a more passionate relationship with Him? For without doubt that is what He wants.

Father, there is in my heart a longing for intimacy, for beauty, for adventure. The intimacy I enjoy with You now is, I know, just a foretaste of what is to come. How I long for that day! Amen.

FURTHER STUDY

1 Tim. 1:12–17; Titus 2:11–14; 3:4–8
1. How did Paul respond to the love of Christ?
2. How are we called to respond to God's love?

What Comes In Must Go Out

FOR READING & MEDITATION – JOHN 4:27–42

'The woman... said to the people, "Come, see a man
who told me everything I ever did."'(vv28–29)

Now we come to the final requirement on our spiritual journey which
brings us closer to God. On this journey it is essential that we do not
simply take in, absorb and assimilate, but also that we share – share what
we have received from God. So the final matter is *sharing the faith*. It is
important for us to take time to share with others the things that God has
shared with us.

What was the instinct of the woman at the well as soon as she had met
the Saviour? It was to share what she had found with others. What I am
saying here may cause some people to feel guilty, especially those who
do not find it easy to share their faith. It is not that we should go out and
accost everyone we meet with the message of salvation, but we should
be alert for every opportunity to do so and take advantage of it.

The four words which summarise the communication of the gospel are
'come... see... go... tell'. We get first-hand knowledge – 'come and see' –
and then the impulse takes over – 'go and tell'. And if there is no 'go and
tell' impulse then perhaps the 'come and see' impulse is not ours – or has
ceased to be a strong instinct in our lives.

A woman once said to me, 'I had a real experience of God and yet
refused to share it with anyone, so it died.' How sad. The first words of
2 Corinthians 9:10 tell us much: 'He who supplies seed to the sower...' Do
you see the inference? God gives seed only to the person who uses it –
the sower. If we won't use the seed then we won't be given it. Our powers
are either dedicated or dead. If they are dedicated, they are renewed by
God. If they are conserved, they die.

**O Father, I ask not for an experience of You – that I already have. I ask
rather for the courage to share it with others. Please give me some seed
today – and help me to sow it in prepared hearts. For Your own dear name's
sake. Amen.**

FURTHER STUDY
Ps. 51:13–19; John 1:43–49; Acts 11:19–26
1. How did David express his desire to 'go and tell'?
2. What courage did the Early Church express in their evangelism?

Let Me Commend My Saviour

FOR READING & MEDITATION – MALACHI 3:1–18

'Then those who feared the Lord talked with each other...' (v16)

We continue with the matter we were talking about yesterday, namely the importance of sharing Christ with others. Experience and expression are the alternate beats of the Christian heart. And if these two essentials are not in operation, the Christian heart ceases to beat. Then what happens? We settle down to dead forms, dead attitudes and dead prayers.

This matter of sharing, however, must not be limited only to evangelism – it applies also to sharing with other Christians the things that God has shared with us. If God has shown you something today from His Word, then why not share it with another Christian? As we have been saying, nothing is fully ours until we share it – the expression will deepen the impression. So in seeking to stay spiritually fresh, discipline yourself to share appropriate issues with your Christian and non-Christian friends. Many do not do this. They are disciplined in their quiet time and their study of the Scriptures, but they have never disciplined themselves to share. Someone has defined a Christian as one who says by word or deed, 'Let me commend my Saviour to you'. What a wonderful definition.

In a newspaper I once saw a cartoon showing a woman putting a garment around the shivering body of a little girl. Behind the woman stood Christ throwing a cloak around her shoulders. The title of the cartoon was this: 'A proven assembly line.' It is, indeed, a 'proven assembly line'. Give out to others and it will be given to you – a good measure, pressed down and running over (see Luke 6:38). Especially running over.

Father, may I reach up to You with one hand and reach out to those in need with the other. Please give me some word or message to pass on to a non-Christian or one of my Christian brothers or sisters this day. In Jesus' name. Amen.

FURTHER STUDY

Ps. 34:1–3; 126:1–6; Eph. 5:15–20

1. What shared experiences does the psalmist recall?
2. How are the Ephesians exhorted to share their faith?

Words and Deeds

FOR READING & MEDITATION – 1 PETER 3:8–22

'Always be prepared to give an answer to everyone who asks
you to give the reason for the hope that you have.' (v15)

Those churches which concentrate on social issues tend to excuse their approach by saying, 'We preach the gospel not with words but with deeds.' Now attending to social issues is important for the Church, but it must never become a substitute for direct evangelism – for sharing our faith.

Suppose Jesus, who is the Word made flesh, had declared, 'I'll be the Word become flesh only. I'll let people see who I am by what I do alone.' That would have been half revelation. It would have been like a bird trying to fly with only one wing. Words and deeds are the two wings of the Christian as he or she soars and sings. Those who call for words alone and those who call for deeds alone are both wrong. We belong to Him who had words and deeds in a living blend. Though it is not necessary to constantly preach at people, we must be ready, as today's text instructs us, to take advantage of every opportunity to share Christ in a manner that is not off-putting.

Suppose the church at Antioch had become completely taken up with food relief when they dispatched Barnabas and Saul to Jerusalem (see Acts 11:27–30), and had concluded, 'Poverty is the main evil in the world. Let's focus on that.' If this had been the case the Christians at Antioch would have lost their way. Poverty is an evil that must be dealt with by the Church. But even if we eradicated all poverty and hunger that would still leave people in need of conversion. We must be balanced about this matter, of course, because hungry people need a meal before they are presented with the gospel. Let us not forget, however, that we are commanded to go into the world to preach the gospel (Matt. 28:19–20). That command will never be annulled.

Father, You have committed to us the greatest work in the world – the work of bringing others to You. Help me here and now to rededicate myself afresh to that task, for nothing counts as much as this. In Jesus' name. Amen.

FURTHER STUDY
Matt. 28:16–20; Jas 2:14–19
1. Use Jesus' great commission to rededicate yourself to Him.
2. How did James link faith and deeds?

Moving Towards God

FOR READING & MEDITATION – 2 CORINTHIANS 3:1–18

'And we, who... all reflect the Lord's glory, are being transformed into his likeness with ever-increasing glory...' (v18)

Today we look back over our last two months together and ask what have been the highlights of our transformational journey. As we do so we remember that we don't all travel this road at the same rate, but that God does take every one of us through certain spiritual experiences and lessons. I have highlighted eight of these experiences. There are unquestionably more, but certainly not less than eight.

In our movement towards God we will encounter a holy God; through suffering, our sensitivity to the needs of others is deepened and widened. In close relationships we learn the art of loving others more than we love ourselves. What about living in the light of eternity? That, too, is a challenge. What has God been saying to you about this, I wonder? Jesus always kept eternity in view. Do you? Can we live with mystery, trusting in God and not dreaming up our own solutions, even if we have to wait until eternity? Can our lives be characterised by a lifestyle of repentance as we continuously return to Him through the door of repentance? Do we rejoice that throughout our entire journey we are accompanied by a passionate God who desires an intimate, vibrant relationship with us? And lastly, do we recall that we are all involved in a rescue mission? Do we share what God has so graciously shared with us?

Well, there it is – the irreducible minimum of what I believe is vital for movement towards God. God is committed to us; can we commit ourselves wholeheartedly to Him? Are we more focused on Him than His cause? Do we realise that what He wants is not just our work but also our worship – not just our service but our love? Take advantage of this moment to offer Him your life once again.

Lord Jesus Christ, help us to love You the way Mary of Bethany did, and may we be as devoted to You as she was. You have done something beautiful for us; help us to do something beautiful for You. Amen.

FURTHER STUDY
1 Thess. 5:16–24; Jude 20–21, 24–25
1. Meditate on God's will for us in Christ Jesus.
2. Give thanks with Jude for the love and mercy of God in Jesus.

MAR
&
APR

Shut Up – To Write

FOR READING & MEDITATION – COLOSSIANS 1:1

'Paul, an apostle of Christ Jesus by the will of God...' (v1)

For the next two months we shall study Paul's letter to the Colossians. This was probably written by him during his imprisonment in Rome in AD 62 or 63. Colosse was one of a group of three towns in the Lycus valley where churches had been established, the other two being Hierapolis and Laodicea. We have no record of Paul having visited Colosse personally, and it is likely that it was Epaphras who had brought the gospel to the area.

The letter seems to have been prompted by Paul's discovery that the Colossian Christians were experiencing a threat to their faith – a threat which Bishop Handley Moule described as 'error that cast a cloud over the glory of the Lord Jesus Christ, dethroning Him and emptying Him of His divinity, thus making Him one of a multitude of mediators... instead of the *only* mediator'. Paul, always ready to defend his Saviour, writes to correct that error and show that Christ is first and foremost in everything. Believers are rooted in Him, alive in Him, hidden in Him, complete in Him, and so are equipped to make Christ first in every area of their lives.

Paul begins his letter by laying down his credentials: 'an apostle of Christ Jesus by the will of God'. Our first reaction might be to think it sad that an apostle should be shut up in prison rather than winning new territories for Christ. But although circumstances prevented him from travelling, his spirit was free to reach out through his pen. Think of it like this: had he not been imprisoned we would not have had the captivity letters – Colossians, Ephesians, Philippians and Philemon. From prison his influence extended to the ends of the earth and throughout the ages. He was shut up – to write.

O Father, help me understand that to a Christian there is no bondage except sin. Physical restrictions may hinder me bodily but my spirit is always free to soar. Circumstances do not have the last word in my life – You do. Amen.

FURTHER STUDY
Gen. 39:20–23; Phil. 1:12–20
1. What did Joseph and Paul have in common?
2. Why should we not fear physical restrictions?

Grace and Peace

FOR READING & MEDITATION – COLOSSIANS 1:2

'To the holy and faithful brothers in Christ at Colosse:
Grace and peace to you from God our Father.' (v2)

When Paul wrote his letters to the churches of the New Testament,' says Dr William Barclay, 'he wrote in exactly and precisely the way ordinary everyday people wrote ordinary everyday letters in the ancient world.' First there is a greeting, then a word of thanksgiving, which is followed by the special contents, and finally a closing greeting. In some instances there is an autographic conclusion.

Paul greets the Colossian Christians with an endearing phrase: 'holy and faithful brothers in Christ'. The faith of the Colossian Christians may have been under attack, but there is nothing to suggest that they had succumbed to error. Certainly there is nothing that comes anywhere near the strong words addressed to the Galatians, who had embraced false ideas concerning the faith. I doubt whether Paul would have called the Colossian believers 'stalwart followers of Christ' (as Eugene Peterson words verse 2 in *The Message*) if they had been moved away from Christ.

He continues: 'Grace and peace to you from God our Father.' Notice the words: *'from God our Father'*. Can grace and peace come from sources other than the Father? Of course. 'Grace' and 'peace' are words often used by non-Christians. Mortgage lenders talk about periods of 'grace'; politicians talk about negotiating 'peace' between warring countries. But what a difference between the grace and peace stemming from human hearts and the grace and peace that come from the heart of the Father. One is temporal, the other eternal; one limited, the other unlimited. The best of men and women are only men and women at best. But what comes from God is always perfect. *Perfect* peace, *perfect* grace.

Father, when the peace and grace You give flow into my life then I need never be impoverished. Your heart is always open to give; may my heart be always open to receive. In Jesus' name. Amen.

FURTHER STUDY
John 1:14–18; 14:25–27
1. Try to define 'grace' and 'peace'.
2. How does the world's peace differ from Christ's peace?

Scripture's Conjoined Twins

FOR READING & MEDITATION – COLOSSIANS 1:3–4

'We always thank God... because we have heard of your faith
... and of the love you have...' (vv3–4)

How encouraging for the Colossians to know they were remembered in Paul's prayers. He had heard good things about them from Epaphras (v7), and so, whenever he prayed for them, he gave thanks to God for their faith in Christ and their love for all their fellow believers.

These words link two important qualities: faith and love. The New Testament often joins these two together; they could be called 'Scripture's conjoined twins'. If you are to have enduring, selfless love for others you must first of all have faith in God. Psychology teaches that love for other people is an integral part of good emotional health, but it has nothing to say on the need for a relationship with God. Without a relationship with God, however, love for others soon runs out of energy.

Some time ago I read about an African government agency which invested a large sum of money in a building programme designed to improve the lifestyle of a certain tribe living in grass huts on a hillside. To replace these flimsy dwellings the government built brick houses at the foot of the hill. The tribespeople, however, felt uncomfortable in their new houses and, after they had lived in them for just a few days, they decided to move back into their old huts. An exasperated official said to the missionaries who lived among them, 'These ungrateful people need a lot of loving. I'm afraid the best we can do is to lift them; we leave it to you to love them.' Love that is not linked to God quickly runs out of impetus. Governments can raise people's standard of living but they can't love them. Only when we have faith in God can we go on loving the unresponsive. No faith in God, no love like God's.

O God my Father, teach me the secret of faith and love, the alternate beats of the Christian heart. My faith draws love from You, and my love expresses that faith in love to everybody. Thank You, Father. Amen.

FURTHER STUDY
1 Cor. 13:1–13; Gal. 5:5–6
1. What is God's love like?
2. How is faith expressed?

A Spring in Our Step

FOR READING & MEDITATION – COLOSSIANS 1:5

'The faith and love that spring from the hope that
is stored up for you in heaven...' (v5)

Yesterday we mentioned the fact that faith and love are sometimes described as Scripture's conjoined twins. Today we ask: Where do faith and love come from? What are their origins? They come, Paul tells us, from the *hope* that is stored up for us in heaven. It is important to remember that the Christian experience is characterised by hope as much as by faith and love.

The concept of hope was something the ancients repudiated. They regarded it as dubious and uncertain. But Christian hope is as certain, if not more certain, as tomorrow's dawn. It is the assurance that however much we enjoy God's presence and blessings here on earth, we will experience something far, far greater in heaven. Some think of heaven as the place where the finishing touches will be added to what we have received on earth. But we are told, 'No eye has seen, no ear has heard, no mind has conceived what God has prepared for those who love him' (1 Cor. 2:9).

Permit me to ask you: How powerfully does the prospect of heaven influence your daily walk with Christ? We have said before that we must be careful, of course, that we do not become so heavenly minded that we are no earthly good. However, we can live in the light of heaven's coming glory. What we have here 'in Christ' is just a foretaste of what is to come. Some of our present spiritual experiences may seem like heaven, but really they are just a little bit of heaven to go to heaven in.

Notice, too, that hope is not a consequence of faith and love but its origin. Faith and love *spring* from hope. When we hold before us the sure and certain hope of eternal bliss in heaven, then out of that hope spring faith and love. They don't just saunter into our lives – they *spring!*

O God, there is so much emphasis on the 'now' that I am apt to forget the truth of what I have been reading about today. Help me keep the prospect of heaven always in mind. Then I know faith and love will 'spring'. Amen.

FURTHER STUDY
Rom. 8:18–25; 12:12; 15:4,13
1. Where does hope come from?
2. What does hope cause us to be?

That's the Truth

FOR READING & MEDITATION – COLOSSIANS 1:5–6

'All over the world this gospel is bearing fruit and growing...' (v6)

The reason Paul tells the Colossians they had heard the true gospel was to hold up before them a standard by which all other gospels could be evaluated. If there were those in the Colossian church who were casting doubt on the completeness of the Christian message as delivered to them by Epaphras, they would, through this letter, have noted Paul's reassurance that what they had learned through him was the word of truth.

How we need in our current times, when people are claiming that what is true for one person may not be true for another, to grasp what Francis Schaeffer described as 'true truth'. And what is 'true truth'? It is the truth contained in the gospel of Jesus Christ. It is the final truth. Nothing can be added to it or subtracted from it. It is the truth, the whole truth and nothing but the truth. Sometimes I find when talking to young adults about Christ, they adopt the attitude, 'Well, that may be true for you, but I have a different truth.' The truth of the gospel, however, is not relative (one thing for me and another thing for you); it is absolute and therefore universal – the same truth for all.

Paul reinforces this point by telling the Colossians that the gospel they had received was the same gospel that was being received all over the then known world – and was bearing fruit. The gospel of Christ cannot be 'enriched' with new ideas; it is divine in origin and so has the power to bear fruit – the power to transform lives. The gospel is 'the grace of God in truth'. God's mercy, not our merit, caused Him to send His Son to save us. That's the truth. Nothing must be added to it and nothing must be taken away.

Father, how grateful I am for the simplicity of the gospel. I can add nothing to it to make it more effective, and if I take anything away it becomes ineffective. May I never be moved from its simplicity. Amen.

FURTHER STUDY
John 14:6; 17:17; Gal. 1:6–12
1. What is truth?
2. What was Paul's concern?

High Praise Indeed

FOR READING & MEDITATION – COLOSSIANS 1:7–8

'You learned it from Epaphras, our dear fellow-servant,
who is a faithful minister of Christ...' (v7)

The Bible is, among other things, a book of biographies. Some are moderately complete, others are short and terse, as is that of Epaphras, the founder of the church at Colosse. Though there is another reference to Epaphras in this letter (4:12), we have enough information here to put together a picture of the kind of man he was: 'our dear fellow-servant, who is a faithful minister'. This is high praise indeed.

The worth of praise is always determined by the one giving the praise. Who was it who praised Epaphras? Paul, the great apostle. I wonder what he had in mind when he called Epaphras a fellow-servant. Did he mean that Epaphras was a man one could easily work with? Probably so. It has been said that the final test of an individual's work is not only to ask, 'What has he or she done?', but also, 'Could other people work with him or her?' Epaphras was such a person – a good co-worker. Yet, in addition, he was a 'faithful minister'. He wasn't merely loyal to his fellow-workers in the ministry; he devoted himself to the needs of those he served.

In emphasising the point Paul continues, 'who also told us of your love in the Spirit'. Epaphras would have been well aware of the faults of the Colossian Christians, but he was not obsessed by them. He was ready to notice and commend the virtues of his people. It still remains a wonderful compliment to say with truth of a particular person, 'You never heard him say an unkind word against anyone.' No greater eulogy, I believe, could be given of any of us at our passing than that we were good colleagues, faithful in our work for Jesus Christ, and swift to see and to speak of the good in others.

O God, may I so live before You that at my passing people may also say of me that I was easy to work with, devoted to Jesus Christ, and saw the good in others more readily than the bad. In Jesus' name. Amen.

FURTHER STUDY
Eph. 5:21; 1 Cor. 4:12; Philem. 23
1. What concerned Epaphras?
2. What is a vital key in being able to work with others?

There's More

FOR READING & MEDITATION – COLOSSIANS 1:9–10

'We have not stopped praying for you and asking God
to fill you with the knowledge of his will...' (v9)

The apostle Paul was not only a great preacher; he was also a great pray-er. Many times when writing his letters he paused to break out in extempore prayer. And his prayers were not rambling petitions but always bore down on particular matters. One of the things I have noticed about those who seem to have a ministry in prayer is that they lose no time in getting to specifics. Though they are careful to worship and adore God, they don't indulge themselves in flowery phrases such as 'O Thou who gildest the heavens and settest the stars in space'. Instead they quickly get down to details. Watch how Paul does this in the verses we have read.

After telling the Colossian Christians that he had prayed ceaselessly for them since the day he had heard about them, he makes the first of his petitions by asking God to fill them 'with the knowledge of his will through all spiritual wisdom and understanding'. Notice the word 'fill'. It suggests that however much the Colossian Christians had received from the Lord, there was still room for more. You see, no one can ever rest and say, 'I am now *completely* Christian.' For the Holy Spirit always has more to teach us about the will of God. Rabindranath Tagore, the Indian poet, said, 'The eternal cry is – more.' Whatever the Colossians knew of God, there was much more to discover.

Also significant is the phrase 'bearing fruit in every good work'. Paul prayed that the life of God might flow through the Colossian Christians and produce substantial spiritual fruit; not fruitless suckers but fruit that the Master can enjoy – on the lowest branches the low-hanging fruit of humility and on the highest branches the knowledge of God.

O God, the days of my life go by at tremendous speed, but You are still pouring, and there is always room in my heart for more understanding of Your will. And the more I receive, the more I long for. I love You Father. Amen.

FURTHER STUDY
Eph. 1:15–23; 3:14–21
1. What did Paul pray for?
2. Why did Paul assume believers could receive even more of God?

You'll Get Through

FOR READING & MEDITATION – COLOSSIANS 1:11–12

'Being strengthened with all power... so that you may have great endurance and patience...' (v11)

One of the words you often hear spoken by Christians is the word 'power'. People say, 'We need more power to witness, more power to work miracles, more power to make the world sit up and take notice.' I agree. My personal burden and prayer over the years has been to see the power of God moving mightily on masses of people in true revival. There's nothing wrong with asking God to demonstrate His power to save, heal and deliver; it's a legitimate prayer concern. But what Paul has in mind as he prays for power to be seen in the lives of the Colossian Christians is power to endure all trials and come through them with thanksgiving.

It will not have escaped your notice, I am sure, that the world in which you live and work is one where you need a full supply of God's power if you are to continue resolutely and persevere despite opposition, setbacks and frustrations. Paul, when writing to the Corinthians, said that through endurance the servants of God commend themselves (2 Cor. 6:4). Today many of you have to go out and contend with fierce antagonism, bitter disappointment, rejection from friends or family, a marriage failure, loss of friendship, a financial reversal, or some other hardship. But listen carefully to me: *you will get through*. And the reason you will get through is because God's power is at work in your life.

You may be shaken but you will not be shattered, knocked down but not knocked out. What is more, you will come through the experience with thanksgiving. You will be thankful because through your difficulties you will be brought closer to God Himself.

My Father and my God, You do not promise to keep me from difficulties, but You do promise me that You will bring me through. On that I can rely. And that is enough. Thank You, Father. Amen.

FURTHER STUDY
2 Cor. 1:8–11; 4:7–18
1. What was Paul's testimony?
2. What did he focus on?

Gone! Gone!

MAR

FOR READING & MEDITATION – COLOSSIANS 1:12–14

'The Father... has qualified you to share in the
inheritance of the saints...' (v12)

Exactly where Paul's prayer for the Colossians finishes we can't be sure. Probably it ends with the phrase 'joyfully giving thanks to the Father' (v12a) because what he talks about next is something the Colossians were already in possession of: a share in the inheritance of the saints, deliverance from the kingdom of darkness, a place in the kingdom of the Son, redemption, and the forgiveness of sins. This was not something they needed to seek; the blessings were already theirs.

When Paul reminds the Colossians that they are qualified to share in the inheritance of the saints, what does he mean? All the conditions necessary for becoming an heir of God and a joint heir with Christ had been met by their acceptance of Christ, and they were now full members of God's new society. But more: they had been 'rescued [by God]... from the dominion of darkness and brought... into the kingdom of the Son he loves'. We must never forget that salvation is a rescue mission – a deliverance. We don't climb out of the darkness; we are delivered from it. That's why the Son gets all the glory, for the glory always goes to the one who saves, not to the one who is saved.

And then there's this: 'in whom we have redemption, the forgiveness of sins'. The Christian faith begins at the point of redemption. We need redemption from sin – that is, release from the bondage of sin – and forgiveness for our sins. Both are provided in Jesus Christ. I know of nothing more wonderful than redemption and forgiveness. The slate is wiped clean. Once I ask for forgiveness from Christ then I am, as far as God is concerned, a person without a past history. I am just like a newborn baby; I have a future but no past. How amazing.

O Father, forgive me if the wonder of redemption and forgiveness does not hit my soul with the force and power it ought. Help me open my heart to the thrilling fact that all my sins are gone. Gone! Hallelujah!

FURTHER STUDY
Luke 15:11–32
1. Why did the prodigal hope for forgiveness but not restoration?
2. How did the father offer redemption?

The Right Way For Everything

FOR READING & MEDITATION – COLOSSIANS 1:15–16

'He is the image of the invisible God, the firstborn over
all creation.' (v15)

Paul's introduction now over, he plunges into the main purpose of his letter, which is to remind the Colossian Christians of the supremacy and sufficiency of Christ. He knows that once they grasp this, it will protect them from error. Jesus is the image of the invisible God, he tells them. Christ takes the place of idols in their lives. Idols misrepresent God – Jesus represents Him.

He goes on to say that 'He is... the firstborn over all creation'. This does not mean, as the Jehovah Witnesses and others claim, that Christ is the first created being. Jesus was 'begotten' by the Father, not 'created' (John 1:14,18 NKJV), and is Himself the One by whom all things were created.

But pause to consider these amazing words: 'all things were created by him and for him'. I wonder if the Church takes these words seriously. It is as if the statement is merely a rhetorical flourish. But nothing in Scripture is more important. If everything is created *by* Christ and *for* Christ then creation is designed to work His way. When it does it works effectively; when it follows some other way it works towards its ruin. What is being said is this: the way of Christ is written not only into the texts of Scripture but into the texture of the whole of creation. If we are created by Christ and for Christ then He is inescapable. Just as you cannot jump out of your skin, so you cannot escape Christ, for His stamp is upon the whole of His creation. Like the watermark in paper, Christ is written into the structure of our beings. This means that Christ's way is the right way to do everything, and all other ways are the wrong way.

Father, I look around and see that the world is finding out how not to live. And finding out painfully – through inner conflict, guilt, and fear. I am so thankful I know You, but I pray for revival, that many others may come to know You too. Amen.

FURTHER STUDY

Matt. 7:24–29; Heb. 1:1–8

1. What happens when we do not follow Christ's way?
2. Why does Christ fully represent God?

Christ – A Centripetal Force

FOR READING & MEDITATION – COLOSSIANS 1:17–18

'He is before all things, and in him all things hold together.' (v17)

These words clinch everything: 'in him all things hold together'. We could also say, 'Out of Him all things fly apart – they go to pieces.' One commentator puts it like this: 'Everything in Him [Jesus] is centripetal; everything outside of Him is centrifugal.' Everything in Christ is bound together in perfect harmony, not simply by power but by love. Further on in Colossians we find these words: 'And over all these virtues put on love, which binds them all together in perfect unity' (3:14).

One man known to me was disinherited by his family when he became a Christian. However, he rose to become a leading figure in society, and made efforts to relate to his family even though they were reluctant to have anything to do with him. Slowly his love for them won through. He held the family together because he was held together within – by being in Christ.

Many years ago, after I had written that the reason why all things in the universe cohere is because they are held together by Jesus Christ, a nuclear scientist shut himself in his office for hours and refused to take any calls because the fact hit him as never before that what holds all creation together is not a force but a Person – Jesus Christ.

Our Lord once said, 'He who is not with me is against me, and he who does not gather with me scatters' (Matt. 12:30). Everything outside of Christ scatters. This is not merely theological opinion; it is working fact. Get among any group of Christians, talk about Christ, and you are together. Talk about our church traditions and you are apart. Let this simple but solemn truth grip your soul with new force today: in Him all things hold together, out of Him all things fly apart.

O Father, I am so grateful that Your Son is my centre and my circumference. In Him I am held together. Let this truth be more than something I hold; may it be something that holds me. In Jesus' name. Amen.

FURTHER STUDY
Luke 7:28; John 1:1–13; 10:27–30
1. Contrast Jesus and John.
2. What does Christ hold in His hand?

The Order of the Resurrection

FOR READING & MEDITATION – COLOSSIANS 1:18

'And he is the head of the body, the church...' (v18)

Colossians and Ephesians have similar themes running through them, but looked at from different perspectives. Ephesians can be described as the letter which portrays the Church of Christ, whereas Colossians depicts the Christ of the Church. Ephesians focuses on the Body; Colossians focuses on the Head.

Here, in today's text, Paul shows us that Christ is not only the Head of creation; He is also the Head of the Church. The formation of the Church is undoubtedly the greatest project God has ever undertaken. An outstanding Welsh preacher, Tom Rees, described it as 'The Divine Masterpiece'. Nothing in heaven or earth can ever eclipse it. And just as Christ being Lord of creation reveals His pre-eminence, so does His position as Head of the Church.

Those of us who are part of Christ's Body, the Church, should remember, as Dick Lucas points out, that 'If a body does not hold fast to its head it can hardly hope to survive'! The Head will never lose contact with the Body, but often the Body loses contact with the Head. When the Church fails to hold fast to its Head it loses co-ordination and direction. We cannot say Christ's pre-eminence is being acknowledged in the Church if the Church refuses to go in the direction which the Head desires and dictates.

What does Paul mean when he says Christ 'is the beginning and the firstborn from among the dead'? He is referring, of course, to our Lord's resurrection. Christ's rising from the dead marked the beginning of a new order – what might be called 'The Order of the Resurrection'. Others who were physically raised from the dead were raised only to die again. Those who die in Christ will be raised *never* to die again.

Father, how glad I am that I belong to 'The Order of the Resurrection'. I can think of nothing more sure and more secure. All honour and glory be to Your wonderful name. Amen.

FURTHER STUDY

1 Cor. 15:35–57; Eph. 5:23–33

1. Contrast the natural and resurrection bodies.
2. What is Christ's relationship to the Church?

Christ – the Pleasure of God

13 MAR

FOR READING & MEDITATION – COLOSSIANS 1:19–20

'For God was pleased to have all his fulness dwell in him...' (v19)

This passage is bursting with meaning. Paul has moved, as we saw yesterday, from thinking of Christ as the originator of creation to Him being the Head of the Church. In case some might think God's relationship to Christ changed when He came to earth, Paul tells us that 'God was pleased to have all his fulness dwell in him'. *Pleased* – note that.

'God dwells in every Christian,' said E. Stanley Jones, 'but He dwells sufferingly. We give Him a great deal of pain. He stays, but not without some degree of travail.' The one Person in whom God dwells without any pain is Jesus. One commentator put it like this: 'God is *at home* in Jesus.' The same commentator said, 'The attempt to impose divine qualities upon the framework of human nature has always resulted in a monstrosity – always except in the case of Jesus.' Others have attempted to make themselves divine; Jesus' divinity is part of His nature. The very essence of God resides in Him. In Him the supernatural is natural. When I consider the sinless life of Jesus, it is no surprise that at the River Jordan God opened the heavens and declared, 'This is my Son, whom I love; with him *I am well pleased*' (Matt. 3:17). No wonder, for He is such a wonderful Son.

Paul also reminds us that Jesus is the One who effects reconciliation for all things. When Christ sacrificed His life on the cross, He took on Himself the curse of sin. The cross makes peace possible in every corner of the universe. Christ restores to the universe the principle of harmony which sin so brutally disturbed.

Father, how I long to be an agent of reconciliation and show others how to be at peace with You. Through Christ's work in me may I bring peace and harmony to my world today. Amen.

FURTHER STUDY
Luke 3:22; John 8:29; 2 Cor. 5:17–21; Phil. 2:1–11
1. What was unique about Christ?
2. What was Christ's attitude?

Three Life Positions

FOR READING & MEDITATION – COLOSSIANS 1:21–23

'Once you were alienated from God and were
enemies in your minds...' (v21)

The verses we have read have been described as some of the most beautiful in the New Testament. The statements Paul makes can be compared with those found in Ephesians chapter 2, for instance Ephesians 2:3 and 2:12. Paul reminds the Colossians – as we all need to be reminded – of what Christ has done. Indeed, we should never tire of hearing it, for the central dynamic of the Christian life is not what we do for Christ, but what He has done for us. Dick Lucas gives a good analysis of these verses when he divides them as follows: what you once were, where you now stand, and how you must go on.

And what were we? 'Enemies,' says Paul. Many are unwilling to apply this term to themselves in their unconverted state. They say, 'I was never at enmity with God, just apathetic to Him.' But dig deep into every human heart and you find not apathy towards God but antagonism. Embedded like splintered glass in every soul is a basic distrust of God. Oh, it's there even though we may not choose to accept the fact. We don't like the idea of God telling us what to do, and so act independently. Yet where are we now through grace? Reconciled. The enmity is over and peace has come to our hearts. We stand in God's presence 'holy... without blemish and free from accusation'.

And how should we go on? We are to 'continue in [the] faith, established and firm, not moved from the hope held out in the gospel' (v23). If we are to continue in the faith then we must remain content with the gospel that brought us to Christ and not try to change it. Those who seek to add or take away from the gospel do not continue in the faith; they contaminate it.

Father, grant that I might never move away from the gospel that challenged me and changed me. May my song ever be, 'On Christ the solid Rock I stand, all other ground is sinking sand'. In Jesus' name I pray. Amen.

FURTHER STUDY
Rom. 8:1–11; Eph. 2:11–18; Jas 4:4
1. Why were we enemies of God?
2. How can we find life and peace?

The Continuing Cross

FOR READING & MEDITATION – COLOSSIANS 1:24

'I fill up in my flesh what is still lacking in
regard to Christ's afflictions...' (v24)

This verse has perplexed many and we must approach it with care. When Paul says he must fill up in his flesh 'what is still lacking in regard to Christ's afflictions' is he suggesting there was some deficiency in Christ's atonement? No, the meaning of the verse is this: Christ had suffered on the cross for the sins of the world and now Paul 'filled up Christ's afflictions by experiencing the added sufferings necessary to carry this good news to a lost world' (*NIV Study Bible*). J.B. Phillips gives a further insight into the meaning of this verse in his translation: 'I am suffering on behalf of you who have heard the gospel, yet I am far from sorry about it. Indeed, I am glad, because it gives me a chance to complete in my own sufferings something of the untold pains which Christ suffers on behalf of his body, the Church.' All the sufferings of Christ's Body are Christ's sufferings. Christ suffers with His people.

Christ shares in the suffering we experience when persecuted for spreading the gospel, but what about the suffering He also undergoes from those who bear His name yet do such ugly things? One church I know has split over the question of Holy Communion. The communion service is a time of blessedness, but it has been turned into a time of bitterness. Christ bleeds again.

Paul, in this verse, is saying something like this: 'Daily I enter into the crucifixion of Jesus, take my share of His sufferings, and bleed with Him and for Him. I am in Christ, therefore I participate in His sufferings for the Church.' Next time you have a cross to bear because of some people in the Church, remember Christ bore a cross for all the people in the Church.

O Father, I accept that because I am in Christ I am involved in His sufferings also. Help me to regard this as a real privilege, and not a problem, as a blessing, not a burden. In Jesus' name. Amen.

FURTHER STUDY
2 Cor. 1:3–7; 11:16–29
1. What was Paul's hope?
2. What did he face daily?

Saying Goodbye to a Text

FOR READING & MEDITATION – COLOSSIANS 1:25

'I have become its servant by the commission God gave me
to present to you the word of God in its fulness...' (v25)

The question is often asked: What constitutes a God-given ministry? The verse before us now gives us the answer: *having the heart of a servant*. There are many definitions of servanthood, but the one I most like is this: 'becoming excited about making other people successful'. True servanthood will always involve a desire to make the Word of God fully known and Christians fully mature... and being excited about the privilege of being used by God.

Take the first of these – the desire to make the Word of God fully known. Listen again to what Paul says: 'to present to you the word of God in its fulness'. How do we make known the Word of God in its fulness? One way is by following closely the principles of exposition. A crying need of God's people and the contemporary Church is for systematic Bible teaching and an understanding of the Scriptures. There is a tendency to devise clever and engaging talks on current events which may commence with a text from the Bible but make no further reference to it. A man once said to me, 'Our pastor always begins with a text from the Bible... then immediately says goodbye to it.' Though there is a place for topical preaching, if a church does not have a regular system of presenting to its people a comprehensive exposition of the Scriptures, then the Word of God will not be fully known or will be misunderstood. As you have no doubt heard it said, 'A text taken out of context quickly becomes a pretext.'

No one can know Christ better without knowing the Scriptures better, and there is no better way of knowing the Scriptures than by doing as we are doing now – going through them verse by verse.

Father, I see that only through systematic study of Your Word can it be fully understood, and only through the Word can Christ be fully known. Help all Your servants handle the Word of God well – myself included. Amen.

FURTHER STUDY
Ezra 7:6–10; Neh. 8:1–12
1. What was Ezra's ambition?
2. What did the Levites do for the people?

FOR READING & MEDITATION – COLOSSIANS 1:26–27

'The glorious riches of this mystery, which is Christ in you,
the hope of glory.' (v27)

A true servant of God, we said yesterday, seeks to make the Word of God fully known and Christians fully mature. Paul claims that he has been commissioned for this task, and clearly he did his work well. But what did he base his work on? It was this great truth: 'Christ in you, the hope of glory.' Paul refers to it as a mystery which though kept hidden for generations had now been made known. 'The mystery... now disclosed' refers, of course, to the fact that Christ indwells Gentiles as well as Jews and welcomes them into His Church on equal terms with Israelites – a revelation that first came through the apostle Paul (see Eph. 3:2–6). This was a sign that a new era had begun, which will culminate in the second coming.

Focus with me now on the phrase 'Christ in you, the hope of glory'. There are many who accept that Christ is for them, but they have no experience of Christ being in them. They may be ready to assert with the rest of us that we have an advocate with the Father, Jesus Christ, the Righteous One (1 John 2:1), but they do not know Him as a power within them. Paul is saying the secret of maturity is having Christ within – thinking, willing and feeling in the heart of His consenting servant.

'Christ *in* you, the hope of glory.' What a phrase. But is it only a hope – a possibility? As we saw the other day, the word hope in Scripture means a sure and certain expectation with no shadow of doubt. To have Christ near to us is not enough. He must be *in* us, subduing the deep selfishness of our nature, ridding us of our moral rottenness. And as William Law said, 'A Christ not in us is... a Christ not ours.'

O Father, what a thought: Christ is not just near to me or around me but living in me, His conquering life overcoming my inward death. How wonderful. All honour and glory be to Your precious name. Amen.

FURTHER STUDY
John 14:15–23; 15:1–8
1. What did Jesus explain to the disciples?
2. How do we remain in Christ?

FOR READING & MEDITATION – COLOSSIANS 1:28

'We proclaim him, admonishing and teaching
everyone with all wisdom...' (v28)

This verse gives us a penetrating insight into the heart and mind of the great apostle. The word 'everyone', which appears twice in this one verse, suggests that Paul was thinking here not primarily of his public ministry but of his personal relationships with believers. Paul had no time for what some people call 'the Church within the Church' – in other words, those Christians who are more committed than others and more ready to respond to profound truths. Maturity is not for a spiritual elite – it is for everyone.

How did Paul go about the task of helping people become mature? By 'admonishing and teaching everyone with all wisdom'. To admonish individuals is to warn them or correct them; to teach is to educate – to lead people into deeper truths and a richer understanding of the things of God. Does this mean that in all our conversations with fellow Christians we ought to be seeking to correct and teach each other? Of course not. I am sure Paul enjoyed some so-called 'small talk' in the same way that we do, but I am sure also that when he saw a need to correct, encourage, or exhort, he would immediately seize the opportunity to do so. Paul concentrated on the goal of bringing others to maturity, and I can imagine him asking at appropriate times questions such as these of his fellow believers: How is your prayer life going? What's your relationship with the Lord like? Are you having any struggles that you might want me to pray about or help you with?

How different relationships would be in the Body of Christ if, when talking with our Christian brothers and sisters, we were as interested in their spiritual health as we are in their physical health.

Heavenly Father, I know that to be mature in Christ is to be mature indeed. May I become excited about encouraging others to grow spiritually. I yield my all to be mature and to help others become mature. In Jesus' name. Amen.

FURTHER STUDY
Gal. 2:11–16; 2 Tim. 3:14–17; Jas 5:19–20
1. What is Scripture useful for?
2. How should we relate to others?

Superhuman Energy

FOR READING & MEDITATION – COLOSSIANS 1:29

'To this end I labour, struggling with all his energy,
which so powerfully works in me.' (v29)

The words 'To this end I labour' sound strained and tense, but then we come to the next part of the verse, which says, 'struggling with all his energy, which so powerfully works in me'. The Amplified Bible (AMPC) expresses it like this: 'For this I labor, striving with all the superhuman energy which He so mightily enkindles and works within me.' Paul's labour did not depend on human energy but the power that came from Christ. He lived using all the energy Christ generated within him. Paul put into his ministry all the energy he could muster, and found that as he did, Christ added His energy also.

Frequently I have heard my friend Dr Larry Crabb talk to counsellors about this verse. He asks them, 'How often when you interact with people in counselling are you aware of an energy flowing through you that doesn't come from you but from Christ?' When he invites a show of hands in response, few are raised. Permit me to ask you a similar question now: How aware are you when you go about your service for Jesus Christ (and I am not just talking about counselling now) of an energy flowing through you and from you that is superhuman? If you were to ask that question of me I would have to confess, 'Too infrequently.'

Paul, however, threw his heart and soul into everything he did and found the energy of Christ matching his every effort. When he said 'I labour' he was using a term (*kopiao* in the Greek) which signifies labouring to the point of weariness. He poured out what was poured in, not with reservation but with *all* the energy which Christ generated within him. Far too often our experience begins and ends in these words: 'To this end I labour, struggling.'

O God, forgive me that so much of my life can be expressed in those words: 'I labour... struggling.' Help me experience the energy of Christ working in me and through me. In His name I pray. Amen.

FURTHER STUDY
2 Cor. 12:7–10; Eph. 3:7–13
1. What did God explain to Paul?
2. What did Paul explain about his ministry?

One Heart and One Mind

FOR READING & MEDITATION – COLOSSIANS 2:1–2

'My purpose is that they may be encouraged in heart and
united in love...' (v2)

Here Paul really opens up his heart to the Colossians and also the believers in Laodicea, to whom his letter would be read (see 4:16). He speaks of his great concern for them – a concern that grew, no doubt, when he heard the news brought to him by Epaphras that a serious error was circulating among them. The apostle longs that they may 'be encouraged in heart and united in love'. The Amplified Bible uses these words: 'that their hearts may be encouraged as they are knit together in love'. How encouraging it is for believers when their hearts are united in love. However, the opposite is also true: discouragement is the consequence of believers realising their hearts are not united in love.

But love is not enough. Paul is aware that lasting unity depends on truth as well as love. The believers at Colosse need to be of one mind as well as one heart; hence his concern that they may have 'the full riches of complete understanding' in order to know the mystery of God, namely Jesus Christ Himself. The false teachers in Colosse believed that revelation could be received outside of the Saviour, but here Paul lays down the thought that all essential truth is found *in* Christ, and they need not look any further than Him for spiritual understanding.

Just as in New Testament times, so today error creeps into the Church if men and women claim to have insight and revelation beyond that which Scripture unfolds. The unity of believers is at risk when the people of God are not of one mind on the things that are essential. A common mind about the truths of the Bible and the supremacy of Christ is the only possible basis for Christian unity. If there is not one mind there cannot be one heart.

O Father, help Your children everywhere to have not only one heart but also one mind. And help us, too, not to sacrifice truth in the interests of unity. In Jesus' name we pray. Amen.

FURTHER STUDY

Rom. 15:1–6; 2 Cor. 13:11–14

1. What was Paul's desire for the Romans?
2. When would God be with the Corinthians?

A Meditation on the Cross

FOR READING & MEDITATION – MATTHEW 27:32–56

'About the ninth hour Jesus cried out... "My God, my God,
why have you forsaken me?"' (v46)

At this time of year, many of us will be observing the festival of Lent, as we look ahead to Holy Week, including the celebration of the resurrection on Easter Sunday. We will pause, therefore, in our meditations on the letter to the Colossians to reflect on the mystery of the cross and the wonder of the open tomb. Three thoughts always form the basis of my meditations at Eastertime. Permit me to share them with you again.

First, *apart from the cross I would never realise the enormity of my sin.* It is tragic that we do not realise the wickedness of sin. We call our sins 'mistakes' or 'failings', and even when we use the right word – 'sin' – we use it lightly. How terrible my sins must be to a holy God if the only way He could expunge them was to allow His Son to die for me.

Second, *apart from the cross I would have no clear focus for my faith.* It was Oswald Chambers who said, 'Life is more tragic than orderly'. Every day we hear of terrible things happening – of horrific accidents and disasters killing innocent people, and many other forms of suffering. Can God be Love and allow tragedies to continue? That is a question many people ask. Whenever a doubt arises in my mind concerning God's love, I stand at the foot of the cross where it is quickly laid to rest. A God who loved me enough to send His Son to die for me has got to be Love.

Third, *apart from the cross I would not have a Saviour.* I need a Saviour. I need an Example, too, and a Teacher, and a Friend. But most of all I need a Saviour. The cross shows me that Jesus Christ has done everything required for my salvation. All I need do is acknowledge my sin, repent of it, reach out to receive the gift of salvation, and it is mine. Mine just for the asking. What marvellous mercy. Apart from the cross I would have nothing.

My Father and my God, thank You for the mercy that streams towards me from Calvary. You do not love me because Christ died, but Christ died because You love me. I am loved, lifted and loosed. Amen.

FURTHER STUDY
Isa. 53:1–12; 1 Cor. 2:1–5
1. Why did Christ die?
2. What was the focus of Paul's preaching?

FOR READING & MEDITATION – LUKE 23:44–56

'The women... followed Joseph and saw the tomb
and how his body was laid in it.' (v55)

How calm and private the tomb was after the shameful public spectacle of the crucifixion. How quiet and still! It is difficult to work out the exact time between our Lord's arrest and His death on the cross, but as far as we can tell it was about eight to nine hours. Eight to nine awful hours! In the brief space of six hours He was examined five times by four different tribunals. He was rushed from Annas to Caipahas, from Caipahas to Pilate, from Pilate to Herod, from Herod back to Pilate again. He was flogged and mocked. And then on to the cross.

Could Jesus not have died in quietness in the company of His loved ones? No, the cup of suffering had to be drunk to its dregs, and the ghastly exposure to public gaze was part of the bitterness of the cross. There was the mix of noise, dust, thirst, jeers and sobs as He hung in agony between earth and heaven. Not long after the cry 'Father, into your hands I commit my spirit' (v46) He bows His head and dies.

And then the tomb. Do you think of a tomb as being cold and eerie? Not this one. It was filled with destiny. Step inside with me for a moment. Our crucified Saviour lies there on a cool bed of rock. In the spirit He waits. What is He waiting for? To fulfil prophecy, to reverse the human verdict passed on Him, to prove that He really died on the cross and did not just swoon, to validate the victory won on the cross. There are many reasons. He waits and waits and waits. And then, to quote Alice Meynell:

All alone, alone, alone,
He rose again behind the stone.

O Father, I never tire of hearing the story of my Lord's death and resurrection. It is the most glorious thing that has ever happened. My salvation is assured because of it. All honour and glory be to Your name for ever. Amen.

FURTHER STUDY
Phil. 2:5–11; Heb. 1:13
1. Why does the Father exalt Christ?
2. What does Christ still wait for?

The New Year's Day

FOR READING & MEDITATION – JOHN 20:1–18

'Then Simon Peter... saw the strips of linen lying there, as well as the burial cloth...' (vv6–7)

As we conclude today our special focus on the events of Easter, let us stand once again at the open tomb and reflect on what happened there. Mary Magdalene comes to the tomb while it is still dark and sees that the stone has been rolled away. She hurries to tell Peter and John the news, and the two of them run to the tomb. John outruns Peter, bends to look into the tomb, glances at the linen cloths, yet hesitates to go in. Peter is not far behind, and when he arrives he doesn't hesitate. Bursting into the tomb he gazes in amazement at the strips of linen clothes lying near the entrance, where Jesus' feet had lain. As he looks further into the tomb he notices the cloth which had been wrapped around Jesus' head. Moments later John follows, and believes that Jesus has risen from the dead.

These verses are full of the most interesting details and are certainly the account of eyewitnesses. And that makes you almost feel you are an eyewitness yourself. Look again at the collapsed linen cloths lying there. What does it all suggest?

When Jesus came back from the dead He did not quietly and laboriously unwind strips of linen used as graveclothes. This was not an unwinding, this was a glorious uprising! The very concept of resurrection is supernatural. The natural process of physical decomposition was not arrested or reversed but superseded. Peter and John were the first to see the evidence of the most sensational thing that has ever happened on this planet. As John Stott puts it, 'We live and die; Christ died and lives.' And because He lives we live also. No wonder A.B. Simpson described Easter as 'The New Year's Day of the soul'.

Lord Jesus Christ, how can I thank You enough that although it was possible for You to die, it was not possible for You to be held by death? And now, because You live, I live also. All honour and glory be to Your wonderful name. Amen.

FURTHER STUDY

Luke 24:13–32; 1 Cor. 15:3–8
1. What did the disciples not understand?
2. Why did Paul believe in Christ's resurrection?

An Exciting Treasure Hunt

FOR READING & MEDITATION – COLOSSIANS 2:3

'In whom are hidden all the treasures of wisdom
and knowledge.' (v3)

There is enough truth in these glowing words to feed our minds and hearts for a whole year! The point Paul has been making is that no essential truths are withheld from anyone who belongs to Jesus Christ. 'All' – notice the 'all' – '*all* the treasures of wisdom and knowledge' are hidden in Him. But notice also that the truth is hidden. That means our Lord conceals as well as reveals. You know and you don't know; you see and you don't see. But what you don't know and don't see spurs you on to further discovery.

For me this perpetual discovery has been the most thrilling thing in my life. The feeling that every day there is some new surprise to be found has kept me on my toes. Throughout my Christian life I have made it a habit to read the Bible daily, and there are times when I am beside myself with excitement as I see something I had never seen before. Christians who go from week to week without ever opening up their Bibles and focusing on some aspect of God's message to them must live dull lives. I fail to understand how they can exist without exploring the treasures of wisdom and knowledge that are found in Christ and revealed to us in the Scriptures.

'This unfolding revelation of Christ,' says one writer, 'puts a surprise around every corner, makes life pop with novelty and discovery, makes life well worth the living.' The Christian life is dynamic, not static. The more you know, the more you know you don't know, and what you know fills you with the longing to know more. The more we know of Christ the more we want to know, and this discovery will go on for ever. We will never go beyond Him. Never.

O Father, I am so glad that what I know of You and Your Son impels me to find out more and more. I am on the most exciting treasure hunt in the world – set to discover the treasures hidden in Christ. Amen.

FURTHER STUDY
Ps. 19:1–14; Prov. 25:2
1. Why is God's Word more precious than gold?
2. What brings glory to God and what to men?

In Good Order

FOR READING & MEDITATION – COLOSSIANS 2:4–5

'I tell you this so that no-one may deceive you
by fine-sounding arguments.' (v4)

The reason Paul told the believers at Colosse and Laodicea that all the treasures of wisdom and knowledge are hidden in Christ and nowhere else is because, as Eugene Peterson puts it in *The Message* (MSG), he didn't 'want anyone leading [them] off on some wild-goose chase, after other so-called mysteries, or "the Secret"'. They must not allow themselves to be deceived.

Sin entered the world, you remember, after Eve allowed herself to be deceived (see Gen. 3). Had she checked Satan's words against the word given by God (Gen. 2:16–17), and held to that, then she would not have succumbed to temptation. If all Christians were to examine carefully what they read in books or hear – even from pulpits – and check it against the infallible Scriptures, then error would have little freedom to circulate. There are many persuasive speakers in today's Church, and although only a few preach error, we would do well to examine everything we hear for the truthfulness of its content and not allow ourselves to be taken in by the attractiveness of its packaging.

Though error was threatening the churches at Colosse and Laodicea, it is obvious from Paul's next words that not everything was bad. 'I... delight to see how orderly you are and how firm your faith in Christ is.' These two go together – orderliness and a firm faith in Christ. It works the other way also: where there is no firmness of faith in Christ there is no order; instead there is disorder. Firmness of faith in Christ and good order are root and fruit. Loss of faith in Christ and disorder are also root and fruit. In Him we are in good order; out of Him we are in disorder.

My Father and my God, I am so thankful that life holds together at the centre when our faith is fixed firmly in Your Son. We stay in good order when we are under Your orders. Amen.

FURTHER STUDY
Acts 17:10–15; 1 Tim. 6:20–21
1. Why were the Bereans commended?
2. What was Timothy to do?

Give, Take, Build

FOR READING & MEDITATION – COLOSSIANS 2:6–7

'Just as you received Christ Jesus as Lord, continue to live
in him...' (v6)

There is no doubt that these two verses sum up the teaching of the entire letter. No better definition of the essentials of the Christian life could be given than this: 'as you received Christ Jesus as Lord, continue to live in him'. These two requirements – receiving and continuing – should be made clear to every new Christian. And those who have been on the Way some time need to be reminded of them also. Some think receiving Christ is the end, but it is only the beginning. The foundation is there to be built on.

How did we receive Christ? By surrender and receptivity. We give to Him and take from Him. Give and take – this is relationship reduced to its simplest terms. Our giving involves giving the one and only thing we own – ourselves. When He has that, He has all. And part of the purpose of giving is so that we may receive. God asks that we give our all in order that He may give His all. Notice the words Paul uses: 'As you received Christ Jesus as *Lord*'. He is 'Lord', remember, not merely Example or Teacher. Lord! And you cannot really call Jesus Saviour unless you call Him Lord. He saves those who submit to Him – no others.

When we continue to depend on Christ and make Him the centre of our lives then we are rooted in Him, built up in Him, and we overflow with thankfulness. These may be different metaphors, but they are telling nevertheless. Rooted in Christ we grow in Him. We hardly bury a seed to see the last of it. Established in Him we are built up in Him. And the final test is how thankful we are. If you do not give thanks regularly for all that God has done for you and given you then you ought to question whether you are indeed a Christian.

Dear Father, I would give, give, give, take, take, take, build, build, build. Let all I take from You enable me to give more. I long to be the best I can be for You. And above all, thank You for saving me. In Jesus' name. Amen.

FURTHER STUDY
1 Cor. 3:6–15; Eph. 4:11–16
1. Why should we be careful?
2. What is necessary for personal spiritual growth?

Godless Philosophies

FOR READING & MEDITATION – COLOSSIANS 2:8

'See to it that no-one takes you captive through hollow
and deceptive philosophy...' (v8)

Paul now challenges the Colossians with a sharp and clear warning:
don't pay any attention to false teachers – those who mix truth with
error, and spout hollow and deceptive philosophies; they will take you
captive. J.B. Phillips words Paul's cautionary message like this: 'Be careful
that nobody spoils your faith through intellectualism or high-sounding
nonsense. Such stuff is at best founded on men's ideas of the nature of
the world and disregards Christ!'

Philosophy is defined by the dictionary as 'seeking after wisdom or
knowledge, especially that which deals with ultimate reality'. Yet any
philosophy that is not built on God's revelation in Scripture leads nowhere.
Philosophical reasoning may sound fascinating but it contains no real
answers to the mysteries of the universe. The truth is found only in Christ.

When Paul used the words 'hollow and deceptive philosophy' he had
in mind the philosophy of the false teachers, who based their reasoning
on human theories rather than on Christ. This teaching seems to have
been an elementary form of Gnosticism. From Paul's emphasis on the
pre-eminence of Christ (1:18), and on the need for a true knowledge of
Christ who is the source of wisdom (2:2–3), it would appear the false
teachers were attempting to persuade believers that Christ was not God's
final revelation and that they could gain a deeper experience of salvation
through enlightenment. This was nonsense, of course, but many fell for this
type of heresy in the days of the Early Church. Mark my words, if something
is not Christocentric it will end up being eccentric – off centre. Our Lord is
the *truth*, as well as the way and the life.

**Gracious and loving heavenly Father, how glad I am that my faith has come
to rest not in a combination of Christ and further enlightenment, but in Him,
and in Him alone. Protect my soul from entertaining error, dear Lord. Amen.**

FURTHER STUDY

1 Cor. 1:18–31; 1 Tim. 1:3–7
1. How does God deal with those wise in their own eyes?
2. Why might we wander from the faith?

Music Vaster Than Before

FOR READING & MEDITATION – COLOSSIANS 2:9

'For in Christ all the fulness of the Deity lives in bodily form...' (v9)

The preceding verses provide the background for this verse. The false teaching was, as we said yesterday, probably an early form of Gnosticism, which also taught that matter is evil and spirit is good. To counter such ideas Paul declares, 'For in Christ all the fulness of the Deity lives *in bodily form*.' God came into matter at the incarnation and made it the vehicle of divine revelation. Nothing could be more important for our existence on earth, environed as we are with matter. The material is not alien; it is an ally.

The spiritual world manifests itself through the material, in material form and material relationships. Listen to these words: 'A body you prepared for me... I have come to do your will, O God' (Heb. 10:5,7). God's will for Christ was to be done in and through a body. The Gnostics of the second century taught that matter was evil. Hindus believe matter is illusion. Christians, however, say matter is God-made ('God saw that it was good', Gen. 1) and can be used to good purposes. The kingdom of God, remember, is within us here on *earth* (Luke 17:21).

And just in case some might claim God came into matter temporarily and partially, Paul says that '*all the fulness of the Deity* lives in bodily form'. There is nothing in God that isn't in Jesus – at least in character and essence. Jesus is God accommodated to human form, not for a short time, but now and always. Christ's body was taken up into heaven and will probably bear the marks of the nail prints through all eternity. His humanity is not something He takes off like a wrap. Christ is both human and divine – for ever. In our Lord, body and spirit were reconciled, and because of that, as one poet put it, 'There beats out music vaster than before'.

O Lord Jesus Christ, the meeting place of God and man, matter and spirit, and the reconciling place of all, grant that I may witness to the Word who became flesh. In Jesus' name I ask it. Amen.

FURTHER STUDY

John 1:1–3,14; 5:16–18; 1 Tim. 3:16
1. What does the Bible teach about Christ and God?
2. Why did the Jews try to kill Jesus?

Fulness of Life in Christ

FOR READING & MEDITATION – COLOSSIANS 2:10

'And you have been given fulness in Christ, who is the
head over every power and authority.' (v10)

Now comes the application of the previous verse: we ourselves have been given fulness in Christ. The false teachers, who regarded the material body as evil, had bypassed the incarnation, saying it was beneath God's dignity to touch matter, let alone enter into it. Instead they taught you could attain fulness of life by knowing God directly. In reality, however, we come to fulness of life in Jesus Christ or we do not come to it at all. Let me pick up Jesus' famous statement once again: 'I am the way and the truth *and the life*' (John 14:6, my emphasis). He is life, and He alone gives us fulness of life – when we are united with Him we share in the very nature of God.

Nowadays some people, in order to accommodate other religions and philosophies, take Christ and someone else: Christ and Mohammed, Christ and Buddha, Christ and Jung. They do this, they say, in the interests of universality. But such thinking is completely misguided, for Christ is universal. To be in Him is to be in everything that is of reality in the universe.

But there's more: the believer also shares in His victory – He is Head over every power and authority. We need fear no longer the prince of darkness or any other power or authority. Christ is the One who is in control of everything and everyone. Dick Lucas says that this verse unfolds two themes: one, the fact that because we have the fulness of God's presence with us here then we have all we can have this side of heaven, and second, with regard to heaven's victory over powers and principalities, we share with Christ all that He has won. To this I say a hearty 'Amen'.

O God, help me to make this my affirmation: in Christ there is fulness of life; outside of Him there is emptiness of life. This is my verdict. May I live by it every day of my life. In Jesus' name. Amen.

FURTHER STUDY
John 1:16–18; Eph. 1:2–10
1. What have we received?
2. What has God made known to us?

Complete in Him

FOR READING & MEDITATION – COLOSSIANS 2:11–12

'In him you were also circumcised, in the
putting off of the sinful nature...' (v11)

Just as happened in the Galatian churches, false teachers seem to have been making circumcision a condition of salvation. In Colosse, however, the false teaching was syncretistic, combining elements of both Jewish and Gentile thought. So, to the Gentile idea of salvation through enlightenment, was added the Jewish tradition of circumcision, dietary rules, and observance of religious festivals.

The false teachers may also have been persuading the Colossian believers to accept the idea that circumcision was an act of dedication and consecration, a second initiation subsequent to baptism. If this were so then Paul is countering the argument by saying circumcision is unnecessary because they already possess a purification of which Christ is the source. At your conversion, he explains, there takes place a circumcision not done by hands – that of being forgiven your sins and cleansed from unrighteousness.

'You were buried with Christ in baptism,' he goes on to tell them. They had already died with Christ so now it followed that as He was raised from the dead so they too were raised with Him. The point being made is that we need not add to what Christ has already done. God can do nothing greater for us than He has done in Christ.

Paul, in verse 10, made the point that Christians are spiritually complete in Christ. Here he adds the thought that we are complete in Christ only when we acknowledge His completeness – when we demonstrate our faith in Him. 'It takes a complete Christ,' said D.L. Moody, 'to make a complete Christian.' It's no good saying Christ is complete then trying to add something to Him. He is either complete or incomplete. Period.

O Father, I see the importance of trusting only in You and in the atoning merits of Your Son. I need nothing for my salvation other than my trust in Him. Thank You, my Father. Amen.

FURTHER STUDY
Acts 15:1–19
1. Why did the apostles and elders meet?
2. What was the conclusion?

FOR READING & MEDITATION – COLOSSIANS 2:13–14

'He forgave us all our sins, having cancelled the
written code... nailing it to the cross.' (vv13–14)

The theme continues: God cannot do for us anything greater than that which He has already done in Christ. When we were dead in our sins His Spirit moved into our lives, cut into our sinful nature, and now continually seeks to render inoperative the energy of sin. Does that mean it is not possible to sin again? No, but it is possible not to sin. God has made us alive with Christ, and when His life pulses through our soul then freedom from sin *is* possible. From this point on Paul launches into a graphic description of salvation. God has not only made us alive with Christ but He has cancelled the written code that was against us, nailing it to His cross. What beautiful word pictures.

Take the first: 'cancelled the written code'. 'Written code' means a handwritten note. It is the Greek term for an IOU – an acknowledgement of a debt and recognition that payment is obligatory, with certain penalties being required if payment is not made. The word translated 'cancelled' (*exaleipho* in the Greek) means to sponge or wipe off. This is what Christ has done with our sins. The written code that condemned us has been sponged off by the blood of Christ. It is as if it had never been.

But Paul uses one more word picture: 'he took it away, nailing it to the cross'. In ancient times the record of a debt, after it had been paid, would sometimes be nailed to a public notice board so that everyone could see the matter was settled. Our Lord has taken the debt we owed and nailed it to the most public place in the universe – the cross. When Christ cried 'It is finished' (John 19:30), He meant that the work of our redemption was complete. The cancelled note hangs on the cross for all to see.

Father, when the hosts of hell try to tell me that my sins are not forgiven, I shall point them to the cross and show them the cancelled note, placarded there for all to see. I am eternally grateful. Amen.

FURTHER STUDY
Eph. 2:11–18; 1 John 1:5–10
1. What has Christ abolished?
2. Why do we need to actually confess sins?

Stripped of Sham Authority

FOR READING & MEDITATION – COLOSSIANS 2:15

'And having disarmed the powers and authorities,
he made a public spectacle of them...' (v15)

This is exciting stuff. To let you feel the impact of Paul's words I will quote this text from two different versions. First that of J.B. Phillips: 'And then, having drawn the sting of all the powers ranged against us, he exposed them, shattered, empty and defeated, in his final glorious triumphant act!' Now Eugene Peterson's paraphrase: 'He stripped all the spiritual tyrants in the universe of their sham authority at the Cross and marched them naked through the streets' (MSG).

There is little doubt that the picture Paul had in mind was that of the triumphal procession that customarily took place after a great conquest in Roman times. Hundreds of weary prisoners of war would be tied to chariots and dragged through the streets so that everyone could witness their misery and shame. For the citizens who belonged to the conquering army it was a wonderful sight, but a terrible and humiliating experience for those who had been conquered.

What a striking illustration this is of the conquest that our Lord achieved for us at Calvary. Just as the Roman citizens could see that they had nothing to fear from the once proud soldiers now defeated and being paraded before them, so we no longer need to fear Satan and his minions, who tried to end the life and ministry of Jesus at the cross. If Satan and his forces have any power over us it is only because we let them. They attempt to masquerade as conquerors but it is all a sham. They have been ignominiously defeated. Satan thought he would have a great victory at the cross but the tables have been turned. It is Christ's victory the cross proclaims. And how!

O Father, I see that Christ's victory on the cross is my victory too. He won it by conquering; I enter into it by just trusting. It sounds too good to be true. But also too good not to be true. Amen.

FURTHER STUDY
John 10:7–11; Heb. 2:14–15; 1 John 3:4–8
1. Contrast the purposes of Christ and the devil.
2. How did Christ destroy the devil?

Shadowlands

FOR READING & MEDITATION – COLOSSIANS 2:16–17

'Therefore do not let anyone judge you by what you eat or drink, or with regard to a religious festival...' (v16)

Yesterday we focused on the triumph of Jesus Christ over every power and authority that is ranged against Him. In the light of this Paul now encourages the Colossian believers to celebrate Christ's victory for them in a life free from unnecessary rituals and ceremonies.

Clearly an attempt was being made in the church at Colosse to persuade the believers to be concerned about such matters as food taboos and keeping religious festivals. This erroneous approach was calculated to make people believe that Christ's sacrifice, and His presence in the life of the believer, were not enough to achieve holiness; other matters such as rituals and ceremonies were essential. Paul will have none of this, of course, and dismisses the idea in no uncertain terms. This is how Eugene Peterson paraphrases in *The Message* (MSG) the opening statement of verse 16: 'So don't put up with anyone pressuring you in details of diet, worship services or holy days.' Strong words – and words most definitely needed if they were to maintain their life of freedom in Christ and assert that He was all that mattered to them.

Paul goes on to say, 'These are a shadow of the things that were to come; the reality, however, is found in Christ.' The shadowland referred to here is the law found in the Old Testament. The rituals it prescribed were to be kept, but they were just *shadows* of what was to come. Their true value lay not in what they were but what they pointed to. Christ is the fulfilment of all that the Old Testament prefigured, and in Him is found all spiritual reality. Those who depend on rituals and ceremonies for their salvation are living in the shadows. Christ is all that is needed. All.

Father, how glad I am that I am in Christ and He is in me. What need have I of standing in the shadows when I can stand in the sunshine of Your love, as shown to me in Christ? Amen.

FURTHER STUDY

Heb. 8:1–7; 10:1–18

1. What did priests and rituals point to?
2. What did they achieve and how did they fail?

Pride Must Die...

FOR READING & MEDITATION – COLOSSIANS 2:18

'Do not let anyone who delights in false humility and the
worship of angels disqualify you for the prize.' (v18)

Paul has given the Colossians several warnings in this chapter and here, in verse 18, is another one. J.B. Phillips translates it in this way: '[Don't] let any man cheat you of your joy in Christ by persuading you to make yourselves "humble" and fall down and worship angels. Such a man, inflated by an unspiritual imagination, is pushing his way into matters he knows nothing about, and in his cleverness forgetting the head.'

Some commentators believe one aspect of the heresy threatening the church at Colossse was the veneration of angels – the idea being to seek out mediators in addition to Christ. If so then it is another indication of the existence of beliefs similar to those of second-century Gnosticism.

Paul has no intention of allowing the false teaching to rob those who are 'in Christ' of their prize, and characterises the individuals concerned in this way: 'Such a person goes into great detail about what he has seen [in visions], and his unspiritual mind puffs him up with idle notions.' Here we see the root of the trouble: those advocating the worship of angels were puffed up with pride. They claimed to have inside knowledge but really they had found a 'spiritual' way (so called) of drawing attention to themselves.

When talking to Christians with strange ideas about the faith, I have found that often the underlying motivation is to be noticed. They have little or no sense of identity, and as aligning themselves with others is not enough of a boost for them, they go in the other direction. Thus they are *different*. The root of all this is, as Paul discerned, pride. William Law put it well when he said, 'Pride must die in us or Christ cannot live in us.'

Father, help me remember that it was pride that turned an angel into the devil and brought havoc to this fair universe. May I be so secure in You that I will find my identity in that, not in being different. In Jesus' name. Amen.

FURTHER STUDY
1 Cor. 8:1–3; 3 John 1–13
1. Why is knowledge good and bad?
2. Contrast different members in the church John wrote to.

Keep Connected

FOR READING & MEDITATION – COLOSSIANS 2:19

'He has lost connection with the Head, from
whom the whole body... grows...' (v19)

Yesterday we considered pride – one of the factors that motivated those who were threatening the Colossian church with serious error. In the verse before us today Paul gives us another reason for the problem: the type of person causing trouble had lost connection with the Head. Apparently they were still part of the congregation, but had not held fast to Christ, the Head of the Church.

A similar situation, you remember, occurred when a group of Christians in the church in Pergamum followed the erroneous teachings of Balaam and the Nicolaitans (see Rev. 2:12–17). And apparently they were still part of the church. The reason why Christ urged them to repent was because it is impossible to remain true to Him and at the same time toy with the error that robs Him of His supremacy and sufficiency.

Paul shows us in this verse – perhaps more clearly than anywhere else in the New Testament – that when we drift away from Christ then we also drift away from each other. Show me a church where the members have lost connection with the Head and I will show you a church whose members have lost connection with each other. That church may have exciting community projects, a wonderful musical programme and clever debates, but if its members are not united with Christ then it no longer functions as a church; it becomes a club. The Head is the source of the spiritual life and health of a church. Its ministers, teachers, musicians, all have a place of course but, as Paul explains, 'the whole body... grows as God causes it to grow'. Growth comes not from men but from God. Aggressive methods and strong appeals can add numbers to a church, but only God can make a church *grow*.

Father, save me from thinking that because a church is increasing in numbers it is therefore growing. I see that growth comes only when we, Your people, are connected to the Head. Help us stay connected, dear Father. Amen.

FURTHER STUDY

Acts 2:42–47; Eph. 4:15–16

1. How did the Early Church keep connected?
2. How does a church grow?

Rules Versus Relationships

FOR READING & MEDITATION – COLOSSIANS 2:20–22

'Since you died with Christ to the basic principles of this world,
why... do you submit to its rules...?' (v20)

These verses imply that some Colossian converts had already succumbed to the false teaching that was circulating in the church. If so, how can we reconcile this fact with Paul's commendation of their faith in chapter 1? The answer, I think, must be that a small number were in danger of being swayed by this error, and it is to those he now expresses his concerns. In these final verses of chapter 2, Paul is at his most trenchant. Why do you live, he asks, as if you still belonged to this world? Why do you submit to its rules? By asking this he is equating the ideas propagated by the false teachers with the religion of the world.

It is obvious that the world cannot do without religion since humanity, having been made in God's image, has an inbuilt desire to worship. Since it rejects Christ as the only way to God, it has to find the elements of its religious structure elsewhere. Satan, the prince of this world, delights in providing people with a religion that satisfies their need to worship but does not ask them to bow the knee to Christ. One commentator puts it like this: 'The closer in language [Satan's] religion can be to the truth, while yet being different, the better this wily prince is pleased.' Rules such as 'Do not eat this', or 'Do not touch that', or 'Do not go near this' are elements of the world's religion and will one day pass away.

Since you died with Christ, says Paul, you are not governed by rules, but by your relationship with Him. You are saved not by what You do but by what Christ has done. God has put the Church in the world, but we must make sure that the world does not get into the Church.

Father, You have taken me from the world and put me into Your Church. Help me not only to tell others where and to whom I belong, but also to show them by my every action, my every attitude. Amen.

FURTHER STUDY
Gal. 3:19–25; 4:1–10
1. What was the purpose of the law?
2. What was the effect of the law?

FOR READING & MEDITATION – COLOSSIANS 2:23

'Such regulations... have an appearance of wisdom, with their self-imposed worship, their false humility...' (v23)

How, I wonder, did those at Colosse who were propagating error respond to Paul's sharp and incisive condemnation of their theories. The false teachers had persuasive arguments, lived lives of self-discipline, and showed great commitment to what they believed, but the motivation behind it all was worldly pride. Outwardly it looked as if these people had a high degree of wisdom but, says Paul, it was merely the *appearance* of wisdom. Their self-imposed worship, their false humility and their harsh treatment of the body made no impression on the mind of the great apostle. He saw these things as just another way of showing off, a way of making themselves look important.

We must pause for a moment to make clear what is meant by 'self-imposed worship'. J.B. Phillips translates this phrase as 'self-inspired efforts at worship'. The people Paul is denouncing worshipped God not in the way He wants to be worshipped but in the way they *thought* He should be worshipped. Referring again to Phillips' translation, he renders the NIV phrases 'false humility' as 'their policy of self-humbling', and 'their harsh treatment of the body' as 'their studied neglect of the body'. These graphic phrases take us to the very heart of their motivation – they were using supposedly spiritual practices as a means to pander to their self-centredness and pride in their own efforts.

It is my opinion that self-centredness lies at the root of most of our spiritual problems. If we could eliminate self-centredness from the human heart we would have very few difficulties. Of that I am sure. And self-centredness is never more deadly than when it is dressed up as spirituality.

Gracious and loving heavenly Father, may I not use my faith in the service of self-centredness and egotism. Help me to have a faith that works by love, and nothing but love. In Jesus' name. Amen.

FURTHER STUDY
Matt. 15:7–9; John 4:19–25; Phil. 3:1–3
1. How did the Samaritans worship?
2. How should we worship?

Our Chief Business

FOR READING & MEDITATION – COLOSSIANS 3:1

'Since... you have been raised with Christ, set your hearts on things above...' (v1)

Paul's letter to the Colossians divides neatly in two, the first half being doctrinal and the second practical. Paul's purpose in this letter, as we have repeatedly seen, is to show that Christ is pre-eminent – that He is first and foremost in everything – and that the life of every Christian should reflect that fact. Eugene Peterson paraphrases Paul's words in this way: 'So if you're serious about living this new resurrection life with Christ, *act* like it. Pursue the things over which Christ presides.' Because we are rooted in Him, alive in Him, hidden in Him, and complete in Him, we must *live* for Him.

Living for Christ is the theme that Paul embarks upon as he begins this third chapter, and he deals with it in terms of *relationships*. First, our relationship with Christ, second, relationships in the local church, third, relationships with the family, fourth, relationship to one's daily work, and fifth, relationships with unbelievers. It has been said that 'The chief business of every Christian is to maintain his relationship with Christ'. If this relationship is not kept intact then it is impossible for other relationships to succeed.

The instruction to set our hearts on things above, where Christ sits, is based on the fact that we have been raised with Him. Think what that means: we have been granted a relationship with Christ, who is at God's right hand. And we are to pursue this relationship by remaining true to Christ, who is the centre and source of all our joy. A Christian is someone who, in a sense, lives in two places at once: in their earthly residence and in Christ. The question we have to ask ourselves is this: Where are we most at home?

Father, in coming to Jesus I have come home. Please help me to be at home in Him – even more at home than I am in my own home. In Your Son's name I pray. Amen.

FURTHER STUDY
Ps. 27:4; 63:1–8; 84:1–12
1. What was the psalmist's desire?
2. What was the psalmist's practice?

At Home in the Heavenly Realm

FOR READING & MEDITATION – COLOSSIANS 3:2–3

'For you died, and your life is now hidden with Christ in God.' (v3)

Our relationship with Christ shapes every other relationship – our relationships with our friends and acquaintances, our working relationships, our marriages, everything. So important is it to grasp this truth that Paul continues with his theme in the second verse. Don't go through life looking down or just looking at the things in front of you, he is saying. 'Look up and be alert to what is going on around Christ – that's where the action is. See things from *his* perspective' (Eugene Peterson, MSG).

Unlike some other world religions, the Christian faith has no geographical centre. Judaism focuses on Jerusalem and Islam on Mecca. The Christian faith, however, focuses on heaven, where Christ is seated at the right hand of God. Without being 'other worldly' and ignoring our responsibilities here on earth, we seek the things that are beyond the earth. We have died in Christ and now we enjoy a new life – a life that is hidden with Christ in God. Why 'hidden'? Well, the union that exists between Christ and His people is hidden from the eyes of the men and women of this world. Though they see us going about our tasks, they are unaware that the strength by which we live and the power by which we practise our faith are drawn from God. But believers can only draw upon this life as they daily reach upwards through prayer and avail themselves of the resources that are hidden with Christ in God.

A wise old Christian was once asked by another believer, 'Where do you live?' With a twinkle in his eye he passed on his business card to the enquirer and said, 'This is where my residence is, but if you really want to know where I live – I live *in Christ.*'

O God my Father, forgive me if my energy is drawn more from the resources that are here below than those that are above. Help me to be at home in the heavenly realm. In Jesus' name. Amen.

FURTHER STUDY
Rom. 6:1–14; Gal. 2:20
1. How has Christ's death and resurrection impacted us?
2. In what sense was Paul both dead and alive?

What a Day That Will Be!

FOR READING & MEDITATION – COLOSSIANS 3:4

'When Christ, who is your life, appears, then you
also will appear with him in glory.' (v4)

Here the thought which Paul has been developing through the first verses of this chapter is brought to completion. The day will dawn when the Christ, whom we worship but do not see, will be revealed to the world in all His glory. If we were to paraphrase this verse it would read something like this: 'When Christ, your real life, shows Himself physically and visibly once again in the world, you, who are His people, will be as glorious as He.' What a day that will be!

I remember as a boy in my native Wales going to the local pit-head to listen to the miners sing as they came up to the surface after their day's work. As the cage brought them up to the pit top they would sometimes sing the chorus of a hymn written by Charles H. Gabriel:

Oh, that will be glory for me,
Glory for me, glory for me,
When by His grace I shall look on His face,
That will be glory, be glory for me.

Although usually just a handful of Christians would start up the chorus, everyone else would join in. Welshmen, as you probably know, love to sing. Often tears would start to flow down their coal-blackened faces as they sang, leaving white streaks. Now, whenever I come to this verse in Colossians, my mind goes back to that chorus and those childhood memories.

When Christ returns it will not just be that His glory is manifested; it will be glory for me also. And for you, if you belong to Him.

Dear Lord, the promise that I will be with You in glory is what keeps me going. What a day that will be! Come, Lord Jesus. Amen.

FURTHER STUDY

1 Thess. 4:13–18; Titus 2:11–14

1. How may we be encouraged in the face of death?
2. What has already appeared and what is still to appear?

An Idol Factory

FOR READING & MEDITATION – COLOSSIANS 3:5–6

'Put to death, therefore, whatever belongs to your earthly nature...' (v5)

Having urged his readers to set their hearts on the things that are above, where Christ is seated at the right hand of God, Paul now invites them to search their hearts. The thrust of his argument is irresistible: if Christ is your life then that means putting to death all things connected with the way of death – sexual immorality, impurity, lust, evil desires, and greed. Setting our hearts on the things that are above, and searching our hearts for those things that hinder Christ's life from flowing through us, go together.

Some Christians, it must be said, are against all forms of self-examination. They believe self-examination to be a negative practice. Concentrate on Christ, they advise, and sinful things will drop away of their own accord. But the phrase 'put to death' suggests that something has to be done to rid us of the evils that reside in our hearts, and that that something has to be done *by us* – utilising the power, of course, that comes from Jesus Christ.

Even though we are Christians and have been saved from the power of sin, that does not mean, as we have already seen, that the roots of sin have been dislodged from our hearts and will never trouble us again. A number believe we can have such an experience of God that sin is completely eradicated, and we reach a state of what they describe as 'sinless perfection'. I do not share that view myself. Even after decades of following Christ and being conscious of His Spirit at work in my life, I am aware that my heart has the possibility of becoming an idol factory. That's why, in addition to setting my affections on things above, I must also search my heart. The one follows on from the other.

Father, I come to You today and ask for Your divine illumination as I search my heart. I want no idolatry within me, no worship of other things. And whatever I find there that is displeasing to You, help me to put it to death. Amen.

FURTHER STUDY

2 Cor. 13:5–6; Eph. 4:17–32
1. How do you feel about spiritual self-examination?
2. What are we to put on and what are we to put off?

I'm In For It Now

FOR READING & MEDITATION – COLOSSIANS 3:6–7

'Because of these, the wrath of God is coming.' (v6)

It has been said that Paul's imperatives are always supported by incentives. In other words, Paul not only presents us with the highest of standards but also provides incentives that encourage us to reach up to them. He gave us in verse 4 the incentive of Christ's appearing, and if that is not enough, he now attaches to his imperative another kind of inducement, namely that 'the holy anger of God falls upon those who refuse to obey him' (Phillips).

The apostle is talking here, of course, not about those who sin and then confess their sin, but those who continue in sin. Those who sin and cry out to God in repentance are at once forgiven and restored. What is more, providing they are open to God, they will receive the empowerment they need to go on and not sin in that way again. But for those who continue in sin things are quite different. The *NIV Study Bible* says in its commentary on this text, 'God is unalterably opposed to sin and will invariably make sure that it is justly punished.' But when? The text is not talking about the judgment that comes at the end of time but the judgment that God metes out while we are still here on earth.

Let's face it, often God does not seem in a hurry to judge. How many times have believers committed sin, not repented, and said to themselves, 'Uh! That was a terrible thing I did. I'm in for it now' but seemingly nothing has happened? The truth is that God's judgments are often silent – something dies within us when we continue in sin. We become less of a person. Our creativity shrivels up, our zest for life is eroded by guilt, our ability to stand stress is reduced. The worst thing about sin is to be the one who has sinned.

O Father, help me to understand that Your judgments are not retributive but remedial. You search me in order to save me. Please drive this point deep into my spirit. In Jesus' name. Amen.

FURTHER STUDY
Matt. 27:1–8; 2 Pet. 3:1–15
1. Identify Judas's thoughts and emotions.
2. Why is the Lord patient and not in a hurry to judge?

Life is Decision

FOR READING & MEDITATION – COLOSSIANS 3:7–10

'But now you must rid yourselves of... anger, rage, malice, slander...' (v8)

From these verses it is clear that Paul is moving on to consider Christians' relationships with one another in the Church. Every one of the six sins mentioned here – anger, rage, malice, slander, filthy language, and lying – has the potential to destroy relationships. This list of sins is not one that he has just plucked out of the air; each one of these sins makes harmonious relationships impossible. What an ugly bunch of words they are.

These things may have been part of our way of life before our conversion, says the apostle, but they should not be practised by those who belong to Jesus Christ. Indeed, he tells us in verse 8 to rid ourselves of these non-Christian practices. Many Christians will no doubt react by saying, 'Easier said than done.' So how do we get rid of anger, rage, malice, slander, offensive language, and lying? We stop ourselves having anything to do with them.

Let me expand on that last statement because to some it might sound like exhortation without explanation. 'Life,' said one philosopher, 'is *decision*.' We can decide to be angry or not be angry, to lie or not to lie, to use offensive language or not to use it. It is foolish to believe that these things just flow out of us of their own accord. Before angry or inappropriate words come from your mouth you have a moment of choice – to stop them or speak them. The moment of choice may be only a second – even a split second – but it is there nevertheless.

If our lives are under the rule of Christ then it follows that our decisions will come under His rule as well. So it is just a question of willpower. You have to decide, 'I will no longer do this'. You supply the willingness – He will supply the power.

Father, I decide now to have done with the old life. I am going to strip off the filthy set of ill-fitting clothes and put them in the fire. Instead, I'm going to have a new wardrobe – custom-made by Christ. Amen.

FURTHER STUDY
Josh. 24:14–27; 1 Kgs 18:21
1. What choice did Joshua offer and how did the people respond?
2. Why did Elijah criticise the people?

FOR READING & MEDITATION – COLOSSIANS 3:11

'Here there is no Greek or Jew... but Christ is all, and is in all.' (v11)

At present we are considering Paul's teaching on relationships. Having spoken of the Christian's relationship to Christ (3:1–4), he is now speaking of the relationship which Christians have with one another in the Church.

Nowadays we live in an age seeking equality of opportunity for all, yet the verse we have read today, written so long ago, is *the* charter of equality. Nothing today can compare with it. Listen: 'Here [in the new nature of those who form Christ's Church] there is no Greek or Jew [no racial distinction], circumcised and uncircumcised [no religious distinction], barbarian, Scythian [people known for their brutality], slave or free [no social, economic or cultural distinction].' Galatians 3:28 adds, 'There is neither... male nor female [no sexual distinction].' The words 'Here there is no Greek or Jew' could be translated, 'Here there *cannot* be any Greek or Jew'. That sweeps the field. There just cannot be any distinctions in Christ. If you hold to distinctions then you cannot be in Christ. You are governed by something else. The equality in Christ's Church is not artificial – a statement of rights not worth the paper it is written on – it is real.

Then notice also the words 'Christ is all, and is in all'. What Paul means is this: Christ is all that matters. If Christ becomes all in all to us we cannot remain the people we were. What is more, everyone else becomes all in all also because we realise Christ dwells in them too. Why is the Church so slow in showing the world what a classless, raceless society is like? I am afraid there can only be one answer: Christ is not all in all.

O Father, You inspired Your servant Paul to sweep the decks of all discrimination, but we, Your people, have been so slow to accept this. Forgive us, dear Lord, and help us fulfil Your purposes. Amen.

FURTHER STUDY
John 4:4–9; Acts 10:15,28; Rom. 3:29; 10:12–13
1. Why was the woman surprised?
2. Why is there no real distinction between people?

Overalls or Evening Dress

FOR READING & MEDITATION – COLOSSIANS 3:12–14

'Therefore, as God's chosen people, holy and dearly
loved, clothe yourselves with compassion...' (v12)

Astonishingly, Paul here takes the characteristic descriptions of Israel and applies them to the Church: 'God's chosen people, holy and dearly loved'. But there's more: the qualities he urges on the Colossian Christians are the very qualities which ancient Israel came to recognise in God's dealing with them: 'compassion, kindness, humility [or lowliness], gentleness and patience'. There is neither the time nor the space to identify the Old Testament texts relating to this fact, but take it from me, they are there in the Scriptures. The reason God chose the people of Israel was because He wanted them to reflect to the other nations the manner in which He related to them. They were to be His 'shop window', so to speak, through which the Gentile nations could look in and see the blessings that come to those who serve the Lord.

Israel, as we know, failed miserably in this respect, but it is Paul's hope and prayer that the church at Colosse – part of the new Israel of God – would treat others as God in Christ treated them. How could this happen? First, by being considerate to each other – despite all provocation – and by forgiving each other. 'Forgive as the Lord forgave you' (v13). This is how the Lord acts towards you, Paul is saying, so it is only right that you follow suit.

Verse 14 is one of my most favourite texts: 'And over all these virtues put on love, which binds them all together in perfect unity.' 'Love,' it has been said, 'is a colour that can be worn with anything – overalls or evening dress.' Or think of it as a kind of overcoat, if you like, a garment that covers all other virtues. It brings harmony to all disharmonies. Love is the garment the world sees. All other virtues are undergarments.

Father, help me to remember that virtues are of no value if love is not present, and that love makes all other virtues blend in unity. And may I not just remember this but live by it. In Jesus' name. Amen.

FURTHER STUDY
Ps. 86:5–17; Lam. 3:19–26
1. What did the psalmist report?
2. How did the depressed prophet find hope?

Every Church a Haven?

FOR READING & MEDITATION – COLOSSIANS 3:15

'Let the peace of Christ rule in your hearts... And be thankful.' (v15)

You may remember that the other day we quoted the saying 'A text taken out of context quickly becomes a pretext.' Perhaps no other verse in the New Testament has been wrested from its context as frequently as this one has been. One interpretation of the verse that I have heard is this: if you don't have a troubled spirit then it indicates that you are walking in the perfect will of God. But there are some Christians whose consciences are so calloused that they are almost insensitive to the pleadings of the Spirit.

Others use the verse to teach that when you wish to know the will of God, imagine yourself going through the different options, and the one which gives you the most peace is the one you should choose. Now there is some sense in that, of course, but that is not what the text is indicating.

Paul is telling us here that when we are under the rule of Christ the inevitable result is that we experience peace in our relationships. Listen to the words of this verse again: '... since *as members of one body* you were called to peace'. Every Christian congregation can be a haven of peace. It is sad that many are not. I once heard a preacher say, when likening the Church to Noah's ark, that 'If it wasn't for the storm on the outside we wouldn't be able to stand the strain on the inside'.

Isn't it a bit unrealistic, though, to expect Christians with different views, different backgrounds and different temperaments to live harmoniously with one another? Some might think so. But Paul wouldn't share that view. When Christ rules in the hearts of believers then peace will rule in that community of believers. Nothing could be more simple yet nothing, it seems, is more difficult.

Gracious Father, we confess that our life strategy is wrong and thus things don't work out right. We become tangled up because we do not take Your way. Help us see that for peace to rule we must come under Your rule. Amen.

FURTHER STUDY
Matt. 18:19–20; Phil. 4:4–9
1. Why can we live harmoniously with other Christians?
2. How can we experience God's peace?

Gratitude for Grace

FOR READING & MEDITATION – COLOSSIANS 3:16

'Let the word of Christ dwell in you richly as you
teach and admonish one another...' (v16)

An interesting exercise is to examine many of the 3:16s of the New Testament. You are familiar, no doubt, with John 3:16 (I imagine you have learnt it by heart), but are you familiar with 1 John 3:16? Look it up and you will see why it is a verse that Christians are more reluctant to memorise. The verse before us today is one of the New Testament's most beautiful 3:16s. We are instructed to let the Word of Christ dwell in us richly. The word 'dwell' (*enoikeo* in the Greek) here has the meaning of permanent residence, of being at home. Eugene Peterson paraphrases it like this: 'Let the word of Christ have the run of the house. Give it plenty of room in your lives.'

How wonderful it is when Christians allow the Word of God to be at home in their hearts, when they draw their spiritual sustenance from the Word of God and not from other things, however exciting they might be. This is not to say that we cannot enjoy spiritual experiences, but we are not to let them divert us from attention to the Word. What is being said here is this: the Word of God must control, not just us personally, but the whole Christian community, and all the ministries of the local church. It is to dwell in us fully as we teach, admonish, counsel, and so on.

It is the Word of God, also, that must guide us as we sing. Some like to differentiate between psalms, hymns and spiritual songs, and they may well be right. However, what Paul has in mind here is not so much the different types of praise and worship, but the *content*. All the songs we sing in church should be consistent with the Word of God – that's his point. A gospel of good news must be echoed by songs of gratitude – gratitude for grace.

O God, save us from being so carried away by the melody of what we sing that we overlook the meaning and content. You have saved us by grace; help us reflect that in the worship we offer to You. Amen.

FURTHER STUDY

Job 23:11–12; Ps. 119:129–144
1. How did Job regard God's Word?
2. How did the psalmist refer to God's Word?

The Jesus Christ Man

FOR READING & MEDITATION – COLOSSIANS 3:17

'And whatever you do, whether in word or deed, do
it all in the name of the Lord Jesus...' (v17)

In this last verse of the section dealing with relationships in the Church, Paul bears down on the truth that everything we do in word or deed must be done in the name of the Lord Jesus. The apostle has emphasised the receptive side of being in Christ, but the receptivity must work itself out in activity. We are to *do* as well as receive and be. Being can only be manifested by doing, and the doing has a definite characteristic: *you do everything in the name of the Lord Jesus.* You are to do everything as representing Him, you are to do it in His name, in His stead, and in His Spirit.

Dr E. Stanley Jones told of riding his bicycle along a country road in India and hearing a young boy who was a cowherd call out to another in the field, 'The Jesus Christ man is going along.' He said that when he heard those words he felt like getting off his bicycle and dropping to his knees in prayer that he might not do anything to destroy the village boys' estimation of him as a 'Jesus Christ man'.

We are all to be Jesus Christ people – to do everything in His name. All that we do is to be done for Christ and in a Christlike manner. As a person once put it, 'We are the only Bible some people will read.' This does not mean we live out our lives in fear and trembling that we might say or do something that misrepresents Him. We are to be controlled not by fear but by a spirit of thankfulness: '... giving thanks to God the Father through him'.

Those who go through life with an attitude of thanksgiving to God for all His benefits soon come to appreciate what He does. The more we focus on how good God is, the more we are set free from fear.

Dear Father, I long to represent You today just as Christ represented You. Grant that my words and my actions may bring You glory. When I speak may it be You speaking. In Jesus' name. Amen.

FURTHER STUDY
2 Cor. 3:1–3; Eph. 6:5–9
1. How can those without Bibles know Bible truths?
2. How can we daily be like Christ?

A Word to Wives

FOR READING & MEDITATION – COLOSSIANS 3:18

'Wives, submit to your husbands, as is fitting in the Lord.' (v18)

Having focused on the Christian's relationship to Christ, and the Christian's relationship to the Church, Paul now takes up the theme of the Christian's relationship to the family. He has a word for each member of the family: for wives it is *submit*, for husbands it is *love* and *understand*, for children it is *obey*. Many Christians approach these words somewhat warily and see them as belonging more to the culture of the first-century Christians than to the contemporary Christian community. Let's understand what Paul is teaching here before we attempt to apply it to the present day.

First, he addresses wives, urging them to submit to their husbands. What does it mean for a Christian wife to submit? Is it doing everything her husband demands of her? I do not believe so. What if a husband asks his wife to engage in something she is not comfortable with because she knows it to be wrong? Is she to obey? Of course not. Submission is a *disposition* – a disposition to defer in everything that is right. It is not to be seen as servility or obsequiousness – those are negative characteristics. A woman who practises biblical submission will have a strong positive desire to support her husband as he fulfils his role in the family. Some claim Paul's teaching here contradicts what he says in Galatians 3:28, where the equality of male and female is celebrated. Equality and submission, they say, cannot co-exist in a relationship. But they can. Christ is equal with God but yet is in submission to Him.

Before a woman can submit to her husband she must first be submitted to God. Without submission to God, submission to one's husband does not constitute a spiritual exercise.

O God, we live in a day when our culture contradicts the teaching of Your Word. Help us in the clash between Christ and culture to take Your way. For Jesus' sake. Amen.

FURTHER STUDY
Eph. 5:22–24; 1 Pet. 3:1–6
1. Why does submission not mean servitude?
2. How should wives relate to their husbands?

FOR READING & MEDITATION – COLOSSIANS 3:19

'Husbands, love your wives and do not be harsh with them.' (v19)

The topic we are discussing at the moment is probably one of the most counter-cultural subjects we could ever touch upon – biblical rules governing the life of the family. A well-known Christian feminist says, 'Many husbands don't deserve a wife who shows a submissive spirit; they mistake it for weakness and exploit it to their advantage.' Well, Paul has a word for such husbands: 'Love your wives and do not be harsh with them.'

It's interesting that here Paul is *commanding* love as if he knows that one of the easiest things in the world is for a husband to say to his wife, 'I love you', but then fail to demonstrate that love in practical ways. A woman once told me, 'My husband's parting words to me when he goes off to work are, "I love you", but then I go to the bathroom, find his shaving kit lying around, the basin filthy, and towels strewn all over the floor. If he really loved me then he would clean up after himself.' I agree. Love is not just something you say, love is something you do.

And here's a further test of love. 'Do not be harsh with them.' Again, I like J.B. Phillips' translation here: 'Husbands, be sure you give your wives much love and sympathy; don't let bitterness or resentment spoil your marriage.' Men can sometimes act in a manner that is overbearing – even somewhat tyrannical. Take this scenario: a woman fails to come up to her husband's expectations of her as a submissive wife, so he turns on her harshly and says, 'The Word of God says you must submit.' In that action he has violated the law of love. He has thought more about himself than his wife's well-being. It's not his wife's problem he needs to be concerned about, but his own.

O God, strengthen my spirit as I follow a way of life that is governed by Your Word and not by the dictates of our culture. May I embrace Your way whether others live by it or not. In Jesus' name I ask this. Amen.

FURTHER STUDY
Eph. 5:25–33; 1 Pet. 3:7
1. How should husbands relate to their wives?
2. Why may a husband's failure have spiritual consequences?

How to Serve the Lord

FOR READING & MEDITATION – COLOSSIANS 3:20

'Children, obey your parents in everything, for this pleases
the Lord.' (v20)

Maybe you are wishing that Paul had dealt more fully with the subject of relationships in the home. Dick Lucas says, 'It is daring to summarise complex relations in such short compass.' Paul, however, is stating basic principles, and although they may be short they are certainly to the point. Now he comes to talk to the children – obviously children who have reached the age of understanding – and tells them that they too must come under the rule of Christ.

On one occasion a family with a young son of 12 came to me. Although the boy had committed himself to Jesus Christ he was being somewhat rebellious towards his parents. He obviously loved the Lord, and as we talked about his Christian faith and what he wanted to do with his life, he told me that he would like to serve Christ in the field of Christian journalism. I asked him if he would be interested in knowing how he could express his desire to serve the Lord Jesus *at the present moment* – and he nodded his head in agreement. So I read him our text for today in J.B. Phillips' translation: 'As for you children, your duty is to obey your parents, for at your age this is one of the best things you can do to show your love for the Lord.' The boy got the point of this verse, and we then prayed together. Later his parents told me that the subsequent transformation in him was remarkable. He is now working for the Lord overseas, not as a journalist but as a preacher of the gospel.

The disobedience and disregard exhibited by young people are frightening features of this present age. I see little hope for the families of the future unless they come under the rule of Christ.

Father, forgive us that we ask for guidance in running our families and yet sometimes balk at the directions You give us. Help us see that we either heed the helm or heed the rocks. In Jesus' name. Amen.

FURTHER STUDY
1 Sam. 15:23; Prov. 6:20–23; Eph. 6:1–3
1. How does God view rebellion?
2. Why should children obey parents?

Problem Fathers?

FOR READING & MEDITATION – COLOSSIANS 3:21

'Fathers, do not embitter your children, or they
will become discouraged.' (v21)

There are two sides to every relationship, and in the verse before us now Paul shows that not all the rights are on one side and all the duties on the other. Fathers, too, have a responsibility to their children – not to 'over-correct [them], or they will grow up feeling inferior and frustrated' (Phillips).

Paul's words here beg the question: Why aren't mothers included in this instruction? I have thought long and hard about this and it is my conviction, based on years of experience in counselling, that by and large fathers tend to be more harsh with their children than mothers. A Christian psychiatrist says, 'Behind most problem children you will find a problem father.' He was speaking in general terms, of course, for we all, I am sure, know children with the most loving parents who, despite their love, have become wayward. However, I think that statistics will support the statement that fathers tend to come down more heavily on their children than mothers.

Hear what Paul says once again: 'Fathers, do not embitter your children, or they will become discouraged.' Coming down hard on children crushes their sensitive spirits. It is no good a father lamenting the fact that his child is not as strong and self-reliant as he himself is if he uses his strength to squash the child's fragile ego rather than develop it. Endless criticism, harsh punishments, unrealistic expectations, will have their effect in the long run. Many a child who is timid, fearful and plagued with deep feelings of inferiority and guilt has developed those characteristics not so much by nature as by nurture. Christ's rule applies just as much to fathers as to anyone.

O Father, our slowness in paying attention to the principles of Your Word has resulted in the devastation, frustration and breakdown of our family life. Give us another chance, and help us to learn the ways of Your Word. In Jesus' name. Amen.

FURTHER STUDY
Matt. 18:1–10; Mark 10:13–16; Eph. 6:4
1. How did Jesus regard and relate to children?
2. Why was Jesus indignant?

Free – On the Inside

FOR READING & MEDITATION – COLOSSIANS 3:22–24

'Slaves, obey your earthly masters in everything... with sincerity of heart and reverence for the Lord.' (v22)

We come now to the section where Paul talks about a Christian's relationship to work. Paul's instruction to slaves to obey their earthly masters in everything has, in more recent times, brought him in for a great deal of criticism. One critic has this to say: 'I cannot help feel a tinge of disappointment that Paul did not use his influence to call for social change as it related to the distressing subject of slavery.' Another comments, 'His instruction that slaves obey their masters puts them on the level of childhood for ever.'

I must confess that in the early days of my Christian life I tended to view Paul's instructions as fastening the yoke of bondage even more firmly on those who were slaves. However, I soon came to see that Paul was writing, not to the leaders of society, but to the Church. If Paul had told slaves to revolt it would have hindered the gospel rather than helped it. The truths he presented in his letters did eventually lead to the abolition of slavery, albeit many centuries later.

Since Paul was unable to deal with the situation horizontally, he focuses on dealing with it vertically. He urges slaves to concentrate on the fact that they are working for the Lord and not for men. This change of perspective, Paul believed, would enable them to find inner freedom. Pagan slaves might obey out of fear of their master, but the Christian slave can obey for a different reason: to do it out of reverence for the Lord. And he reminded them of the reward they will receive – the divine inheritance. Paul was unable to give the slaves of his day the status of freedmen, but he certainly showed them how to be free on the inside.

Father, help me learn the lesson that even when I cannot change what is happening outside of me, I can change inwardly and find freedom in You. I am so thankful. Amen.

FURTHER STUDY
John 8:31–36; 1 Cor. 10:31–33; Titus 2:9–10
1. What is true slavery and what is true freedom?
2. Why should slaves/employees obey their masters/employers?

A Heated Talking Point

FOR READING & MEDITATION – COLOSSIANS 3:25–4:1

'Masters, provide your slaves with what is right and fair,
because... you also have a Master in heaven.' (4:1)

The break imposed when the Bible was divided into chapters suggests that Paul's exhortation to the slave masters does not start until the beginning of chapter 4. But it is difficult to read the last verse of chapter 3 without feeling that Paul had in mind not only Christian slaves but their Christian masters also.

Once again (4:1) Paul presents the other side of an issue and, having addressed slaves, he has a word for their masters. Who was the greater wrongdoer, the slave who did not work as hard as he could or the master who was not considerate and did not give a proper reward? It must have been a new thought for slave masters that they should show consideration towards slaves, and I can imagine it becoming a heated talking point in the slave markets. Did you notice how often the word 'Lord' (or 'Master') is mentioned in the verses to do with slavery? Five times. 'Lift up your eyes and see the Lord as your Master,' Paul says to the slaves. And, to the slave masters, he says the same: 'Don't forget for a minute that you, too, serve a Master – God in heaven' (Eugene Peterson, MSG). Just as Christ showed fairness in the way He dealt with those who were slave masters, so they, in turn, are to show fairness in the way they deal with their slaves.

Now that we have surveyed Paul's teaching on the subject of slavery (albeit briefly), do you agree that Paul was doing the right thing in not calling for the abolition of slavery? He laid down, nevertheless, some basic principles which eventually led men such as William Wilberforce to crusade to set men, women and children free. The weapons Paul forged hundreds of years ago helped bring that victory.

Father, I see that to have mastery in life I must bow my knee to the Master. Your ways, and Your ways alone, are the ways of mastery. Help me follow them in all of life's situations. In Jesus' name. Amen.

FURTHER STUDY

Prov. 14:31; Mal. 3:5; Jas 5:1–6
1. How does God identify with oppressed workers?
2. Why did James criticise rich people?

First Talk to God

FOR READING & MEDITATION – COLOSSIANS 4:2–4

'Devote yourselves to prayer, being watchful and thankful.' (v2)

Paul now focuses on the Christian's relationship to outsiders – those who were not part of the family of God. At first glance these verses might seem to contain a random list of admonitions, but really they are a tightly constructed section which shows us how to relate to those of our friends, acquaintances, and families who have not committed themselves to Jesus.

He begins by pointing out that before we talk to others about God we ought to talk to God about others. Evangelism is best undertaken in a spirit of prayer – by praying for people before talking to people. Paul asks for the prayers of the Colossian Christians, that even though he is in prison, God will grant him many opportunities to preach the gospel. 'Pray that every time I open my mouth,' he says, 'I'll be able to make Christ plain as day to them' (Eugene Peterson, MSG). There is a God-dependence here that is touching. Paul does not rely on his gift of apostleship, or his previous experience of planting new churches; he knows that without prayer his efforts will not bear fruit. And this prayer is not to be occasional, but persistent.

Sometimes I am astonished when I read training courses on evangelism and notice how little emphasis is placed on the need for personal, powerful intercessory prayer. Evangelistic techniques, methods, systems, and procedures all have their place. However, they are of little value unless they have come from a heart that is given to prayer. Notice that when Paul talks about prayer he also adds this: 'being watchful and thankful'. Prayer needs to be coupled with praise, just as praise needs to be coupled with prayer. The one fuels the other.

Father, drive this truth deep within my spirit – that before I talk to people about You, I must talk to You about people. Help me be more than just a hearer in this issue; help me be a doer. In Jesus' name. Amen.

FURTHER STUDY

Luke 18:1–8; Phil. 4:4–6

1. Why may we sometimes seem not to receive answers to our prayers?
2. How did Paul link prayer and praise?

The Right to Say 'No'

FOR READING & MEDITATION – COLOSSIANS 4:5–6

'Be wise in the way you act towards outsiders...' (v5)

Though Paul is coming to the close of his letter, his thoughts flow as beautifully as they do in his opening remarks. Eugene Peterson's rugged paraphrase of these verses is well worth considering: 'Use your heads as you live and work among outsiders. Don't miss a trick. Make the most of every opportunity. Be gracious in your speech. The goal is to bring out the best in others in a conversation, not to put them down, not cut them out.'

Many are not wise in the way they share their faith. They are insensitive and intrusive. A dear old Christian wrote in the flyleaf of my Bible: 'To win some be winsome.' When Paul talks about our conversations being 'always full of grace, seasoned with salt, so that you may know how to answer everyone' he is not thinking of memorising systematically prepared theological arguments so that we can give biblical answers to questions that may be asked of us. That, of course, can be helpful, even important. No, he is thinking not only about *what* we say but *how* we say it. Our conversation is not to be insipid but to have a point – to be 'seasoned with salt' – and we are to speak in a pleasant manner.

How many times have you felt pressurised by a salesman, and have bought something just to get rid of him? Evangelism should never be a 'hard sell'. We take advantage of every opportunity to share Christ, even offer Him, but we must always respect the right of the person to whom we are witnessing to say 'No'. There was an occasion when Jesus talked to a rich ruler, who could not accept what Jesus told him and turned away (Luke 18:18–25). Did Jesus run after him, and try to press him into making a decision? No, He let him go because He respected his right to say 'No'.

Father, forgive me if I put people off by insensitivity and aggressiveness. May I present the gospel clearly and in a gracious manner, but also respect the right of others to say 'No'. In Jesus' name. Amen.

FURTHER STUDY
Gen. 4:1–8; 1 Pet. 3:15–16
1. What right did God grant Cain?
2. How should we answer people?

Paul – A People-Person

FOR READING & MEDITATION – COLOSSIANS 4:7–9

'Tychicus... a dear brother, a faithful minister
and fellow-servant in the Lord.' (v7)

When we come to this section we can see at once that Paul had a great affinity with people. He was a true people-person. He did not just remember names; he cared deeply for those whom he counted as his friends. Paul was greatly loved because he loved greatly. This final section of his letter is rich in personal messages and greetings. Only his letter to the Romans can be compared to it. Paul wants his friends to realise something of his tremendous concern for them.

He begins with Tychicus and Onesimus. Onesimus was a runaway slave who had almost certainly robbed his master, then escaped, met Paul and accepted Christ. He is the subject of the letter to Philemon, in which Paul urges the slave owner to welcome Onesimus back as a brother in the Lord because he had been so helpful to the apostle.

Tychicus was a companion of Paul and represented him on a number of different occasions. He is described as 'a dear brother, a faithful minister and fellow-servant in the Lord'. The most significant thing about Tychicus was that he was 'a faithful minister'. He had a call and was faithful to that call, and that gave him drive and direction. But he did not allow this single-mindedness to prevent him being a dear brother and a fellow-servant.

Some Christian workers are faithful servants but not very 'dear', and not good 'fellow-servants' either. This is particularly true of the strong, devoted, driven types. They are extremely busy and absorbed in fulfilling their mission, but no one would ever refer to them as 'dear'. And they are so taken up with their own ministry that they cannot work with others. Tychicus was a well-rounded person, faithful in his ministry, a dear brother and a fellow-worker.

Father, I too would be a well-rounded person. Help me submerge my will and affection in a larger Will and Affection, for it is only then that I can expect to attain wholeness and loveliness of character. In Jesus' name. Amen.

FURTHER STUDY
Philem. 1–25
1. How did Paul feel about Philemon?
2. How did Paul refer to Onesimus?

FOR READING & MEDITATION – COLOSSIANS 4:10–13

'Epaphras... is always wrestling in prayer for you...' (v12)

Paul adds four more names to his greetings list in this section: Aristarchus, Mark, Justus and Epaphras. Aristarchus was a Macedonian who accompanied Paul on some of his missionary travels and was seized during the riot in Ephesus (Acts 19:29). Paul refers to him here as 'my fellow-prisoner', so obviously Aristarchus was with Paul in prison, probably on a voluntary basis.

Mark is also mentioned. Remember him? Paul and Barnabas had a violent quarrel over Mark, and Paul appeared to have little confidence in the young man who seemed ready to run at the first hint of trouble (see Acts 15:36–40). Now, about twelve years later, the wound has been healed and Mark is clearly one of Paul's fellow-workers. Elsewhere he is described by Paul as 'helpful to me in my ministry' (2 Tim. 4:11). Justus is an unknown colleague of Paul and there is no other record of him.

We met Epaphras, you may recall, in the opening days of our meditations on Colossians. There Paul told us several things about him; now he adds, 'He is always wrestling in prayer for you'. The foundations of this man's character were set deep in the soil of prayer. The phrase 'wrestling in prayer' suggests that his prayers were largely intercessory. What an insight Paul must have gained into the character of Epaphras during their time together in Rome as he listened to him pray for the church back at Colosse. There is no doubt in my mind that the secret of Epaphras's spiritual success lay in his prayer life. He was great in soul because he prayed much, and because he prayed with the unselfishness which marked all he did. Earnest and persistent prayer was the secret of his sanctity. That secret is available to us all.

Father, forgive me if I do not commune regularly with You and intercede for others in prayer. Prayer moments are the only real moments. Help me to see prayer as not just a luxury, but a necessity. In Jesus' name. Amen.

FURTHER STUDY
Gen. 18:16–33
1. What does Abraham's prayer teach us about intercession?
2. What does it teach us about God?

Final Greetings

FOR READING & MEDITATION – COLOSSIANS 4:14–16

'After this letter has been read to you, see that it is also
read in the church of the Laodiceans...' (v16)

Paul ends his greetings with the names of Luke and Demas. Luke often accompanied Paul on his travels and was with him in Rome during his imprisonment. Demas was also a companion of Paul, but sadly later deserted him because of his love for this world (see 2 Tim. 4:10).

Paul then turns from sending specific greetings to giving more general greetings – to the brothers at Laodicea, and to Nympha and the church in her house. For the most part the Early Church met for worship, instruction, and fellowship in homes, as we can see from such verses as Romans 16:5, 1 Corinthians 16:19, Philemon 2 and Acts 12:12.

Paul asks that his letter be read in the Laodicean church as well, and the Colossians in turn were to read the letter from Laodicea. Obviously Paul also wanted the Laodicean believers to be aware of possible threats to their faith. This exchange of letters shows the importance of reading all we can. The more Scripture we absorb the stronger our defences against false teaching will be.

The reference to the letter from Laodicea, however, is puzzling. It could mean that the Laodiceans were to lend the Colossians a letter Paul had originally written to them and is now lost. Many think the letter referred to here was Paul's letter to the Ephesians, which was making its rounds as a circular. It was the practice in the Early Church to read letters aloud to the assembled congregation. Imagine, therefore, what a thrill it must have been for those Christians to receive a letter from the apostle Paul. Little did they realise that what they were reading then would be read by the whole world close on 2,000 years later.

Father, may I be diligent in my reading of Scripture. I am living in days when there are just as many threats to my faith as in the days of the Colossians. Help me learn all I can so that I may not waver in my faith. Amen.

FURTHER STUDY
John 3:16; 2 Tim. 4:9–13; 1 John 2:15–17
1. Contrast Demas and Luke.
2. How can we love and yet not love the world?

FOR READING & MEDITATION – COLOSSIANS 4:17

'Tell Archippus: "See to it that you complete the
work you have received in the Lord."' (v17)

Though it is dangerous to read between the lines, I can't help feeling that there is a slight suggestion in these words that Archippus was a man who did not find it easy to follow through on things. Even Paul's description of him as a 'fellow-soldier' in Philemon 2 does not dissuade me from thinking that here he was drawing attention to a matter that Archippus needed to work on. J.B. Phillips was obviously of the same opinion, for he translated the verse this way: 'God ordained you to your work – see that you don't fail him!'

Was Archippus, I wonder, the kind of man who allowed himself to be so absorbed by the marginal that he had little drive left for the central issues of his life? I have met many servants of Christ like that. They have been called to minister to people – to save them, develop them, and lead them to maturity – yet have ended up doing everything but that. Paul said on one occasion, you remember, 'But one thing I do' (Phil. 3:13), not 'These forty things I dabble in'. Those who focus on what they are supposed to be doing leave a mark; those who don't, leave a blur.

The temptation to do the easier things and not to follow through on issues plagues us all. Paul's words – 'See to it that you complete the work you have received in the Lord' – strike home to every one of us I am sure. Notice the words *you have received in the Lord*. Everybody *in the Lord* is in service for the Lord. It means being involved in the Lord's plans for us. Let no unimportant weeds choke the fine wheat of the kingdom of God. Say 'No' to the marginal so that you can say 'Yes' to the central. And do not give up, but complete the work God has given you to do.

Lord Jesus Christ, You fulfilled Your Father's purposes in everything that You had to do. Help me, too, fulfil the ministry You have chosen for me. Amen.

FURTHER STUDY

Luke 10:38–42; Rev. 2:1–7
1. Why were Martha's good intentions bad?
2. How had the Ephesians become preoccupied with the marginal?

Closing Words

FOR READING & MEDITATION – COLOSSIANS 4:18

'I, Paul, write this greeting in my own hand. Remember
my chains. Grace be with you.' (v18)

We come now to Paul's last words to the Christians at Colosse. As you will know, it was his custom to dictate his letters and then pen a few greetings in his own hand at the end. His personal signature was the guarantee that the letter had come from him.

Paul's closing words are as rich as any of the others in this highly personal letter: 'Remember my chains. Grace be with you.' This was a plea, of course, to the Colossians to remember him as he remained in prison. But what do we remember of Paul's chains? Nothing, because they have rusted away. However, although the chains have gone, his words have not. They leap across the centuries and come home to our hearts with as much force as they did to those to whom they were directly addressed.

I wonder what we would say if we found ourselves in a similar position – locked up in a jail because of our passion for the gospel. Probably this: 'Remember my chains. Ask God to give me grace.' But listen again to Paul's words: 'I am in chains. Grace be with *you*'. One of the greatest evidences of spiritual maturity is the desire, when under personal pressure or pain, to still reach out and give to others. Paul was such a man. In the midst of overwhelming difficulties his final thought is for others.

So ends an important letter, one written with the desire to prevent believers being drawn away from the truth of the gospel, and one in which Paul has encouraged us to see Christ as all-sufficient and all-supreme. Christ is 'all, and is in all' (3:11). As we end our time reflecting on the words of the great apostle Paul, let me put my last thought in the form of this highly personal question: We are all in all to Christ, but *is Christ all in all to us*?

O Father, I offer myself to You again today and pray that just as Your Son is the centre of all things in Your universe, so may He be the centre of all things in my universe. In Christ's precious name I pray. Amen.

FURTHER STUDY
Luke 23:26–43; John 19:25–27
1. What concerned Jesus as He faced death?
2. How could you be more aware of others' needs?

MAY
— & —
JUN

A Counsellor Par Excellence

FOR READING & MEDITATION – JOHN 14:1–17

'I will ask the Father, and he will give you another
Counsellor to be with you for ever...' (v16)

We focus in the next two months on Jesus' amazing words in John 14:16, about the promised Holy Spirit. As a way of describing all that the Holy Spirit would be to the disciples, Jesus used the phrase 'another Counsellor'. But first let me set the scene.

It is the night before Christ is to be crucified, and He is closeted with His disciples in an upper room in the sacred city of Jerusalem. The air is heavy with the atmosphere of imminent events. The Passover has been celebrated, Judas has just left, and suddenly Jesus announces that He is soon to leave this world and return to His Father in heaven. We read these words of our Lord with calmness, but I can imagine that when they were first spoken the disciples were anything but calm. Their stomachs must have churned within them as they heard their Friend and Master say He was going away. For over three years He had been their Teacher, their Confidant and their Guide. He had comforted them when they were sad, inspired them in times of doubt, and encouraged them whenever their footsteps began to flag. He had been to them a Counsellor *par excellence*. But now He was going. How were they to handle things in His absence? What were they to do when they didn't know which course of action to take? Who was to be their inspiration and guide? Another Counsellor is to take His place.

The Spirit came, as we know, at Pentecost, to be to the disciples all that Jesus was – and more. And He has remained in the world to be our Counsellor too. But how dependent are we on His counsel? How often do we draw on His resources? Sadly, all too seldom and too little. God has appointed a divine Counsellor to assist us, yet so often we prefer to muddle along on our own.

O God my Father, forgive me if I treat Your Holy Spirit as a Counsellor only in name, and lean more on my own understanding than on His. Show me how to take hold of the resources of this divine Counsellor more. In Jesus' name I pray. Amen.

FURTHER STUDY

Isa. 53:6; 55:1–11

1. Why do we need God's counsel?
2. Why are logic and intuition insufficient for godly living?

A Permanent Presence

FOR READING & MEDITATION – JOHN 14:18–31

'I will not leave you as orphans; I will come to you.' (v18)

The statement 'I will ask the Father, and he will give you another Counsellor' is found in the section of John's Gospel known as 'The Upper Room Discourse' – chapters 14 to 16. Think with me again about how the news that Christ was leaving the world to go to the Father would have been received by the disciples. For more than three years they had been inseparable. When they went to sleep at night they knew that Jesus would be there in the morning to lead and inspire them. Now all that was about to change – for ever. No more meals together, no more quiet talks around the camp fire at night, no more shared laughter, no more deep spiritual discussions.

Speaking of His departure from the world, our Lord used the word 'orphans', as we see from our text today. Why orphans? The disciples were adults, not children. Ah, the sting of His departure left them feeling as bereft as a child who has lost both parents. Yet His promise, remember, was *not* to leave them as orphans. I am sure it was difficult for the disciples to believe at that time that they would ever get over the feelings they experienced as they heard their Master was going away, but subsequent events show that they did overcome them.

When the promised Holy Spirit visited them at Pentecost, the dispirited disciples came alive again and appeared to become twice the men they were when Jesus was with them. Why? Jesus had been *with* them, but the Holy Spirit was *in* them and would *remain* in them. There was no fear that *He* would leave. And this made them bold. He would stay with them always. And what He was to them He is to us also – a permanent presence.

Gracious God and heavenly Father, what joy fills my heart to know that Your Spirit has come not as a temporary guest but a permanent one. Your Spirit within me is as permanent as my choices – and more so. I am so grateful. Amen.

FURTHER STUDY

Esther 2:1–11; Matt. 28:16–20

1. In what sense was Mordecai like the Holy Spirit?
2. How can Christ be with us always?

Glorious 'Foreverness'

FOR READING & MEDITATION – JOHN 1:19–34

'The man on whom you see the Spirit come down and remain...
will baptise with the Holy Spirit.' (v33)

We continue to consider the fact that the Holy Spirit 'remains'. When Jesus announced that the divine Counsellor would abide with His disciples permanently (and subsequently with the whole Church), keep in mind that it had never been like this before, not even in the lives of the Old Testament greats. But from now on... yes! Remember too that the pattern the disciples had of the coming of the Holy Spirit, as seen in the Old Testament, was of temporary endowments of power for temporary tasks. In other words, He came and went. Yet in John 14:16–17, as we saw, Jesus announced that following His return to the throne in heaven, the Holy Spirit's coming would be permanent.

This 'foreverness' of the Spirit is intimated in the passage before us today. Note the words *and remain*. These words and the phrase used in John 14:16 – *to be with you for ever* – strike the same note. The idea of an occasional visitation is replaced by a permanent coming.

The Holy Spirit is a Counsellor who is available all day and every day. Human counsellors have to set aside special times to see people and often have difficulty in fitting everyone into their schedules. This, however, is not a problem to the divine Counsellor. You can approach Him any time of day or night, and though He may be involved at the same time in supporting, empowering, and guiding many people around the world, He will give Himself to you as if you were the only one on the face of the planet. And you don't have to look for Him in any other place than in your own heart. The Holy Spirit is not only the divine Counsellor but a dependable Counsellor. He is available to you and me – permanently.

O God my Father, I am grateful for all You have done for me through Christ, but I am especially grateful that Your Spirit has taken up a permanent place in my heart. Help me understand all the deep implications of this. In Jesus' name. Amen.

FURTHER STUDY
Ruth 1:1–17; Heb. 13:5–6
1. How did Ruth demonstrate a quality of the Holy Spirit?
2. Why should we not be afraid?

Another Counsellor

FOR READING & MEDITATION – ACTS 16:1–10

'Paul... travelled throughout... Phrygia... having been kept
by the Holy Spirit from preaching... in... Asia.' (v6)

Permit me to remind you again of Jesus' words which form the basis of our current meditations: 'I will ask the Father, and he will give you another Counsellor' (John 14:16). Note the word *another*. Without that word we have no point of comparison; the word 'Counsellor' would be unanchored. Counsels us how? And to do what? He counsels us in the same way and with the same principles that Christ followed when He counselled His disciples. The Spirit's counsel was to be the same as Jesus' counsel. In the very nature of things it could not be different.

Did you notice in today's reading that the terms 'Holy Spirit' and 'Spirit of Jesus' are used interchangeably? Look at it again: 'having been kept by the Holy Spirit from preaching the word' (v6), and 'the Spirit of Jesus would not allow them to' (v7). The Holy Spirit seemed to the disciples to be the Spirit of Jesus within them. They were one. The counsel given to every believer by the Holy Spirit will accord with the counsel given to the disciples by Jesus when He was here on earth. If God is a Christlike God, then the Spirit is a Christlike Spirit.

There are many matters about which I know little or nothing, but one thing I do know about is counselling, as I have been involved in it for most of my life. When I meet a counsellor I can usually tell what school of thought he or she belongs to by listening to that person talk. It is the same with the Holy Spirit. Having observed how He functions in the lives of men and women (and in my own life) over the years, I can tell what school He comes from. It is the 'The Jesus School of Counselling'. He counsels in the same way as Christ.

O Father, I am so grateful that the counselling ministry of Jesus and of the Holy Spirit are one. This means that He will lead me in the same way that Jesus would lead me were He here at my side. I can trust Him wholly – and I do. Amen.

FURTHER STUDY

Isa. 11:1–3; Luke 4:18–19; Acts 8:26–40

1. How did the Spirit work in Christ's life?
2. How was Philip helped by the Spirit and what was the result?

The First Thing

FOR READING & MEDITATION – JAMES 1:1–11

'If any of you lacks wisdom, he should ask God...' (v5)

Our heavenly Father has given us the Holy Spirit to be our Counsellor, yet how much do we avail ourselves of His resources? Across the world the Christian Church and secular society are experiencing what some describe as a 'counselling explosion'. While this has many benefits, the danger is that we put our faith in human help rather than in the divine Counsellor.

I remember a time in the Church when counselling was regarded by many as an unnecessary ministry. If you have a problem, it was said at that time, never look to others for help; instead, get down on your knees and talk to God about it – the Holy Spirit will show you what to do. That, of course, was an extreme position. Very often it does help to talk through a problem with a Christian counsellor. As David Seamands puts it: 'A counsellor [ie, a Christian counsellor] is a temporary assistant to the Holy Spirit.' But the Church nowadays seems to be going to the opposite extreme by suggesting that when anyone has a problem the *first* thing they should do is to discuss it with a Christian counsellor.

No, the *first* thing we should do whenever we have a problem that cannot be solved using our own resources, is to turn to the divine Counsellor and invite Him to help us. If light does not come, *then* seek the help of a wise and godly friend. But seeking help from others should not be our first recourse; our first recourse should be to God. The Holy Spirit, as we said the other day, is a Counsellor *par excellence*. To seek counselling from another Christian is, of course, quite valid, but that kind of counselling might be needed less if we depended on the Holy Spirit more.

O God, forgive me if my first thought when I am in need of help is not of You. If I have dropped out of the habit of opening my heart to You before I open it to anyone else, help me recover that habit. In Christ's name I pray. Amen.

FURTHER STUDY

1 Kgs 3:5–14; 2 Chr. 16:7–14
1. What was the first thing Solomon asked for?
2. Why was Asa foolish?

FOR READING & MEDITATION – EPHESIANS 4:17–32

'And do not grieve the Holy Spirit of God...' (v30)

We must spend another day on the subject we discussed yesterday – the need to avail ourselves more fully of the resources of the Holy Spirit, whom Jesus described as the divine Counsellor. We are saying that we are in the midst of what is being called a 'counselling explosion', and are in danger of falling into the trap of taking our problems first to counsellors rather than bringing them straight to God.

Why do we do this? There are many possible reasons. Maybe we prefer a visible counsellor to an invisible one. Perhaps we are not sure how to establish contact with the divine Counsellor or how to recognise His voice when He speaks to us. Or possibly we are not quite certain that the divine Counsellor is interested in the likes of us. We can believe He guides and counsels such people as Billy Graham, Luis Palau or Nicky Gumbel – but ordinary people like us? Ah, that's different.

It is these issues and many others that I want to come to grips with over the next two months, but let me lay this down in your mind right away: the services of the divine Counsellor are yours for the asking. If you are a Christian then His resources are available to you – completely free and for the taking. It is customary for anyone who is charged with an offence and brought to court to have a professional advocate to counsel them and plead their case. If they cannot afford one, one is provided for them – free of charge. God and Christ do for you, as one of God's children, what any good government will do; they provide you with counsel. When we spurn the services of the divine Counsellor we sadden Him. For He is not merely an influence; He is a *Person*.

O God my Father, if I have been living too independently and relying on my resources rather than on Yours, once again I humbly ask Your forgiveness. Teach me how to be more God-dependent and less self-reliant. In Jesus' name I pray. Amen.

FURTHER STUDY

Luke 21:10–15; 1 Thess. 5:12–24

1. What did Jesus promise?
2. How may we sadden the Spirit and put out His fire?

'He' - Not 'It'

FOR READING & MEDITATION – ACTS 13:1–12

'The Holy Spirit said, "Set apart for me Barnabas and Saul..."' (v2)

We ended yesterday with the thought that the Holy Spirit is not merely an influence but a divine *Person*. This is why, when we talk about Him, we refer to Him as 'He' and not 'it'. Some Christians believe He is an impersonal influence, yet use personal pronouns such as 'He' and 'His' when referring to Him. I remember on one occasion pointing out the illogicality of this to someone who held this view, and this was his reply: 'I use a personal pronoun when talking about the Holy Spirit in the same way that people use the term "Jack Frost" when speaking about icy conditions.' How sad.

The Holy Spirit is not the personification of an influence, the sense of fellowship Christians experience when they get together, or even spiritual enthusiasm. He is a Person in the same way that you and I are persons – only, of course, much more so. He has individuality, intelligence, hearing, knowledge, wisdom, sympathy, and so on. He can see, speak, rejoice, love, whisper and, as we have seen, when we spurn Him by turning to other resources, or resist Him when He seeks to work within us, He is hurt in the same way that a close friend would be hurt. The Bible says He is God, with the very same attributes as God. In Job 26:13 He is seen as having the power to create. In Psalm 139:7 He is shown to have omnipresence – being everywhere present. In Hebrews 3:7–9 He is spoken of as issuing commands – something only God can do. And in 2 Corinthians 3:17 He is referred to as 'Lord'.

My dear friend, if you are a Christian there is an unseen Deity in your life – the Holy Spirit. He doesn't want to hide from you, and He doesn't want you to hide from Him.

O God, before I go any further, let this thought sink deep into my heart – the Holy Spirit is a Person with whom I can commune, and from whom I can draw resources. Help me become better acquainted with Him. In Jesus' name. Amen.

FURTHER STUDY

John 16:12–15; 2 Cor. 13:14

1. How did Jesus refer to the Holy Spirit?
2. What is 'the fellowship of the Holy Spirit'?

Who is the Real You?

FOR READING & MEDITATION – ROMANS 7:7–25

'What a wretched man I am! Who will rescue me from this body of death?' (v24)

Before we move on to compare the Holy Spirit's counselling ministry with that of Christ's – particularly as it relates to helping us become the kind of person God sees that we can be – we must ask ourselves the question: to whom do we refer when we describe ourselves by the personal pronoun 'I'? In our personalities is there anything so constant and reliable that we can honestly refer to it as 'I'?

'Human nature is so changeful,' said one philosopher, 'and so subject to swiftly alternating moods, that when I say "I", I am not sure what "I" I am talking about.' Who is the real man or real woman? The man who sings heartily in church, but then shouts at his wife and children on the way home in the car? The woman who enjoys leading a Bible study group and shows great wisdom, but who blows her top when the meal she has prepared turns out wrong? The same person can be so many different persons. Whom do others mean when they say 'you', and whom do you mean when you say 'I'?

Aristotle claimed there were six different Aristotles. Faust declared: 'Two souls, alas, dwell in this breast of mine.' Ernest Renan, the French author, admitted: 'I am two people; one part of me laughs while the other part of me cries.' Even Paul, in the passage before us today, talks about another self dwelling within him: 'For what I want to do I do not do...' (v15).

Some might try to explain this as 'dual personality', but the elements of what we are talking about are in us all. The real 'you', so I believe, is not the person others see, not even the person you see, but the person God, Christ and the Holy Spirit see. Only They know the real you and recognise your true potential.

O Father, how consoling it is to know that the Trinity see me not only as I am but as I can be. And You are all working to bring me up to my full height in Christ. Thank You, my Father. Amen.

FURTHER STUDY
Ps. 139:1–24
1. What did the psalmist explain?
2. What did he desire?

Double Vision

FOR READING & MEDITATION – JOHN 1:35–42

'Jesus... said, "You are Simon son of John. You will
be called Cephas" (which... is Peter).' (v42)

If, as we have been saying over the past few days, the Holy Spirit is our Counsellor, then what are some of the ways in which He makes His counsel available to us? How does He go about this important task? I pointed out earlier that when Jesus said 'The Father... will give you *another* Counsellor', He meant that the Holy Spirit would counsel us in the same way that Jesus counselled His disciples. So if we can see something of the way Jesus counselled them, we will have a clearer picture of how the Holy Spirit goes about the task of counselling us.

Take first the way in which our Lord came alongside Simon Peter, described in the passage before us today, and sought to help him see himself as the man he could be. One of the characteristics of a good counsellor is to have a clear vision of a person's potential so that he or she can encourage that person to move towards it. By potential I mean not so much human potential but our potential in Christ. Jesus looked at Simon and declared, '"You are Simon... You will be called Cephas" (which... is Peter).' What was Jesus really saying here? He was saying that He saw within Peter the potential to be a rock, for that is what the name 'Peter' means. Simon was the kind of vacillating character who could walk on the water with Jesus and yet 'followed at a distance' (Luke 22:54) when he was on the land. But Jesus had the insight, as many counsellors do, to see people not just as they are but as they can be.

This is a characteristic of the Holy Spirit also. He sees us as we are, loves us as we are, but yet loves us too much to let us stay as we are. Lovingly and gently He prods us towards perfection.

O God, how grateful I am that You have 'double vision'. You see me not just as I am but as I can be. May Your Spirit be at work in my life this day and every day, gently prodding me to perfection. In Jesus' name I ask it. Amen.

FURTHER STUDY

1 Sam. 16:1–13; 17:41–51

1. Contrast how people saw David and how God saw him.
2. Why could little David be confident against Goliath?

FOR READING & MEDITATION – COLOSSIANS 2:1–11

'And you have been given fulness in Christ, who is the
Head over every power and authority.' (v10)

We continue looking at Simon, the Galilean fisherman, the brother of Andrew and the son of John, to emphasise the point we are making, namely, that Christ saw him not as he was but as he could be. And, of course, everything that Christ did in Simon Peter's life was designed to draw him up to his full height spiritually. This too, as we have started to note, is the way the Holy Spirit works with us. But more of that a little later.

So, how many Simons were there? There were at least three: Simon as his friends saw him, Simon as he saw himself, and Simon as Christ saw him. What was Simon like in his friends' eyes? I can only conjecture, of course, but I imagine his friends might have described him like this: blustering, impulsive, loud mouthed – but clearly endowed with leadership qualities nevertheless. What was Simon like in his own eyes? Certainly he did not perceive himself as the same man that his friends saw. We rarely see ourselves as others see us. Indeed, we do not even see ourselves as others see us *physically*. When we look in a mirror the image we see is always reversed. And mentally and spiritually it is the same; it is another self we see from within. The poet Robert Burns (1759–1796) said:

Oh wad some power the giftie gie us
To see ourselves as others see us!

To see ourselves as others see us may be helpful, but what is more helpful is to see ourselves as God, Christ and the Holy Spirit see us. They see us, as we have been saying, not merely as we are, with dark marks on our soul, but as we can be – complete in the Godhead.

O God, once again I want to confess my gratitude for the fact that though You see me as I am, and love me as I am, You love me too much to let me stay as I am. You are working to bring me to completeness. I surrender to Your purposes. Amen.

FURTHER STUDY
Rom. 8:28–39; Eph. 1:3–14
1. What has God planned for us?
2. What have we received in Christ?

False Self-Images

FOR READING & MEDITATION – LUKE 4:38–44

'Simon's mother-in-law was suffering from a high
fever, and they asked Jesus to help her.' (v38)

We are beginning to realise that no matter how perceptive we may be, we never see ourselves as we really are. Some psychologists have suggested that we gain our sense of self through a series of 'mirrored appraisals'. Let me explain what is meant by this.

The view is that I, for example, do not see myself solely through my own eyes or solely through the eyes of others; I see myself as I *think* others see me! If this is the way we come to conclusions about ourselves, we are in a very perilous position as, generally speaking, we are poor judges of what others actually think. If we are to make any progress in the Christian life, we need to begin to see ourselves as God sees us, and let this form and transform every thought. This takes trust, time and courage – trust in the fact that God's Word is true; time spent 'soaking' ourselves in God's Word; and courage to see what needs to be changed, deal with it with the Spirit's help and step forward as the person God sees you can be.

I wonder, was the picture Simon had of himself a flattering one? No doubt he thought of himself as a good judge of other people, a good husband, and perhaps even a good son-in-law. Certainly, as we see from the passage before us today, he appeared to have a great concern when his mother-in-law was ill. If someone had said to Simon, 'Are you without fault?' I think he might have answered, 'No, I do have some faults.' But I don't think he would have particularised them. Usually people don't until they are serious in the pursuit of holiness. Then, and only then, will we search deeply into our faults, itemise them, pray over them and say, 'This, and this, and this is sin within me.'

O God, help me to become serious in the pursuit of holiness. If there are faults or sins within me that I can't see, or even others can't see, then give me Your light. For it is only in Your light that I can see light. In Jesus' name. Amen.

FURTHER STUDY

Luke 18:9–14; 1 John 1:8–9

1. Why did the Pharisees have a false self-image?
2. What did John explain?

A New Name

FOR READING & MEDITATION – 1 PETER 2:1–10

'See, I lay a stone in Zion, a chosen and precious cornerstone...' (v6)

We look now at the Simon Jesus saw. I think if we were speaking with full understanding as well as accuracy we would say that our Lord saw *two* Simons. First, Simon as he was (which was neither the Simon his friends saw nor the Simon he himself saw), and second, the Simon Christ could make of him. The two were so different that they required a different name. Our Lord, looking at Simon, said, 'You are Simon son of John,' and then, envisaging the Simon he could make, said: 'You will be called a rock. That is the man I'll make you' (see John 1:42). What a change: Peter, who could be swayed by even the gentlest wind would, under the counselling ministry of Christ, become a rock.

Did that happen? Through the combination of Christ's counselling and later the Holy Spirit's counselling, the impulsive blusterer became clear in judgment and firm in will. One commentator says: 'The man who could curse and swear and deny all knowledge of his best friend to save his own skin, became a valiant leader at Pentecost and the unshaken champion of the sect which was itself to change the world.'

In today's passage Peter speaks of Christ as the living Stone – rejected by men but chosen by God. It is interesting that Peter talks so much about Christ being a Rock, for under the tuition of the 'Rock', he himself had become a rock. Not, of course, that Peter could be compared to Christ, but he had taken on the characteristics of his Lord which were foreign to his own nature. 'This is what I will make of you,' Jesus had said, 'a rock.' And He did. What could the Holy Spirit have planned for your life?

O God, if You could turn Peter the unstable into Peter the rock, then what can You do with me? With You nothing is impossible. Help me be open to all the changes the divine Counsellor wants to bring about in my life. In Jesus' name. Amen.

FURTHER STUDY

Judg. 6:11–16; Luke 22:54–62; Gal. 2:7–9

1. How did weak Gideon become a mighty warrior?
2. How was Peter regarded by the Early Church?

Divine Enticement

FOR READING & MEDITATION – GENESIS 17:1–15

'No longer will you be called Abram; your name will be Abraham...' (v5)

It is always a powerful moment when one person stands before another and paints for them a picture of the kind of person they can be. This is something all good counsellors, as well as people helpers and friends, know how to do.

Please pardon the personal reference here, but when counselling I have often found myself saying something like this to a husband who has told me he feels weak and inadequate: 'In Christ you have the potential to be the man who can strongly move into your wife's world, to be the kind of husband to her that Christ is to the Church – initiating, loving and considerate.' I remember on one occasion talking to a woman who had been raped in her teens and was finding it difficult to give herself fully to her husband: 'You believe deep down that because you were violated you cannot now give your attractiveness to anyone. However, in the strength and power of Christ, your femininity which you now want to hide can blossom into an attractiveness that will not only bring out your own inner beauty but *His* also.' The changes those God-inspired remarks made in those people's lives are something I thank God for to this day. To Him be all the glory.

Our Lord's dealings with Simon Peter, particularly in respect of putting before him a vision of what he could be, set a pattern the Holy Spirit follows in His counselling ministry with us. Tell me, have you ever been at prayer and caught a vision, if only for a moment, of what it would mean to be the person you longed to be? That was the ministry of the divine Counsellor at work within you. He sees with double vision, and to get more of that double vision we must determine to spend more time with Him.

Loving heavenly Father, my mind is made up to spend more time with You – beginning today. Show me how to manage my time so that I can bring more of You into my day. The more You have of me the more I have of You. In Jesus' name I pray. Amen.

FURTHER STUDY
Jer. 1:4–19; Eph. 2:1–10
1. How did God change Jeremiah's view of himself?
2. How have we been changed?

Confined in a Cage!

FOR READING & MEDITATION – GENESIS 35:1–15

'God said to him, "Your name is Jacob, but you will no longer
be called Jacob; your name will be Israel."' (v10)

Who is the real you? Is it the person you yourself see? No! Positively no! Unless your powers of introspection are heightened by the Holy Spirit, you do not know yourself. Psychology is not enough. Psychologists and psychiatrists can be amazingly unaware of themselves, and some appear to need the treatment they give to others. Is the real you the person others see? Again I have to say a definite 'No'. It may be an act of faith on my part, but I am ready to assert that the real you is the person the Holy Spirit wants to make you. You were not made to be undermined, to be beaten and frustrated by sin. You were made for God Himself, and seated deep in your heart there are longings to know Him and be like Him.

In a zoo some years ago I looked at eagles in their cage. Somehow the sight hurt me. The great birds were made for the skies but here they were, confined in a cage! So many of us are like that – made for higher things but confined in a cage of doubt, fear, denial, perhaps even sin. Just as Jesus looked on Simon the unstable and saw Peter the rock, so the Holy Spirit looks on you and sees you may feel ineffective, beaten, cowed and fearful, but He also sees you as confident, effective, sanctified, and strong, moving ahead along the Christian pathway with great strides.

Oh, if only we could see ourselves as He sees us! What a difference that would make. If only we could move closer to Him, stand at His side and get that double vision – the vision of the men and women we are and the men and women we might be. But what stops us getting close? Mainly it is our unwillingness. When our *will* is intent on getting closer, we *will* find a way.

O Father, help me to be willing. I know that my potential can never be realised without spending time with You, but the cost of that is sometimes more than I am willing to pay. Forgive me and help me. In Jesus' name. Amen.

FURTHER STUDY

Dan. 6:16–23; Acts 12:1–14

1. Why did Daniel escape his cage?
2. How was Peter released from prison?

The Person God Meant

FOR READING & MEDITATION – 2 CORINTHIANS 3:7–18

'And we... are being transformed into his likeness
with ever-increasing glory...' (v18)

We spend one more day considering the fact that the divine Counsellor is at work within us seeking to make us into the kind of person He sees that we can be. Ralph Waldo Emerson (1803–1882) said:

Could'st thou in vision see
Thyself the man God meant,
Thou never more could'st be
The man thou art, content.

How does the Holy Spirit enable us to see the man or woman God meant? He can only do it, as we have said, when we get close to Him or allow Him to get close to us. No counsellor is effective unless he or she has the confidence, trust *and* attention of the person being counselled. Charles Swindoll, when talking to a group of preachers and Bible teachers, said: 'As theologians and teachers of the Word we study the Holy Spirit from a safe doctrinal distance; we are loath to enter into any of the realms of His supernatural workings or even to tolerate the possibility of such. Explaining the Holy Spirit is one thing; experiencing Him another.'

I believe with all my heart that the Holy Spirit yearns to transform us in the same way that Christ yearned to transform Simon Peter. But it requires confidence and trust from us. It means taking time to develop our relationship with Him. Once we do that, however, He goes to work, inflaming, enlightening, guiding, enticing and moving us on until the difference in us is so marked that we need a new name. To you now, as to one long ago, the Spirit says: 'You are... But you shall be...'

Loving Father, burn into me by Your Holy Spirit the truth that unless we travel together – You, me and the other members of the Trinity – I shall never be the person You see that I can be. Today I put my hand in Yours. Lead me on. Amen.

FURTHER STUDY
Rom. 12:1–2; Col. 3:1–17
1. What are the keys to transformation?
2. Describe the process of transformation.

No Prayer – No Power

FOR READING & MEDITATION – LUKE 18:1–8

'Jesus told his disciples a parable to show them that
they should always pray and not give up.' (v1)

We have seen over the past week something of the way in which our Lord counselled Simon Peter by painting for him a picture of the man He saw he could be. We noted also that the Holy Spirit, the divine Counsellor, follows that same pattern in His ministry with us. He too seeks constantly to set before us an image of the man or woman He sees we can be, and the more we give ourselves to Him the more He can give Himself to us.

We look now at another occasion when Jesus guided and directed His disciples – this time a group counselling session. And we shall consider later that just as Jesus did in this case, so the Holy Spirit, the divine Counsellor, seeks to encourage us. So look first with me at how Jesus instructed His disciples concerning the subject of prayer. The passage before us is just one of many passages in the Gospels in which Jesus unfolded to His disciples the power and importance of prayer. The particular aspect of prayer which our Lord brings out in this parable is that of *perseverance*. We are to pray and not faint.

Often when we are overcome by troubles and trials we find it difficult to pray. Time and time again when counselling I have asked people (never immediately, but at some appropriate moment), 'What's your prayer life like?' More often than not they have responded, 'I find it very hard to pray.' It's not easy to pray when things all around us are falling apart, but hard though it may be to accept, that is the time we need to pray the most. Indeed, one of the goals of a godly counsellor is to help a person establish a consistent prayer life, for without one there is little chance of spiritual survival. If we do not pray, we faint.

O God, just as Jesus counselled His disciples to pray, may the Holy Spirit counsel me along these lines too. For I see that if I do not pray, I faint. Divine Counsellor, my heart is open and You have my total confidence. In Jesus' name. Amen.

FURTHER STUDY
1 Kgs 18:41–46; 2 Kgs 13:14–19
1. How did Elijah show perseverance?
2. What would result from Jehoash giving up too quickly?

Running From the Crowds!

FOR READING & MEDITATION – LUKE 5:12–16

'But Jesus often withdrew to lonely places and prayed.' (v16)

Over and over again in the Gospels we catch sight of Jesus helping His disciples to pray. Why? He spent so much time on this issue because He knew that prayer opens us to God and to the resources of the Holy Spirit. Like an old-fashioned watch, life has a tendency to run down. It needs rewinding. Prayer rewinds the springs of life by opening our spirits to the Holy Spirit. You don't have to tamper with the hands of a watch to make them go round if the mechanism is fully wound. They go round of their own accord. Likewise, when we are in an ongoing relationship with God through prayer, the Holy Spirit supplies the energy we need to get through every day. And not merely get through, but sail through – victoriously.

Counsellors can never take anyone farther than they have gone themselves, and if a counsellor doesn't know the value of prayer then he or she will not be able to convey that to others. Our Lord is the perfect example of a Counsellor who practised what He preached. In the passage before us today we read that following the healing of the leper, the news about Christ's great ministry spread widely until the crowds flocked from near and far to hear His words and be healed of their diseases. But on many occasions, we are told, He escaped from the crowds to pray. Just think of it: Christ moved away from the multitudes to get alone and pray. That shows how much of a priority our Lord gave to prayer.

We preachers are far too often crowd-conscious. We run *from* praying *towards* the crowds, eager for praise and affirmation; our Lord ran from the crowds in order to pray. Prayer helps us revise our lives and renew them. Jesus needed to pray. So do we.

Lord Jesus Christ, You are the greatest man who has ever lived and yet You needed to pray. May the Holy Spirit work in me so that I too shall be primarily prayer-conscious and secondarily people-conscious. For Your own dear name's sake. Amen.

FURTHER STUDY
Mark 14:32–42; Luke 6:12–19
1. What battle did Jesus face in prayer?
2. What did Jesus do prior to choosing the disciples?

Pray! Pray! Pray!

FOR READING & MEDITATION – 1 THESSALONIANS 5:1–23

'Pray continually...' (v17)

Put quite simply, prayer is the heart of our faith. People have spoken to me over the years and said something like this: 'I am no theologian. Put it to me in the clearest terms: What is the heart of Christian living? How do I grow in grace and power?' Prayer is the way. However, I know that many of our ideas concerning prayer are confused, and many find it difficult to pray, even when no problems are crowding into their lives.

A pastor tells of a woman who told him she was leaving the church and never returning. When he asked why, she said that her daughter had sat for a scholarship, and although she and her little girl had prayed hard, she had not passed. Indeed, not only had she failed to pass but she had come bottom of the list. That proved, the mother claimed, that there was nothing in prayer, and therefore she was not attending church any more. The pastor concluded, 'It struck me as I listened to her that I had not taught her much about prayer.' He knew the daughter well and realised she could not have passed a scholarship if her life had depended on it. She was a lovely girl and would go on to fulfil a satisfying role in life, but did not have the ability to pass this scholarship. Think of a mother losing faith in prayer because of that.

Some see prayer as simply the means to get something from God. So, they pray only when they want something. You may have heard of the little boy who told his vicar that he didn't pray every day because there were some days when he didn't want anything. What would you think of a friend who turned up to see you only when he wanted something? Is that how we treat God I wonder?

O God, wean me from the idea that prayer is simply asking for things. And help me understand that when You say 'No' to my prayers it is because You know best. Teach me to pray, to really pray, dear Father. In Jesus' name. Amen.

FURTHER STUDY

Acts 4:23–31; Col. 4:2–4

1. What happened when the Early Church prayed?
2. How should we pray?

When Disinclined to Pray

FOR READING & MEDITATION – EPHESIANS 6:10–20

'And pray in the Spirit on all occasions with all kinds of prayers and requests.' (v18)

Prayer, as we saw yesterday, is much more than asking for things. In fact, those who see it as such are in prayer's kindergarten. But even those who see prayer as more than that often tell me they find it difficult to pray. The need for prayer is apparent, the command to pray is recognised, but the *longing* to pray is not in them. They have to push themselves to get down on their knees. What a tragedy. The very thing we need most, we desire the least. How can we escape from this impasse?

Thankfully, the divine Counsellor is willing to come to our aid. Paul says, 'The Spirit helps us in our weakness.' (Rom. 8:26) You will know, I'm sure, that some Bible translations use the word 'Helper' rather than 'Counsellor' in the text which provides the theme for our studies – John 14:16 – and I do not object to that, for that is precisely what the Holy Spirit does – He *helps*. And never more so than when He helps us pray.

At one time in my life I went through a dark period when prayer lost all its appeal for me. I continued preaching and writing in a kind of mechanical way, and as far as I can tell, no one noticed any difference. My words were carefully thought out, my sentences studiously crafted, but they were not soaked in prayer. Then the Spirit drew near and challenged me about my prayer life. 'But I don't *feel* like praying,' I complained. 'Then I will help you,' He seemed to say. He did, and by His grace He lit the flame of prayer once again in my heart.

Is the divine Counsellor, I wonder, talking now to you about this very problem? Then ask Him to help you. And do it without any further prevarication – today.

O God, You put within me the desire to pray and can also help me overcome any disinclination I have to pray. Touch me today by Your Spirit and give me a greater passion for prayer than I have ever known before. In Christ's name I ask it. Amen.

FURTHER STUDY
Deut. 8:6–18; Phil. 4:4–9
1. Why may we be disinclined to pray?
2. How can we follow Paul's example?

The Spirit is Praying!

FOR READING & MEDITATION – ROMANS 8:18–27

'The Spirit himself intercedes for us with groans that
words cannot express.' (v26)

Yesterday we said that our divine Counsellor helps us overcome any disinclination we may have to pray. The passage before us today tells us that on some occasions He will actually pray in us and through us. These words spell out one of the most astonishing truths about the Holy Spirit contained anywhere in the Word of God. The Holy Spirit, says the apostle Paul, intercedes for us 'with groans that words cannot express'.

I find very little has been written about this aspect of the Spirit's work, so I can only tell you what *I* think is meant here. The Holy Spirit (like any good counsellor) does not despise human frailties or reprimand us when we don't know how to pray or what to pray for. Instead, He makes our weakness the reason to plead our interests before God. We all experience occasions when we lack clarity about the subjects for which we should pray, and at such times our prayers are very superficial. Thus the needs we express in prayer are lesser needs, and not the things we really ought to be praying about. But sometimes our divine Counsellor, knowing that prayer brings about God's redemptive purposes, takes up the task of intercession for us 'with groans that words cannot express'. The relationship between God and the Holy Spirit is so close that the prayers of the Spirit need not be audible. The sighs of the Spirit are clearly interpreted by God, because it is for God's own purpose for each one of us that the Spirit is pleading.

It is an awesome moment when one senses that one is being prayed *through*. All one can do is to silence every other voice that rises up in the soul and say, 'Hush! The Holy Spirit is praying!'

O God, how wondrous are the ways of Your Spirit. Help me understand, however, that being prayed through is more occasional than general, and I must not use it as an excuse for not initiating prayer. In Jesus' name I ask it. Amen.

FURTHER STUDY

1 Sam. 1:9–20; 19:14–23

1. What happened when Hannah groaned?
2. What happened when people encountered the Holy Spirit?

The Groan of God

FOR READING & MEDITATION – JOHN 11:32–44

'Jesus... was deeply moved in spirit and troubled.' (v33)

We see in our reading for today that our Lord was deeply troubled in spirit. The New King James Version translates the text in this way: 'Jesus... *groaned* in the spirit and was troubled' (my emphasis). God was about to use Jesus to bring Lazarus back to life, yet immediately prior to this momentous event our Lord groaned deep within His soul. Why was this? Let us consider some words of the late Dr W.E. Sangster in his *Westminster Sermons*: 'All true progress in this world is by the echo of the groan of God in the heart of His people.' What did he mean? An illustration might help to make things clear.

In previous centuries, much to our shame, Britain was engaged in the nefarious business of slave-trading. How did it eventually come to an end? Did every Briton wake up one morning and say, 'This is most definitely wrong – we must free the slaves immediately'? No! One man woke up one morning and found the Spirit groaning in his soul. That man was William Wilberforce; he and his friends laboured until that most notable hour in our history when we paid a sum larger than our national debt of the time to free the slaves.

Progress in spiritual things is not mechanical. It does not come from ourselves alone. Progress results from the groan of God in the hearts of His people. Was the groan that Jesus felt as He confronted death God groaning within Him? Was it the spiritual precursor of something mighty and momentous? I think so. If it is true, as Sangster says, that 'all true progress in this world is by the echo of the groan of God in the hearts of His people', then ought we not to ask ourselves: When did we last feel the groan of God in our soul?

O God, I feel saddened today to think that I might block some aspect of spiritual progress in this world because I am insensitive to Your groan echoing in my soul. Tune me in more closely to Your purposes, dear Lord. In Jesus' name. Amen.

FURTHER STUDY
Rom. 10:1; Gal. 4:8–20; 2 Pet. 3:8–9
1. Why did Paul groan?
2. For what does God groan?

Three Groans!

FOR READING & MEDITATION – 2 CORINTHIANS 5:1–10

'For while we are in this tent, we groan and are burdened...' (v4)

We spend one last day reflecting on the way in which the Holy Spirit, our divine Counsellor, encourages us, as did Jesus, to explore the depths and heights of intercessory prayer. The verse before us today takes our minds back to Romans 8, where the apostle Paul reminds us about three kinds of groans. He tells us there that the whole creation groans (8:22), we ourselves groan (8:23), and the Spirit makes intercession for us with groans that cannot be expressed in words (8:26).

First then, let us consider that *the whole creation groans*. Who can doubt it? Everything that lives is subject to disease: human beings, animals, fish, birds, trees, plants. Life seems strangely poisoned at the fount. Second, we read that *we groan within ourselves*. A.W. Tozer said: 'We have not progressed very far in the Christian life if we have not felt the groan that goes on in creation... and felt also the groan in our own hearts – the longing to be released from bondage and be with Christ.' This is, in fact, what the text before us today is talking about – the longing that there is in all redeemed hearts to be free from sin's bondage and corruption. Third, and most astonishing of all, Paul says that *the Spirit groans within us*. Is the groan of the Spirit the answer to the groan in creation? Is this God's way of ensuring spiritual progress in this world? I think it is.

Three groans! Hear the groan of creation. Hear the groan within yourself. Hear too the Spirit making intercession for you with groans which cannot be put into words. But know this also: God's last word is not a groan. God's last word is joy, joy, joy! The Spirit is our deposit, guaranteeing this promise.

O Lord, while I am thankful for knowing about these three groans, I am thankful also for this reminder that Your last word is joy. May I keep that thought always before me, that I might live with a full understanding. In Christ's name. Amen.

FURTHER STUDY
Matt. 23:37; Luke 19:41–46; Rev. 21:1–4
1. Why did Jesus groan and weep?
2. When will groaning cease?

FOR READING & MEDITATION – JOHN 4:1–26

'Jesus said to her, "You are right when you say you have no husband."' (v17)

So far in our meditations we have examined just two aspects of our Lord's counselling approach which we see reflected also in the counselling ministry of the Holy Spirit. First, the way in which He holds out for us the vision of the person God sees us to be, and second, the importance of building a good and meaningful prayer life. Counselling focuses, of course, on many different issues, but the two aspects we have considered are regarded as pivotal and fundamental by all those who seek to counsel according to Scripture.

Another aspect of good counselling, and one which we see demonstrated both by our Lord and the Holy Spirit, is bringing important issues to a head through *loving confrontation*. This involves moving people away from symptoms on the surface to face the significant issues.

Look with me first at how Christ demonstrated this skill in His encounter with the woman at the well. How did Jesus get to the root problem in the heart of the Samaritan woman without seeming to invade sanctities? Did He say bluntly: 'Woman, you are living an adulterous life'? No, He highlights her problem in a more delicate way: 'Go, call your husband' (v16). She replies weakly, 'I have no husband.' That was true, He acknowledged, recognising her honesty before touching the deeper areas of her life. It was just a step from there to confronting her with the real issues for which she needed help, and soon her heart was open and exposed. Christ always saw past the surface issues to the major ones, and never hesitated, though always respectfully, to bring the hidden things to light.

O God, perhaps I too need a lesson here, though I may not be a counsellor. Help me to be concerned not about winning arguments but winning people, and how to respect people even though I may disagree with their behaviour. In Jesus' name. Amen.

FURTHER STUDY
Gen. 3:1–23; Mic. 3:8; John 16:7–8
1. How did God respond to Adam's sin?
2. Why was Micah filled with the Spirit?

FOR READING & MEDITATION – GALATIANS 6:1–10

'Brothers, if someone is caught in a sin, you who
are spiritual should restore him gently.' (v1)

❝In almost every life,' said Dr E. Stanley Jones, 'there is an issue which needs confronting, which becomes the decision point from which we swing toward darkness or toward light – toward spiritual malformation or spiritual transformation. If that central issue is not faced then the process of transformation is blocked. If faced courageously then the process and power of redemption is at our disposal.' Powerful words. If it is true that in almost every life there is 'an issue which needs confronting', then what is to be done about it? It must be faced and faced courageously.

However, when confronting issues such as sin or moral failure, great care must be taken. We saw yesterday how expertly our Lord dealt with the woman at the well. He pointed out her moral need in a delicate way that showed both readiness to confront her over her sin and yet respect for her as a person. Did you notice in yesterday's reading that Jesus said at the beginning of the conversation: 'You are right', and at the end, 'What you have said is quite true' (John 4:17–18)? He pointed out the good in her at the very moment He touched the terribly sore depths.

There is a form of Christian counselling known as 'nouthetic counselling', *noutheteo* being the Greek word for 'to warn, admonish, confront'. This type of counselling may be experienced as confrontational, because some of its practitioners (though not all) have in the past appeared, in their enthusiasm, to be more interested in exposing sin than restoring the sinner. Our text for today reminds us that where there is moral failure, it is restoration, not exposure, that ought to be the overriding consideration. To confront does not mean to affront.

O Father, how much less pain there would be in all our relationships if we, Your children, could follow the example of Jesus and hate sin but not hate the sinner. Help us learn that lesson and learn it quickly. In Christ's name. Amen.

FURTHER STUDY
Gen. 4:1–16; Matt. 12:1–8
1. How did God show Cain both justice and mercy?
2. What did Jesus explain?

FOR READING & MEDITATION – JAMES 1:12–18

'But each one is tempted when, by his own evil
desire, he is dragged away and enticed.' (v14)

One of the abilities of a good counsellor, we have been saying, is to bring important issues to a head through loving confrontation. Note the word *loving*. Some people just love to confront – period. But if confrontation is to be successful it must be done in a certain way. It must enable the person being counselled to understand the damage and devastation caused by sin, but be done in a way that shows deep respect for the person. Jesus models this. And so too, of course, does the Holy Spirit.

An old hymn by Alfred H. Vine (1845–1917) describes the Holy Spirit as a Counsellor, and contains the lines:

Christ is our Advocate on high,
Thou art our Advocate within.
O plead the truth and make reply
To every argument of sin.

The arguments of sin? What does that mean? Psychologists (with their love of awkward phrases) call it 'the rationalisation of desire'. Let me explain what that involves. One day you find yourself being tempted by something that hitherto you have always resisted. But this time you begin to look at it a little differently. Perhaps you begin to talk to yourself like this: 'The pressures in my life at the moment are so strong that surely a little escape from them can be justified. After all, the world is not a Sunday school. Standards change from age to age. No one can blame me for just one lapse – just one.'

You see how it leads on? That is what the psychologist calls 'the rationalisation of desire', and that is what the hymnwriter had in mind when he spoke of the *argument* of sin.

O God, how encouraging it is to know that when the arguments of sin are heard in my soul, I have an Advocate who rises at once to rebut them. Thank You, my Father, for appointing the Holy Spirit as my Advocate. In Jesus' name. Amen.

FURTHER STUDY
Luke 4:1–14; Eph. 4:25–27
1. How did Jesus overcome the arguments of sin?
2. What did Paul warn against?

David's Great Sin

FOR READING & MEDITATION – 2 SAMUEL 11:1–27

'But the thing David had done displeased the Lord.' (v27)

We spoke yesterday of the ease with which we can slip into what psychologists call 'the rationalisation of desire'. Keep in mind that what makes temptation powerful is the desire within us for the thing with which we are tempted. Where there is no innate desire, temptation has little appeal. King David knew all about 'the rationalisation of desire', as we see from the passage before us today. He wanted the wife of Uriah, one of his officers, and while Uriah was on active service fighting the king's battles, David seduced the woman. Then, fearing the consequences, he 'arranged' the death of her husband and added murder to lust. The 'man after God's own heart' was immersed in murder and manipulation.

How did he ever get to that point? By 'the rationalisation of desire', by the arguments of sin. It would have happened like this: A desire dropped into David's mind. He could not help this, of course, but he dwelt on it when he should have blacked it out. He fed his imagination on it when he should have blasted it with prayer. He told himself later that Uriah had died in the discharge of his duty. Gallant soldiers do fall in battle ...! And then he married the woman and thought he had resolved the problem. He was a victim of the arguments of sin.

David was so self-deceived that on this occasion even the Holy Spirit was unable to get through to him (He will plead but never overpower), and so the Spirit used Nathan as one of His 'temporary assistants'. Nathan's barbed little parable did its work. Soon the wail of Psalm 51 arose: 'Have mercy on me, O God... blot out my transgressions... wash me, and I shall be whiter than snow' (Ps. 51:1,7).

O God, help me never to get into the state where my conscience is drugged and I become self-deceived. I tremble that my soul could become so insensitive to sin that the Spirit would be unable to get my attention. Save me from that. Amen.

FURTHER STUDY
2 Sam. 12:1–10; Jas 1:22–25
1. How did Nathan confront David?
2. How can we avoid self-deception?

He is Always There!

FOR READING & MEDITATION – EPHESIANS 1:1–14

'You were marked in him with a seal, the promised Holy
Spirit... guaranteeing our inheritance...' (vv13–14)

A question I have often been asked concerning the Holy Spirit is this: Does the Spirit withdraw from our hearts if we ever fall into sin? I have thought long and hard about this, and I have to say: I don't think so. He is hurt by our sin, even deeply saddened by it, but He remains with us and in us nevertheless. Some would *like* to believe that He *does* leave when we fall into sin, for the thought of a grieved and hurting Spirit residing in the soul greatly increases their spiritual discomfort. Experiencing the sting of one's own conscience when one has sinned is bad enough, but the thought that the Holy Spirit is there in the soul also – hurting, grieved, and pained – seems to make the sin more heinous still.

Many years ago, when I was living in the city of Sheffield in the north of England, the local newspaper carried a report about a barrister who had to plead 'invisibility' at the Sheffield Quarter Sessions because he was not wearing a wig and gown. In a British court a barrister (known as an advocate in Scotland) is obliged to wear a wig and a gown in the court room otherwise officially he is not present. 'I cannot see you,' said the judge as the barrister arose in court. 'You are invisible to me.'

That, I believe, will never happen in the heart of one of God's children. The Spirit is always 'dressed' for the occasion. He will not desert you. You may sadden Him and turn a deaf ear to Him, and if you do not heed Him it is possible that His voice may grow faint within you. But I don't believe He will leave. The promised Holy Spirit is our guarantee. We are sealed by the Spirit until the day of redemption. *He is always there.*

O Father, how thrilling it is to know that Your Spirit is unwilling to leave me. He knows the worst about me but still will not desert me. My words cannot convey my gratitude. In Jesus' name. Amen.

FURTHER STUDY
2 Kgs 6:8–17; Hag. 2:1–5
1. Why does the Spirit's invisibility not imply His unavailability?
2. What reassurance did the prophet give?

The Purifying Spirit

FOR READING & MEDITATION – ACTS 15:1–11

'[The Holy Spirit] purified their hearts by faith.' (v9)

The work of the divine Counsellor in pleading against the arguments of sin is perhaps needed more now than at any other time in history. I say this because moral permissiveness is so commonplace that we are in danger of being brainwashed by the world into reducing our standards to less than those to which Christ has called us.

Society tolerates things today that years ago would have brought an expression of absolute horror to most people's faces. Take the area of entertainment. (I speak mainly of the scene here in the British Isles.) On stage and screen where people used to worry about whether or not nudity was gratuitous, it is now more or less compulsory. On TV we are treated to the most intimate and shameless sexual disclosures. In sport, footballers provide us with displays of loud-mouthed arrogance. Much of sport is marred by vindictive and threatening gestures and talk. Business people line up to boast about this or that takeover, and almost everyone in politics seems to be hard at work on self-aggrandising memoirs. Recently I watched a TV panel programme during which one person objected to the low standards being accepted everywhere today. A member of the panel retorted, 'But it's only human nature.' That sums up the spirit of the world: 'It's nature and therefore hardly sin.'

This attitude of compromise must not be allowed to invade the Church. Many are interested only in the power aspect of the Holy Spirit's ministry. But we must never forget that the Spirit's *greatest* work is helping us to be cleansed from sin and to overcome sin. He is, we must always remember, the *Holy* Spirit.

My Father and my God, by Your Spirit You are bringing things to the surface – not to shame us but to save us. Give us grace as Your Church to follow through – from exposure to experience. In Jesus' name we pray. Amen.

FURTHER STUDY
2 Cor. 6:14–7:1; Gal. 5:16–26
1. What is the result of reverence for God?
2. Contrast acts of human nature with the fruit of the Spirit.

Sensitivity to Sin

FOR READING & MEDITATION – 1 JOHN 1:1–10

'If we claim to be without sin, we deceive ourselves...' (v8)

Today we ask ourselves: Is a sense of sin old-fashioned? Our fathers used to talk a lot about the way the Holy Spirit convicted of sin, but 'conviction of sin' is a phrase we don't use much nowadays. It is true, of course, that earlier generations indulged in the most extravagant descriptions of their own sinful nature, and a glance through old hymnbooks certainly confirms that. Here is a typical example from a hymn by John Wesley (1703–1791):

Me, the vilest of the race,
Most unholy, most unclean.
Me, the farthest from Thy face,
Full of misery and sin...

The Christians of a bygone age seemed to delight in their depravity. One Victorian commentator tells of a village shopkeeper, a devout member of a local Methodist church, who week by week used the same phrase in his prayers to describe his spiritual condition: 'My soul is a mass of putrefying sores.' Yet he was by all accounts a perfectly honest and upright man. Today we regard such attitudes as 'old-fashioned' and are apt to say with a touch of satisfied complacency, 'We are not at all like that.'

Let us be on our guard, however, lest in our unwillingness to express ourselves in the self-depreciating language of previous generations we grow smug in our attitude to sin. It is perilously possible that, without realising it, we may have been affected by the tendency of this age to reduce the eternal distinction between right and wrong to a question of taste. Ask yourself now: Am I as sensitive to sin as I think I am?

O God, again by Your Spirit You are bringing issues to the surface and confronting me with the reality of what may be going on within me. Help me not to indulge in my depravity, but help me not to overlook it either. In Christ's name. Amen.

FURTHER STUDY
Ps. 119:9–16; Isa. 5:18–24
1. How can we avoid sin?
2. How may some regard good and evil?

The Scrutiny of God

FOR READING & MEDITATION – PSALM 139:1–24

'Search me, O God, and know my heart...' (v23)

I want to instil a thought in your mind that I hope will be helpful to you not only now but in the years to come: The safest form of self-examination is that which is carried out in the presence of the Holy Spirit and under the guidance of the Spirit. Some Christians seem to be *always* examining their hearts and thus become unhealthily introspective. Others never examine their hearts and become spiritually indolent and lethargic.

Reviewing our relationship with God should be a regular activity. I know many Christians who examine their hearts every Sunday. They claim this is the best time, when work and other pressures can be dismissed from the mind. Whenever it is performed (and one can hardly get by with less than once a week), first invite the Holy Spirit to be present and to guide. The whole purpose of spiritual reflection is to identify the things that should not be in our lives and to bring them to God so that they may be uprooted. If the Holy Spirit is not invited to the moment of self-examination then it is possible that we could end up in a state of self-pity rather than contrition. The Spirit never moves us to self-pity; the Spirit moves us to repentance. Self-pity is an enemy of repentance because it is an attempt to remove the soul's pain by humanistic means rather than by entrusting oneself to God and His Holy Spirit.

The psalmist, as we see today, had the right idea when he prayed: 'Search me, O God... See if there is any offensive way in me...' (vv23–24). Begin with that prayer, wait before God to see what He will make you conscious of. Then ask Him for forgiveness and go out into the day – forgiven and cleansed.

O Father, help me to regularly open up the depths of my heart to Your Spirit, the divine Counsellor. May He search me and see if there is any wicked way in me – anything that hinders the flow of Your life through me. In Jesus' name. Amen.

FURTHER STUDY

Matt. 5:21–24; 1 Cor. 11:23–32; 2 Cor. 13:5–6
1. Why might we postpone worship?
2. When is it especially important to examine ourselves?

God Where it Counts

FOR READING & MEDITATION – ACTS 2:1–21

'All of them were filled with the Holy Spirit...' (v4)

In today's meditation, we remind ourselves that the coming of the Holy Spirit has put the resources of the Trinity where they count – *within*. I love the definition of the Holy Spirit given by a little boy in Sunday school: 'The Holy Spirit is God in action.' He is! The disciples were so fearful prior to Pentecost. They seemed to lack nerve, to lack direction, and to lack a sense of reinforcement within... Until the Holy Spirit came, that is. Then they were transformed and became unstoppable.

You know, most likely, that there is a great debate among theologians as to whether the last twelve verses of Mark's Gospel are part of his original text. Some say they were added by a later writer. If this is so then Mark's Gospel ends with the words of chapter 16 verse 8: 'They said nothing to anyone, because they were afraid.' Suppose there had been no Day of Pentecost. Then the gospel story would have ended at this point. We would have had the record of our Lord's birth, His ministry, His three-year involvement with His disciples, His death, His burial, His resurrection, His ascension. But the end of it all would have been that the disciples 'said nothing to anyone, because they were afraid'. The four Gospels without the Upper Room would have proclaimed a powerless gospel.

But let's not go down this road any longer. Such was not the case, for the Holy Spirit came to put the Spirit of Jesus within the disciples. Jesus said He would go away but that He would come again to them – in the power and presence of the Spirit. And the coming of the Spirit has put God and Christ in the most vital place – within.

O God, on this day when we Your people celebrate the descent of the Spirit at Pentecost, come again and flood us out by a deluge of Your Spirit. Enlarge our vision and set our hearts on fire. Give us more of Your Spirit, dear Lord. More. In Jesus' name. Amen.

FURTHER STUDY

Mark 16:9–20; Acts 1:4–8

1. What happened when the disciples went out?
2. Why could the disciples not preach straight away?

Whose Voice Was It?

FOR READING & MEDITATION – ROMANS 8:1–11

'You... are controlled not by the sinful nature but by the Spirit,
if the Spirit of God lives in you.' (v9)

A central thought has occupied our minds over the past several days. I refer to the truth that the Holy Spirit, our divine Counsellor, is at work within our hearts pleading against the arguments of sin. He, like our Lord, never hesitates to make us aware of important issues in our hearts, but He does so in the same way that Jesus did – tenderly, delicately, and respectfully. Would that all Christians followed their example.

But tell me now before we move on: Do you know anything about what we have been calling 'the arguments of sin'? Something tells me that you do. Cast your mind back over your life for a moment. Can you recall times when temptation has come to you and you felt some sinful desire rise within you? In the courtroom of your soul did you hear the plea of the arguments of sin? And did you hear another voice also, a voice that was low but clear and insistent, speaking to you of past victories, of the people who love you, of home, of your family, of the Church? Who was that, pleading like a skilful advocate in front of a judge, calling to mind every good point from the past in order to help His case? Do you remember moments like that? Whose voice was it?

Yes, you know, don't you? It was your divine Counsellor. He was pleading the truth and making reply to every argument of sin. Where would you and I be today, I wonder, were it not for that blessed ministry of the Spirit? What if, when the arguments of sin arose, He had left us without a word? It doesn't bear thinking about. Jesus loved people enough to plead with them to give up their sin. The Holy Spirit does so too.

Dear Father, I lay at Your feet the tribute of gratitude that fills my soul today as I reflect on the many times Your Holy Spirit has pleaded in my heart against every argument of sin. My gratitude is Yours for ever. Amen.

FURTHER STUDY
Num. 22:7–39; Isa. 30:21
1. How many times did God warn Balaam?
2. What is God's promise?

A Piercing Question

FOR READING & MEDITATION – JOHN 6:60–70

'"You do not want to leave too, do you?" Jesus asked
the Twelve.' (v67)

We look now at a fourth characteristic of an effective counsellor – the ability to summarise a confused situation in such a way that the person being counselled sees clearly the direction in which they ought to go. An example of how our Lord demonstrated this ability is seen in the passage before us now.

It was a critical moment in Jesus' public ministry. The loud burst of applause which had been there right from the start was now over. The crowds were melting away, and so too were many of His disciples when they heard His hard sayings. Had He deliberately wrecked His chance of success? Surely He was making things unnecessarily difficult they must have thought; converts would soon find out for themselves the cost of discipleship. Why frighten them off early with a too-realistic recital of the facts?

Discerning the unspoken thoughts of His followers and perceiving the confusion they were in, Jesus brought the issue to a head by startling them with this clear and concise question: 'You do not want to leave too, do you?' Our Lord's remark probably caused the disciples' minds to range far and wide. Who would replace Jesus? Where could one find a satisfactory alternative? Reflectively and with painstaking care Peter considered the possibilities. Would Hillel do? Or Shammai? Or Gamaliel? No. The Saviour's dramatic question had put the whole issue into clear perspective. Peter's reply was magnificent: 'Lord, to whom shall we go? You have the words of eternal life' (v68). No more perplexity, no more confusion. The Master's piercing question had left them in no doubt about the direction in which they should go. They would follow Him.

Father, how reassuring it is to know that the ability which Your Son had to help the disciples resolve confusion has been granted to the Holy Spirit. Help me draw on that gift rather than resorting to my own resources. In Jesus' name. Amen.

FURTHER STUDY
Luke 18:18–25; 20:20–26; John 8:3–11
1. How did Jesus clarify the ruler's heart issue?
2. How did Jesus avoid the Pharisees' traps?

Light for the Way Ahead

FOR READING & MEDITATION – PSALM 73:1–28

'You guide me with your counsel...' (v24)

One of the characteristics of a good counsellor is the ability to summarise a confused situation in such a way that the person being counselled sees clearly the direction in which to go. Yesterday we observed the way our Lord pierced the fog in the minds of the disciples by asking a powerful and perceptive question. Time and time again when the disciples seemed unsure about what they should do or which way they should go, Jesus would step in and say something that illuminated the path ahead.

This is the work of the Holy Spirit also. Our text today tells us that God guides us with His counsel, but it is the specific ministry of the Spirit to apply that guidance to our hearts. 'He,' said Jesus, speaking of the Holy Spirit, 'will *guide* you into all truth' (John 16:13, my emphasis). It is the Spirit who helps to clarify the issues that puzzle us and assists us in seeing clearly the next step we must take. All of us, I am sure, can remember moments when we dropped to our knees in confusion and cried, 'Lord, what shall I do now?' And all of us too, I imagine, can remember moments when, through the Holy Spirit's ministry of guidance, that prayer was answered.

Without railroading through our personalities and therefore making us overly dependent, the divine Counsellor remains at hand to bring clarity and illumination to our minds whenever we need it. That guidance, of course, comes in different ways – through Scripture, through circumstances, through sanctified reasoning or through the Spirit speaking directly to our hearts. But whichever way it comes, the end is always the same – light for the way ahead.

O God, You know how many times my emotions get tangled up and I can't think straight. At such times I am so glad that Your Holy Spirit, the divine Counsellor, is at hand to help me. All honour and glory be to Your precious name. Amen.

FURTHER STUDY

Acts 10:1–29

1. How did the Spirit guide Peter?
2. Why did the Spirit need to guide Peter?

A Sense of Being Led

FOR READING & MEDITATION – ROMANS 8:12–17

'Those who are led by the Spirit of God are sons of God.' (v14)

Today we consider again the subject of guidance. Why is it so necessary for Christians to receive divine guidance as they make their way through this world? Well, mostly because we are carrying out purposes that are not our own. Thus every one of us, if we are to be at our best, must have a sense of instrumentation, of being guided by our God, of fulfilling a will that is ultimate. Francis Schaeffer in a recorded talk I once heard put it like this: 'Christians simply must have a sense of being led.' Without that sense of being led, life hangs at loose ends, lacks a goal and lacks also the dynamic necessary to attain a goal.

'Anybody got a car that is going anywhere?' asked someone at the end of a weekend Christian conference. Everyone laughed, for the question didn't make sense. It sounded as if that person wanted to go somewhere but the destination didn't really matter. Much of our life may be like that – lacking direction and goals. If we lose the sense of being led by the Spirit we become victims of our circumstances. Then we are circumstance-directed instead of Spirit-directed. Guidance by the Holy Spirit is the very essence of Christianity. If there is no sense of leadership we will have no sense of sonship.

In some Christian circles to talk of being guided by the Holy Spirit brings an adverse reaction, as if it were a strange and superstitious thing to be led of God, directly and first-hand. This reaction is most revealing. It shows how content we are to have a knowledge of God but not a relationship with God. If we are not being led by God, how can we claim to be His sons and daughters? Schaeffer was right; we simply must have a sense of being led.

O God, forgive us for forgetting so often that as Your children we are carrying out purposes that are not our own. Help us walk through life with a sense of being divinely led. Not merely sometimes, but at all times. In Christ's name. Amen.

FURTHER STUDY

Joel 2:28–30; Acts 13:1–5

1. How may the Spirit guide us?
2. When did the Spirit speak in Antioch?

Sub-Christian Living

JUN

FOR READING & MEDITATION – PSALM 48:1–14

'For this God... will be our guide even to the end.' (v14)

We focus again on the point we were considering – that the Holy Spirit is our Guide. 'If we are not conscious of being guided in our lives day by day,' said Dr C. Jones, a Welsh theologian who lived in the late nineteenth century, 'then we are living at a level that is sub-Christian.' These are strong words. But are they true? I think they are. God wants to guide us not only in times of emergency but at all times. Our text for today makes that point crystal clear: 'For this God... will be our guide even to the end.' One of the blessings of having the Holy Spirit within, as we saw the other day, is that we gain the sense of being led. And not just the *sense* of being led but the practical benefits that come from it.

How aware are we of this? Something that will surprise us when we get to heaven, I think, is discovering how many times while we were on earth we tried to muddle through on our own instead of entering into and enjoying the direction of the Holy Spirit. I was struck by this statement made to a group of ministers in the United States by an evangelist with a reputation for 'telling it as it is': 'Some of the most active Church leaders,' he said, 'well known for their executive efficiency, people we tend to admire, will have a shock in heaven when in the X-ray light of eternity they will be seen as agitated, half-committed, wistful, self-placating see kers to whom the power and serenity of the Everlasting had never come.'

God being who He is – the Architect of fine detail – has a plan, a purpose for every life. If we turn our backs on that idea then, as Dr C. Jones put it, we are at a level that is sub-Christian.

Gracious Father, You have fashioned the lowest cell with Your hands. Have You no plan for my life? I believe You have. Help me to find that plan, pay the price of working out that plan, and make it the adventure of my life. Amen.

FURTHER STUDY
Acts 9:5–22; Jas 4:13–16
1. How did God guide Saul and Ananias?
2. Why did James criticise some people?

Continuous Guidance

FOR READING & MEDITATION – 2 CORINTHIANS 5:11–21

'We are therefore Christ's ambassadors...' (v20)

God being who He is, we said yesterday, has a plan and purpose for every life. After He made each one of us He apparently broke the mould because we are all different. Each life has significance. If we find the plan of God for us and work within it, we cannot fail. Outside of it we will not find true peace or rest. To be the instrument of the purposes of God is the highest thing in life.

On one occasion I heard a preacher say that whenever he stands up to preach he reminds himself of a verse God gave him at the beginning of his ministry: 'You did not choose me, but I chose you and appointed you to go and bear fruit...' (John 15:16). God gave me that verse also and, like the preacher I heard, I rarely stand up to preach without repeating it to myself. Repeating it gives me the sense of being sent, of having the backing of the Eternal One, and of speaking in a name not my own. But it does something else as well – it lays on me a sense of obligation to surrender and be obedient to the working out of God's plan. It gives life a sense of mission and submission.

'Ah, that may be fine if you are a preacher,' I hear you say, 'but what about me? I have not been called to preach.' Maybe not, but as our text for today makes clear, you have been called to be an ambassador – for Christ. An ambassador must weigh his words carefully, for they represent the views of his country – he is speaking on behalf of his government. Everyone is, in one sense, a representative. We are speaking, thinking, acting in a name that is not our own. That is why guidance is not a matter of the occasional but the continuous.

O God, I begin to see that if I am to live, I must live in You. You are the way to life and my way of life. When I find Your plan I find my person. Give me an understanding of what it means to be guided continuously. In Jesus' name. Amen.

FURTHER STUDY

Acts 4:5–14; 9:36–42

1. Why were the religious leaders astonished?
2. How did Dorcas represent Christ without preaching?

Guidance Demands Surrender

FOR READING & MEDITATION – PSALM 25:1–22

'He guides the humble in what is right and
teaches them his way.' (v9)

Although we are focusing on the Holy Spirit's ministry of providing us with guidance in times of confusion and uncertainty, we must say a few more words about the necessity of being guided not occasionally but continuously.

All of us, if we are Christians, can walk through the world with a sense of mission. 'The significance of life', I have read, 'is determined by the significance of what it is identified with and what it represents.' A sense of mission brings a sense of submission. Instead of making you proud and cocky it has the opposite effect. You feel awed and humbled. You want to walk softly before God. You are on what has been called 'the adventure of humility'.

The whole thought of guidance, whether it is occasional or continuous, strikes at the citadel of the personality and demands the surrender of self-sufficiency. Mark that, for it is extremely important – guidance demands surrender. That is why some find the subject of guidance intimidating; they don't like the idea of giving up their independence. If we are to be guided then there must be a shifting from self-will to God's will. That will, not your own, becomes supreme. God's will and guidance become your constant frame of reference.

Guidance is not a spiritual luxury to be enjoyed by only a few souls; it is the minimum necessity for every Christian. Do you remember the text of a few days ago: 'Those who are led by the Spirit of God are sons of God' (Rom. 8:14)? Guidance, I say again, is the very essence of Christianity. It gives mission to life. But the mission demands submission.

Father, I have been made in the very structure of my being for Your ways. Your will is my peace. My will is my war. I am eager to know Your mind, not only in moments of confusion but always and in every area of my life. For Jesus' sake. Amen.

FURTHER STUDY
Jas 4:4–10; 1 Pet. 5:5–7
1. What happens when we submit to God?
2. What are the benefits of humility?

Healthy Dependency

FOR READING & MEDITATION – ISAIAH 8:11–22

'Should not a people enquire of their God?' (v19)

It's surprising how many Christians there are who, though they know God, know little about His guidance, either occasional or continuous. Hence their impact upon life is at times unnoticed. We have seen that God wants to guide us not just sometimes but at all times. But the divine Counsellor's concern for us is the same as Christ's concern for His disciples – to guide and not to override. He wants to guide us, yet at the same time create initiative in us.

In the little Welsh village where I was brought up, milk was supplied by two farmers who brought it daily to each home on a horse-drawn cart. Villagers would take out their jugs to the milkman and have them filled. I noticed that one farmer would lead his horse from one house to the next. The other had trained his horse to move at a command – stop or go. The first horse was helpless without the step-by-step guide. The other had more freedom.

The Spirit guides us in a way that does not override our personality or weaken it, but brings us to a point of healthy dependency. Some would say that dependency on another is unhealthy. 'You Christians are so weak and lacking in courage,' said a man to me once, 'that you have to look to God before you make any move in life.' He had no idea of what he was saying, for if he had known how deeply entrenched in all of us is a spirit of independence, he would have realised that one of the biggest struggles we have as Christians is to bring our independent and stubborn natures into submission to the divine will. Our need to be guided is often, I am afraid, greater than our willingness.

Gracious Father, I bring my independent spirit to You for You to harness it and bring it under Your control. I recognise there is still something in me that prefers my way to Yours. But I want Your way to be my way. Help me, dear Father. Amen.

FURTHER STUDY
Josh. 9:1–19; John 5:19–20
1. What was Joshua's mistake?
2. How independent was Jesus?

Five Forms of Guidance

FOR READING & MEDITATION – ACTS 8:26–40

'The Spirit told Philip, "Go to that chariot and stay near it."' (v29)

The task facing the Holy Spirit of giving us guidance is similar to that of every thinking and concerned parent. The Holy Spirit not only guides us, but also develops us as persons. To lead us and at the same time produce initiative in us is a task worthy of divine wisdom. 'Many parents are benevolent tyrants,' says a child psychologist whom I know, 'who snuff out all initiative and personality in their children. Guidance must be such that each person is guided into a free, self-conscious, choosing, creative personality.'

These are the general routes to guidance: First, guidance according to the character of Christ. We know who God wants us to be like – He wants us to be like His Son. Anything Christ would not do we should not do. Second, guidance through His Word. The Spirit makes the Bible come alive to us, and throws a beam of light on the path ahead. Third, guidance through circumstances – putting us in situations where the circumstances indicate the direction in which we ought to go. Fourth, guidance through the counsel of good and godly people. Fifth, guidance through the direct whispering of the Spirit within us.

This last form of guidance is the one to which we are giving special attention at this time and in our meditation for tomorrow – the direct voice of the Spirit in our hearts. Some look on this method of guidance as strange and mysterious. It is capable of being abused, I admit, but it is a form of guidance that is clearly laid down in Scripture. Some call it 'the inner voice'. However, we must always be sure that the inner voice we follow is the Spirit's voice, not our own voice.

Father, I am thankful for all the ways You guide me, and also for all the times You have guided me. But teach me more about how to distinguish Your inner voice from the other voices that are heard in my soul. In Christ's name I ask it. Amen.

FURTHER STUDY

Heb. 3:7–19; 1 Pet. 1:10–12; 2 Pet. 1:19–21

1. What may prevent us experiencing God's blessings?
2. Why were the Scriptures written?

Listen!

FOR READING & MEDITATION – 1 SAMUEL 3:1–21

'Then Samuel said, "Speak, for your servant is listening."' (v10)

If, as we have been saying, our divine Counsellor is ready and willing to guide us, how do we recognise His voice when He speaks to us? That is the issue with which we must come to grips today.

'My sheep know My voice,' Jesus told His disciples categorically (John 10:3–5). When I go to the telephone and hear my mother's voice, I know immediately who is speaking. I know it is not my sister or my secretary, for I have heard that voice thousands of times during the course of my life. 'Ah,' you say, 'but a voice in your ear is a lot easier to discern than a voice in your soul.' Granted, but there is a way to tune in to the voice of the Spirit and learn to hear His accent in Your soul. Here's how it is done.

Train your spiritual ear to *listen*. When the king complained to Joan of Arc that he never heard the voice of God, she replied, 'You must listen, then you will hear.' There are two main reasons why people fail to hear the Spirit's voice: their spiritual ears are untrained or they are unwilling. Many of us don't want to listen to the voice of God because we are afraid that if God reveals His will to us, it will be disagreeable. 'Your will be done' becomes 'Your will be borne'.

When you commune with God, give as much time to listening as you do to talking. At first you will not be able to distinguish the voice of the subconscious from the voice of the Spirit, but in time the differentiation will be possible. Sometimes, of course, the Spirit booms so loudly in the soul that His voice is unmistakable. But that is more the exception than the rule. Usually He speaks quietly, and to a soul that sits quietly before Him.

O God, forgive me if I attempt to take short cuts in my spiritual life by desiring the benefits without being willing to go through the training. Help me to talk less and listen more in my daily communion with You. In Jesus' name. Amen.

FURTHER STUDY
Ps. 46:1–11; John 18:37
1. How do we come to know God?
2. Who will listen to Jesus?

The Great Teacher

FOR READING & MEDITATION – JOHN 3:1–15

"'You are Israel's teacher," said Jesus, "and do
you not understand these things?"' (v10)

Yet another quality a counsellor should possess is a basic ability to explain and teach. Those who are practitioners of what is called 'non-directive counselling' will, I know, be horrified by that statement as they see counselling not so much as giving people direction, but helping them clarify their own thinking concerning their problems and then come to their own conclusions. There is a lot to be said for this approach as it is one way of showing respect for a person's individuality and encourages them to develop their own decision-making processes.

However, while it is true that Christian counselling is at times non-directive, it is at other times directive. Individuals who are struggling with a problem need clear direction on how to take advantage of Christ's resources, and to provide that one needs, as I have said, a basic ability to teach. Note the word 'basic'. A counsellor does not need to be an expert teacher, but he or she does need to be able to show a person how to take the steps that lead from where they are to where they should be.

Our Lord, of course, provides the supreme example of what and how to teach. He is seen in the Gospels teaching huge crowds, and at other times small groups. In today's passage we see Him teaching an individual – Nicodemus – the principles of what we call 'the new birth'. Around nineteen such private conferences are recorded in the Gospels, when Jesus is seen closeted with a seeking soul and teaching him or her the steps to effective, abundant living. Our Lord taught as no others have taught – before or since.

Loving heavenly Father, how can I thank You for the arrival on earth of Your Son, Jesus? What He has taught the world is wonderful, but what He did for us on the cross is even more wonderful. My gratitude will last as long as eternity. Amen.

FURTHER STUDY
Luke 11:1–10; 1 Tim. 3:1–2; 4:11–13
1. What did the disciples desire?
2. What is required of church leaders?

FOR READING & MEDITATION – MATTHEW 7:15–29

'He taught as one who had authority, and not as their
teachers of the law.' (v29)

Before examining some of the ways in which the divine Counsellor applies to our hearts the teaching of Jesus, we must spend a few more moments looking at why our Lord's great teaching ministry was so powerful while He was here on earth.

We see from the passage before us today that the crowds were simply spellbound by the things He said. A verse similar to our text is found in Mark: 'The people were all so amazed that they asked each other, "What is this? A new teaching - and with authority!"' (Mark 1:27). Obviously it was the 'authority' with which Jesus spoke that arrested people's attention. Other teachers *quoted* authorities, but Jesus spoke *with* authority. What was that authority? An authority imposed from without? No, it was the authority of the facts. He was lifting up the meaning of life, the meaning of the laws and principles underlying life. He was uncovering Reality – Reality with a capital 'R'.

A good many people make the tragic mistake of regarding Jesus as a moralist imposing a moral code upon humanity which humanity was not made for. But Jesus was not a moralist in that sense at all. He was the Revealer of the nature of Reality. He revealed first the nature and character of God, and went on to show how the nature and character of God is the ground of God's conduct and ours. He then lifted up the laws of effective living which are written into the universe and into every nerve and tissue of our being, and showed us that there is just no other way to live. It was not imposed idealism but exposed realism. Reality itself was speaking. No wonder it was 'authoritative'. Here was the indicative become the imperative.

Lord Jesus, when I look upon You, I am looking at Life. In You is every pure dream fulfilled, every pure longing becoming fact. Your words take me to the heart of reality – the nature and character of a loving God. I am so thankful. Amen.

FURTHER STUDY
Matt. 13:31–52; 22:15–16
1. What style of teaching did Jesus often use?
2. Why was Jesus such an effective teacher?

The Spirit – Our Teacher

FOR READING & MEDITATION – 1 JOHN 2:18–27

'His anointing teaches you about all things...' (v27)

Our Lord's expert teaching ministry was not lost to the Church when, after His death and resurrection, He returned to heaven. The promised Holy Spirit, the divine Counsellor, continues that ministry, and is here to teach us all things and bring to our remembrance everything that Christ taught His disciples when He was with them here upon earth.

What did Jesus mean when He said 'all' things (John 14:26)? Before answering that, permit me to draw your attention to the views of one agnostic. 'The great difference between Christianity and science,' he claimed, 'is that Christianity is fixed but science isn't. Science is open and progressive,' he went on to say, 'because it is not fixed in terms of absolutes and non-optional dogmas.'

While this is entirely true, it is not true entirely. In the Person and teaching of Christ we have God's full and complete disclosure. But, of course, we could not see or comprehend all that is involved in His teaching in one classroom encounter, any more than we could fully understand mathematics by having a three-hour lesson. The revelation which God has given us through Christ is final in the sense that nothing will be taught that is different from it, but we must see that it is also progressive and unfolding. In what respect? In the way that the Holy Spirit brings out from the words and teaching of Christ new understanding, new challenges and new insights. These are all found in our Lord's words, in embryonic form at least, but the Spirit takes them, applies them to our hearts and leads us to deeper comprehension. The divine Counsellor will teach us *all* Jesus taught but not *other* than Jesus taught.

Father God, here is both conservatism and radicalism, going hand in hand. The Spirit conserves all that Jesus taught, but at the same time opens up from it radical new dimensions. Truth is fixed yet unfolding. I am so grateful. Amen.

FURTHER STUDY
John 14:25–26; Eph. 3:1–11
1. What two functions would the Spirit fulfil?
2. What is one example of the Spirit's teaching?

Lopsided Christianity

FOR READING & MEDITATION – JOHN 16:5–16

'But when he, the Spirit of truth, comes, he will guide you into all truth.' (v13)

We linger on the words of our Lord in John 14:26: 'The Counsellor the Holy Spirit... will teach you *all* things...' (my emphasis). A similar affirmation is given in the verse before us now. We concluded yesterday that the Holy Spirit, acting as our divine Counsellor, is at work in our hearts, unpackaging and unfolding all the words recorded for us in the Gospels, and thus leading us into all truth.

There is another aspect of the word 'all' which I would like to consider with you now. It is this: When we are not under the Holy Spirit's guidance, we can soon become focused on *some*thing that Jesus taught and neglect the 'all'. This is a trap any one of us can fall into – and many have. They concentrate on one aspect of Jesus' words and make that the whole issue. Francis Schaeffer pointed out many years ago that the Church in every age has made the mistake of taking some of Jesus' words, putting a fence around them and claiming a particular emphasis as their own. The consequence of this is a lopsided Christianity with an overemphasis on some things and an under-emphasis on others.

My next statement might be slightly exaggerated but I make it simply for the purpose of illustration: Whole denominations are built around one truth. This is not to say they don't believe other aspects of Christian teaching, but the truth they are always emphasising appears to make other truths less important by comparison. They live on *a* truth instead of on *the* Truth. Thus they have to be controversial to justify their lopsidedness. Christians who are truly open to the movement of the Holy Spirit in their lives will be creative rather than controversial.

O God my Father, move me from living on just one truth or even a cluster of truths. I want to live on all the truth, for I know I will become what I feed upon. Help me, my Father. In Jesus' name I pray. Amen.

FURTHER STUDY
Acts 18:24–19:6; 20:26–27
1. Why were the Ephesian disciples lopsided?
2. What could Paul declare?

Go the Second Mile

FOR READING & MEDITATION – JOHN 15:18–27

'When the Counsellor comes... he will testify about me.' (v26)

The Holy Spirit is not only our divine Teacher but also our divine Remembrancer. He promises to bring back to our remembrance all that Jesus said. What does this mean?

It does not mean that the Holy Spirit will magically bring into our minds the words of Jesus if we have not taken the time to read them in the Bible and ponder them. Some time ago I met a man in Scotland who told me that although he regularly read the Old Testament and the Epistles, he never read the Gospels because he believed the Holy Spirit's ministry was to bring home to him the things Jesus said. I pointed out that Jesus promised: '[He] will *remind* you of everything I have said...' (John 14:26, my emphasis). *Remind*, I suggested, implies that Jesus' words are already in our memory, and the Holy Spirit's work is to prompt us in ways that make sure we do not forget them. The man was unconvinced. He suggested (not in the politest terms, I am sorry to say) that I had lost my faith in the supernatural.

The fact that the divine Counsellor is ready to remind us of the words of Jesus is one of the greatest arguments for soaking our minds in Scripture, particularly the Gospels, where Jesus' words are recorded. The more we expose ourselves to His words, the more easily the Spirit can remind us of them. Just before writing these lines a colleague and I were struggling to come to a decision about an important issue. We didn't know what to decide, then the Spirit reminded us of Jesus' instruction: 'Go the second mile.' We laughed together for we knew that naturally it was not what we wanted to do. The divine Counsellor, however, thought differently.

O God, I am thankful for everything contained in Your Word, but especially the words of Jesus. They are my life, my energy, my spiritual substance. May I take every opportunity to expose my mind to them. For Jesus' sake. Amen.

FURTHER STUDY

John 6:61–69; 2 Tim. 3:14–17

1. What is special about the words of Jesus?
2. What is the purpose of the Scriptures?

Truth Hurts

FOR READING & MEDITATION – JOHN 16:5–16

'But when he, the Spirit of truth, comes, he will guide you
into all truth.' (v13)

Our text for today, which we also looked at two days ago, tells us that the Holy Spirit will guide us into all truth. What does this really mean – *guide* us into truth? Sometimes a teacher is able to teach a certain truth but is unable to guide someone into it. When this happens in a church setting (a Bible study for example) it is a matter of concern, but when it happens in a counselling session it is even more worrying. A counsellor should be able not only to teach the truth but guide a person into it also.

To be fair, counsellors have a better opportunity to guide individuals into truth than preachers or teachers who present truth from the pulpit, because they can ask questions such as these: Do you understand what I have been saying? How do you respond to what I have just said? Counsellors are taught never to present an insight to someone without checking that the person understands what is being said and making sure they are following them every step of the way. Counsellors know too that if they present to someone a truth that is challenging or demanding, the personality more often than not becomes adept at looking for ways of escape. It puts up defences or seeks to minimise the impact of a challenging truth through such means as denial and rationalisation. Thus skill is needed not only to present the truth but to outmanoeuvre the objections, overcome the difficulties, gently rebut the arguments, and thus guide people into possession of the truth.

The Holy Spirit is expert not only in teaching truth, but also in guiding us into it. You and I wouldn't be where we are now in our spiritual lives unless He had been at work in this way.

My Father and my God, I recognise the truth of this and am deeply humbled by it. I can only wonder and cry, 'Thank You, my Father.' In Jesus' name. Amen.

FURTHER STUDY
Acts 15:1–20,27–31
1. Why was there a dispute in the Church?
2. How did the Holy Spirit guide them into the truth?

The Spirit of Truth

FOR READING & MEDITATION – 1 CORINTHIANS 2:10–16;
GALATIANS 1:11–12

'We speak, not in words taught us by human wisdom
but in words taught by the Spirit...' (1 Cor. 2:13)

We spend one last day pondering and, I trust, giving thanks to God for the wondrous ministry of the divine Counsellor who not only teaches and unfolds the truths Jesus taught, but so expertly guides us into the possession of them.

I wonder sometimes whether we have a rather too limited view of the statement made by Jesus that the Counsellor will guide us into all truth. Clearly, He was thinking of the truth of His words and the insights He had shared with His disciples, but could the promise mean more than that? Could it be that the Holy Spirit wants to lead us also into the truth about *everything*? Think about times in your past when the Holy Spirit has guided you or disclosed something to you that put the truth about a matter into clear perspective. Can't that be understood as the Spirit guiding you into all truth? Have there been occasions in your life when you needed to understand the truth about a matter that was causing you confusion and then, to your surprise, in a relatively short time everything seemed to open up and the fog of confusion was blown away? Who brought that about? Could it have been the Holy Spirit?

I know that kind of situation has occurred a thousand times and more in my own life, but I have never until now thought of it in terms of the Spirit of truth making matters clear. Can the promise of being guided into truth be seen also in the way the Spirit opens up a difficult scripture, or the truth regarding both options in a difficult decision? Why can't these be part of the truth which Jesus promised would be disclosed to you and me? I see no reason why not. Our Lord was an expert Teacher. And the Holy Spirit also.

Father, when I think of the insights I might have missed in the Bible – hidden things You have brought to light – I realise more than ever that You are truly the Spirit of truth. I both revel and rejoice in it. In Jesus' name. Amen.

FURTHER STUDY

Acts 20:17–25; Col. 1:24–29
1. What truths did the Spirit reveal to Paul?
2. To whom are mysteries revealed?

Being There

FOR READING & MEDITATION – MATTHEW 16:21–28; 17:1–11

'After six days Jesus took with him Peter, James
and John the brother of James...' (17:1)

The last (but not least) qualification of a counsellor that we shall consider is this – the ability to come alongside someone who is hurt and to support them in their pain. This is often referred to as 'being there for someone'. One illustration of our Lord 'being there' for His disciples is seen in the passage before us today. It is suggested by the simple but intriguing phrase 'after six days' (17:1).

There is, of course, a distinct connection between this verse and the events immediately preceding it. Dr G. Campbell Morgan deduced that when the disciples discovered their Master was going to a cross, they drew back in dismay. Follow the clue in the words 'after six days' carefully, he advised, and it will be seen that during this period there was a sense of estrangement between the disciples and the Master. Peter, at one point, had gone so far as attempting to dissuade Christ from even thinking about going to a cross. Christ's foretelling of His death seemed to make the idea he held of Messiahship impossible. The disciples wanted to reign with Jesus; He knew He was heading to the cross.

The six days of confusion would be ended by the act of Transfiguration, but before that, what must it have been like for our Lord and His disciples as they walked together through the northern part of Israel? He, no doubt, was pained by their failure to understand, and they were pained by the revelation that their concept of Messiahship did not appear to match His. But did He leave these misunderstanding disciples and go it alone? No, He stayed with them. He was there for them even when they were not there for Him.

My Father and my God, the more I see of Your Son the more my heart adores Him. And I know that in adoring Him I am adoring You. For You are One. Indeed You are Three in One, and One in Three. I cannot understand it but I stand upon it. Amen.

FURTHER STUDY
Isa. 43:1–7; Heb. 13:5–6
1. What has God promised?
2. What can we say with confidence?

Nonverbal but Empowering

FOR READING & MEDITATION – JOB 16:1–22

'I have heard many things like these; miserable comforters
are you all!' (v2)

We saw yesterday how our Lord was there for His disciples when, because of their bewilderment, not one of them was fully following Him. *Being there* is not giving advice; it is saying in nonverbal ways: 'This is not the time for talking but, as far as I am able, I want to bear the pain with you.'

I remember being faced with a distressing problem early in my Christian life. Everyone I consulted suggested there must be some sin in my life, otherwise I would be free from problems. I felt towards them as Job must have felt towards his 'comforters' when he spoke today's text. Finally, a man who had a problem with stuttering and was unable to complete a single sentence started to put his arm around me, and then drawing back placed his hands together in an expression of prayer as if to say, 'I can't help you on the verbal level, but I will be there for you in prayer.' That meant more to me than any words. It was nonverbal, but empowering all the same.

A little while ago I talked to a man in South Africa who told me that his wife had made his life almost impossible for a number of years. She humiliated him in front of friends, telephoned his boss and told lies about him, ran up debts that he was expected to pay, and ill-treated him in a whole host of other ways. 'How are you handling all this?' I enquired of him. His reply moved me deeply: 'My only wish is that I might be able through a Christlike attitude to give her a taste of how much God loves her, and, above all else, my longing is to be there for her until she leaves this world for eternity.' I thought as I listened, 'Why, you could almost put those same words on the lips of the Holy Spirit.'

O God, thank You for those in my life who have been there for me during a time of pain or sorrow. May I in turn be there for someone who needs me now or at any time in the future. I ask this through Your Son's worthy and wonderful name. Amen.

FURTHER STUDY

Job 4:1–4; 1 Cor. 16:17–20
1. What kind of comforter was Job himself?
2. Why was Paul glad?

Counsellor and Comforter

FOR READING & MEDITATION – ISAIAH 66:5–13

'As a mother comforts her child, so will I comfort you...' (v13)

Let's face it, some of the problems we encounter are not going to go away however hard we pray. So what sort of help can we expect to receive from our divine Counsellor? Great help, for we can be sure that He will be there for us – empowering us with His comforting presence, sharing our pain and entering into all our sorrows.

The translators of the New International Version, the version I use for these daily notes, (though in my personal study I much prefer the New King James Version) were all scholars. When deciding upon a name in English for the Holy Spirit they therefore leaned towards a word that suggests the giving of advice or verbal direction. This is not said in any derogatory way or to suggest that the translators were not people of feeling. But I have often noticed when going through the NIV that the translators chose words with an intellectual ring – words which seem to be lacking in feeling. For instance, 2 Corinthians 5:14 is translated, 'Christ's love compels us' in the NIV, whereas the NKJV translates it, 'the love of Christ *constrains* us' (my emphasis). Do you see what I mean? The word 'constrains' has a feel (in my opinion) which the word 'compel' does not have.

The Greek term for the Holy Spirit is *parakletos*, derived from *para* (beside) and *kaleo* (call), and means 'one who comes alongside to help'. I wish the word could be translated 'Counsellor and Comforter' – a phrase which would convey the fuller idea that the Holy Spirit is not just someone who gives us advice but someone who feels *for* us and *with* us also. Oh, He *feels*, does this blessed Counsellor and Comforter. And more than we will ever know.

O Father, how is it possible that the Holy Spirit feels for me and with me in my problems and at the same time with all my brothers and sisters also? What resources He must have! And those resources are available to me. Thank You. Amen.

FURTHER STUDY

Jer. 8:21–9:1; 1 Thess. 2:7–12

1. What happened when God's people felt crushed?
2. How did Paul relate to the Thessalonians?

The Ultimate Counsellor

FOR READING & MEDITATION – 2 CORINTHIANS 7:1–16

'But God, who comforts the downcast, comforted
us by the coming of Titus...' (v6)

We continue reflecting on the thought that the Holy Spirit is a Counsellor who does more than give us advice; He enters into our hurts, empathises with our pain and is there for us in every difficult situation of life. Listen to how the Amplified Version translates our focus verse for these meditations, John 14:26: 'But the Comforter (Counselor, Helper, Intercessor, Advocate, Strengthener, Standby), the Holy Spirit, Whom the Father will send in My name... He will teach you all things.'

The Holy Spirit is a Counsellor who has everything. The ability to give good advice? Yes. The ability to empower with divine strength? Yes. The ability to be our Advocate? Yes. The ability to pray through us when we don't know what to ask in prayer for ourselves? Yes. The ability to stand by us when we are overcome with worry? To comfort us? Yes! Yes! Yes! There isn't a single thing we need in life that He isn't able to provide.

The word Comforter – from the Latin *con* (with) and *fortis* (strength) – means one who strengthens you by being with you. It's astonishing what strength we draw from someone just being with us when we are going through a painful experience. Prior to her death, my wife spent many hours sleeping. At first I would steal away to my study and work after she had gone to sleep, but she told me on one occasion that even in her sleep she could sense whether or not I was there. 'Just being there,' she said, 'just sensing you are at my side is more of a comfort to me than I can ever explain.' I have had the same thought at times in relation to the Holy Spirit, haven't you? Simply sensing He is at our side is a comfort that we can never explain.

Gracious Father, as I learn more of Your Spirit my heart becomes increasingly grateful. Your Spirit is a Counsellor who has everything. He specialises not in one thing but in all things. Help me absorb all this. In Jesus' name. Amen.

FURTHER STUDY
Heb. 2:10–18; 4:14–5:10
1. Why is Christ an effective comforter?
2. What can we receive from God?

The Spirit's First Work

FOR READING & MEDITATION – ACTS 2:29–41

'Repent and be baptised... And you will receive the gift of
the Holy Spirit.' (v38)

There are those who claim that the first task of the Holy Spirit is not really a work at all. Primarily, they say, He is there to be with us. What He does in us and through us is important, but His primary service is *to be there for us*.

If this is so (and it is difficult to argue against it), then we must see that our preoccupation with gifts rather than the Giver is entirely out of place. Many Christians seem to be more taken up with possessing the gifts of the Spirit than possessing the Holy Spirit Himself. *He* is the gift, and although we are instructed by Paul in 1 Corinthians 14:1 to 'eagerly desire spiritual gifts', this does not mean that we are to think more highly of the gifts than the Giver. In the text before us today Peter talks about the Holy Spirit being *the* gift. He is the Gift of gifts, and when He is with us and in us, He supplies us with the gifts that enhance our spiritual effectiveness.

Early in my Christian experience I made the mistake many make today. I was brought up in a church where a great emphasis was placed on the gifts of the Spirit but little on the Giver. As a result, I eagerly went over all the gifts mentioned in the New Testament – the gifts in Romans 12, those listed in 1 Corinthians 12, and those mentioned in Ephesians 4. I then laid out my shopping list before the Lord and said to Him, 'Father, these are the gifts I want from You.' But the Spirit whispered to my heart, 'Are the gifts more important than the Giver?' This gentle rebuke helped me to see that I was more interested in the gifts of the Spirit than the Spirit who gave the gifts. This is a danger we must all avoid.

O Father, forgive me if I have been making more of the gifts than the Giver. I don't want to do anything that will hurt, grieve or quench the Holy Spirit in my life. Steer me away from all dangers, dear Lord. In Jesus' name. Amen.

FURTHER STUDY
Ps. 105:1–4; Acts 8:4–24
1. What should we do before we seek God's power?
2. What astonished Simon, but what did he actually want?

Trust My Love

FOR READING & MEDITATION – JOB 42:1–17

'My ears had heard of you but now my eyes have seen you.' (v5)

As we said a few days ago, there are occasions in life when problems don't go away despite our most ardent praying. At such times the divine Counsellor ministers to us His comfort and supernatural strength.

Just before starting this page I recalled a vivid memory of when I was a little boy being taken to hospital to have my tonsils removed. When I entered the place, smelt the distinctive smell that hospitals had in those days and saw the white-coated doctors and nurses, I became very frightened. Looking up into my mother's face I said, 'Do I have to go through with this? Will it hurt? What is it all for? Will I die under the anaesthetic?' Well, what can you say to a small boy about to have such an operation? My mother could have given me all the medical reasons why the operation should be performed, but I would not have understood. So she simply said, 'I can't save you from it, my dear. For your own good this has to be done, but some day you will understand. You must trust my love. I shan't leave you and I will be here waiting for you when you come out of the anaesthetic.'

That boyhood experience has been a parable to me. There have been many times in my life (and I am sure in yours also) when the Holy Spirit has whispered in my soul, 'I cannot shield you from this. You will have to go through it, and you may feel some pain. But I will be with you all the way.' Job, as we see from today's passage, never got the answers he wanted to his questions, but he received something better: he came through his experiences with a richer sense of God's presence than he had ever felt before.

O God my Father, Your presence made real in my soul through the Holy Spirit is worth more to me than anything. I would far rather have a problem-filled life with You than a problem-free life without You. Thank You, Father. In Jesus' name. Amen.

FURTHER STUDY
Luke 8:22–25; Acts 27:13–26
1. Contrast how the disciples and Paul were saved.
2. Why was Paul unafraid?

Supernatural Comfort

FOR READING & MEDITATION – ACTS 9:19B–31

'The church... was strengthened; and encouraged
by the Holy Spirit, it grew in numbers...' (v31)

The comforting ministry of the Holy Spirit is not simply a theory; it is a glorious fact. Who, reading these lines, has not felt the divine Counsellor's consoling presence steal into their souls during a time of personal difficulty or distress?

Early in my ministry I thought it was my task alone to bring comfort to people who were disheartened. However, I remember on one occasion receiving a gentle rebuke from the Lord that put the matter into its true perspective. As a young minister, every week seemed to bring its batch of special difficulties and duties. I confess there were times when my spirit rebelled. Constant contact with people who were plunged into sudden tragedy and horrendous pain drained me of nervous energy. This drove me, of course, to prayer, but sometimes my prayers became complaints. I said to the Lord, rather petulantly I am afraid, 'I can't keep going into the homes of tormented people who are repeatedly submerged in sorrow, give them sympathy and talk about a God of love.'

It was then that God taught me a vital lesson. He spoke to me and reminded me that above and beyond any comfort I could give was that of the Holy Spirit. His work was to bestow not human comfort but *supernatural* comfort. I must do my part and trust the divine Counsellor to do His. When I realised that Another was ministering along with me to the sick, the suffering, and the bereaved, I began to relax and turn over the major part of the task to Him. I was working with His help. All who belong to Christ's Body are expected to minister comfort to each other, but the biggest share belongs to the Holy Spirit. We comfort; He is the Comforter.

O Father, how reassuring it is to know that Your Spirit is moving through Your Body even now, using some to bring comfort to others, but also adding His own supernatural brand. Thank You, my Father. Amen.

FURTHER STUDY
2 Cor. 1:3–11; Col. 1:28–29
1. How does Paul describe the process of comfort?
2. Of what was Paul aware?

Grace - Simply Amazing

FOR READING & MEDITATION – 2 CORINTHIANS 12:1–10

'Three times I pleaded with the Lord to take it away from me.' (v8)

How reassuring it is to know that when we need comfort and consolation the Holy Spirit is more than equal to the task. Others can *bring* us comfort but He *is* comfort. The passage before us now gives us a classic example of how the Spirit ministers grace and comfort in the midst of difficulty.

The apostle Paul doesn't tell us what his problem was but uses a metaphor – a thorn in the flesh – which is used elsewhere in Scripture to convey a troublesome issue. Many have speculated about that 'thorn', but no one knows for sure what it was. Perhaps opthalmia or epilepsy or neurasthenia? A harassing evil spirit that stirred up strife everywhere he went? We don't really know. One preacher joked that Paul had a thorn in the flesh and no one knows what it was; if we have a thorn in the flesh everyone knows what it is! How true that often is! Paul asked the Lord three times to take it away but the answer each time was 'No'. The problem was to remain. But in the midst of his trouble God began to pour into Paul a special supply of His comforting grace; grace to accept the 'No', grace to endure the discomfort, and grace to handle the pain.

But how does grace work? Like this: you find yourself undergoing a period of testing and your heart becomes heavy. You lose your appetite, struggle with insomnia, and become increasingly irritated. Then you go to prayer. As you pray the heaviness in your spirit continues, but then suddenly, it is as if a weight is lifted from you. You breathe more easily and your spirit feels a little lighter. What has happened? Some might call it 'a spontaneous sense of relief'. Those who know call it grace.

O Father, this is something I always wanted to see but hardly dared believe – You never allow a problem to remain in my life without supplying me with the comfort and grace that sees me through. All glory be to Your matchless name. Amen.

FURTHER STUDY
Eph. 1:3–10; 2:1–9; Phil. 4:4–7
1. What is so amazing about grace?
2. How can we overcome anxiety?

Brave if not Blithe

FOR READING & MEDITATION – ISAIAH 49:8–16

'Shout for joy, O heavens... For the Lord comforts his people
and will have compassion on his afflicted ones.' (v13)

In a fallen universe like this we are confronted with issues which produce almost inconsolable pain. Sir Arthur Conan Doyle tells in his autobiography, *Memories and Adventures*, what made him a materialist in early life. As a physician he constantly saw sights which he could not reconcile with the idea of a merciful providence. He tells of going into a humble home where there was a small cot, and by a gesture made by the mother he sensed that the problem lay there. He picked up a candle, walked to the cot and stooped over it, expecting to find a young child. What he saw, he says, was a pair of brown sullen eyes full of loathing and pain which looked up in resentment to his. He could not tell how old the creature was. Long thin limbs were twisted, the face malignant. 'What is it?' he asked in dismay. 'It's a girl,' sobbed the mother. 'She's nineteen. Oh, if only God would take her.'

What answer can we give to explain circumstances such as those? There is no adequate answer. It's easy to brush perplexing matters aside and say they are the result of living in a fallen world, but that still leaves huge issues unresolved. Why did God allow sin to strike the universe in such a way? Could He not have modified its consequences so it would not have affected us as it has? These are easy questions to ask, but even if God gave us clear answers I am not sure we would be able to understand them. We will understand everything one day, but meanwhile God simply says, 'Here's My comfort, that has a depth and sufficiency.' In moments of bewilderment it is not answers we need; it is comfort. That comfort may not keep us blithe but it will keep us brave.

O God my Father, I see that no matter what happens to me and no matter how many problems I am called upon to face, You provide all the comfort and strength I need to carry on. Others may fail me but You – never. Thank You, dear Lord. Amen.

FOR READING & MEDITATION – PSALM 86:1–17

'You, O Lord, have helped me and comforted me.' (v17)

Sooner or later every one of us needs comfort. It does not matter how strong we may be, how composed and free from sentimentality, the time will come when we need to feel God's solace. The Holy Spirit is the minister of grace. He is the One who brings into our hearts the resources of the Godhead. Let us never forget that.

Some, when needing comfort, turn to drink. But there is no real comfort to be found in the cup. Too much champagne at night produces real pain in the morning. Drink can no more cure our sorrows than an anaesthetic can cure a cancer. Robert Burns, Edgar Allan Poe and others have tried it and discovered that it only aggravates the trouble it was taken to heal. Others turn to literature. 'The anodyne you need,' they say, 'is reading. Relief can be found in a library. Turn for consolation to the infinite resources of literature.' I love literature and have made it a habit to read several books a week. But in the time of real sorrow there is no adequate comfort in books. Some comfort perhaps, but not enough to heal a heart that is torn. Is Dickens your favourite author? You will not find him very comforting when the doctor diagnoses a serious medical problem. Do you like Scott? The Waverley novels will not be very effective on the day you come home from the cemetery.

What about nature, or music, or art? They can be helpful supplements but they can never be substitutes. They are not a fount of comfort in themselves. They can offer a pleasurable or exciting diversion but this soon fades. I can tell you from a lifetime of facing trials, including bereavement, that the only sure comfort when all the world has gone grey is the comfort of God.

O Father, how reliable is Your comfort? There are few things in life I can depend on but I can depend on this. May the truth of it grip my soul and strengthen it every hour of today and every day. In Christ's name I ask it. Amen.

FURTHER STUDY
Prov. 31:6–7; Isa. 66:10–13; Jer. 6:13–15
1. How may we treat serious wounds lightly?
2. How may God act like a mother?

Is Optimism Enough?

FOR READING & MEDITATION – JEREMIAH 8:14–22

'Is there no balm in Gilead?' (v22)

There are in the Christian Church those who advocate optimism as the way to approach life's problems. You sometimes see posters outside churches designed to catch people's attention with a cheerful word. But those who choose the words for some of these posters, as well as those who display them, often seem to have no understanding of what is relevant to the needs of the general population. Once I was on my way to a home that had been stunned by an awful bereavement, wondering what I would say to the distressed family. As I passed a church I caught sight of a large poster that advised: 'Cheer up – it may never happen.' I remember shouting out in my car: *But it has happened.*

There is no lift in optimism in an hour like that. Like the nerveless needle of a broken barometer it continues to point, even in a thunderstorm, to 'Very Fair'. No, the only reality we can depend upon in this barren world is the consolation and comfort of the Holy Spirit.

One of the things that saddens me about the day in which we live is that few people read the biographies of the early missionaries any more. Many of them contain dramatic instances of the way in which the Holy Spirit comforts and consoles. Take Allan Francis Gardiner for example, the intrepid missionary to South America. He and his companions found themselves on Picton Island in the most difficult circumstances imaginable. It is hard to read the story without tears coming to one's eyes. Yet in his diary he wrote: 'Great and marvellous are the loving kindnesses of my gracious God to me.' Many things may be absent. But God's comfort – never. It can always be relied upon.

Father, thank You for the balm that is available to Your wounded children through the gentle and comforting ministry of the Holy Spirit. I have known this solace, as will millions more who need it this day. Blessed be Your name for ever. Amen.

FURTHER STUDY

Jer. 29:16–32; Rom. 15:1–5

1. Why did the prophets give people false hope?
2. What are two reliable sources of encouragement?

Understood One Day

FOR READING & MEDITATION – REVELATION 20:11–21:5

'He will wipe every tear from their eyes.' (21:4)

We have been emphasising that we are not always going to receive answers to the difficult questions that arise during our lifetime. Questions such as these: Why has God allowed this? What possible good can come from it? How can a loving God permit such a thing?

I can imagine that such questions might have been asked by the Curé D'Ars. His story illustrates my point. He was a godly French priest, who many years ago was sent to the little village of Ars. The village had sunk low in its morals, and had a bad reputation. Sunday services were ignored by most of the villagers, the dance halls were full, ignorance was widespread, foul language was common in the streets, and drunkenness, blasphemy and lying were all features of the villagers' lives. The faithful priest instantly declared war on this wickedness. When he did, the villagers struck back by besmirching his reputation. They spread slanderous stories about him, saying he attracted girls to his house for immoral purposes. He was the subject of obscene songs and scurrilous letters. A prostitute paraded under his window night after night, accusing him in the most filthy language of the being the father of her child. It was all lies, of course, but the faithful man of God bore it with courage, with dignity, and with grace. The humiliation lasted 10 years, but eventually he won. God used his unwavering faith in a wonderful way, and the time came when the dance schools closed down, foul language was heard no more in the streets, and the churches were crowded with worshippers.

The answers you don't get here, you will get in eternity. Maybe the pain you are facing now is accomplishing something special that you will one day understand, if not in this life, then in the one to come?

O Father, I've no guarantee that all my questions will be answered down here, but I am guaranteed strength, grace, and comfort to carry on. Thank You, dear Lord. In Jesus' name. Amen.

FURTHER STUDY
Ps. 73:1–22; 2 Cor. 4:7–18
1. Why was the psalmist confused, and when did he understand?
2. Why did Paul lose heart?

What Happens Now?

FOR READING & MEDITATION – JAMES 4:1–17

'Come near to God and he will come near to you.' (v8)

We end our meditations on this note: as we make our way towards heaven, life may be hard and perplexing, but God promised and has given us His Holy Spirit to be our Counsellor along the way. And what a Counsellor He is! Run your mind back with me over the characteristics of this matchless Counsellor which we have looked at during the past two months.

(1) He seeks to draw out of us all the potential that God has built into us, and is continually at work developing us into the kind of persons God sees us to be. (2) He prods us to prayer, and on those occasions when we don't know how to pray as we ought He takes over and prays in us and through us. (3) He brings hidden things to light in our souls and seeks to rid us of all sin. (4) He shines the laser beam of knowledge and wisdom through the fog that sometimes surrounds us, and guides us in ways of which we are both conscious and unconscious along the path He wants us to take. (5) He teaches us as no other could teach us, and leads us into what our hearts were built for – truth. (6) He comforts us whenever we are in need of solace, and strengthens our hearts to go on even though we have no clear answers to our predicament.

How sad that with all the resources of our divine Counsellor available to us we prefer so often to muddle through on our own. When we refuse to open up to Him, to depend on Him and consult Him, we deprive ourselves of the love, wisdom, and spiritual sustenance we need to live effectively and dynamically. He will open up to you, but only if you will open up to Him. I encourage you today, take one step towards Him and He will take two towards you.

O God, You have shown me the resources that are available to me through Your Holy Spirit. Now I must avail myself of them. I open my heart fully now. Seal my commitment with an overwhelming sense of Your presence. In Christ's name. Amen.

FURTHER STUDY
Ps. 73:23–28; Luke 11:9–13; John 14:15–17
1. What is good for us?
2. What did Jesus promise?

JUL
— & —
AUG

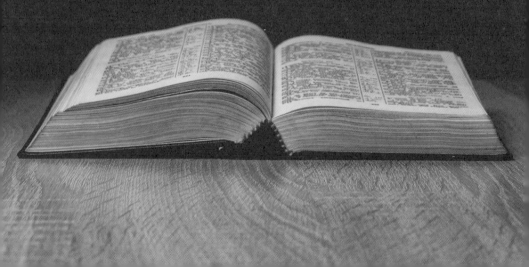

Wise Up and Live

JUL

FOR READING & MEDITATION – PROVERBS 1:1–19

'For attaining wisdom and discipline; for understanding
words of insight...' (v2)

Over the next two months, we set out to explore some of the great
and thrilling themes of the book of Proverbs. I was introduced to this
book within weeks of becoming a Christian, and I have no hesitation in
saying that, as far as practical matters are concerned, it has influenced my
thinking and coloured my judgments more than any other book of the Bible.

I shall never forget my pastor taking me aside just after I had been
converted and telling me, 'I am going to teach you to steal, to drink, to lie,
and to swear.' Looking at my expression, and seeing my astonishment, he
quickly went on to say, 'I want to teach you how to steal time out of every
day to read something from the book of Proverbs. And then I want to teach
you how to drink from its clear, refreshing waters, to lie on your bed at night
and meditate on its great themes, and to swear that by the grace of God
you will put into practice its wonderful teaching.' My pastor's rather novel
approach laid deep in my mind the importance of this powerful book, and
the truths I have learned from it I now long to share with you.

We begin with the question: What is the purpose of Proverbs? Our text
for today gives us the clue. Listen to how the Living Bible paraphrases it:
'He [Solomon] wrote them to teach his people how to live – how to act in
every circumstance...' This, then, is what Proverbs is all about – wisdom
for living. Millions of people know how to make a living but do not know
how to live. They know everything about life except how to live it. I tell
you, the more you understand the book of Proverbs, and the more you
put its truths and principles into practice, the more effective will be your
living. I guarantee it.

**O Father, help me come to grips with the wisdom that enables me not just
to live, but to live abundantly. I long to know what I need to do to get on in
life. Through the ancient but inspired words of Proverbs please teach me
how. Amen.**

FURTHER STUDY
Eccl. 7:11–19; Matt. 7:24–29
1. What are the benefits of wisdom?
2. What are the similarities and differences in Jesus' parable?

Wisdom Personified

FOR READING & MEDITATION – PROVERBS 1:20–33

'But whoever listens to me will live in safety and
be at ease, without fear of harm.' (v33)

Before settling down to focus on our theme, which is Wisdom for Living, it will be helpful if we acquaint ourselves with some background information concerning the book – hence these opening days will be more of an introduction to the book than an exposition of it.

You will not get far when reading Proverbs before you begin to notice that both wisdom and its opposite, foolishness, are personified as women – Lady Wisdom and Lady Folly – each of whom attempts to persuade people to follow her ways. This personification of wisdom and of folly is a literary device that the writer uses to add punch and power to his points, particularly in the first nine chapters. We use a similar form of expression when we personify natural laws and refer to them as 'Mother Nature'. For example, we may hear people comment, 'Mother Nature is bringing out the spring flowers early', or, 'Mother Nature is doing her thing'. This is a poetic and colourful way of referring to the principles and laws that govern the universe in which we live.

Notice how wisdom is personified in these words taken from the passage we have read today: 'Wisdom calls aloud in the street, she raises her voice in the public squares; at the head of the noisy streets she cries out, in the gateways of the city she makes her speech' (vv20–21). Later on in the book of Proverbs you will see how similar language is used of Lady Folly. The purpose of this personification is to make the reader vividly aware that over and against the fatal attraction of folly, wisdom brings security and contentment. Wisdom is the soul's true bride and true counsellor. Wisdom is good for us; it is what our personalities were designed for by God Himself.

O Father, help me to grasp the truth that I am made for a certain way of living – Your way – and when I try to live against that way then I am nothing but a fool. Make me wise, dear Lord, with the wisdom that comes from You. Amen.

FURTHER STUDY
Ps. 112:1–10; Eccl. 2:24–26
1. How can we live without fear of bad news?
2. How do we gain wisdom?

The Source of All Wisdom

FOR READING & MEDITATION – PROVERBS 2:12–22

'Wisdom will save you from the ways of wicked men...' (v12)

Yesterday we touched on the thought that in the book of Proverbs, particularly in the first nine chapters, wisdom and foolishness are seen as persons. Jesus was also using the device of personification when He concluded His address to the crowds on the significance of John the Baptist with the words, 'But wisdom is proved right by her actions' (Matt. 11:19). Some have expressed the view that the personification of wisdom in the Scriptures indicates that wisdom is to be seen as a person, perhaps a member of the angelic hierarchy, who visits men and women and imparts divine wisdom to them. But this, in my opinion, is taking things too far. The writer is simply using a literary device to make a point.

Having said that, however, most evangelical commentators are agreed that the device of personification when used in connection with wisdom is to prepare the way for the apostle Paul's great statement in 1 Corinthians 1:24, namely that Christ is 'the power of God and the wisdom of God'. If this is so then it suggests that the divine purpose underlying the personification of wisdom in the book of Proverbs is not simply to acquaint us with an absorbing set of guidelines or helpful suggestions by which to run our lives, but to hint that true wisdom lies in a Person – that Person being none other than Jesus Christ.

The Christian message moves beyond the wise proverbs of Solomon, which, by the way, commend themselves to non-Christians as well as Christians, and points to the fact that the highest wisdom comes from a relationship with the One who is the fount of all wisdom – Jesus. Knowing the principles of wisdom is one thing; knowing the Person in whom all wisdom resides is another.

O Father, how can I sufficiently thank You that by faith I am linked to the source of all wisdom – the Lord Jesus Christ? Let the wonder of this relationship – that I am in Him and He is in me – sink deep into my soul today. Amen.

FURTHER STUDY

Isa. 11:1–5; 1 Cor. 1:30–31

1. What would rest on Christ?
2. What is Christ to us?

Sophomores – 'Wise Fools'

FOR READING & MEDITATION – PROVERBS 4:1–9

'Do not forsake wisdom, and she will protect you;
love her, and she will watch over you.' (v6)

Having seen why the writer of Proverbs uses the device of personification in connection with wisdom, and having understood that the main message of the book is to provide us with wisdom for living, it is time now to ask ourselves: What exactly is wisdom? How is it to be defined?

Some say wisdom is synonymous with knowledge and use the two words interchangeably. There is, however, a world of difference between knowledge and wisdom, as writers and philosophers down the ages have pointed out. Knowledge is the capacity to comprehend and retain what we are taught; wisdom is the ability to put that knowledge to best effect. If knowledge is the same thing as wisdom then, as Paul Larsen points out, 'There are many "wise" men who are fools.' Schools and universities cram information into the minds of the students who attend them, and so they graduate knowing a good deal about such matters as the solar system, microbiology, history, psychology, the laws of physics, art, and so on. However, knowledge by itself does not stop them from making a mess of their lives. In the United States a second year university or high school student is called a 'sophomore', a term derived from the Greek words for 'wise' and 'foolish' – in other words, a 'wise fool'. How revealing! When we reach the higher stages of education we think that we know it all, but if this attitude is not changed then we will soon demonstrate what it means to be a fool.

A 'fool' in Proverbs is not someone who can't pass a simple literacy or numeracy test; he or she is someone who thinks they know what life is all about but does not. Those whom the world recognises as 'wise' may, from heaven's standpoint, be the biggest fools.

Father, I begin to understand what Paul meant when he said 'we are fools for Christ'. My lifestyle may appear foolish to those around me, but help me never to forget that if I am following Your principles it is the highest wisdom. Amen.

FURTHER STUDY

Rom. 1:18–23; 1 Cor. 1:18–29

1. Why are wise people foolish?
2. Contrast human wisdom and God's foolishness.

The 'Wisdom Literature'

FOR READING & MEDITATION – PROVERBS 5:15–23

'For a man's ways are in full view of the Lord, and he examines
all his paths.' (v21)

There are just a few more important general points to make concerning
Proverbs before we start to focus on our theme for these two months –
Wisdom for Living. Proverbs is a book considered to be part of the 'wisdom
literature' of the Old Testament. These books are associated with a class
of people called 'wise men' or 'sages'. Wise men were highly regarded
both in Israel and in the surrounding nations, as 1 Kings 4:34 reveals.

The Old Testament consists of three sections: first, the Law, second,
the Prophets, and third, the Writings – answering to the three groups of
leaders outlined in Jeremiah 18:18: 'For the teaching of the law by the
priest will not be lost, nor will counsel from the *wise*, nor the word from
the *prophets*.' Included within the category of the Writings are the wisdom
books – Job, Psalms, Proverbs, Ecclesiastes, and Song of Songs. While
the prophets and the priests dealt with the religious life of Israel, the wise
men were called upon to give advice about more philosophical matters.
They were the ones who made the point that the world was designed for
wisdom, and those who followed wisdom would find that the world was
made for them.

The book of Proverbs, which was largely written by Solomon, whose
wisdom was legendary, is crammed with the best advice it is possible to
get, and it is a tragedy that it is not part of our educational system. But
perhaps a greater tragedy is the fact that in some parts of the Christian
community (though not all) Proverbs is an unexplored book. I do not
hesitate to say that any church that does not encourage its people,
especially its young people, to delve into the book of Proverbs is doing
them a major disservice.

**Gracious Father, help me develop a love for Your wisdom literature.
Grant that these days of searching and exploring may result in a new
understanding of wisdom, and that new evidences of Your wisdom may be
seen in my life. Amen.**

FURTHER STUDY
Ps. 119:97–104; Dan. 2:20–23
1. How could the psalmist be wiser than his teachers?
2. What did Daniel give thanks for?

FOR READING & MEDITATION – PROVERBS 28:1–17

'A man of understanding and knowledge maintains order.' (v2)

Yesterday we ended with the comment that any church which does not encourage its people, especially its young people, to delve into the book of Proverbs is doing them a major disservice. Earlier I mentioned that I was introduced to Proverbs when I myself was young – within weeks of becoming a Christian, in fact. Now, several decades later, I can testify that this book, perhaps more than any other in the Bible, has supplied me with wisdom for living and has enriched my life. What is more, the teaching in this book has greatly empowered both my ministry and my writing. Every child, young adult, man and woman needs to be steeped in the book of Proverbs as there is nothing to be found in literature that can so prepare them for life.

Alexander Maclaren, a famous preacher from a past generation, said, 'Proverbs is portable medicine for the fevers of youth.' How true. And, as with any medicine, what matters is that you take it whether or not you know the doctor who prescribed it. A number of young men and women known to me have told me that they came to faith in Jesus Christ through reading the book of Proverbs. One said to me, 'When I applied the principles of Proverbs, and saw that these wise and witty sayings really worked, I was drawn to search for the One whose hand was so clearly present in the book and also in my life. After reading the instruction manual I wanted to know the Instructor.'

Not everyone, of course, will react in that way. However, I myself am convinced that encouraging and exposing people, especially the young, to the wise sayings and principles found in the book of Proverbs is one of the greatest forms of outreach that can be conducted.

O Father, help me use any influence I have with the young to motivate them to read and absorb what is found in the book of Proverbs. But first, let me dwell deep within it myself. In Jesus' name I pray. Amen.

FURTHER STUDY
2 Kgs 20:1–7; Ps. 107:17–22
1. How may God heal us?
2. How was Hezekiah healed?

Invoked or Not...

FOR READING & MEDITATION – PROVERBS 8:12–36

'Blessed is the man who listens to me, watching daily at my doors...' (v34)

We spend just one more day considering the book of Proverbs as a whole before embarking on our theme – Wisdom for Living. The more you read and study Proverbs, and the more you apply its words to your life, the more you will find that its wise and witty sayings 'work'. They work because God has set things up to work this way. It was said of Carl Jung, the famous psychologist, that written over his study door were these words: 'Invoked or not, God is present.' This interesting statement provides us with a clue to understanding Proverbs, for whether or not men and women invoke the Creator, His creative and sustaining wisdom goes on giving them a world where wisdom operates and where things make sense to humankind.

One person has described Proverbs as 'the scrapbook of common grace'. 'Common grace' is the phrase theologians use to describe the grace that God gives to humanity in general so that, whether they turn to Him or not, they are enabled to live more effectively and wisely on the earth. 'Wisdom,' says Charles G. Martin, 'writes the handbook of instruction in God's workshop, and when people despise wisdom, that is, true wisdom, they blot the copy book of life.'

Of course, we must accept the fact that some may pursue wisdom for the wrong reasons – out of self-interest, for instance, or just because wisdom 'works'. But, as Archbishop William Temple once put it, 'The art of politics is so to arrange matters that self-interest prompts what justice demands.' Leaving aside for the moment the wonderful prospect of heaven, it has to be said that life on earth would be a great deal better if wisdom, rather than folly, prevailed.

Father, I am so thankful for Your 'common grace'. Your love reaches down to help people live life in a sensible and profitable way even though they may never come to know You personally. What a wonderful God You are. Amen.

FURTHER STUDY
Josh. 1:1–9; Ps. 1:1–6
1. How would Joshua be successful?
2. How can we be fruitful?

Come Into my House

FOR READING & MEDITATION – PROVERBS 9:1–9

'Wisdom has built her house; she has hewn out its seven pillars.' (v1)

Having looked at some background information concerning the book of Proverbs, we are ready now to begin focusing on our main theme. As I shall be taking you to different sections and passages of this book, and not covering every single verse, I would encourage you to sit down during the next few days and read through the whole book, preferably in two or three sittings. This will prepare you for our daily meditations over the next few weeks.

Our text for today tells us that wisdom is like a house built on seven pillars. There are two main ways of interpreting this verse. One view is that both wisdom and folly have a house to which humankind is invited. Wisdom has a much larger house than folly, being built upon 'seven pillars' – a sign in ancient times of wealth, status, and prestige. There is no doubt that this interpretation of the text has much to commend it, but it is the other view that I am following in these studies – namely that wisdom has seven major aspects. The book of Proverbs does not state categorically what these seven aspects are, so, based on my study and understanding of this great book, my intention is to give you what I consider to be the seven chief aspects of wisdom.

Never in the history of the human race have there been so many problems, so much confusion, and so many conflicting philosophies concerning how to live. Those who lack wisdom do not have the perspectives that enable them to discern the connection between cause and effect, and therefore they don't understand what they are stumbling over, or, if they do avoid problems, they don't understand why they avoid them. We need wisdom to live – and the book of Proverbs will give it to us.

Gracious and loving heavenly Father, my appetite is whetted and now I am ready to begin my study. Grant that as I expose myself to the truths of Your Word, wisdom may become more deeply imprinted upon my spirit. In Jesus' name I pray. Amen.

FURTHER STUDY
Ps. 73:1–17; Prov. 9:13–18
1. When did the psalmist gain understanding?
2. Why should we decline some invitations?

The Ability to Trust

FOR READING & MEDITATION – PROVERBS 3:1–18

'Trust in the Lord with all your heart and lean
not on your own understanding...' (v5)

We turn now to consider the first of the seven pillars on which I believe that wisdom is built – *trust*. The theme of trust occurs throughout Proverbs; it appears in almost every passage and on every page. The word 'trust' itself occurs quite often, the frequency varying according to the translation you read (in the Authorised Version, for example, 'trust' appears nine times). Trust in God is shown in Proverbs to be of far greater value than any human endeavour, however well planned and clever. According to Rabbi Bar Kappa, the verse which is our text for today is the pivot around which all the essential principles of Judaism revolve. He claims that these words summarise the teaching of the whole of the Old Testament and give a clear focus to the fact that the wise are those who trust God and follow His directions for living.

But what exactly is trust? How important is it to daily living? Why does the theme of trust occur so many times, not only in Proverbs but in other parts of Scripture as well? The dictionary defines trust as 'a firm belief in the reliability, honesty, veracity, justice, and strength of a person or thing'. Basically, trust is confidence – confidence that what we believe about a person or thing is true.

We tend to think of trust as being a spiritual quality, but actually it is an essential part of life for everyone. It would be very difficult to get through a single day without the exercise of trust. All government, all economics, all institutions, all marriages, and all relationships between people are fundamentally governed by trust. We cannot relate well to God or others unless we have the ability to trust.

Father, I see that trust is an essential thread that runs through the whole of life. Teach me the art of trusting, for an art it is. Help me to relax and maintain complete confidence in You – hour by hour and day by day. Amen.

FURTHER STUDY
Ps. 37:1–11; 56:1–4
1. How do we trust in the Lord?
2. What did the psalmist do when afraid?

Trust is Good For Us

FOR READING & MEDITATION – PROVERBS 14:14–26

'A simple man believes anything, but a prudent
man gives thought to his steps.' (v15)

We saw yesterday that all relationships, both human and divine, are fundamentally governed by trust. Without trust, society would deteriorate into paranoia – the feeling that everyone is out to get you. Mental health specialists see an inability to trust as a symptom of emotional ill health. Erik Erikson, a developmental psychologist whose studies on the subject of trust are well known among psychologists, says that the capacity to trust is the foundation of good emotional health, and conditions such as chronic anxiety, nervousness or paranoia could be caused by an inability to trust. Although people may let us down and betray our trust, we must be careful that we do not allow those experiences to lead us to the conclusion that everyone we meet is a conspirator.

On the other hand, you may have come across the expression 'a trusting fool' – a term used to describe a person who is unable to discern any cunning schemes that are being devised to exploit him. Erikson also says, 'Unless we have a balanced approach to life – a basic trust together with a certain degree of caution – then we will never achieve emotional maturity or wholeness.' Please take careful note of his words 'a *balanced* approach to life'. Therein lies the secret. We must learn how to trust while at the same time exercising a certain amount of caution.

Our text for today tells us that 'a simple man believes anything'. However, that should not cause us to go to the other extreme and believe that everything people tell us is a lie or a fabrication. The point is that we should not be gullible. Truth is a narrow column and we must watch that we do not lose our balance and fall off.

O Father, help me to be a balanced person – one who stands on the narrow column of truth without falling off into one extreme or the other. Remind me that error is often truth taken to an extreme. Please keep me always in the truth. Amen.

FURTHER STUDY
Num. 13:25–14:4; 1 John 4:1–3
1. Why is caution bad?
2. Why is caution good?

A Snake in the Grass

FOR READING & MEDITATION – PROVERBS 16:10–20

'Blessed is he who trusts in the Lord.' (v20)

Picking up from where we were yesterday – talking about the need to maintain a proper balance between trust and caution – we ask ourselves: Why does the Bible present us with the idea of caution? The simple answer is because we live in a fallen world. God made the first human pair, perfect in every way, and put them in a beautiful garden. They trusted Him for everything they needed and not once did He let them down. However, there was a 'snake in the grass' who hatched a plot to which they succumbed, and so they were brought down to ruin. Their downfall, in turn, plunged the whole human race into chaos and uncertainty (see Gen. 3).

Because of the Fall, life is beset with problems, especially when it comes to the matter of trust. I can't rely entirely on nature – sometimes it rains too much and at other times not enough. I can't rely entirely on family or friends – sometimes they won't or can't help, and at other times they may help too much. Sin has struck so deeply into human relationships that it would be unwise not to recognise that at times and for a variety of reasons people may let us down.

In one way or another the Fall has played havoc with this issue of trust, but we must be careful that we do not allow the failures of trust we may experience on the human level to affect our view of God. Let me spell it out as clearly as I can: you can put your trust in God without fear of ever being let down. The apostle Peter expresses it like this: 'The one who trusts in him will never be put to shame' (1 Pet. 2:6). Drop your anchor into the depths of this reassuring and encouraging revelation. Whoever else you may not be able to trust – you can trust your heavenly Father.

O Father, what encouragement this thought gives me: whoever else I cannot trust, I can trust You. I have heard this truth so often and read it so many times; now help me take hold of it. In Jesus' name I pray. Amen.

FURTHER STUDY

Ps. 20:7; Isa. 31:1–3; Jer. 17:5–6
1. What did the psalmist affirm?
2. Why may trusting people be wrong?

Why is Trust Difficult?

FOR READING & MEDITATION – PROVERBS 28:18–28

'He who trusts in himself is a fool, but he who
walks in wisdom is kept safe.' (v26)

Today we ask the question: Why do some people find it so difficult to trust? Many have said to me, 'My problem is I find it so hard to trust.' Something I have observed in talking to people over the years is this: a person who finds it difficult to trust on a human level often finds it difficult to trust on a spiritual level. Let me suggest what I think lies behind the inability to trust.

Trust is a learned response, and we begin learning it the moment we are born. A newborn baby arrives in the world with a great deal of vulnerability, and among other things has to learn the art of developing a basic trust. If the parents are loving, reliable, predictable, and trustworthy the child soon gets the idea, 'I can trust these people who are looking after me. They don't always respond the way I would like them to but generally they are there for me when I need them.' If, however, there is no reliable and consistent input of love and affection into a child's personality in the early years, if the parents are perceived as unconcerned and unpredictable, the child gets the idea, 'People are not to be trusted'. And in cases where parents are not just unconcerned, but are unkind and even abusive, then the development of a basic trust is hard – some would say impossible.

My experience in counselling has shown me that people with an inability to trust are usually those who experienced serious privation, abuse, or cruelty in their early developmental years. This is no reason to despair, however, for when we have faith in Jesus Christ we become children of God – we have a new parent and a new parentage. And He enables us to overcome whatever difficulties there may have been in our past.

Father, may my focus not be on what has been but on what can be, and on what will be when I am rightly related to You. Please help me grow up spiritually. In Jesus' name I ask it. Amen.

FURTHER STUDY
Luke 12:22–34; Rom. 8:15–17
1. Why can we trust God?
2. What have we received?

How to Forgive

FOR READING & MEDITATION – PROVERBS 30:21–33

'As twisting the nose produces blood, so stirring
up anger produces strife.' (v33)

If, as we said yesterday, difficulties concerning basic trust which occur on a natural, human level can hinder our ability to trust at a spiritual level, how do we overcome this problem? The first thing we must do is demonstrate a willingness to forgive those who deprived us, hurt us, or betrayed us. 'That's hard,' you might say, and my reply is this: 'Yes, particularly if you have been badly let down or abused, it is indeed hard – hard, but not impossible.'

Here's how you go about it. You focus first on how much you have been forgiven. One of the keys to forgiving others is to enter into a realised awareness of how much God has forgiven you. When people have told me during a counselling session, 'My problem is that I can't forgive,' I have usually responded by saying, 'No, that's not your problem. Your problem is that you don't know how much you have been forgiven.' It may be difficult for some to see this, especially those who have experienced betrayal and gone through deep hurt, but nothing others have done to us is as awful as what we have done to God.

If you have difficulty with that last statement it is because you do not understand the true nature of sin. Sin is taking the Creator of the universe and relegating Him to irrelevance; it is saying to the One who made us, 'I can run my life on my own terms.' Sin is insanity – and you and I have been guilty of that. Yet, because Jesus Christ died on the cross for our sins, God has forgiven us, pardoned us, and bestowed upon us His royal favour. Having been given such forgiveness can we, dare we, withhold it from anyone who has hurt us or betrayed our trust, no matter how awful or painful that hurt has been?

Father, Your Word is frank and open; help me to respond to it in the same way. Take from me every trace of hesitancy, every fear and apprehension, every refusal to accept responsibility. In Jesus' name I pray. Amen.

FURTHER STUDY
Matt. 18:21–33; Eph. 4:30–32
1. What did the unmerciful servant fail to recognise?
2. Why should we forgive others?

FOR READING & MEDITATION – PROVERBS 14:1–13

'There is a way that seems right to a man, but in the end it
leads to death.' (v12)

Today we continue looking at the steps we need to take in order to rid ourselves of the things that hinder our ability to trust. Forgiveness, we said yesterday, is the first step – but what is the second? It is the recognition of the fact that, having been let down by others, we have determined in our hearts that we will never trust another person again.

The determination never to trust another person again may be a human reaction, but it is not God's way. So many times I have heard many people say, 'I can trust God but I can't trust other people.' But the Christian faith is all about relating to people. The essence of reality is passionate, other-centred relationships, as is evidenced by the perfect relationships of the Trinity – God the Father, God the Son, and God the Holy Spirit. If we draw back from others because we are afraid of being betrayed then what we are in reality saying is this: 'I can't trust God enough to hold me when others let me down.' Those, therefore, who say, 'I can trust God but I can't trust people', are not making sense. It is more honest to say, 'I can't trust God and I can't trust people.' What we can say, if we really believe the truths of the New Testament and are willing to give ourselves to them, is this: 'I can trust God to hold me when I relate to others, irrespective of whether I am accepted or rejected.'

The determination to stay safe and self-protected is evidence that our trust is not what it should be. We must therefore bring this self-protective determination to preserve our own soul before God in an act of repentance, and indicate by an act of resolve that no matter how others may treat us, we will confidently place our trust in Him.

O Father, I must ask myself: Can I trust You enough to hold me when others do not come through for me? The determination to stay safe seems so right, yet it is so wrong. I turn from my way to Your way. Hold me secure. In Jesus' name. Amen.

FURTHER STUDY
Acts 13:2–5; 15:36–41; 2 Tim. 4:11
1. Why did Paul and Barnabas argue?
2. What did Paul later confess about Mark

Is Trust Idealistic?

FOR READING & MEDITATION – PROVERBS 29:19–27

'Fear of man will prove to be a snare, but whoever trusts in
the Lord is kept safe.' (v25)

The truths I have been putting before you in the past few days are
extremely challenging – especially for those who have been badly let
down or betrayed. Sometimes someone has said to me, 'Isn't it idealistic
to expect me to be vulnerable to further hurt after I have been let down
and betrayed?' My answer is to point them to Jesus. If He can do it then so
can we – providing we depend on His strength and not ours. Jesus knows
better than anyone what it means to be let down and betrayed. In all the
heaped-up pain of His passion, few things would have hurt Him more than
being betrayed by His disciples. Take Peter's betrayal, for example (see
Matt. 26:69–75). Did our Lord's experience of Peter's denial cause Him to
conclude, 'Never again will I trust that man'?

Come with me to Galilee and let us see. Simon Peter, no doubt feeling
disappointed and disillusioned, returns to his trade as a fisherman,
whereupon Jesus pursues him and puts Himself in a position of being hurt
once again. He says to Peter, 'Do you truly love me...?', using the strong
Greek word for love – *agapao*. Peter responds, 'Yes, Lord, you know that
I love you' (John 21:15–16). Jesus opened Himself up to Peter despite the
hurt He would still have been feeling from Peter's earlier betrayal and
despite the possibility of further rejection. Jesus' openness with Peter
opened up again the possibility of relationship and also opened up the way
for Peter to enter into an important new role within the fledgling Church.

Jesus did not allow the hurt He felt to deter Him from continuing, even
pursuing, the relationship. *That's* what I mean by vulnerability. *That's* what
I mean by love.

**Father, is it possible that You can make me so secure that I, too, am able
to be vulnerable in my relationships? I must believe it; I do believe it. Help
me to demonstrate it in every relationship I am called by You to pursue. In
Jesus' name. Amen.**

FURTHER STUDY
Luke 22:31–34,54–62; John 21:15–16
1. Why was Peter unreliable?
2. How did Jesus react to Peter's betrayal?

Yours Trustingly

FOR READING & MEDITATION – PROVERBS 11:25–31

'Whoever trusts in his riches will fall...' (v28)

We spend one more day meditating on the important issue of trust. What have we been saying? We have concluded that trust is an essential ingredient in our relationships – both human and divine. The reason we can demonstrate trust in all our earthly relationships is because we recognise that there is One who is guiding and governing our lives, One in whom we can place our fullest confidence. We can give ourselves to others knowing that even though they let us down, He will hold us in His arms and not allow us to be destroyed.

Take careful note of what I say here because many people hold God to promises He never made and are then disappointed when He doesn't do what they believed He had promised He would do. God does not promise to keep us from being hurt in our relationships, but He does promise to keep us from being destroyed.

The more you trust in God, the more effective you will be in your relationships with others. Because your ultimate trust is in God you will be free from unconscious manipulative or exploitative techniques and, drawing your security from Him, you can give yourself more freely to others. 'Love does not begin,' someone has said, 'until you expect nothing in return.' When your trust is wholly and fully in the Lord Jesus, you can love like that.

If you have never done so before, decide now to put in God's hands all the hurts, traumas, and betrayals of the past. Forgive all those who have let you down. Lift up your head and look into the face of the One who will never betray you. Give Him all your trust. And, I say again, keep in mind the fact that trust is not only an essential attitude in life, it is also the first step in wisdom. The wise are those who trust in God.

O God, break down any last barrier that may be hindering me from putting my trust fully in You. I would have the doors of my spirit turn out, not in. Help me begin and end every day by saying, 'Yours trustingly'. In Jesus' name. Amen.

FURTHER STUDY
Ps. 52:1–9; Jer. 17:7–8
1. What was the result of trusting in God's love?
2. Why can we be free from fear in difficult times?

Integrity - 'Profound Wisdom'

FOR READING & MEDITATION – PROVERBS 10:9–17

'The man of integrity walks securely, but he who
takes crooked paths will be found out.' (v9)

We move on now to look at what I consider to be the second pillar of
wisdom – *integrity*. This theme, like trust, is one that is continually
emphasised in Proverbs for, as we shall see, no one can be truly successful
in life without integrity.

What is integrity? The dictionary definition puts it like this: 'wholeness,
soundness, trustworthiness, uprightness, honesty'. You can see at once
that integrity is a moral quality, and morality is an essential characteristic
of wisdom. One of the mistakes many people make when thinking about
wisdom is to confuse it with learning, intelligence, brilliance, or cleverness.
How many times do we read in the newspaper of those who have climbed
the ladder of success, have been highly educated, or have achieved great
prominence in the world, only to then come tumbling down because of
some issue of personal or corporate integrity?

Many professional people have a great deal of knowledge but lack
wisdom. For example, you see this in the marriage counsellor who, in
spite of all his credentials, can't hold his own marriage together; in the
psychiatrist who, overcome by her own problems, slides into depression; in
the economist who goes bankrupt playing the stock market; in the church
leader who causes chaos and hurt when leaving his family for another
woman. Learning, understanding, intelligence, and professional training
are important – please don't hear me demean them – but if we are to be
experts in the art of living, as Proverbs sets out to teach us to be, then
we must see that without wisdom the things I have listed don't count for
much at all.

'The simplicity of integrity is the profundity of wisdom,' says Paul Larsen.
How true! How very true!

**O God, give me in addition to trust a high degree of integrity. I want not
only to trust others but I want them to trust me. You know my need and also
my desire. Grant me these facets of wisdom. In Jesus' name I ask it. Amen.**

FURTHER STUDY

1 Kgs 9:1–5; Job 2:1–10

1. What was God's promise to Solomon?
2. Why did Job not curse God for his troubles?

I Would Rather Be Right...

FOR READING & MEDITATION – PROVERBS 8:1–11

'For wisdom is more precious than rubies, and nothing
you desire can compare with her.' (v11)

Today we continue with the thought that another aspect of wisdom is integrity. Both we and the universe are made for truth and integrity, and both the world and we are alien to untruth and dishonesty. The universe is made for the same thing that we are made for – righteousness.

The same moral law that God has revealed in Scripture He has also stamped on human nature. He has, in fact, written His law twice – once in the text of the Bible and once in the texture of human nature; once on stone tablets and once on human hearts. The moral law is not an alien system that is unnatural for people to obey; it fits perfectly, as a hand into a glove, because it is the law of our own created being. There is a fundamental correspondence between God's law in the Bible and the one written on our hearts. We can discover our true humanness by obeying it.

Charles Spurgeon wrote to the then Prime Minister of Britain, William Gladstone, in these words: 'You do not know how those of us regard you who feel it a joy to live when a Prime Minister believes in righteousness. We believe in no man's infallibility but it is restful to be sure of one man's integrity.' What makes us so suspicious of politicians, even though politics can be a noble profession, is not that they might make mistakes, but that sometimes staying in office is more important to them than honour and candour. Henry Clay, when about to introduce to the American Congress a bill that was heavily weighted in favour of morality, was told, 'If you do this, it will kill your chances of becoming president.' His reply was, 'I would rather be right than be president.' I can almost see King Solomon's head nodding in favour of that attitude.

Tender and skilful Invader of my soul, I yield myself to You for the inrush of divine life that brings with it wisdom. Father, I see that the reason I am not wiser is that I do not have enough of You. Please fill me with Your Spirit. Amen.

FURTHER STUDY
2 Sam. 18:9–13; 2 Kgs 5:13–27
1. What is a mark of integrity?
2. Contrast Elisha and Gehazi.

A Lie Has Short Legs

FOR READING & MEDITATION – PROVERBS 28:18–28

'He whose walk is blameless is kept safe, but he whose
ways are perverse will suddenly fall.' (v18)

Yesterday we said that both we and the universe are made for integrity. Let's take that thought a stage further by asking: Will the universe sustain a lie? I have no hesitation in saying that it will not, for I believe that the universe is not built for the success of a lie. The Tamils in South India have a saying that goes like this: 'The life of the cleverest lie is only eight days.' A lie may not break itself upon the universe today or tomorrow, but one day it will.

Before World War II the Germans used to say, 'Lies have short legs', meaning that they were bad in the long run. During the war that saying was changed to 'Lies have one short leg'. Why? Because Goebbels, the propaganda minister, had one short leg!

In a moral universe nobody gets away with anything. Dr Cynddylan Jones, a famous Welsh preacher, claimed, 'The worst thing about doing wrong is to be the one who does the wrong.' I don't know about you, but I used to think the text 'Be sure that your sin will find you out' (Num. 32:23) meant 'Be sure your sin will be found out'. The verse doesn't say that, though. It says your sin will find *you* out. It will register in you and demean you. We may be free to choose, but we are not free to choose the consequences of our choosing.

Any philosophy or ideology that dismisses the moral universe and tries to establish its own ideas about what is right and wrong is doomed to fall. This is what brought about the downfall of the great empires of Assyria, Greece and Rome. 'There is nothing concealed that will not be disclosed' (Matt. 10:26). We either work with the moral universe and gain benefits or we work against it and face the consequences. It is as simple as that.

Gracious and loving Father, I see that You have designed a moral universe and that those who run against it go against the grain. Help me to be a person of integrity and truth, and thus get results, not consequences. In Jesus' name. Amen.

FURTHER STUDY
Ps. 101:1–8; Acts 5:1–11
1. What did David promise?
2. Why is lying so serious?

Can a Lie be Justified?

FOR READING & MEDITATION – PROVERBS 19:1–9

'He who pours out lies will perish.' (v9)

We continue looking at the question we raised yesterday: Will the universe sustain a lie? Contemporary society is increasingly facing and needing to deal with 'situational ethics', which would have us believe that sometimes, under certain situations, a lie is admissible. I think that is a dangerous and deadly path. A lie is never right – no matter what attempts we might make to justify it. 'God is not a man, that he should lie', we are told in Numbers 23:19, and in 1 John 2:21 we read, 'No lie comes from the truth'. God Himself cannot lie, and He will never delegate to you the task of lying for Him. When we weave lies and dishonesties into the tapestry of our lives we actually weave fire into our very being – here and hereafter: 'All liars shall have their part in the lake which burns with fire and brimstone' (Rev. 21:8, NKJV).

Situational ethics often proposes possible scenarios to justify a position, such as, 'What if someone came to your house to murder a member of your family and asked if that person was in. Would it not be right to lie in those circumstances?' Can you see the thrust of this question? It is the argument, 'This is what we must and ought to do because it makes sense'. But once we view sin as a 'must' and as an 'ought' it is magically turned into something that is 'good'.

The Bible does not advise that anyone, in any situation, *ought* to sin. 1 Corinthians 10:13 teaches that because God is faithful, we will never find ourselves in a situation where we *must* sin, and promises that there will always be a way of escape. God never puts us in such a situation or calls upon us to break one of His laws in order to keep another of His commands.

O Father, in a world that seems to be always looking for excuses and exceptions, help me to steer my life by the clear statements of Your revealed will. I want to conform to the rules – Your rules. In Jesus' name. Amen.

FURTHER STUDY

John 8:42–47; Col. 3:9–10
1. Where do lies originate?
2. What are the marks of the old and new natures?

Two Important Facts

FOR READING & MEDITATION – PROVERBS 6:12–19

'There are six things the Lord hates... a false witness who
pours out lies...' (vv16,19)

We return to the question we started to consider yesterday: What if someone came to your house to murder a member of your family and asked if that person was in – how would you respond? Would it not be right to lie in such circumstances? Situational ethics may demand a 'Yes'. The Bible, in my opinion, says, 'No'.

Situational ethics is notorious for putting forward hypothetical situations in which a person *must* sin because that is what *ought* to be done. But when we view sin as a 'must' and an 'ought' we are finished. A Christian view of ethics rejects every constructed situation which situational ethics advances if it fails to take into account two important biblical facts. First, *God's sovereignty*. God will always prepare a way out for His people. God is still alive today. Second, *the Holy Spirit's power*. The believer is encouraged not to worry about what he or she has to say in difficult situations. Jesus has promised, 'At that time you will be given what to say, for it will not be you speaking, but the Spirit of your Father...' (Matt. 10:19–20). Also, we are told, 'Trust in the Lord with all your heart and lean not on your own understanding' (Prov. 3:5).

God is not ignorant or stupid. He did not fail to see that sometimes His laws would seem to contradict one another. He knew full well that there would be occasions when it might appear prudent from a human point of view to ignore one of His principles – hence His promise to us in 1 Corinthians 10:13. Those who try to excuse the breaking of any of God's moral laws on the pretext that it feels 'right' or seems 'good', sow the seeds of disruption in their own inner being. It is not the way of wisdom.

Father, forgive us that so often we prefer human wisdom to divine wisdom simply because it 'feels' right. Help us to trust Your Word even when it runs counter to our own feelings. In Jesus' name we pray. Amen.

FURTHER STUDY
Deut. 19:16–20; 1 Kgs 21:1–23
1. What was the result of false witness?
2. How would God deal with Ahab and Jezebel?

Dishonesty is Doomed

FOR READING & MEDITATION – PROVERBS 14:1–13

'A truthful witness does not deceive, but a false witness
pours out lies.' (v5)

We need to fix it as an axiom in our thinking that nobody gets away with anything, anywhere, any time, if that 'any thing' is dishonest or untrue. The whole history of the human race is a commentary on this. The first lie uttered by Satan was 'You will not surely die' (Gen. 3:4). And he keeps repeating that well-worn but discredited lie to every man and woman who comes into this world.

Something dies the moment you are dishonest or fail to be a person of integrity. Self-respect dies within you. Degeneration begins to damage your heart the moment dishonesty enters it. You are not so much punished for your sin as by your sin. You are punished *by* sin *for* sin. In one sense, sin is its own punishment.

The first time I was in Chennai, India, I had a meal with a family who told me the story of their milkman. He had to drive his cow and calf from door to door in the hot sun and milk the cow in the presence of each housewife. 'What a clumsy way of delivering milk,' I commented. 'Ah,' said my host, 'but you see, he was discovered putting water in the milk and now, because he can't be trusted, he has to milk the cow before the eyes of everyone he serves.' The milkman's dishonesty doomed him to drudgery. The moral universe had the last word.

'Dishonesty puts sand in the machinery of life,' says one writer. I would add, 'And honesty and integrity puts oil into it.' We can choose to live with either sand or oil in our inner mechanism. I cannot say whether or not I would ever lie. I would like to think not – but I have to acknowledge I am fallible and human. However, I know this: my moral joints will creak if I am dishonest. I am made for integrity and I will not function well without it.

O Father, help me grasp this simple but important fact – that I am designed for truth and honesty. When I work with truth, I go leaping into life. When I work without it, I limp. Drive this truth deep into my being, I pray. Amen.

FURTHER STUDY
Jer. 9:1–6; Mic. 6:9–16
1. What happens to a society when there is deceit?
2. Why may people be dissatisfied?

Truth is Truth is Truth

FOR READING & MEDITATION – PROVERBS 30:1–9

'Keep falsehood and lies far from me...' (v8)

Increasingly, in our society, integrity is in short supply. Some time ago I asked a successful businessman, 'What would you say is the greatest need in your sphere of business?' He thought for a moment, looked me straight in the eye, and said, 'Integrity.' When I asked him why, he explained, 'Almost daily I am faced with dishonesty and duplicity, and whenever I confront it people take the view that dishonesty is only a problem when it is found out.' It's interesting, however, that those who laugh at dishonesty become deeply upset when they are the victims of it.

The following statement is one that I once caught sight of in one of my grandson's books: 'An honest fisherman is a pretty uninteresting person.' Another statement made in the book was this: 'There are two things essential if you are to succeed in business – integrity and sagacity. Integrity is keeping your word and sagacity is never giving your word.' Is it any wonder that we find the thought of no moral absolutes so appealing? It is only fair to say, though, that despite the present-day trend away from honesty and integrity, there are still millions of people who would not claim to be Christians but who, nevertheless, see it as their duty to be honest, upright and decent. May their tribe increase!

Christians who lack integrity hinder the progress of the gospel in this world and set Christ's message in a false light. Determine to be honest in thought and speech and act. Lay this down as a cornerstone of your life, especially you who are young, and begin building from there. Whatever you do, shun like a plague the temptations of situational ethics and admit no exceptions. Truth is truth is truth.

O God, You who are the Designer of the great design, help me mould my life by it and be fully surrendered to its purposes. If I run from truth I run from myself, for I am made for truth. Keep me true, dear Lord. In Jesus' name. Amen.

FURTHER STUDY
Ps. 119:25–32; Eph. 4:20–29
1. What did the psalmist choose?
2. How should we speak to others?

Self-Exploratory Surgery

FOR READING & MEDITATION – PROVERBS 23:15–25

'Buy the truth and do not sell it; get wisdom, discipline
and understanding.' (v23)

We spend one more day meditating on the importance of integrity. In one of his books, Charles Swindoll tells how many years ago in New York a doctor by the name of Evan O'Neil became convinced that most major operations could be performed while patients were under a local anaesthetic, thereby avoiding the risks of general anaesthesia. On 15 February 1921 he operated on himself and removed his appendix while under a local anaesthetic. The operation was a success, and it was said that he recovered faster than usually expected of patients who were given general anaesthesia.

Today I invite you to undertake some self-exploratory surgery of the soul. While fully conscious and fully aware, allow the Holy Spirit to assist you by handing you the only instrument you need for soul surgery – the infection-free scalpel of Scripture. 'The word of God is living and active. Sharper than any double-edged sword, it penetrates even to dividing soul and spirit, joints and marrow; it judges the thoughts and attitudes of the heart' (Heb. 4:12).

This is not just an interesting idea, it is something we are required to do because Scripture commands it: 'But let a man examine himself' (1 Cor. 11:28, NKJV). Right now, in God's presence, ask yourself: Am I honest? Am I a person of integrity? Can my word be trusted? Remember, only you can perform this surgery on your soul – only you. No one else but you knows the truth about yourself. You can rationalise and twist the facts and no one will know the difference – except you. And remember, too, that there can be no wisdom without morality, no expertise in living without truth and honesty. The wise are those who have integrity.

Father, I realise that when truth is not present in me there is as much pain as with a diseased appendix. By Your Word, and through Your Spirit, right now cut away in me all that is untrue and dishonest. For Jesus' sake. Amen.

FURTHER STUDY

Ps. 139:14–24; 2 Cor. 13:5

1. What did the psalmist recognise about himself?
2. Why should we examine ourselves?

Take Another Path

FOR READING & MEDITATION – PROVERBS 5:1–14

'Keep to a path far from her...' (v8)

Following on from integrity, we look now at what I believe to be the third pillar of wisdom – *personal purity*. This, too, is a major theme in Proverbs, for throughout the book we come across statements that encourage us to be chaste, virtuous, self-disciplined, and pure in our relationships, especially with the opposite sex.

First, I would like to deal with the subject of chastity, as Proverbs speaks particularly to this. We live in an age that largely ignores the biblical teaching that enjoins us to keep sexual intercourse until marriage. Some sections of the Church now accept 'the new morality' which says that sexual relationships outside marriage are fine providing they are conducted in a loving and a non-manipulative relationship. I have no hesitation in rejecting this, both as not biblical and anti-relationship. The passage we have read today describes most clearly the destiny of sexual relationships outside marriage. They are fundamentally destructive.

The second half of the chapter is given over to a description of how fulfilling sexual relations can be within marriage. The emphasis of Proverbs at this point is to avoid putting yourself in a position of temptation – to keep well away from the danger of seduction. The words 'Keep to a path far from her' mean, 'Keep your distance from such a woman' (*The Message*), in other words 'Avoid an immoral woman as you would avoid a plague.'

A man once went to the great American preacher D.L. Moody with a tale of personal moral disaster and said, 'Now, Mr Moody, what would you have done if you had got into such a situation?' Moody replied, 'Man, I would never have got into it.' That's more than just common sense – that's wisdom!

O God, help me to help myself. Please show me how to avoid circumstances that make a fall almost inevitable. For I cannot ask You to help me out of situations unless I help myself not to get into them. Amen.

FURTHER STUDY

Job 31:1; Matt. 5:27–32
1. What did Job pledge?
2. What did Jesus teach about chastity?

Don't Go On His Ground

FOR READING & MEDITATION – PROVERBS 4:10–27

'Let your eyes look straight ahead, fix your gaze directly
before you.' (v25)

We continue looking at the issue of sexual experience and the need for it to be kept within marriage. If every man and woman were to accept and put into practice the principle of not allowing themselves to get into difficult situations where great strain is placed on physical intimacy, it would make a world of difference to the matter of temptation.

Some temptations cannot be avoided; some, however, can. Anatole France has an apocryphal story in which God and the devil are talking of a beautiful young girl. God asks, 'How dare you tempt such a lovely creature as that?' The devil replies, 'Well, she came on to my ground.'

R.W. Everrood tells another story. A young man seeking his fortune was travelling across a desert when he came across an oasis where a beautiful young girl sat spinning on a loom. Thirsty, he asked for a drink, and she responded, 'Certainly, providing you let me put these threads around you that I am spinning.' He agreed, thinking he could easily brush away the thin gossamer threads as one would brush away a spider's web. After drinking the water he fell asleep, and awoke to find himself tied by thick, strong cords. And what was more, the beautiful young girl had changed into a repulsive and ugly hag.

The best strategy with temptation is not to go near it. Paul's advice to young Timothy was 'Flee from all this' (1 Tim. 6:11). John Ruskin says, 'No one can honestly ask to be delivered from temptation unless he has honestly and firmly determined to do the best he can to keep out of it.' My advice to every unmarried man and woman reading these lines – and married people, too – is this: Keep out of the devil's territory. Don't go on to his ground.

O God, make me alert to the dangers that beset my path, and if I do move towards them unsuspectingly, grant that warning bells may ring in my heart. I know You will do Your part; help me do mine. In Jesus' name I ask it. Amen.

FURTHER STUDY
Gen. 39:1–12; 1 Cor. 6:18; Eph. 4:27
1. How did Joseph overcome temptation?
2. How may the devil gain access to our lives?

Take It On Faith!

FOR READING & MEDITATION – PROVERBS 6:16–26

'My son, keep your father's commands and do not
forsake your mother's teaching.' (v20)

The real truth about sex and sexual satisfaction is difficult to fully understand outside of marriage. Many young people say to me, 'Why all these negatives in the Bible concerning sex before marriage? What is the point of all these dos and don'ts, all these prohibitions? Isn't sex a beautiful thing?'

This is what I say to them: 'Once you are married you will begin to see why there are so many negatives; it is so that you may better enjoy the positives. God doesn't give His prohibitions because sex is a bad thing; they are there to protect us from engaging in a good and beautiful thing in the wrong context. Within marriage, sexual activity is the doing of the right thing in the right place. It is only when you are married that you begin to see the purpose of all the dos and don'ts spelled out in the Bible.'

Christians are, or should be, people who take God on trust. There's not much point in confessing to be a follower of Jesus Christ if you don't believe what He tells you in His Word and change it to suit your convenience. Passion has always been a problem, but wisdom and passion must be properly related. You must recognise the necessity of learning to wait, which is one of the first evidences that you are growing in maturity. A young child desires immediate gratification and will cry and howl until he gets what he wants. When that child grows older and becomes more mature then the desire for gratification is brought under control. The concept of deferred satisfaction is a vital one for every young person to grasp, for without it there can be no real maturity. You must learn to deny yourself now so that in the future you may experience the right thing in the right way.

Father, take me by the hand lest I succumb to the temptation of immediate satisfaction. If I get off the track here I will find myself in a jungle that gets more and more tangled every moment. Please guide me and hold me. Amen.

FURTHER STUDY

2 Sam. 13:1–20

1. What principle did Amnon ignore?
2. What was the result of Amnon's sex with Tamar?

FOR READING & MEDITATION – PROVERBS 6:1–11

'Go to the ant, you sluggard; consider its ways and be wise!' (v6)

We continue looking at the important principle of deferred satisfaction. As is apparent from verses 6 to 8 of today's reading, this is evident even in the insect world. The harvester ant doesn't spend all its time eating. Instead it runs back and forth carrying food into the nest so that it may survive the winter when there will be no food.

This picture of the ant is one that you should keep continually in your mind. It is an image included in the Word of God in order to bring instruction to the heart. Prepare for the future in every way you can, not only by denying yourself the things that God puts out of bounds, but also by giving yourself to the things you need to know to increase your effectiveness in your chosen profession or vocation. Whatever you plan to do in the days ahead of you – prepare for it. Prepare by study and also by prayer.

The wisdom of learning to wait and preparing for the future applies to everyone regardless of age. Whenever you have to do anything, whatever it might be – either public or private – prepare for it. This may require you to put something else off for the time being so that you can give yourself to the task in hand. There are no short cuts to success. I prepared myself for years by filling my heart and mind with the Word of God, and then, when the time came, God called me to launch these Bible notes that you are now reading. Frequently people have asked, 'How can you continue to write year after year after year?' I know that this would not have been possible had I not, many years ago, denied myself many things so that I could prepare.

Whatever God asks you to do, don't take His blessing for granted – *prepare.*

Father, Your knife cuts deep but Your cuts are always redemptive. Forgive me for taking so much for granted and for not giving myself to the tasks to which You have called me. Help me to be a prepared person. In Jesus' name I ask it. Amen.

FURTHER STUDY

Exod. 31:1–11; 36:1–7; Ezra 7:6–10

1. How did God and the Israelites prepare to build the tabernacle?
2. What did Ezra prepare for?

Giving All to God

FOR READING & MEDITATION – PROVERBS 8:1–11

'Choose my instruction instead of silver, knowledge
rather than choice gold...' (v10)

People who struggle with this concept of deferred satisfaction, in other words, learning to wait, ought to take another look at the contestants who prepare for sports events – especially the Olympic Games. You see men and women pushing themselves almost beyond endurance in order to gain a prize for themselves, their club or their country. I don't think that all the training is unmitigated pleasure. Indeed, I know it isn't. The rigorous regime involves going through the pain barrier. So why are they doing it? They are demonstrating the principle of deferred satisfaction. They are willing to endure suffering now in order to win in the future. The pressure, the denial of legitimate pleasures, the strong self-discipline, the tough training, are all outweighed by the hope of winning.

You see, the idea of deferred satisfaction is not a uniquely Christian idea. It has been recognised by reflective people throughout more than 2,000 years of history. Plato talks about it, and so does Socrates. Greek philosophy talks about the control of the passions by self-discipline and encourages the development of virtue by self-denial.

The Christian message teaches us that God came to this world in the Person of His Son in order to set up a rescue mission to save us from an everlasting hell. If we believe that Jesus is God's Son we are saved, but not that we might sit back and indulge ourselves in the thought. We are saved to serve. If non-Christians can deny themselves present satisfaction for future gains and go to such lengths to win a prize, how much more ought we, who serve the risen Christ? Dare we stand by and watch them do for gold what we are not prepared to do for God?

Father, Your school is strict but the end is redemption. Your instructions, however hard and uncompromising, are ultimately my salvation. Help me to see the end from the beginning and to use all my powers in reaching for the goal. Amen.

FURTHER STUDY

1 Cor. 9:19–27; Phil. 3:12–21; 1 Tim. 4:8

1. Why should we deny ourselves pleasure?
2. How are exercise and discipleship compared?

Sin Breaks God's Heart

30
JUL

FOR READING & MEDITATION – PROVERBS 6:27–35

'But a man who commits adultery lacks judgment;
whoever does so destroys himself.' (v32)

We have talked about chastity; let's talk now about faithfulness. Chastity is purity prior to marriage; faithfulness is virtue within marriage. Love cannot be love unless it includes faithfulness, and God wants everyone who enters into marriage to be loyal and true. When we say that God is love (1 John 4:8), we are also saying that God is faithful because, I repeat, love cannot be love unless faithfulness is an integral part of it.

Marriage is a covenant. Many people argue, 'It's just a piece of paper and fifteen minutes of a couple's time.' But hold on a minute. If you understand that life is fundamentally based on relationships, that the only ethical relationship is love, and that love is faithfulness, then the covenant of marriage is the most precious thing in life. Both in the Old and New Testaments a theme that appears constantly is the covenant aspect of love. We read, 'He is a faithful God, keeping his covenant of love...' (Deut. 7:9). And when you study the covenants of Scripture you will find this: that God keeps His covenants even though they are broken by the other side. The relationship between Jehovah and Israel is often pictured as the relationship between a husband and a wife. Israel becomes the wayward, unfaithful wife who commits adultery. But God is still faithful to His covenant. God says, 'I will never break My covenant. You can count on it. I am God.'

People may shy away from commitment in a relationship, claiming they want to be 'free' – but without commitment is it really love? Love is a commitment, and when men and women indulge in sex before marriage or a so-called affair, they don't just break God's laws; they also break His heart.

O Father, in an age when anything goes, may I be an exhibition to the world around of what it means to be a follower of You. Help me to keep all my relationships pure. For Your dear name's sake. Amen.

FURTHER STUDY

Gen. 6:5–6; Isa. 54:1–10; Hos. 2:16–3:1
1. Why does God allow Himself to feel pain?
2. Describe the nature of God's love.

Be a Person of Passion

FOR READING & MEDITATION – PROVERBS 29:1–18

'Where there is no revelation, the people cast off restraint...' (v18)

O ver the past few days we have been talking about the subject of passion – the romantic passion of a man or a woman. Prior to marriage the passion has to be managed, and within marriage it is focused on one's partner – and on one's partner alone.

But how do we keep passion moving along the right lines? Do you remember the story of Odysseus in Greek mythology? He sailed with his crew past an island inhabited by the Sirens – creatures who had the bodies of birds, the heads of women and very beautiful voices. When the Sirens began to sing, passing sailors were so entranced that they sailed towards the island, only to be dashed to pieces and destroyed on the jagged rocks. So Odysseus asked Orpheus, the greatest harpist in the ancient world, to play for him as they sailed past the island, and the music he created was far more beautiful than that provided by the Sirens. One passion overwhelms the other.

What every one of us needs in our lives is a passion so powerful that it transcends all other passions. In God we find that passion. When our lives are touched by Him and we drink from His life-giving stream, our hearts are filled with a passion that keeps every other passion under control. Is not this what happened to Joseph? When Potiphar's wife tried to seduce him he fled from the house crying, 'How then could I do such a wicked thing and sin against God?' (Gen. 39:9). His passion for God overwhelmed all other passions.

When Christ, who is the wisdom of God and the power of God, is allowed to live at the centre of our lives then His passion keeps every other passion where it ought to be – under control.

O Christ, come into my being afresh this day and light the fire of passion for You that will bring every other passion in my life under its complete control. This I ask for the honour and glory of Your precious name. Amen.

FURTHER STUDY

2 Cor. 5:11–20; 6:14–7:1

1. What compelled Paul?
2. Why should we live holy lives?

Honeysuckle Christians

FOR READING & MEDITATION – PROVERBS 11:25–31

'A generous man will prosper; he who refreshes
others will himself be refreshed.' (v25)

Now we come now to what I consider to be a fourth pillar of wisdom – *generosity*. This subject, too, is a favourite theme of the book of Proverbs. Our text for today tells us that when we move out of ourselves and give to others, we ourselves are refreshed. An old Welsh proverb says, 'The greatest joy in giving is to be the one who gives.'

Now, we must not take today's text to mean that we ought to focus on generosity because it brings rewards. Generosity that is exercised simply for the purpose of reward is not true generosity. The reward simply comes as a by-product of giving. I have heard ethicists – those who study questions of right and wrong – pull today's text to pieces. They say that this, and similar statements found in the Word of God, make Christianity a form of sophisticated selfishness. Christians, they claim, give to others because it makes them feel good, not because it is the right thing to do or the right way to live. Christianity, they conclude, is an indirect form of selfishness. Well, we must admit that some Christians may look at things in this way, but I imagine they are few and far between.

I love the way in which Charles Harthern, a preacher of a different generation, described giving: 'Some give like a sponge – only when they are squeezed. Some give like Moses' rock – only when they are hit. True Christians, however, give like the honeysuckle – because they delight to give.' That's the secret – giving because we delight to give. The generous hand comes from a generous heart. If the heart is not generous then, however much the hand gives, there is no true generosity.

Gracious and loving heavenly Father, I ask for the blessing not only of trust, integrity, and personal purity, but of generosity also. And I ask not just to get a blessing but to give a blessing. In Jesus' name I pray. Amen.

FURTHER STUDY
Acts 20:35; 2 Cor. 9:1–15
1. What did Jesus explain?
2. What was Paul's concern in giving?

Divine Mathematics

FOR READING & MEDITATION – PROVERBS 11:16–24

'One man gives freely, yet gains even more; another
withholds unduly, but comes to poverty.' (v24)

We continue to meditate on the wisdom of generosity. What all the passages in the book of Proverbs that talk about generosity really reveal is that selfishness short-circuits human happiness and that the route to joy is liberality – liberality with our talents, our treasure, and our time.

Today's text is, of course, difficult for some to accept because it violates all the rules of mathematics. How can it be that the more you give away the more you have, and the less you give the poorer you become? It doesn't seem logical! Well, let Lord Bertrand Russell, one of the greatest mathematicians of the twentieth century, comment on that: 'Mathematics and logic have nothing to do with reality.' David Rivett, an accountant and former Director of Waverley Abbey, said that in working with the ministry he has found that God has a quite different arithmetic from that to which he, as an accountant, is accustomed. For example – what do five and two make? Seven? Yes, in man's arithmetic, but not in God's. In God's arithmetic five and two make five – thousand. How come, I hear you say? Well, five loaves and two fish – the little lunch which a boy once gave to Jesus – were taken by Him and turned into enough food to feed five thousand (see John 6:1–13). And just to add to the point – twelve baskets of leftovers were gathered up by the disciples after everyone had eaten their fill!

Nature, we are told, abhors a vacuum; it is the same in the spiritual realm. Liberality and generosity create a vacuum into which God flows, enabling us to give and to go on giving. I cannot explain it, but I have witnessed it countless times. Over the decades I have seen it happen again and again and again.

O God, You who are always reaching out to me in generosity and love, help me this day to do the same. Grant that I may quicken and awaken some life by the generosity that comes from my life. For Your own dear name's sake. Amen.

FURTHER STUDY

1 Kgs 17:7–16; Eccl. 5:13

1. What was the result of the widow feeding Elijah?
2. Why might wealth harm us?

Giving With a Warm Hand

FOR READING & MEDITATION – PROVERBS 22:1–9

'A generous man will himself be blessed...' (v9)

Today we ask the question: Does being a generous person mean you will always have plenty of money or material goods to give away? Not necessarily. This would be a naïve interpretation of the principle we are discussing. No text should be taken in isolation. Verses of Scripture must be put into context if we are to get a more complete picture of the truth under discussion. Some Christians cannot be trusted with large amounts of money or lots of earthly goods; they just would not know how to manage them.

That said, we should note that you do not have to be rich in order to be generous. A pauper can give like a prince, providing he or she has the right spirit. An old Jewish saying puts it like this: 'The man who gives with a smile gives more than the man who gives with a frown.' It is the *spirit* of generosity that the Bible focuses on first of all – the spirit that gives, not because it wants to get something in return, but because it simply delights to give. One person has defined generosity as 'giving with a warm hand'. I like that. Who likes to receive anything from a cold hand?

As you know, the opposite of generosity is selfishness, and just as generosity is a facet of wisdom, so selfishness is a facet of foolishness. A teacher once said to a class, 'Unselfishness means voluntarily going without something you need. Can anyone give me an example?' A little boy raised his hand and said, 'Yes, sometimes I go without a bath even though I need one.' We smile, but how many of us do something very similar by turning a truth on its head to take the pressure off ourselves?

'The love of liberty,' said William Hazlitt, 'is the love of others. The love of power is the love of ourselves.'

O God, help me to be a person who gives 'with a warm hand'. Melt any coldness and iciness there may be in my spirit and please make me a magnanimous and generous person. Fire me with a passion to give. In Jesus' name I ask it. Amen.

FURTHER STUDY
Luke 18:18–25; 21:1–4
1. Why may religious people lack real faith?
2. Contrast the ruler and the widow.

The Generous Eye

FOR READING & MEDITATION – PROVERBS 28:18–28

'He who gives to the poor will lack nothing...' (v27)

We continue meditating on the subject of generosity. Not only the book of Proverbs but the whole Bible has a great deal to say on this subject. Jesus made a powerful statement, recorded in Matthew 6:22, which in the Moffatt translation reads: 'If your Eye is generous, the whole of your body will be illumined.' 'If your Eye...' These words indicate that if your whole outlook on life, your whole way of looking at things, is generous then your whole personality is filled with light.

Jesus was generous towards all – the poor, the outcasts of society, the sinful, the unlovely – and His whole personality was full of light. When we are in touch with Jesus, the fount of all wisdom, then He generates that same generosity within us. We begin to see everyone and everything with the same generous eye.

It is generosity that is at the heart of all good relationships. On occasions I have had the privilege of visiting Sweden and Norway, and I used to wonder why it is that the Swedes and the Norwegians have such a brotherly attitude towards each other. They seem to have an unbreakable bond that ties them as one people. Then I discovered that in 1905, when Norway wanted to break free from Swedish control, the Swedish people responded by recognising Norwegian independence. The Swedes responded according to the Christian ethos of the ruling family who were in power at that time, and King Oscar II renounced his claim to the Norwegian throne. This generosity in giving freedom without war or bitterness created a basic soundness that now flavours all their contacts with one another.

The generous eye fills the whole body of relationships with light. Generosity, like love, never fails.

Lord Jesus, Your generous eye saw in me things I could never see in myself. Help me this day to make generosity the basis of all my dealings with everyone. May Your generosity generate generosity in me. In Jesus' name I pray. Amen.

FURTHER STUDY

1 Sam. 25:1–42

1. Contrast the attitudes of Nabal and Abigail.
2. Contrast the consequences of their attitudes.

Suppose... Just Suppose...

FOR READING & MEDITATION – PROVERBS 3:19–35

'Do not say to your neighbour, "Come back later; I'll give it tomorrow" – when you now have it with you.' (v28)

Throughout the Bible we find the truth that the generous generate generosity in others. When Ananias, a potential victim of Saul's spite and rage, put his hands on the blinded zealot and generously said, 'Brother Saul' (Acts 9:17), that generosity, I believe, touched something deep within the newly converted disciple. It helped to start the greatest Christian missionary of the centuries on his way.

Suppose, just suppose, the little boy who gave his loaves and fishes to Jesus (John 6:9) had said to himself, 'This meal is mine and I won't share it with anyone.' If he had done that he would not have witnessed one of the most amazing miracles of all time. And suppose, also, that the disciples, instead of serving the multiplied bread and fishes to the crowd, had decided to pile it high in one place and make a charge for it in order to boost their funds. What do you think would have happened? I doubt if we would ever have heard of them again. They would have sunk into obscurity. And again, suppose the man who owned the colt on which Jesus rode into Jerusalem (Matt. 21:1–3) had said, 'This colt is mine and I will not let it go to anyone else.' What would have happened? For the rest of his days he would have had an inner debate over whether or not he was justified in keeping it for himself.

I have no doubt that today, and certainly in the immediate future, we will come across opportunities to be generous. If we fail to respond to these opportunities, who knows what rivers will never flow, what great ministries will never be initiated, what mighty things will not get done? God has opened His doors and been generous to us; let us not fail to open up our doors and be generous to others.

O Father, may I be the channel and not the stopping place of all Your generosity to me. When I see how generosity has opened up such power in the life of others, I fear that I may fail. Help me, dear Father. In Jesus' name. Amen.

FURTHER STUDY

Luke 10:25–37; Jas 2:15–17

1. What instruction did Jesus give to the lawyer?
2. What did James explain?

A Framework for Generosity

FOR READING & MEDITATION – PROVERBS 11:1–10

'The Lord abhors dishonest scales, but accurate weights
are his delight.' (v1)

As we have seen over the past few days, generosity is an important life principle, so now we ask ourselves: How do we go about establishing a framework for generosity? Here are my suggestions.

First, decide that nothing you possess is your own but that everything you have belongs to God. This puts God in His place and you in yours. You are now ready to manage His possessions, not as you like but as He likes. This is real freedom. It gives you a sense of accountability to Another – God. You get your life orders not from a whim, a notion, self-impulse or whatever takes your fancy, but from the One who saved you and redeemed you.

Second, go over your life and see what can be classed as your needs and what merely constitutes your wants. Your needs are important, and God has promised to supply them (Phil. 4:19), but what about your wants? Ah, that's another matter. You need as much as will make you fit – spiritually, physically and mentally – for the purposes of God while you are here on the earth. Beyond that, what you have belongs to the needs of others. How do you decide what can be classed as your needs? No one can decide this question for you – though they can make suggestions – for you are accountable to God. Go over your life item by item and ask Him for directions. Your family should figure prominently in your concerns, but you must check everything with the Lord.

Third, fix it as an axiom in your mind that you will be generous to people, not for the good feelings that generosity brings, but because you are determined to bless them in some way. We should never be generous in order to get a blessing; we should be generous in order to be a blessing.

Father, I am thankful that my life is fixed in You and from that foundation I am able to build a framework for generosity. From now on please help me to give freely and willingly. In Jesus' name I pray. Amen.

FURTHER STUDY

1 Chr. 29:1–18

1. What did David acknowledge?
2. How did the people give to God's work?

FOR READING & MEDITATION – PROVERBS 14:27–35

'Whoever is kind to the needy honours God.' (v31)

We spend one more day looking at how to build a framework for generosity. My fourth suggestion is this: give at least a tenth of your earnings to God's work. The giving of a tithe is seen by many as legalistic, but the tithe is really an acknowledgement that all that we have, including the remaining nine-tenths, belongs to God. The Hebrews waved the firstfruits of the harvest before the Lord as an acknowledgement that the coming harvest belonged to Him (Lev. 23:9–11). Some will be able to give far more than a tenth of their income, but the tithe is a good place to begin.

Fifth, make your will under God's direction and maintain a balance between responsibility for your family and the continuing work of God. Make sure your relatives don't waste what God has given you to invest in His kingdom. You might need help and advice here from a mature Christian.

Sixth, remember that the principle of generosity applies not only to your treasure but also to your talents and your time. Each day ask God to show you ways of using your talents and time for Him. I have referred before to John Wesley's advice but I believe it is worth repeating: 'Make all you can; save all you can; give all you can.'

Seventh, accept the smallest opportunity to be generous as a training ground for faithfulness. 'You have been faithful with a few things; I will put you in charge of many things' (Matt. 25:21). Don't wait for the big opportunities to be generous, but start with the next opportunity that comes your way – no matter how small it may be. Get ready for the larger opportunities by doing the small ones well.

Why does the Bible make so much of generosity? Because the truly generous are the truly wise.

Father, just like Simon Peter, who gave Your Son his boat from which to preach, I give You my treasure, my talents, and my time for You to use as Your pulpit – today and every day. In Christ's name. Amen.

FURTHER STUDY

Acts 4:32–37; 11:27–30; 1 Cor. 16:1–2
1. What was the practice of the Early Church?
2. Is emergency relief a government or personal responsibility?

A Disturbing of Complacency

FOR READING & MEDITATION – PROVERBS 13:1–10

'The sluggard craves and gets nothing, but the
desires of the diligent are fully satisfied.' (v4)

Today we come to what I believe is the fifth of the seven pillars of wisdom – *diligence*. The wise are those who persevere, who persist in following that which is right, who stick with it and never give up. One of the great needs of our day, in my opinion, is for diligence to become an essential part of life again – particularly, some might say, among the young. A Christian educator writes, 'Diligence in the young is something that is built into them not by precept but by example. In today's world there are not enough examples of diligence to inspire or guide.' Some may consider this an exaggeration, but I think I myself would have to say that diligence seems no longer to be esteemed in the way it once was.

Prior to my conversion, I was greatly lacking in diligence, not from lack of encouragement or example, I hasten to add, but simply because I chose not to apply myself to anything. Then in my teens Jesus Christ came into my life, and by His coming disturbed my complacency and challenged me to apply myself to the things that needed to be done. The result? I covered more ground in the first year following my conversion than I did in the previous two or three years. A year or so after my conversion an uncle of mine said to my father, 'I wondered whether he had been really converted, but by his diligence I can see he has found God.'

Forgive the continued personal emphasis, but if it had not been for the diligence I learned at the feet of Christ I would not have been able to write *Every Day with Jesus* for over forty years. I learned diligence from the One whose life and character were the very epitome of this quality – Jesus. He is diligence personified.

Gracious and loving Father, I also long for this facet of wisdom – the quality of diligence. Prune from me all inertia and indolence, all lethargy and dodging of responsibility, all complacency and pride. In Jesus' name I ask it. Amen.

FURTHER STUDY

Matt. 16:21–23; Luke 9:51–56; John 17:1–4; 19:30
1. How did Jesus respond to obstacles?
2. What could Jesus say?

A Second Wind

FOR READING & MEDITATION – PROVERBS 10:1–8

'Lazy hands make a man poor, but diligent hands bring wealth.' (v4)

Yesterday we ended with the statement 'Jesus is diligence personified'. Here is an example of what I mean. One day the disciples said to Jesus, '"A short while ago the Jews tried to stone you, and yet you are going back there?" Jesus answered, "Are there not twelve hours of daylight?"' (John 11:8–9). What was Jesus saying in this rather puzzling statement? He was saying that it is not a question of what will or will not happen. There are twelve hours in the day – enough time for what must be done – and He must get on and complete His task. What a sense of inward drive is conveyed by these words. The purpose for which He had come into the world was inwardly pressing Him forward, despite the threats and obstacles that came His way, and He would pursue the task right to the end.

It is possible, of course, to be a person of diligence without knowing Jesus Christ, but those who know Him have an added passion which motivates them and drives them forward to the completion of a task. Yesterday I said that when Christ came into my life He disturbed my complacency. Someone else sums up his experience like this: 'When Jesus came into my life He became the conscience of my conscience.' A middle-aged lady I knew who found the Lord said, 'Christ gave me a second wind in the race of life.'

I wonder, as you read these notes, are you on the point of giving up a task in which you know you are rightly engaged? Have lethargy, inertia, and indifference crept in and threatened to take over your soul? Reach up and put your hand in the hand of Jesus. Talk with Him now and draw from Him the strength you need. Then in His name go out and throw yourself once again into the task.

Loving Father, I am thankful for all the benefits of 'common grace' but I am even more thankful for the special grace that is mine through Christ Jesus. Help me to be diligent and use that special grace to Your praise and glory. Amen.

FURTHER STUDY
2 Thess. 3:6–13; 2 Tim. 4:6–8
1. What was Paul's rule?
2. What could Paul say?

FOR READING & MEDITATION – PROVERBS 4:10–27

'Above all else, guard your heart, for it is the wellspring of life.' (v23)

Today we pause to make clear the difference between diligence and obstinacy. Some people known to me have experienced spiritual shipwreck because they didn't discern the difference between these two characteristics. They thought they were being diligent when actually they were being obstinate. When asked to clarify the difference between perseverance and obstinacy, a student wrote, 'One is a strong will and the other is a strong won't.' Diligence is dogged perseverance; obstinacy is dogged inflexibility and self-will.

A certain man whose life was full of promise as far as the Christian ministry was concerned now spends his days in sadness and regret because he did not know the difference between diligence and obstinacy. He embarked on a project that he thought was God's will for him, and when things started to go wrong, instead of checking his guidance, he continued to press on and ended up in failure. He did not listen to his family, friends, and those who loved him, refusing to change course, and carried on regardless. Having set himself to complete a particular task, he did not have the wisdom to realise that what he was doing was not being diligent but obstinate. The result is that he lives in perpetual disillusionment.

When Jesus came to Calvary, He said, 'I have finished the work which You [the Father] have given Me to do' (John 17:4, NKJV). Notice the word 'You'. There were many who would have liked Jesus to do this and that, to go here and go there, but He did only what the Father required Him to do. Saying 'yes' to God's will and pursuing it is diligence. Saying 'yes' to a thing that is not God's will and pursuing that is obstinacy. We had better learn the difference.

Father, help me differentiate between diligence and obstinacy so that at the end of my time here on earth I, too, will be able to say, 'I have finished the work which You have given me to do.' Amen.

FURTHER STUDY

Prov. 23:26; Jas 1:1–8

1. How can we guard our hearts?
2. How can we know God's will?

The Secret of Survival

FOR READING & MEDITATION – PROVERBS 12:11–28

'Diligent hands will rule, but laziness ends in slave labour.' (v24)

A couple of days ago I said that many non-Christians advocate the value of diligence. It goes back to the subject of 'common grace' that I talked about at the beginning of these meditations. There are many people who, even though they are not Christians, catch sight of the fact that the universe is made for wisdom and that to live effectively on this earth we have to search for wisdom and cultivate it. Through rational thought and intuition these people come to the conclusion that without diligence life is more like a cage than a challenge.

Victor Frankl was one such person. Frankl, a Jew, was an Austrian neurologist and psychiatrist as well as a survivor of the Holocaust and the horror of the concentration camps. He was the founder of logotherapy and existential analysis. Sadly his father died in the Theresienstadt ghetto; his mother, brother, and wife all died in Auschwitz. Throughout his years in a concentration camp he gave himself to the task of finding out why it was that despite tremendous odds some survived while others gave up the will to live. He discovered that the reason why some people gave up was because they had no sense of meaning. Those who had a meaning or purpose to live for, such as the hope of seeing a loved one again, found it easier to keep going despite the greatest odds, while those who had no meaning or purpose simply gave up.

Frankl discovered by empirical means what another Jew discovered by revelation – that in order to persist, we need hope. That other Jew was the apostle Paul, and he showed greater understanding than Frankl when he said, 'Christ in you, the hope of glory' (Col. 1:27). Christ *with* us is one thing; Christ *in* us – now that's another.

O Father, how can I sufficiently thank You for the joy of having Christ within? His presence within gives me a hope that provides meaning in the deepest and darkest moments of my life. For this, Lord, I am eternally grateful. Amen.

FURTHER STUDY

1 Cor. 9:7–10; Heb. 6:10–20
1. Why do people work?
2. What is an anchor for our souls?

So Wise – Yet So Foolish!

FOR READING & MEDITATION – PROVERBS 2:1–11

'Applying your heart to understanding... then you will...
find the knowledge of God.' (vv2,5)

We pick up from where we left off yesterday when we said that in order to persist we need hope. We made the point, you remember, that having Christ *with* us is one thing; having Him *in* us is another.

Permit me to continue to explore a little more of Victor Frankl's thinking. Although he became a well-known and highly respected psychiatrist, Frankl seemed unable to accept the divine perspective. Listen to this: 'The reason so many people are unhappy is because they fail to understand what human existence is all about. Until we recognise that life is not just something to be enjoyed but rather is a task that each of us is assigned, we will never find meaning in our lives and we will never be truly happy.' So near yet so far! So wise yet so foolish! He understood that without meaning life is drab and difficult, but he failed to go on to the next step and say that true meaning can be found only in Christ. He was both a delight and a disappointment – a delight because he said, 'Life is a task', but a disappointment because he failed to recognise that we need Christ to help us perform that task.

Yes, in many ways life is a task – a tough one that is sometimes well-nigh unbearable. That's why we need to have Jesus at the centre of our lives. We then pursue the divine task with the help of divine grace. Both the writer of Proverbs and Victor Frankl said that life works better when we give ourselves to it with diligence, but there is much more to it than this. Why do you think God inspired the writer of Proverbs to personify wisdom? Because, as we saw, it prepares us to face the fact that true wisdom is not merely found in principles but in a Person. And that Person is Jesus Christ.

O Father, how sad when the wise of this world show themselves to be so foolish. They get so close – yet fall at the crucial moment. Thank You, Father, that through Jesus I dwell in wisdom and am indwelt by it. Amen.

FURTHER STUDY
Ps. 18:25–32; Phil. 4:10–13
1. What could David proclaim?
2. Why was Paul undaunted?

What's the Point?

FOR READING & MEDITATION – PROVERBS 21:1–15

'The plans of the diligent lead to profit as surely as haste
leads to poverty.' (v5)

Today we ask ourselves: What is the point of diligence? Why keep persevering with a task? I'll tell you why. It is because it is in the arena of perseverance that true character is forged, shaped, tempered, and polished. It is in the daily grind – in the hard and often tedious duties of life – that the character of Jesus is given the maximum opportunity to be reproduced in us, replacing what Charles Swindoll calls that 'thin, fragile internal theology with a tough, reliable set of convictions that enable us to handle life rather than escape from it'.

Listen to what the apostle Paul says about this in Romans 5:3–4: 'We also rejoice in our sufferings, [why?] because we know that suffering produces perseverance; perseverance, character; and character, hope.' Because life is a task, we need strength to face it, not speed to escape from it. When the foundations shake beneath our feet, when Christian friends or even leaders allow themselves to fall into immorality, when the anchor points of civilisation disappear, when the bottom of our world seems to drop out and brutal blows push us up against the ropes and pound the very life out of us, we need what diligence and perseverance offer us – willingness to face whatever comes, determination to stand firm, knowing that Jesus is not just with us but in us, insight to see Christ's hand in everything, and character enough to continue.

Without diligence, we will stumble and fall. With it, we can survive and overcome. The astute of this world are wise enough to recognise that no advances can be made in life without diligence. How much more ought we, who name the name of Christ and have Him living within us, recognise this also?

O God, help me see that out of the raw materials of human living I must fashion the important quality of diligence. Help me never to forget that the rewards are far greater than the cost. In Jesus' name. Amen.

FURTHER STUDY

2 Cor. 11:23–33; Jas 1:12

1. What difficulties did Paul overcome?
2. What is the reward of those who persevere?

The Four Spiritual Flaws

FOR READING & MEDITATION – PROVERBS 20:1–13

'A sluggard does not plough in season; so at harvest
time he looks but finds nothing.' (v4)

Yesterday we saw that diligently ploughing through life's tasks and problems produces in the end something exceedingly precious – character. Have you ever heard about the 'Four Spiritual Laws'? They have been used greatly by many evangelists, but today I would like to talk instead about the 'Four Spiritual Flaws'. These are four common misconceptions concerning the tough questions and difficult tasks of the Christian life, and unless they are nailed, diligence will have no meaning.

Flaw No. 1: Once you become a Christian, you will never have any more problems. It's not true. In fact, quite the opposite may happen – your problems may increase. What is true, however, is that Christ will be there to share our problems and get us through them.

Flaw No. 2: If you are having problems then you must be lacking in some way spiritually. A number of problems can arise because of this, but certainly not all. Some of the most godly people I know have wrestled with gigantic problems. If you have any doubt about this, read the story of Job.

Flaw No. 3: Never admit to anything being a problem; if you do, negativism will take over your life. This is complete nonsense. If you don't face a matter fairly and squarely then you will live in denial, which is, by the way, the opposite of integrity.

Flaw No. 4: All problems can be resolved by the application of the right verses of Scripture. Again, this is not so. After many years I still have unanswered questions concerning God's dealings with me, and know I might have to wait until I arrive in eternity to see things clearly. Here on earth we are big enough to ask questions but not big enough to understand the answers. Diligence must keep us going.

Father, I would be rid of all flawed thinking. Show me that I am not called to understand, but to stand. Give me grace to keep going even in the face of every one of life's unanswered questions. In Jesus' name I pray. Amen.

FURTHER STUDY

Prov. 26:12–16; 1 Cor. 13:12

1. What is the difference between an excuse and an evasion?
2. What did Paul explain?

Diligence Does Pay Off

15
AUG

Diligence Does Pay Off

FOR READING & MEDITATION – PROVERBS 24:23–34

'Thorns had come up everywhere, the ground was covered
with weeds...' (v31)

For one more day we think about the subject of diligence. What are diligence and perseverance all about? They involve sticking to a task you know God wants you to do until it is completed, irrespective of the difficulties and frustrations.

Diligence does pay off. Have you heard the story of the two frogs who fell into a bucket of cream? They tried very hard to get out by climbing up the side of the bucket, but each time they slipped back again. Finally, one said, 'We'll never get out of here,' so he gave up, stopped kicking and drowned. The other frog persevered and kicked and kicked and kicked. Suddenly, he felt something hard beneath his feet and discovered that his kicking had turned the cream into butter. He hopped on top of it and was able to leap out to safety.

Someone has described diligence as 'an archaic word'. Even though it may appear diligence does not play a big part in today's world, it certainly plays a big part in the kingdom of God. Those who have done great exploits for God have been men and women of persistence and perseverance. One of the greatest examples of diligence in the Bible is the life of the apostle Paul. The verses that best illustrate this are these: 'We are hard pressed on every side, but not crushed; perplexed, but not in despair; persecuted, but not abandoned; struck down, but not destroyed' (2 Cor. 4:8–9). Paul kept going when others would have given up.

I love the story of Sir Winston Churchill who, during his last years, and though failing and feeble, stood up to address a group of university students and said, 'I have just one thing to say to you: Never give up. Never, never give up. Never, never, never give up.' He sat down to a standing ovation.

Father, I see that life can be made or broken at the place of continuance. Give me, I pray, this aspect of wisdom so that, like a postage stamp, I will stick to one thing until I get there. In Jesus' name I ask it. Amen.

FURTHER STUDY
Matt. 15:21–28; Luke 11:5–10; 18:1–8
1. What preceded the daughter's healing?
2. What did Jesus teach about prayer?

The Weight Of Words

FOR READING & MEDITATION – PROVERBS 10:9–17

'The mouth of the righteous is a fountain of life, but
violence overwhelms the mouth of the wicked.' (v11)

We look now at the sixth pillar of wisdom – *watchfulness with words*. Anyone who fails to understand the importance of words and the effect they can have for good or bad is not a wise person. The book of Proverbs has a great deal to say about the power of words, and this is without doubt one of its major themes. Today's text implies that there is a transfer of wisdom from one person to another when wise words are used, but that unwise words have the opposite effect.

Whenever I have been involved in preparation for marriage or marriage counselling, I have talked to couples about the weight of their words. I have given them examples of the emotional scars that can be left by bitter words. How many adults, for example, still struggle from bitter words spoken to them when they were children – words such as 'I wish you had never been born!'? Many a man and woman has told me that a statement such as 'I'm sorry I ever married you', carries as much force as a physical blow. Words have the potential to destroy or build up, to hurt or heal, to bless or blister, to bring comfort or consternation.

Some Eastern religions teach that ultimate reality is silence. Lao-tse, the famous Chinese philosopher, said, 'The word that can be uttered is not the divine word; that word is Silence.' I believe that ultimate reality is relationship – relationship with a God who speaks. God broke the silence of eternity with the words 'Let there be light' (Gen. 1:3). Lao-tse had to say that ultimate reality was silence for he knew nothing of a God who speaks. With words, God created a world. We do the same. Our words create a world of order or disorder, of cosmos or chaos. Be wise – watch your words.

Father, I see that when You spoke, You created a world, and that when I speak, I do the same. Give me the wisdom to use words in a way that will build up and not pull down, construct and not destruct. This I ask in Jesus' name. Amen.

FURTHER STUDY

Gen. 1:26–31; 1 Sam. 4:12–22
1. How did God affirm and inspire Adam and Eve?
2. Why may Ichabod have disliked his name?

Words That Scar

FOR READING & MEDITATION – PROVERBS 12:11–28

'Reckless words pierce like a sword, but the
tongue of the wise brings healing.' (v18)

Have you ever said or sung these words in the school playground when you were a child: 'Sticks and stones may break my bones, but words will never hurt me'? It's not true. Words do hurt and produce emotional scars that can stay with us for life. I remember counselling a woman who could not break free from the bondage of a name her father gave her when she was a child: 'The devil's daughter'. She was freed from it eventually, but not without hours of deep counselling and intense struggle.

Unkind or cutting words are like deadly missiles that penetrate all the soul's defences and blast a hole in the personality, creating damage that may take years to repair. On the other hand, words that are encouraging can lift and cheer the soul in a way that is quite amazing. C.E. Macartney tells how, passing through the corridor of a hospital one day, he saw sitting on a bench a minister whom he had known. The man was well advanced in years and broken in health. As a result of his condition he had given up his church responsibilities, and was unable to participate in any kind of pulpit ministry. Macartney says, 'I turned to speak to him, expecting to hear from him some word of melancholy reminiscence or present gloom, but I received a pleasant surprise. He told me that a woman going by had just spoken with him and told him that a message he had given many years ago had been the means of bringing her to Christ. The glow on his face was something I shall never forget.'

How wonderful it will be if today you and I can say a cheerful and encouraging word to someone that will bless them, lighten their darkness, and minister the life of God into their soul. At least let's try!

O Father, may I not be like the person who looked into a mirror and then went away, forgetting what he looked like. Having looked into the mirror of Your Word I see what I should be. Please help me to be that person. In Jesus' name. Amen.

FURTHER STUDY
Ps. 64:1–4; Jas 3:1–13
1. What did the psalmist ask of God?
2. What does James explain about the power of words?

Driven Personalities

AUG **18**

FOR READING & MEDITATION – PROVERBS 18:1–24

'The tongue has the power of life and death...' (v21)

Today we continue meditating on the awesome power of words. It is important not to think that your words will be overlooked or easily erased. Even to this day I can remember the words of a teacher who made me stand up in a crowded classroom and said something that pierced my heart, leaving a deep scar. The hurt has gone now and forgiveness has dealt with the residual effects, but the memory burned within me for years. Any counsellor will tell you that the words spoken to a child in the early years have shaped and moulded that child's life either for good or for bad.

A minister tells of talking to a 42-year-old man who was frantically working himself into a state of exhaustion – 'a volatile human being whose temper exploded at the slightest hint of disagreement or criticism'. He found that during his childhood this man's father repeatedly told him, 'You are not going to amount to anything.' Every time his father lost his temper he would repeat this statement to the boy. Thirty years later the man still bore the pain of his father's verbal malpractice and was *driven* to prove his father wrong. This is an example of what people mean when they refer to those who are *driven*. This man was *driven* by the lash of bitter and cruel words spoken to him years earlier.

Take, on the other hand, this example of another man to whom I talked some time ago. He told me that his father used to hug him every day and say, 'You are so special to me. There is no one in this world who could take your place.' That man grew up full of life and with a personality characterised by optimism. Proverbs is right: death words destroy, life words build up and give increasing strength.

Father, I would be a builder and not a destroyer of human personalities. Forgive me for the many foolish and unwise words I have spoken. From this day forward help me keep a check on my speech and use words as You would use them. Amen.

FURTHER STUDY
Josh. 1:1–9; Job 4:4
1. What did God urge Joshua to do and what would be the result?
2. Why was Job commended?

FOR READING & MEDITATION – PROVERBS 15:1–15

'The tongue that brings healing is a tree of life...' (v4)

We have been emphasising how devastating it can be to receive cruel and unkind words, and how long-lasting their effect can be. Today we focus on the healing power of kind and encouraging words. When Sigmund Freud found that symptoms of emotional distress could be relieved simply by talking in certain ways to his patients, he was deeply interested and intrigued. His training in what is known as 'the medical model' had conditioned him to think of people as merely biological and chemical entities whose problems arose from physical malfunctioning.

If Freud had spent some time reading the book of Proverbs he might have been less surprised to discover that words have such a powerful impact. Most effective psychotherapy has to do with letting people talk. When people put their feelings into words it seems as if the pent-up emotion flows out through the words. I once heard of a special phone line you can ring where, after you have given your credit card number, a person will spend three minutes giving you some encouraging and heartening words. The service, I understand, is now a growing industry.

As I was preparing this page I thought hard and tried to recall the most influential and healing words anyone has ever spoken to me. While I was thinking I remembered a friend coming up to me at my wife's funeral and saying, 'You will be in my thoughts every hour of the day.' How different from the sincere and well-meaning person who said to me at the same event, 'Be brave.'

We can't change the things we said yesterday, but think of the possibilities ahead of us today and tomorrow. Don't wait another day – start now. Thank God that life, as well as death, lies in the power of the tongue.

Father, help me minister life through my tongue this very day. Give me opportunities to put into action what I have heard, and help me recognise those opportunities. I would be all You want me to be. In Jesus' name I ask it. Amen.

FURTHER STUDY

Gen. 21:14–21; Mark 5:35–43; John 11:43–44

1. Why did Hagar stop crying?
2. How did Jesus bring faith and healing?

The Most Powerful Word

FOR READING & MEDITATION – PROVERBS 25:11–28

'As a north wind brings rain, so a sly tongue brings
angry looks.' (v23)

It's astonishing the effect that words can have upon you. This is why the writer of Proverbs returns so frequently to the matter of words and the way they ought to be used. I shall never forget sitting in a London airport one day in 1968 waiting for a flight to the USA and, to my horror, hearing an announcer say, 'The flight to New York is ready for its final departure'!

Here's a teaser I would like to drop in that highlights the way words can be used. Professor Ernest Brennick of Columbia University, USA, is credited with inventing the following sentence, which can be made to have eight different meanings by placing the word 'only' in all possible positions in it: 'I hit him in the eye yesterday.' Please don't write requesting all the permutations; work them out for yourself. Someone has compiled a list of the most powerful words in the English language: 'The bitterest word – alone. The most revered word – mother. The most feared word – death. The coldest word – no. The warmest word – friend.'

What, I wonder, is the most powerful word you have ever come across? I will tell you mine – Jesus. Charles Colson, one of President Nixon's right-hand men who, after the Watergate affair, was wonderfully converted to Christ, tells of visiting a man on death row. The man had been in a foetal position for months and would speak to no one. Charles told him the gospel and asked him to say the name Jesus. A week later he returned to find the man sitting in his chair, shaven, and the cell swept clean. When he asked what had happened, the man said, 'Jesus lives here now.' He went to the electric chair but his last words to the executioner were these: 'I'm going to be with the Lord.'

O Father, when I utter the name Jesus, something profound happens within me. It is like an oratorio in two syllables, a library compressed into a single word. May I learn and appropriate all the power that lies behind that name. Amen.

FURTHER STUDY
John 16:23–24; Acts 4:12; Phil. 2:5–11
1. Why is Jesus' name special?
2. How can we use His name?

A Disciplined Tongue

FOR READING & MEDITATION – PROVERBS 10:18–32

'He who holds his tongue is wise.' (v19)

I'm glad God included in the book of Proverbs the words found in our text for today, as it is so easy to think that all we have to do is talk, talk, talk. It's important to talk, but talking too much is as bad as not talking at all. Sometimes a well-chosen sentence has more power than a whole paragraph. Proverbs extols rationing our words.

Once, when Thomas Edison, the inventor, was at a reception, the toastmaster stood up and complimented him on his many inventions, especially the talking machine. After the toastmaster sat down, the aged inventor rose to his feet and said, 'Thank you for those remarks, but I must correct one thing. It was God who invented the talking machine. I only invented the first one that can be shut off.'

A doctor told me that once, while writing out a prescription, he asked a woman to put out her tongue. When he had finished she said to him, 'But, doctor, you never even looked at my tongue.' The doctor replied, 'It wasn't necessary, I just wanted you to keep quiet while I wrote the prescription.' Amidst the humour of today's notes, don't miss the point: words are important but don't overdo them.

I like the advice of an anonymous poet who wrote:

If your lips would keep from slips
Five things observe with care:
Of whom you speak, to whom you speak,
And how and when and where.

A wise person is someone who has a disciplined tongue. Many need to learn this for, just like the tongue in old lace-up shoes, our tongue is often the last thing to be worn out. If that is true of you, ask God to help you, for an undisciplined tongue is an unloving tongue.

Father, I realise that often my tongue is the most difficult thing to bring under control. Yet I have the promise of Your help even in this. I give you my tongue to be bridled – please take over the reins. In Jesus' name I pray. Amen.

FURTHER STUDY
Prov. 17:27–28; Jas 1:19–21
1. What is the advantage of not talking?
2. What is the difference between speaking and listening?

We Become What We Say

FOR READING & MEDITATION – PROVERBS 21:16–31

'He who guards his mouth and his tongue keeps
himself from calamity.' (v23)

At present we are thinking about the need for a disciplined tongue. Why is this self-discipline so important? It is because the expression of a thing deepens the impression. A word uttered becomes a word made flesh – in us. We become the incarnation of what we express. When speaking to the Pharisees Jesus warned, 'By your words you will be acquitted, and by your words you will be condemned' (Matt. 12:37). After I saw that a person becomes what he says, I looked at this verse in a different light. If you tell a lie, you become a lie. Earlier, when dealing more fully with the subject of integrity, I said that the greatest punishment for telling a lie is to be the one who utters that lie. That person has to live with someone he cannot trust.

Now look at what I am saying from the opposite perspective. When we express good things, positive things, loving things, scriptural things, these things go deeper into us. How many times, when expressing something to someone, have you said to yourself, 'Because I expressed it so clearly I understand it more clearly myself.' And why? Because clear expression deepens impression. A brilliant young physicist says that he often discusses complex issues relating to physics with his wife, who doesn't know the first thing about the subject. He told a friend, 'I describe in detail what I am doing and she doesn't understand a word. But sometimes when I'm through – *I do.*'

If it is true – and I believe it is – that we become the incarnation of what we express, then how careful we ought to be to ensure that what we say is guarded and governed by truth, integrity, and kindness. Always remember: every word you utter becomes flesh – in you.

O Father, how awesome is the thought that I become the incarnation of what I express. Cleanse me deep within so that I may be pure in soul as well as speech, and honour You in all I do. Grant it please, dear Father. In Jesus' name. Amen.

FURTHER STUDY
Jer. 1:4–19; Phil. 4:8
1. Why did God rebuke Jeremiah and how did He encourage Him?
2. What should be the content of our 'self-talk' thoughts?

The Cause of Most Friction

FOR READING & MEDITATION – PROVERBS 16:21–33

'Pleasant words are a honeycomb, sweet to the soul and
healing to the bones.' (v24)

Now that we have seen something of the power and importance of words, there is just one more thing I would like to add: be careful to watch your tone of voice. An old Chinese proverb says this: 'If you have a soft voice, you don't need a big stick.' I am convinced that most of the friction in human relationships is caused not so much by the words we speak as by the tone of voice in which we speak them. What we say is important, of course, but how we say it is also important. Our speech conveys our thoughts; our tone of voice, however, conveys our mood. How easy it is to say, 'I love you', in a tone that conveys the very opposite.

Proverbs does not actually say we should focus on the right tone of voice but the implication is clearly there in the command to use words that are kind and gentle and tender. Of course, you can say things in the right tone of voice without any real feelings of kindness at all. That is why the Bible urges us to do more than seek a change in behaviour, but a change that goes right down to the core of our being. Change must always come from the inside out otherwise it will not be real change. 'Take once again the infection-free scalpel of the Spirit – the Word of God – and, if necessary, let it cauterise your tongue. Indeed, let it go deeper – into the 'thoughts and intents of the heart' (Heb. 4:12, NKJV).

What is our conclusion after meditating these past eight days on the subject of words? Is it not this: the wise are those who understand how their words can impact another person, for good or for bad, and commit themselves to using words only as Paul instructs us in Ephesians 4:29 – words that are 'helpful for building others up'.

O God, I ask once more that You will help me to hold my tongue when I should and to speak when I should. My tongue can have sourness or sweetness, but it cannot have both at the same time. Give me the wisdom of a right way with words. Amen.

FURTHER STUDY
Isa. 50:4; Hos. 2:14–23
1. What can the Lord teach us?
2. How would the Lord speak to Israel?

A Single Soul in Two Bodies

FOR READING & MEDITATION – PROVERBS 22:10–16

'He who loves a pure heart and whose speech is
gracious will have the king for his friend.' (v11)

The final pillar of wisdom to occupy our attention is that of *friendship*. The wise are those who know how to make friends and remain loyal to them. The book of Proverbs emphasises the whole area of relationships – love and respect for parents, love for one's spouse, kindness to one's neighbours, and so on – but it pays particular attention to the matter of friendship. Why is friendship such an important theme in Proverbs? What exactly is friendship? And how do we go about the task of developing good friendships? These are some of the questions we must come to grips with over the next few days.

First, what exactly is friendship? Many years ago a Christian magazine offered a prize for the best definition of friendship sent in by its readers. Hundreds of definitions were received and the one that was given first prize was this: 'A friend is the one who comes in when the whole world has gone out.' My own definition of friendship is this: 'Friendship is the knitting of one soul with another so that both become stronger and better by virtue of their relationship.' I like also the definition of an ancient philosopher who said that friendship was 'a single soul dwelling in two bodies'.

The word 'friendship' is usually used in connection with non-sexual relationships between people of the same sex, but of course it can be applied equally to people of opposite sexes. It goes without saying, I think, that romantic relationships, such as courtship and marriage, should demonstrate the qualities of friendship, and it is sad when married couples live together without also being the closest of friends. If married, one's life partner ought also to be one's best friend.

Father, teach me the art of making friends. Help me see at the very beginning that being a friend is more important than having a friend. Save me from getting the wrong perspective on this. In Jesus' name I ask it. Amen.

FURTHER STUDY
Gen. 2:19–25; 1 Cor. 4:15–17; Phil. 2:19–23
1. What did God say about Adam?
2. Describe Paul's relationship with Timothy.

FOR READING & MEDITATION – ECCLESIASTES 4:1–12

'Though one may be overpowered, two can defend themselves.
A cord of three strands is not quickly broken.' (v12)

Today we start to consider the question: Why is friendship so important? The reason I have turned your attention for the moment away from Proverbs and focused it on the book of Ecclesiastes (another book in the library of Wisdom Literature) is because today's reading includes verses that show us better than any other verses in the Bible the reason why friendship is so important. What they are telling us is this: it's good to have a friend because if you fall down a friend can help you up, or, if you are suffering the effects of the cold, a friend can help keep you warm.

It is interesting to note that to begin with the emphasis is on two people – '*two* are better than one', 'if *two* lie down' – but at the end the writer adds something very strange: 'A cord of *three* strands is not quickly broken.' Most commentaries dismiss these words as a literary device for the sake of emphasis. The *NIV Study Bible*, for example, describes it as 'a climactic construction'. But I believe it is much more than that; the words contain a powerful truth which it is to our disadvantage to miss or not understand.

The point being made is this: when you are in a close relationship with another person you not only have what the other person gives to you in the friendship, or you to the other person, but you have a third quality – a strength and a power which comes out of the relationship and which you could never have known had you both stayed apart. In other words, in the fusion of friendship you discover a power that could never be discovered were you not bound together in the relationship of friendship. Your strength plus your friend's strength produces a new and even greater strength.

Father, now I see into the heart and meaning of friendship. Out of it comes a power and a strength that is greater than the sum of the two parts. Teach me more, dear Father. In Jesus' name I ask it. Amen.

FURTHER STUDY
1 Sam. 18:1–4; 19:1–7; 20:30–33,42
1. Define the phrase 'one in spirit'.
2. How did Jonathan prove his friendship with David?

Synergy

FOR READING & MEDITATION – PROVERBS 17:1–17

'A friend loves at all times, and a brother is born for adversity.' (v17)

Today we continue with the point we made yesterday, namely that in friendship we find the creation of a new energy that was never there before. The word that is often used to describe this is 'synergy'. The dictionary defines the word as 'the combined effect of two things that exceeds the sum of their individual effects'. It simply means that the whole is greater than the sum of its two parts.

Synergy is seen everywhere in nature. The roots of plants known as 'legumes' produce nitrogen. So if, for example, you plant beans and sweetcorn together, the beans will climb up the sweetcorn and the sweetcorn will benefit from the nitrogen in the soil. When you put two pieces of wood together in a certain way they hold much more than the total of the weight held by each separately. One plus one equals three or more. Stephen Covey describes synergism in this way: 'The relationship which the parts have to each other is a part in and of itself. It is not only a part, but the most catalytic, the most empowering, the most unifying, and the most exciting part.' This is why, when understood correctly, friendship is so exciting because you don't quite know what exactly is going to happen or where it will lead. Christians, of course, who bring their friendships under the authority of God and His Word need not be concerned about anything that comes, for they have – or should have – an internal security which enables them to deal with anything and everything.

A friendship can be exhilarating, exciting, and at times exhausting. But it can also open up new possibilities, new trails, new adventures, new territories, and new continents. We live deprived lives if we live without friends.

Father, I see that I am made for relationships, not isolation. Help me understand this principle of synergy and how it can work to the extension of Your kingdom. This I ask in Jesus' precious and incomparable name. Amen.

FURTHER STUDY
Lev. 26:8; 2 Tim. 1:13–18
1. When does addition produce multiplication?
2. What was special about Onesiphorus?

A Friend with Skin On

FOR READING & MEDITATION – PROVERBS 27:17–27

'As iron sharpens iron, so one man sharpens another.' (v17)

Sometimes I have heard Christians say, 'Why do I need friends? God is my Friend – isn't that enough?' Such questions demonstrate a lack of understanding of the purpose of human relationships. Yes, God is our Friend – our closest Friend – but, as a little boy once put it, 'We need friends with skin on also.'

'To be,' said someone, 'is to be in relationships.' You won't know who you are until you are in a relationship. Paul Tillich, a well-known writer and theologian, made the same point in these words: 'You don't really know yourself until you are put over against someone other than yourself.' You see, if no one ever gives you an idea of how well or otherwise you come across, never challenges your presuppositions, never confronts you, never encourages you to open up about your problems, then parts of you remain undiscovered. Others, of course, who are not your friends can do this, but it is best done by someone who knows you well.

The other day we looked at some good definitions of friendship, but I have kept my favourite one until now as it fits in beautifully here: 'A friend is someone who knows all there is to know about you and loves you just the same.' Looking back on my life, I can see how valuable my friends have been to me. Because I have felt safe with them I have been able to reveal myself, and in the revealing I have come to know myself in a way that I could never have done with a mere acquaintance.

Yes, God is our Friend, but we need human friends also. This might be difficult for some to accept, but the more effectively we relate on a horizontal level with our human friends, the more effectively we will relate on a vertical level with our heavenly Friend.

Father, I see that my best friend is someone who brings out the best in me. Help me to be a best friend to someone – and to bring out the best in that person. In Jesus' name I ask it. Amen.

FURTHER STUDY
2 Sam. 10:6–13; Gal. 2:11–16
1. What was the agreement between Joab and Abishai?
2. How was Paul a friend to Peter?

Steps to Friendship

FOR READING & MEDITATION – PROVERBS 18:1–24

'A man of many companions may come to ruin, but there
is a friend who sticks closer than a brother.' (v24)

Everyone needs at least a small circle of friends – even those who are
married. I feel deeply sad for anyone who does not have a friend. So
today we ask ourselves: If friendship is so important, how do we go about
making friends?

The first step is *be friendly*. The New King James Version of our text for
today says, 'A man who has friends must himself be friendly.' You should
not, however, become friendly just in order to gain a friend. This is an
unhelpful motive because you are more interested in gaining a friend than
being a friend. Self-centredness will get you nowhere.

Friendliness is the art of going out of yourself and appreciating others
as much as you appreciate yourself. It is really a mind-set, an attitude. Dale
Carnegie, in his book *How to Win Friends and Influence People* – a secular
approach to the subject of friendship but full of good sense nevertheless
– said, 'You can make more friends in two months by becoming interested
in other people than you can in two years by trying to get other people
interested in you.' The main reason why some people have no friends is
because they demonstrate an unfriendly attitude. To have a friend – be
one.

The second step is *allow time for friendships to develop*. In friendship
it is futile to try to force doors open. Instead, be like Christ in the book of
Revelation (Rev. 3:20); stand reverently at the door – and knock. Only if the
door is opened from within should you go through it. Some relationships
you have with people may never develop into close friendships. Don't be
upset about that. If you are open and friendly then God will guide you and
show you where deep friendships are to be developed.

**Father, help me be a friend who does the knocking before I enter instead of
knocking down after I have left. And show me not only how to sympathise
with my friends' weaknesses, but also how to draw out their strength. In
Jesus' name. Amen.**

FURTHER STUDY
John 1:35–39; 15:9–17; Rev. 3:20
1. How did Jesus show friendship?
2. What is the mark of a true friend?

FOR READING & MEDITATION – PROVERBS 27:1–9
'Wounds from a friend can be trusted...' (v6)

We continue looking at the steps we need to take in order to win friends. The third step is *be prepared to be vulnerable*. By this I mean be prepared to be hurt. No relationship is free from pain this side of eternity – so don't expect perfection in your friendships. If your goal in life is to stay safe and comfortable, then don't get involved in developing friendships. Friendships demand that you leave the comfort zone of base camp and confront an entirely new and unknown wilderness. There will be times when your words or actions are misunderstood, but stay with it when this happens. This is what friendship is all about – sticking closer than a brother. It is loving as you yourself are loved.

Fourth, *love your friend enough to talk with him or her about anything you feel is not right*. One of the greatest tests of friendship is to ask yourself: Am I prepared to lose this friendship in the interests of God's kingdom? If not, then you haven't got a true friendship. You are in it for your own reasons, not God's. You are not a true friend. Where you see wrong, deal with it, but do so lovingly, gently, and firmly. You see, that's what friends are for – to help us see what we might otherwise be missing.

Fifth, *allow your friend to have other friends also*. Don't suffocate your friend by being possessive and demanding that he or she maintain just your friendship and no one else's. It is this attitude, more than any one thing, which is responsible for the death of friendships. Give your friend the freedom to move out into other relationships, to make new contacts and see new people, and be happy for them when they do so. You will desecrate a friendship if you try to dominate it.

O Father, may I never suffocate a friendship by being possessive. And help me to have such a secure relationship with You that I can risk losing a friend if it is in the interest of that which is right. In Jesus' name I pray. Amen.

FURTHER STUDY
Isa. 41:8–14; Matt. 26:47–50; Jas 2:23
1. How did God reveal friendship?
2. How did Jesus regard Judas?

No-one Has a Double

FOR READING & MEDITATION – PROVERBS 27:10–16

'Do not forsake your friend...' (v10)

Today we consider the sixth and final step to developing friendship: *stay loyal and loving to your friends as far as you possibly can.* I say 'as far as you possibly can' because they may commit and continue in some sin, such as adultery, for example, and this demands action by the church as described in Matthew 18:15–17. Discipline may have to be given and you will need to reconsider the grounds upon which your friendship can continue. Loyalty and love in this case would mean continuing in prayer for your friend – prayer, by the way, that may take hours, not minutes.

Clearly, the matter of friendship is of major importance and those who ignore it do so at their peril. You see, the opposite of friendship is isolation. And how much emotional damage is the result of that? 'The world is so empty,' said Goethe, the German poet and philosopher, 'if one thinks only of mountains, rivers, and cities, but to know someone here and there who thinks and feels with us and, though distant, is close to us in spirit – this makes the earth an inhabited garden.'

God made us for relationships and it is His will that we cultivate a circle of friends. Every friend is different. No one has a double in friendship. The more we have, the richer we are. Dr Lawrence Crabb says, 'Every day we ought to move out from our base in the home and say to ourselves: Lord, help me reach out and touch someone deep in their being today, not for the rewards it brings me in terms of good feelings, but for the blessing I can be to them.'

This is the way in which Jesus lived and related to others. Perhaps this is why they called Him 'a *friend* of... "sinners"' (Matt. 11:19). He hated sin, but He loved the sinner.

Father, one thing is clear: the wise are those who know how to make friends. Guide me in my future days so that in every relationship I may be able to apply the principles I have just learned. In Jesus' name I ask it. Amen.

FURTHER STUDY

Matt. 9:9–13; 11:19; 1 John 1:1–7

1. What caused the Pharisees to call Jesus a friend of sinners?
2. What is the basis of deep fellowship?

Growing in Wisdom

FOR READING & MEDITATION – PROVERBS 9:10–18

'The fear of the Lord is the beginning of wisdom, and
knowledge of the Holy One is understanding.' (v10)

It is my hope that what I set out to do two months ago has now been accomplished – namely, to have encouraged you to steal, drink, lie, and swear as much as possible. Just in case you have forgotten, let me hasten to remind you what I mean by that statement: that from now on you will steal time out of your schedule to read continually from the book of Proverbs; that you will drink regularly from its clear refreshing waters; that you will lie on your bed at night and meditate on its great themes; and that you will swear by the grace of God to put its powerful principles into practice every day.

If you feel that I have not touched on some aspect of Proverbs then I have served you well. It will stimulate you to deeper and further study. The 'seven pillars of wisdom' I have suggested, you must remember, are the themes that I believe are the dominant ones in Proverbs. Others will have different views and different observations. Read what they have to say, too – it will help you gain even greater understanding.

My prayer is that these meditations will stimulate thousands to pursue that most glorious of all qualities – divine wisdom. But remember, do not seek wisdom for its own sake. Seek it so that you might more effectively represent Jesus Christ. And beware of legalism, that soul-destroying attitude that takes greater pleasure in principles than in the Person who is behind them – our Lord Jesus Christ Himself. If you still don't know Him, then bow your head this very moment, repent of every sin you have committed, and quietly surrender your heart and life into His hands. Committing your way to God is the beginning of wisdom; continual trust in Him will see it develop and grow.

Father, please grant me this wisdom, not so that I might have an advantage over others, nor to fulfil selfish needs, nor even to advance my fortunes. I seek it that I might know You better, love You more, and do Your perfect will. Amen.

FURTHER STUDY
Prov. 1:7; Col. 3:1–17
1. Why is fearing God good for us?
2. Contrast a person before and after conversion.

SEP
— & —
OCT

Nothing Missed

FOR READING & MEDITATION – JEREMIAH 29:1–14

'"For I know the plans I have for you," declares the Lord...' (v11)

One of the most exciting ideas I have come across in my journey through the Christian life is the thought that in every believer's life a divine story is being written. Through all the countless occurrences of our lives, a guiding hand is at work, taking the raw material of life and making from it a story-line that, even though it may be hidden from us at the moment, will, when viewed from the vantage point of eternity, astonish us.

Over the next two months I hope to be able to bring home to you the realisation that if you believe in the Lord Jesus Christ and have accepted Him as your Saviour then your life is not a series of haphazard events, but a narrative. God has the ability to take everything that happens to us and make out of it a story – a story that has coherence and purpose and that fits into the bigger story He is telling. A story has a beginning, a middle, and an ending. Everything in it has a point. Nothing need be irrelevant.

The writer Thornton Wilder says we should think of our lives in terms of a great landscape that extends far beyond what the eye of our experience can see. 'Who knows,' he says, 'how one experience so horrible to us can set in motion a chain of events that will bless future generations?' This is the thought that must grip us as we begin our meditations: behind the seemingly chaotic and indiscriminate events of our lives a bigger story, a *divine* story, is being written. A writer has been defined as 'someone on whom nothing is missed'. The Divine Author, I assure you, misses nothing. It was said of one short-story writer that he could make a story out of a grocery list. God can do infinitely better: He can make a story out of anything.

O Father, drive deep into my spirit the truth that nothing is being missed in my life. Everything that happens to me is being used to form a story. You turn everything into something meaningful. And I am so grateful. Amen.

FURTHER STUDY
Gen. 50:15–21; Acts 2:22–24
1. What was God's purpose in Joseph's story?
2. Explain why Joseph is a type of Christ.

More Than Just Facts

SEP

FOR READING & MEDITATION – COLOSSIANS 3:1–17

'For you died, and your life is now hidden with Christ in God.' (v3)

We began yesterday by affirming that in every Christian's life a divine story is being written. My dictionary defines a story as 'a piece of narrative, a tale of any length told or printed in prose or verse of actual or fictitious events'. A story consists of much more than the stringing together of certain facts. It has rhythm and movement, highs and lows, light and shade, plot and counterplot.

I can tell you about my life by giving you a list of facts, but that will not tell you the *story* of my life. It is only when those facts are fleshed out with details of the dramas that have gone on in my life – with the rhythms – that it becomes a story. Dan Allender, professor of counselling psychology at Mars Hill Graduate School illustrates the difference between a set of facts and a story in this way: 'If I say, "The king died and the queen died," then all I have are facts. But if I say, "The king died *and the queen died of grief*..." now I have the basis of a story.'

We must learn to see our lives as far more than a compilation of facts, otherwise we are in danger of regarding a person merely as a biological machine. Even in the seemingly most humdrum life a story is being created that, seen from an eternal perspective, would be breathtaking. You may think your life is boring and routine, but if you are a Christian then the sovereign God is at work, weaving every fact into a story. Don't get caught up, I beg you, with the world's ideas to such an extent that you forget, as our text for today puts it, that 'your life is now hidden with Christ in God'. Any life that is in Christ has a meaning that extends far beyond what is obvious from the happenings down here on earth.

O Father, how can I ever thank You enough for the fact that my life is hidden with Christ in You? Reveal to me day by day all the implications of this tremendous truth. Help me be fully aware of its wonder. In Christ's name I ask it. Amen.

FURTHER STUDY
John 6:5–13; 1 Cor. 12:12–27
1. How did a boy's packed lunch become part of the divine story?
2. Why are we all immensely important?

The Elements of Story

FOR READING & MEDITATION – 1 THESSALONIANS 5:12–28

'And we urge you... be patient with everyone.' (v14)

Today we continue thinking about what constitutes a story. When I first began my ministry of writing, I enrolled in a course for writers, one section of which dealt with the technique of short-story writing. I was told that a story should have four elements: (1) characters; (2) a plot; (3) movement; (4) dénouement. Take the first element: *characters*. A good story has many different characters – lead characters, supporting characters, antagonists, and so on. In your story and mine there is a variety of characters: friends, enemies, people who are for us, and people who are against us.

My pastor used to say to me when I was a young Christian, 'Always remember that the people you relate to are part of God's purpose for your life.' Non-Christians go to their graves with their character flaws largely unaltered, but with you and me it is different. Though the finishing touches will be made when we see our Lord face to face, the major shaping of our characters takes place in the here and now. God wants to make us like Jesus, and one of the ways He goes about this is by using the people who cross our paths as tools to shape us and make us more like Christ.

The people in your life, I believe, are hand-picked by the Lord to expose your temper, pride, stubbornness – whatever your struggles and difficulties might be. And running away from them is no answer. It's not worth it because God has many more such people to replace them. Make a list of all the people with whom you find it difficult to get on and ask yourself: What is God trying to show me about myself through them? Be assured of this: the characters who appear in your story are being used by God to develop your own character.

O Father, help me grasp the fact that relationships do not so much cause problems as reveal problems. Grant that I may not miss the lessons You are trying to teach me through the people You allow into my life. In Jesus' name. Amen.

FURTHER STUDY

Rom. 12:14–21; Gal. 2:11–16

1. How do we become more like Christ?
2. How was Peter's fault exposed?

The Divine Plot

FOR READING & MEDITATION – ROMANS 8:28–39

'For those God foreknew he also predestined to be conformed
to the likeness of his Son...' (v29)

Yesterday we said that a good story contains four elements: characters, plot, movement and dénouement. Today we look at the second of these elements: *plot*. The dictionary defines 'plot' as a 'plan of main events or topics in a play, poem, novel, etc'. I am always intrigued when occasionally (very occasionally) I read the writing of a good, clean-minded novelist who takes the raw data of existence and makes out of it a story. Storytellers who are able to devise a plot and carry one along through its various twists and turns have provided me with some satisfying reading over the years. This kind of writing is not something I am able to do. Only once in my life have I written a short story, and no publisher seemed at all interested in it!

God, as we have been saying, is in the story-telling business too. But what is His plot? John Stott expresses it like this: 'God is making human beings more human by making them more like Christ.' In the beginning God created us in His own image, which we spoiled by our sin and disobedience. Now He is busy attempting to restore that lost image.

The Living Bible brings this out most beautifully when it paraphrases our text for today in this way: 'For from the very beginning God decided that those who came to him – and all along he knew who would – should become like his Son...' God is so excited about His Son Jesus Christ that He wants to make everyone like Him, not in appearance, of course, but in character. And He uses everything that happens to us – good, bad, and indifferent – to make us more like Him. What a difference it would make if we would really get hold of the truth that God allows into our lives only what He can use.

My Father and my God, help me grasp the fact – really grasp it – that You allow into my life only those happenings – including trials and tribulations – that further Your intention to make me more like Your Son. In Jesus' name. Amen.

FURTHER STUDY

Col. 1:24–27; 1 Pet. 2:13–25

1. What mystery did God plot that Paul revealed?
2. Why is becoming like Christ not an easy process?

FOR READING & MEDITATION – 1 CORINTHIANS 13:1–13

'When perfection comes, the imperfect disappears.' (v10)

Now we look at the third aspect of good story-telling: *movement*. This has to do with the way a story unfolds. Eugene Peterson defines Christian counselling as 'listening to someone's story and looking for the movement of God'. He makes the assumption that God is always actively doing something in a Christian's life. Yet how can we believe that, when life comes to a stop and nothing seems to be happening? And what about those times when, to use the words of Shakespeare, 'Sorrows... come not single spies but in battalions'?

Often when I have sat with a person in whose life tragedy has occurred they have asked, 'What can God be up to in allowing this to take place?' My usual response is, 'I don't know, but whatever is happening, He is going through it with you.' The time of tragedy is not a time for speaking about the ultimate problems of the universe. It is time for the upward look and trustful silence. Not every person, of course, is strong in faith and able to praise God in the midst of trouble and believe that He is bringing about something good. Most of us perhaps, myself included, would identify with a man who once told me, 'The best I can do in times of trouble and tragedy is to demonstrate mute obedience.'

Certain dark problems have occurred in my own life that I have never been able fully to understand. *Some* light shines upon those problems, but no *complete* solution is to hand. However, whatever God's intention, I am told in Scripture that it is good. And I hold on to that. Enough light beats on our path for us to pick our way along it. But for the final explanation we must wait until we get home, and then our heavenly Father will explain it to us Himself.

My Father and my God, help me in those moments when I can find no answers to develop the upward look and the trustful silence – to trust You even when I cannot trace You. In Christ's name I ask it. Amen.

FURTHER STUDY

Job 13:15; Rev. 21:1–7
1. How did Job express ultimate faith?
2. What is God's ultimate intention?

All's Well That Ends Well

FOR READING & MEDITATION – 2 CORINTHIANS 4:1–18

'For our light and momentary troubles are achieving for
us an eternal glory that far outweighs them all.' (v17)

The fourth aspect of good story-telling is *dénouement* – the final resolution. Soon after it was published I read *The God of Small Things* by Arundhatiti Roy, the book which won the Booker Prize for literature in 1997. Though there are some passages in the book a Christian finds unacceptable, nevertheless I was thrilled by her wonderful use of the English language, the way in which she peeled away layer after layer of mystery, and her ability to stir emotions with words. It is indeed a masterpiece of writing. But in my opinion the beauty of the book is its *dénouement*.

After reading it I could not help but ponder the question: How will the story of my own life end? What special skill will the Divine Author apply to the final details of my personal narrative? As I mused, I remembered a quote by C.S. Lewis, which came home to me with great force: 'We ride with our backs to the engine... we have no notion of what stage of the journey we have reached... a story is precisely the sort of thing that cannot be understood till you have heard the whole of it.'

I do not know how God will write the final pages of my personal story, but I am sure of this: it will eclipse anything written by the greatest novelist. I trust Him to do this. And so, my friend, must you. Because your life is hidden with Christ in God, you are not just a statistic in the divorce rate, a victim of menopausal depression, an 'uneducated misfit' or a 'square peg in a round hole'; your life is a drama for which, perhaps, some of the best action and speeches are yet to be written. G.K. Chesterton said, 'You cannot finish a sum how you like, but you can finish a story how you like.' All of God's stories end well.

Loving heavenly Father, help me see that though You have the ability to turn all things to good, I have some responsibility too. May I so live that nothing I do will hinder You writing the conclusion You have planned for my story. Amen.

FURTHER STUDY

Job 42:1–16; Rev. 22:1–5
1. How did Job's story end?
2. How will our story end?

God at Work

FOR READING & MEDITATION – PHILIPPIANS 2:1–18

'It is God who works in you to will and to act
according to his good purpose.' (v13)

Today we continue reflecting on the fact that in every believer's life a divine story is being written. We simply have to believe this. Not to believe it means that our lives fragment into a series of random events, jerky starts and meaningless cul-de-sacs. Many of us go through times when what occurs doesn't seem to make sense. But because God is at work in our lives, we can be assured that a wonderful story is being written, in which all the puzzling parts will finally fit – everything will eventually come together.

Have we not all found that years after a perplexing event has happened, suddenly it all seems to fall into place? The realisation that God was at work dawns on us and we say to ourselves, 'Oh, so that's what *that* meant.' The Almighty is not helpless in the face of the sad and tragic things that happen to us. He is busy transforming them. And He can do this with such amazing power that sometimes we look back on the occasion of the evil that became the opportunity for the Author to do so much good.

This is not the first time I have used the illustration of the beautiful park and boating lake in Scarborough, Yorkshire, called The Mere. Not many who are impressed with its charm know that it was created out of a garbage heap. Originally it was one of Scarborough's refuse dumps, but with scientific thoroughness and the strictest regard for hygiene the city fathers transformed it into a thing of beauty. And if man can do that, what of God? These lines sum it up beautifully:

Deep in unfathomable mines
Of never failing skill
He treasures up His bright designs
And works His sovereign will.

Gracious Father, how can I thank You enough that Your transforming power is constantly at work in my life? Things are never static. I am following an unfolding Mind and an expanding Will. Blessed be Your name for ever. Amen.

FURTHER STUDY

Gen. 1:1–5,26–31; 2:7; 1 Cor. 1:26–31
1. What does God work with?
2. What is the result of His work?

An Unfolding Creation

FOR READING & MEDITATION – MATTHEW 18:1–9

'If your hand or your foot causes you to sin,
cut if off and throw it away.' (v8)

When we begin to look at our lives as stories then everything changes. Existence is not flattened out on the graph paper of analysis but comes alive in the movements of a drama – some of which is yet to be written. Many Christians have told how the concept of their lives being a story has engaged their attention and fired their imagination in a way that nothing else has done. William Kilpatrick, a Christian psychologist, claims that 'the Christian life and the imaginative life can grow up together'.

J.R.R. Tolkien went so far as to say that a Christian could, through sanctified imagination, actually 'assist in the unfolding and enrichment of creation'. Some of the great story writers, such as George MacDonald, C.S. Lewis, G.K. Chesterton, and Dorothy Sayers, were not only wonderful writers but were, at the same time, lucid apologists for the Christian faith. They opened up worlds to us because of the world that was opened up to them as they soaked their thoughts in Holy Scripture.

Do you remember C.S. Lewis's wonderful story *The Silver Chair*? The beautiful Queen of the Underworld nearly convinces the children from the Overworld that her own dismal kingdom is the only reality, and theirs but an imagined dream. The young prince, the two children, and their companion, a Marsh-wiggle, are in danger of falling prey to the Queen's blandishments when the Marsh-wiggle, to prevent the Queen's words taking hold, thrusts his foot into the fire. The shock helps him face reality, and as he speaks up, the children see the point he is making, run to his side, and escape. Can you think of anything that more imaginatively builds on the words of our Lord that we have read in today's text?

O Father, one of the reasons why I know Your Word is inspired is because it inspires me. Everything comes alive within me as I read it. Help me open up new worlds to others as You open up new worlds to me. In Jesus' name. Amen.

FURTHER STUDY

Ps. 119:18; John 16:12–15; 1 Cor. 2:7–15
1. How does God open our imagination?
2. Why can we understand spiritual mysteries?

Is This Idea Biblical?

FOR READING & MEDITATION – PSALM 94:1–23

'Does he who implanted the ear not hear?
Does he who formed the eye not see?' (v9)

It is possible that you might be saying to yourself at this stage: What biblical foundation is there for believing that God is a story writer? Where does this idea arise in Scripture? Well, I know of no text that explicitly states that God is a story writer, but several verses suggest God is the Author of our story. One is Ephesians 2:10: 'For we are God's workmanship.' This text could also be translated 'We are God's *poem*.' The Greek word used here is *poiema*, from which we get the word 'poem'. Another is 2 Corinthians 3:3: 'You show that you are a letter from Christ.' If we combine these two texts we see that a Christian is to be God's poetry and God's prose. Our lives are to enshrine a divine mystery – poetry – and at the same time express a divine message – prose.

There are three occasions recorded in Scripture when God wrote. The first was on Mount Sinai when He inscribed the Ten Commandments on two stone tablets (Deut. 4:13), the second at Belshazzar's feast (Dan. 5:5), and the third when, in the Person of His Son, He wrote in the sand (John 8:6). But it is when I consider the text at the top of this page that I am most convinced God is a story writer.

Whenever I read a story that grips me with its intricate plot and keeps me on the edge of my seat as I follow its twists and turns, I say to myself: If God can gift people with such imagination, what powers of imagination must He Himself possess. He who puts imaginative ideas in the hearts of men and women, is not He the same? If we find excitement in a thrilling novel then what can we expect to find in real life when the Author is none other than the Almighty God?

Gracious Father, help me to truly enter into the excitement of seeing my life not simply as 'a tale to be told' but as a story that is scripted by the world's most innovative and inventive story writer. In Jesus' name. Amen.

FURTHER STUDY
Ps. 19:1–5; 2 Cor. 3:1–6; 2 Tim. 3:15–17
1. Where does God write His story?
2. What is the purpose of His writings?

Always Ahead

FOR READING & MEDITATION – MARK 16:1–8

'He has risen!... He is going ahead of you into Galilee.' (vv6–7)

When I first understood that in every believer's life a divine story is being written, it changed my whole approach as a pastor and a counsellor. I have to confess that when I was a young minister I sometimes found it exceedingly dull listening to people talking about their personal problems. Then one day, while preparing an Easter sermon, the Lord spoke to me from the words in today's passage: 'He has risen... He is going ahead of you into Galilee.'

As I studied this passage the realisation dawned on me that whenever I sat down with someone to listen to their personal problems, *the risen Christ had gone there ahead of me.* He was in that person's life, doing something, saying something, that with the Spirit's help I needed to understand. I realised that my task was much more than to perform the traditional pastoral role, read a few comforting texts and pray; I needed to be alert to the story God was writing in that person's life.

As soon as I became aware that I was coming in on something that was already happening, and that the events in a person's life should not be looked upon in isolation as problems but as part of a continuing story, counselling changed from being an exacting task into something stimulating and exciting. My task then was to help individuals interpret that story, to encourage them to go back over a line or even a page they had missed or misread, to recover an essential piece of memory. I discovered that the more people understood that beyond the story of their lives a bigger story was unfolding, the more productive counselling became. This is one of the most powerful and transforming of all concepts. We are what we are because of a divine story.

O Lord, I need more light and guidance on this matter. I ask You to wash my eyes and cleanse my heart that I may see. Show me even more clearly that no matter what happens to me, You are always ahead. Amen.

FURTHER STUDY

Esther 4:1–17

1. What two messages did Mordecai give to Esther?
2. How had God gone ahead in this story?

Prevenient Grace

FOR READING & MEDITATION – PSALM 139:1–6

'You hem me in – behind and before;
you have laid your hand upon me.' (v5)

Yesterday I said that as soon as I became aware that everyone's life is a story, a complete change took place. Counselling ceased to be an exacting task and became instead something that was stimulating and exciting. As people grasped the idea that their life was a story they changed before my very eyes. Stories enhance, elaborate, and develop. One person was so excited that he said to me, 'This idea almost blows my mind. If I am part of a story then nothing that goes on in my life is irrelevant.'

Earlier I mentioned that Eugene Peterson defined counselling as 'listening to someone's story and looking for the movement of God'. Notice the words *the movement of God*. Eugene Peterson, as I pointed out, makes the assumption that at any given moment God is *doing* something. This is a thought I usually introduce when talking to ministers and counsellors. In response, more than one has told me how encouraging it is to realise that as they sit down with someone who is going through a crisis, the Master has gone ahead of them.

I happened to speak about this matter when I was attending a pastors' conference in Singapore. Afterwards a Chinese pastor said to me, 'From now on I will see my hospital visits and counselling sessions in a new light. Whenever I walk into a counselling room or a hospital ward I shall say to myself, "Christ has risen and is going before you."' And then he added, 'I am so intrigued with the idea that the Master is always ahead of me, that when I meet up with His children I am coming in on something that is already in progress. It has revolutionised my ministry.' Theologians call this 'prevenient grace'. Grace is *there* – even before we need it.

O Father, how wonderful it is to realise that Your grace is prevenient – that it is there even before I need it. Help me to trust the transforming power of that grace even when darkness hides it from my sight. In Jesus' name. Amen.

FURTHER STUDY
Ps. 139:7–18; Matt. 28:1–7
1. What did the psalmist understand?
2. What did the angel explain?

Paul's Thorn in the Flesh

FOR READING & MEDITATION – 2 CORINTHIANS 12:1–10

'Three times I pleaded with the Lord to take it away from me.' (v8)

Following on from what I said yesterday, I predict that unless Christian counsellors start to recognise that everyone's life is a story, unless they learn to listen to the story that God is telling in a person's life and go along with it, then they will fail to help people in the way they need to be helped. Overlooking the issue of story is a mistake that is often made. Some time ago I spoke to a young Christian counsellor in training and asked him what goal he set for himself when trying to help others. He replied, 'Well, obviously the removal of the problem.' I suggested to him that Christian counselling must have a much higher goal than that of solving problems; the goal must be *to know God in the problem.*

Imagine that young man sitting down with the apostle Paul who, in today's reading, talks about a problem he was experiencing and describes it as 'a thorn in my flesh'. If his goal was the removal of Paul's problem he would have been working against the purposes of God. Clearly, the Lord was allowing the problem to continue because it served to make Paul a more dependent and defenceless person.

Frequently, I have sat with a person in difficulty and, after seeking to understand what part their problem played in God's story, I have said something like this to them: 'You have to stay with this problem for a little while longer as God is using it to deepen your character and draw you into a closer relationship with Himself.' The highest goal we must have when attempting to help anyone spiritually is not the resolution of the problem but to attempt to understand the story-line that God is writing. Anything less than this will fail to draw out God's plans and purposes.

My Father and my God, thank You for reminding me that the solution of problems is not the highest goal for a Christian. Knowing You is the highest goal. Make me fully aware of this truth, I pray. In Jesus' name. Amen.

FURTHER STUDY
2 Cor. 1:3–11; 4:7–18
1. How can we help those in trouble?
2. What did Paul explain?

The Character on Page 29

FOR READING & MEDITATION – EPHESIANS 1:11–23

'According to the plan of him who works out everything
in conformity with the purpose of his will...' (v11)

It is unrealistic to expect that we will be able to make sense of our lives every step of the way. But that does not mean there is no sense. When I pick up a novel, I become so caught up with the plot that I carry on an imaginary conversation with one of the characters who might appear early in the book (perhaps page 29), and say to him or her, 'You are in a bit of a mess right now, and I wonder how your creator is going to get you out of this.' Then, as I read on and see how, later, the author rescues the character from distress and turns the whole situation around, I go back in my imagination to the character on page 29 and remark, 'There now, you worried unnecessarily didn't you? Things didn't make sense at the time but you were in good hands... your creator had the way out already planned.'

The character on page 29, could he or she have talked back to me, would not have made sense out of what was happening at that point because he or she was unaware that a bigger story was being written. And life is very much like this. Maybe that is how you are feeling at the moment. Things are happening in your life that just don't make any sense to you. So what have I to say to you? This: *you are only on page 29*. Take heart: up ahead the Divine Author is going to show you the significance of what is happening to you. Remember, He 'works out everything in conformity with the purpose of his will'.

The important thing now is that you trust the Author and play your part well. That may involve helping another person, not letting others down, doing the loving thing even though you don't feel like it. You are part of a story – a much bigger story – and what you do counts – infinitely.

O Father, help me to trust in Your plans at all times. Remind me, I pray, that things are working according to plan – to Your plans, not my plans. In Jesus' name I ask it. Amen.

FURTHER STUDY
Acts 16:16–34
1. How did the apostles respond to trouble?
2. What was the result of their faithful actions?

Tell Me a Story

FOR READING & MEDITATION – MARK 4:21–34

'He did not say anything to them without using a parable.' (v34)

As a lifelong student of human nature I have come to the conclusion that people have an appetite for stories just as they do for food and drink. Children, as you know, love nothing better at bedtime than to be told a tale. Tonight, in millions of homes all over the world, parents will hear their children ask as they tuck them in for the night, 'Will you tell me a story?'

The desire to be told a story is as old as humanity itself. And when we become adults we do not lose this longing. In this respect we never really grow up. André Malrux, in his book *Anti memoirs*, writes about one of his acquaintances, an elderly and experienced country priest, who said, 'There's no such thing as a grown-up person. We are all children at heart. Some of us know how to disguise it better.' Jesus knew full well the power of a story and used it to great effect in His ministry. The words of our text today make that very clear. In *The Message* Eugene Peterson paraphrases it in this way: 'He was never without a story when he spoke.'

One reason why Jesus used so many stories was because He knew how expert men and women were at arming themselves against the entrance of truth. And human nature doesn't change. Many of us, when we go to church, listen to the sermon that is preached from behind a mental barricade. We are on our guard lest something challenging gets past our defences and touches our conscience. But we listen to stories differently. A story glides unhindered into the very citadel of our mind, and the truth it conveys gains access before we guess its purpose. The story touches our conscience until it stings in confirmation of the point. The flag of surrender goes up and our soul capitulates.

Father, I see that You have given me an appetite for a story. Please give me a greater appreciation of this fact, and may I understand how to use stories in my ministry to others. In Jesus' name I pray. Amen.

FURTHER STUDY

Matt. 7:24–27; Luke 10:25–37
1. Why may a story have greater impact than a principle?
2. What did Jesus want His stories to do?

Saved – By a Story

FOR READING & MEDITATION – 2 SAMUEL 12:1–14

'Then David said to Nathan, "I have sinned against the Lord."' (v13)

We continue exploring the thought that everyone longs to hear a story. It seems that God has built this desire into the very fabric of our nature. And not just to listen to stories but to tell them also.

The writer Thomas Howard argues – and argues quite successfully – that humankind is a story-telling species, and without story our lives would be much poorer. 'All those stories,' he says, 'about orphan boys who set out on a journey and remember faithfully what they were told by the old beggar woman, who battle with temptation, see through false disguises, and find at the end of their journey that they are not orphans at all but the son of a king – all those stories ring bells in our imagination because that, in fact, is *the* story.' J.R.R. Tolkien, the man who inspired C.S. Lewis and gave him so many ideas for his stories, said, 'Man is a story-telling animal and for this reason God has given him a story to live.'

The passage we have read today shows how God saved David through a story after committing adultery with Bathsheba. It was probably the only way he could have been saved. God sent the prophet Nathan to him with a simple story about a rich man who had large flocks but who stole from a poor man his one little lamb and killed it. David was moved by the story, but because he had deceived himself so completely he could not see in it any application to himself. Almost before the story ended he burst out angrily, 'As surely as the Lord lives, the man who did this deserves to die!' (v5). The next moment the prophet challenged him with these words: 'You are the man!' (v7). The lie was exposed. The sophistry was at an end. David had been found out – by a story.

O Father, I pray that I might never become so self-deceived that I see no application to myself in the truths, principles, and stories You have recorded for my benefit in Scripture. Help me develop self-awareness, dear Lord. Amen.

FURTHER STUDY
Gen. 41:15–40
1. How was Egypt saved by a story?
2. What happened to the storyteller?

The Most Appealing Stories

FOR READING & MEDITATION – JOSHUA 24:1–18

'Choose for yourselves this day whom you will serve...' (v15)

Our need for a story does not mean we settle for any story. Novelists know that the most appealing ones are those which contain an element of romance and adventure. All good romances and adventure stories contain certain ingredients: the power of a great love, the presence of good and evil, the threat of danger, the eventual judgment of evil, a quest or a journey, and, most importantly, a hero or heroine who passes various tests to save the day or even his or her life.

Many sections of the Bible would lose something if the elements of adventure or romance were absent. Imagine if, in fairy tales, the evil prince or the wicked uncle could sin without impunity, if the dragon could easily be overcome, or if the good prince could save the day by sitting in his castle and studying philosophy. If this were the case then nobody would read them. Those who wrote those ancient stories knew the necessity of including threats of danger, time limits, rescue bids, and so on. People have to make important decisions within a time frame: 'If the stone is not returned to its proper place in the tower before the morning sun strikes the eastern wall, your kingdom and your bride are forfeit.'

The story before us today is just one of the many Bible passages that show us that out of all the choices we are called upon to make in life, the most important one is to come over onto the Lord's side. But we certainly need to keep in mind that Bible stories, though full of romance and adventure, are not fairy tales but fact. These life-and-death issues are crucial. We must never forget this awesome truth: 'Man is destined to die once, and after that to face judgment' (Heb. 9:27).

Help me, dear Father, to read the Bible not as a page torn from the past but as a mirror that reflects where I am in my own personal journey of faith. May I constantly expose myself to the truths of Your Word. In Christ's name. Amen.

FURTHER STUDY

Deut. 30:11–20; 1 Cor. 10:1–13

1. What did Moses and Joshua emphasise?
2. Why does the Bible contain so many stories?

The Process of Being Known

FOR READING & MEDITATION – PSALM 32:1–11

'I will instruct you and teach you in the way you should go...' (v8)

Some Christians find it difficult to accept that their lives are part of a bigger story. Several years ago, during a counselling session, I tried to convey to a woman who was struggling with the ups and downs of life that through it all a wonderful story was being written. However, she simply could not believe that to be true. 'My life is just a series of random happenings,' she responded, 'with no semblance of sense or design.' Though I tried to explain, she would not listen, and left the counselling room muttering, 'I can't believe it... I can't believe it.'

After much thought about why some Christians find it difficult to accept the concept of story, I have decided there are several reasons. The first reason, I think, has to do with feelings of self-rejection. It's surprising how many people go through life rejecting themselves. They never felt accepted by those who nurtured them and, believing themselves unworthy of acceptance, they develop a sense of self-hate and self-rejection. They cannot believe that any human being could take an interest in them, let alone God.

C.S. Lewis, in *Letters to Malcolm: Chiefly on Prayer*, defines prayer in this way: 'Prayer is taking part in the process of being deeply known.' How profound. God knows everything there is to know about an elephant, but the elephant cannot join in the process of being known. Only a person made in the image of God can do that. There are some who cannot joyfully join in the process of being known because they are convinced that if they were deeply known, they would be rejected. They live with a fear of being fundamentally dull. I tell you with conviction that God regards no one in this way. No one.

O Father, what a thrilling thought that through prayer I can join in the process of being known. What a friend You are to me – You know everything there is to know about me yet You love me just the same. Thank You my Father. Amen.

FURTHER STUDY
Luke 5:1–11; 15:21–24
1. What did Peter ask of Jesus?
2. How did the Lord respond?

God Is Interested

FOR READING & MEDITATION – PSALM 139:7–24

'How precious to me are your thoughts, O God!' (v17)

Another reason why some Christians doubt that their lives are part of a bigger story is this: they are not sure that God takes an interest in what happens to them. Many things make it hard for them to believe God takes a personal interest in their affairs – the vastness of space, for example. An astronomer who claims to be a Christian once said something like this to me: 'When I look up at the stars and study the bewildering immensity of space it seems so pitifully naïve to say, "God cares for me, for a tiny person like myself."'

Samuel Chadwick, in his book *The Path to Prayer*, tells of a critic who could not accept the fact that God is at work in the lives of His children, and accosted every believer he met with these words: 'I do not believe you when you say God is interested in the affairs of your life. God is great.' By saying 'God is great' this man meant, of course, that He is too great to be interested in the people who live on planet Earth.

However, we hold to God's personal care and interest in our lives not *in spite* of God's greatness but *because* of it. Though He is far beyond the scope of our thoughts, we dare believe that He stoops to ask for the love of our poor hearts. And even though whirring worlds move at His word, He says to us, 'Be still, and *know* that I am God' (Ps. 46:10). Managing directors and chief executives may leave some details to their colleagues, but not the Almighty. He does not delegate the responsibility of developing the story-line of our lives. He does this Himself. Let this amazing thought sink into your consciousness today: the God before whom angels veil their faces condescends to involve Himself in the tiniest details of your life.

O God, the thought that You stoop to ask for the love of my heart and have a personal interest in all the details of my life is more than I can take in. Yet I must believe it for it is true. 'I do believe, help me overcome my unbelief!' Amen.

FURTHER STUDY
Matt. 6:25–34; 10:29–31
1. How did Jesus explain God's interest in us?
2. What was His conclusion?

Knowing God

FOR READING & MEDITATION – PHILIPPIANS 3:1–11

'I want to know Christ and the power of his resurrection...' (v10)

Consider now a third reason why some people find it difficult to believe that God is sufficiently interested in them to compose a story in their lives: they do not know Him well enough.

Some time ago I was intrigued to read about the rules a person has to follow when presented to the reigning monarch at Buckingham Palace. There are guidelines concerning dress. Lessons in deportment are advised for some. One is expected to be at the palace well ahead of time and to be prepared to wait. It is appreciated if women curtsy and men bow. Contrast this with attendance at the court of heaven – with having an audience with the King of kings. All may come – there is no question of social standing. No introductions are necessary, no seeker is hindered, and no one need delay in order to improve their deportment or dress. Now, as ever, 'The sacrifices of God are a broken spirit; a broken and contrite heart, O God, you will not despise' (Ps. 51:17). Yet how many neglect the privilege and act as though the door is barred against them.

Time and time again I have been somewhat baffled when Christians have told me in a counselling session that they know their families better than they know the Lord. How sad, as Christ can be the Person best known to everyone everywhere! How do we get to know Him? By spending time with Him in prayer and the study of His Word. Those who do not know Him well are the ones who struggle with the idea that He is composing a story in their lives. Of course, discipline is essential. It amazes me that people happily set aside several hours to master some hobby yet blandly suppose they can get to know God during a few sleepy moments at the end of the day.

O Father, how I long to know You better. Yet there is a cost in terms of discipline and time. Help me pay the price, for the knowledge of You is of far greater value than the cost. In Jesus' name. Amen.

FURTHER STUDY
Matt. 11:25–30; Eph. 2:18; Heb. 4:14–16
1. How can we come to know God?
2. Why is it easier to know God than an earthly king or queen?

The Bible – A Story

FOR READING & MEDITATION – EPHESIANS 1:1–10

'The mystery of his will... to bring all things in heaven
and on earth together under... Christ.' (vv9–10)

We move on now to consider the fact that the Bible itself is pre-eminently a story. 'Some people,' says John Stott, 'seem to think of the Bible as trackless jungle, full of contradictions, a tangled undergrowth of unrelated ideas. In fact, it is quite the opposite, for one of the chief glories of the Bible is its coherence.' He adds, 'The whole Bible, from Genesis to Revelation, tells the story of God's sovereign purpose of grace, his master plan of salvation through Christ.' When we read Scripture we are reading a series of stories that blend together to tell an overall story.

Many Christians approach the Bible in the same way they do the internet – as somewhere to go when they are in trouble and need information or advice. They see it only as a book that contains texts they can apply to their daily struggles. There is nothing wrong, of course, in looking up appropriate verses when we are downcast or in need of spiritual help, but we must realise that the Bible has much more to yield than prescriptions on how to stop worrying, how to avoid anger, and so on. First and foremost the Bible is a story – a story of how God is at work, moving from a plan laid down in eternity to a climax within history, and then on beyond time to the future. The story that God is telling in each of our lives is wonderful, but more wonderful still is the story that God tells in the Scriptures.

Over the years, in my own walk with God, I have found a strange thing: the more I get caught up in the story God is telling in the Bible, the less preoccupied I become with my own personal problems. I can assure you that nothing empowers daily living more than being caught up in *His* story.

O Father, open my eyes to see the big picture which the Bible unfolds. Now I have glimpsed the fact that You have a story that is bigger than my story, I am on fire to know more. Lead me on, dear Father. In Jesus' name. Amen.

FURTHER STUDY
Luke 24:13–27; John 20:30–31
1. What did Christ have to explain?
2. Why was John's Gospel written?

The Illusion of Depth

FOR READING & MEDITATION – JOHN 10:1–21

'I am the gate; whoever enters through me will be saved.' (v9)

Yesterday we said that the Bible is composed of a series of stories that tell an overall story. Howard Hendricks puts it like this: 'The Bible does not come to us as systematised doctrine but as narrative. *And the story form is as important as the story it tells*' (emphasis mine). In the early days of my ministry I became so preoccupied with analysing the Bible that I missed out on the fact that first and foremost it is a story.

One of the things I have noticed in my study of psychology is that few schools develop the theme of story. Psychology mostly focuses only on what it means to be a 'person' and has no comprehension of what it means to be an heir to a kingdom prepared by God from the beginning of time. And because it misses out on story, it fails to tell the whole story. How refreshing it is to turn from the world of psychology to the world of the Bible and find that Scripture does not deaden our imagination or dull our desire for a story, but actually incites it, encourages it, and supplies us with some of the most exciting stories that have ever been told.

The disciplines of psychology and sociology have their place in the scheme of things, of course, but in themselves they lack depth. They are like a hall of mirrors, where you see different reflections of yourself. But that is all you see. Eventually you tire of seeing yourself and want to get out, you want to find the door. Jesus talked of Himself as the door or the gate, as we see from today's text. If you are looking for a new world – a world with depth – you will have to find the door. That door is Christ. And going through that door brings you to a much more exciting world than you could ever have imagined.

O Father, how glad I am that I have found that door. Through Your Son I enter a world that surpasses my greatest imagination. Enable me to help others find that door. In Jesus' name I pray. Amen.

FURTHER STUDY
Col. 2:1–8; Rev. 3:20
1. Why do we have to be careful?
2. What does Jesus promise?

FOR READING & MEDITATION – GENESIS 24:1–67

'So they... asked her, "Will you go with this man?"
"I will go," she said.' (v58)

We continue reflecting on the thought that most of the Bible is written in story form. If we lose sight of this fact we lose sight of one of God's great abilities for, as G.K. Chesterton put it, 'God is the world's best story-teller.' The stories in Scripture prepare us for great truths. For example, the story we have read today gives us an insight into the wonderful way in which God sent His Holy Spirit into the world to seek out a Bride for His Son. Just as the servant in the story moved under the guidance of God until he at last found the one whom God had elected to be Isaac's wife, so the Spirit has moved (and is moving) through the world, seeking God's elected ones and preparing them for the day when the Bride (the Church) and the Bridegroom (Jesus Christ) will be joined together for all eternity. One of the best descriptions I have heard of the Old Testament is this: *God's wonderful storybook.* It is.

A dangerous trend in today's society is that the value of story-reading is seemingly being lost. It is said that nowadays many children become restless when they are asked to listen to a story being read. It was very different when I was young. In my primary school the last fifteen minutes of the day were given over to the reading of a story by our teacher. If someone misbehaved badly, one of the punishments meted out was for the class to be deprived of the daily story. Whenever that happened, the culprit would be so taunted on the way home from school that he or she would think twice before misbehaving again. I will tell you what concerns me about this trend in our society. If Satan destroys our interest in story then I am afraid we will lose our interest in the story of God.

O God, save me from the harmful trends in today's society. You have given me a most wonderful storybook. I neglect it at my cost. Help me never to lose sight of its tremendous and awesome importance. In Christ's name I ask it. Amen.

FURTHER STUDY
Matt. 4:4; 11:10; 21:13; 26:31; Acts 8:26–39
1. What did Jesus often do?
2. What prepared the Ethiopian for salvation?

History – God's Story

FOR READING & MEDITATION – GALATIANS 3:15–25

'So the law was put in charge to lead us to Christ
that we might be justified by faith.' (v24)

The Bible tells God's story, and He has given us through the stories in the Bible what Thomas Howard describes as '*the* story of all stories, the only story there is finally'. What is 'the only story there is finally'? Frederick Buechner, in his book *The Complete Literary Guide to the Bible*, summarises the whole message of Scripture in this way: 'God creates, loses and restores.' He goes on to say, 'Christianity is not just a set of presuppositions, or philosophical ideas – it is a story that captures the imagination.'

Dr Larry Crabb sums it up a little differently when he says that God's story consists of seven chapters: (1) God in Trinity; (2) God and the angels; (3) Evil begins; (4) Paradise created; (5) Paradise lost; (6) Glory revealed through Christ; (7) Glory enjoyed for ever. Paul, in his letter to the Ephesians, captures as no other New Testament writer does the eternal sweep of God's purposes. But here, in today's reading in Galatians, he condenses into just 11 verses the story of the Old Testament – a period of about 2,000 years. It is as if he is describing a mountain range whose peaks are Abraham and Moses, with the highest peak – the Everest – being Jesus Christ. His message is simply this: God's promise to Abraham was confirmed by Moses and fulfilled in Jesus Christ.

In these verses Paul is teaching the unity of the Bible, while at the same time giving us a sense that through history God has been at work, pursuing a purpose that might have been unseen at the time but was nevertheless part of an eternal plan. 'There is a great need in the Church today for a Biblical Christian philosophy of history,' writes a contemporary. There is, for history is *His story*.

O Father, the more I learn about the story You are telling, the more I want to learn. Take me deeper into this subject, dear Lord. And whatever other book I ignore, help me to never ignore Your inspired Word. In Jesus' name. Amen.

FURTHER STUDY

Acts 14:8–17; 17:22–34
1. How did Paul speak to Gentiles?
2. What were the key elements in his message?

Salvation History

FOR READING & MEDITATION – ACTS 3:11–26

'He must remain in heaven until the time comes for God to restore everything, as he promised long ago...' (v21)

Yesterday we ended with this statement: 'There is a great need in the Church today for a Biblical Christian philosophy of history.' John Stott says, 'Many of us are so preoccupied with current affairs... that neither the past nor the future has any great interest for us. We cannot see the wood for the trees. We need to step back and try to take in the whole counsel of God, his everlasting purpose to redeem a people for himself through Jesus Christ.'

Some Christians have little time for the Old Testament as they regard it merely as history. But to understand God's universal epic we must realise that He has been at work not only in the centuries after Christ but in the centuries before also. The ancient Greeks regarded history as a complete circle going nowhere in particular and never reaching an identifiable goal. Similarly, G.N. Clarke, in an inaugural address given at Cambridge University, said, 'There is no secret and no plan in history to be discovered.' André Maurois, a French biographer, wrote, 'The universe is indifferent. Who created it? Why are we here on this puny mud heap spinning in infinite space? I have not the slightest idea, and I am quite convinced no one has.'

The God of the Bible is the God of history – the history of the Old Testament as well as that of the 2,000 years that have passed since Christ was here on the earth. The Almighty, who calls Himself the God of Abraham, Isaac, and Jacob (Exod. 3:6), chose Israel out of many nations to be His covenant people, and came to us in the Person of His Son at a recorded moment in history. The history the Bible recounts is 'salvation history', and the salvation it proclaims was achieved by historical events.

Father, I see so clearly that the history Your Word records is 'salvation history'. You have been working through history to achieve Your purposes. Truly, history is Your story. Thank You my Father. In Jesus' name. Amen.

FURTHER STUDY
Acts 2:14–41
1. What did Peter explain?
2. What was the result?

Taking the Long Look

FOR READING & MEDITATION – HEBREWS 6:13–20

'God wanted to make the unchanging nature of his purpose
very clear...' (v17)

Today we reflect a little more on the fact that our God is the God of history. Henry Ford, in his libel suit with the *Chicago Tribune* in 1919, said, 'History is bunk.' Rudolf Bultmann wrote, 'The question of meaning in history has become meaningless.' And some would echo these words: 'The most accurate chart of the meaning of history is the set of tracks made by a drunken fly with feet wet with ink, staggering across a piece of white paper. They lead nowhere and reflect no pattern of meaning.' Are they right? Of course not. These views fail to see things from God's perspective, from an *eternal* point of view. When we look at the fragments of history they tell us very little, but when we take 'the long look' we can see, as C.S. Lewis put it, that 'History is a story written by the finger of God.'

Historians and cosmologists who see the past as merely one senseless crisis after another have no answer to the question: Where have we come from and where are we going? And because they consider history has no sense or pattern, they soon become prey to the philosophy of existentialism, which embraces the present to the exclusion of both the future and the past. Yet amid the tides of modern philosophies the believing Christian stands fast and realises that despite all the difficulties sin has caused, there is a divine design which runs throughout history.

Rest assured, my friend. Pause and consider the bigger picture: history is not a random succession of events, each effect having its cause, and each cause having its effect, yet the whole betraying no overall pattern. The God revealed in the Bible is working to a plan and is accomplishing all things according to the purpose of His will (see Eph. 1:11).

Father, forgive me if I am so taken up with the present that neither the past nor the future has any great interest for me. Help me step back and take in the whole purpose of God – to take the long look. In Jesus' name. Amen.

FURTHER STUDY

Acts 7:40–60

1. How did Stephen embrace his past, present and future with story?
2. Why did people not like his story?

Invitation to a Wedding

FOR READING & MEDITATION – REVELATION 19:1–10

'The wedding of the Lamb has come, and his
bride has made herself ready.' (v7)

Having spent three days reflecting on the fact that history is *His story* – God's story – we move on now to ask ourselves: What exactly is the overall story which the Bible is telling? What is the big story of God? It is a *love story*. This is the thought we touched on a few days ago when we looked at the account of Abraham sending his servant Eliezer to find a bride for Isaac (Gen. 24:1–67), but now I would like to deal with it in more detail.

George Macdonald wrote, 'When we unravel the facts of history, together with the many statements of Scripture, we stumble across a love story of immense magnitude – the love of the Father for the Son, and the love of the Son for His Bride.' A.W. Tozer put it like this: 'The end which God had in mind for His universe when first He created it was to provide His Son with a Bride. This and this alone unfolds the meaning behind all history and makes it comprehensible.' So the big story of God – His universal epic – is essentially a romantic one.

God's concern to provide a Bride for His Son is laid down in the types and shadows of the Old Testament. It is unfolded more fully for us by the apostle Paul, and brought into final focus in the passage we have read today. The greatest event in the eternity to come will be the wedding supper of the Lamb. Many years ago the poet T.S. Eliot penned these depressing words: 'This is the way the world ends. Not with a bang but with a whimper.' For Christians, the end of all things will not be a whimper, but a wedding. We will 'rejoice and be glad ... for the wedding of the Lamb has come'. We who have been wooed by Christ and won to Him will one day be wed to Him. Hallelujah!

O Father, this is something I can hardly take in. It would be enough to be saved from hell and given a place in heaven. But to be joined to You, to be one with You, almost blows my mind. All I can say is: Thank You dear Lord. Thank You. Amen.

FURTHER STUDY

Matt. 22:1–14; 25:1–13

1. What is required of wedding participants?
2. What may prevent us responding to God's wedding invitation?

The Big Story of God

FOR READING & MEDITATION – EPHESIANS 5:22–33

'This is a profound mystery – but I am talking about Christ and the church.' (v32)

We continue meditating on the fact that the universal epic God is writing is a love story – of His concern to provide a Bride for His Son. All of us are familiar with the fairy story that tells of a princess who kisses a frog and by so doing turns him into a handsome prince. God's big story is about a Bridegroom touching the lives of stubborn, independent sinners such as you and me, and by His grace turning us into people fit to be joined in marriage to Him, to be His companions for all eternity.

The apostle Paul, when talking about the fact that a husband and wife become one flesh, goes on to say, 'This is a profound mystery – but I am talking about Christ and the church.' What is the 'mystery' that engages his attention here? It is the 'mystery' that just as a married couple become one flesh, so the Church will be one with Christ in eternity. Not a buddy but a bride, not a pal but a partner.

Non-Christian historians cannot conceive that behind the universe is a love story. Once, on a plane, I found myself sitting next to an historian. During the course of our conversation I asked the man what lessons he drew from his study of history. He paused for a moment and said, 'There seems no sense in history.' As I tried to explain to him that through all the seeming chaos a divine scheme is being worked out – a romantic one – he looked at me in amazement. Obviously keen to avoid further discussion, he shuffled his papers and said that though he would like to talk more about the matter, he had a lot of work to catch up on. When, at the end of the flight he told me he was catching another plane and going on somewhere else, I could not help but think: I wonder where.

O Father, what a prospect – what a story! We who were deep-dyed sinners but are now washed and made clean through the blood of Your Son, are to be joined with You for ever. I still can't get over it, dear Lord. Blessed be Your name for ever. Amen.

FURTHER STUDY
Isa. 62:1–5; Hos. 2:14–3:1
1. What causes God to rejoice?
2. How would the Israelites refer to the Lord?

A Divine Intimation?

FOR READING & MEDITATION – GENESIS 2:15–25

'Then the Lord God made a woman from the rib he had taken out of the man, and he brought her to the man.' (v22)

For one more day we reflect on the thought that God's chief purpose from the beginning of time was to provide His Son with a Bride. There appears to be an intimation of this truth in the story of Eve's creation from Adam, recounted in our reading today. A great Welsh preacher of the nineteenth century, Dr Cynddylan Jones, expressed this viewpoint: 'What happened in the first few pages of the Bible is a dress rehearsal for what takes place in the last few pages of the Bible, when the Church, the Bride of Christ, who was *in* Him and came *out* of Him, will be joined *to* Him in a marriage that will last for all eternity.'

In these words he was saying that the creation of the woman is a picture of the Christian Church. First, the woman was in the man – conceptually at least. Then she was taken out of him when God opened up Adam's side. Around the rib that was taken from him God 'built' a woman. Lastly, God gave the woman back to the man, and saw that as the act of holy matrimony (v24).

Isn't this creative act similar to the conception, creation, and consummation of Christ's Bride, the Church? In Ephesians 1:4 we are told that God saw us *in* Christ before the foundation of the world. In verse 7 we see that we have redemption through His blood – the blood, you remember, that came from His riven side when a soldier pierced Him with a spear (John 19:34). In Ephesians chapter 5 we read that we who were *in* Him and came *out* of Him will be joined yet again *to* Him.

Cynddylan Jones said, 'God couldn't wait to tell the world how He planned to provide a Bride for His Son, and so He built the truth in typological form into the original creation.' Was he right? You decide.

My Father and my God, whether or not Your purpose when You created Eve from Adam was to typify what I have read about today, one thing is sure: my salvation came from You and my destiny is to be joined to You. Hallelujah! Amen.

FURTHER STUDY

Ruth 4:1–17; S. of S. 4:7–15

1. How are Boaz and Ruth like Christ and the Church?
2. How would Christ speak to His Bride?

The Central Character

FOR READING & MEDITATION – MATTHEW 1:18–25

'This is how the birth of Jesus Christ came about…' (v18)

There is usually a central character in a story – the star or headliner of the story. And the central character in God's big story is Jesus. Some think of Jesus as the central character of the New Testament only, but He is the central character of the Old Testament too. 'To see the story of Jesus as confined only to the New Testament,' says one commentator, 'is to misunderstand the purpose of the Bible.'

No doubt you were relieved today's reading started at verse 18 and not verse 1. Yet Matthew gives our Lord's genealogy for a particular reason. He will not allow us to read about Jesus' birth before we have ploughed through a list of historical figures because until we see Christ in the context of His ancestors we will not properly understand His story. Jewish genealogies established the right to belong to the community of God's people. Ancestry gave people their identity and status. And Jesus' very mission necessitated Him belonging to the people who were to bring blessing to the earth; He was the fulfilment of all the Old Testament promises that related to the Messiah. Jesus has to be seen in the light of a bigger story that goes back many centuries.

The Old Testament, says Chris Wright in his book *Knowing Jesus through the Old Testament*, tells the story which Jesus completes. 'Without the Old Testament,' he claims, 'then Jesus quickly loses reality and either becomes a stained-glass window figure – colourful but static and undemanding – or a tailor's dummy that can be dressed to suit the current fashion.' Jesus without the bigger story would not be the Person we know He is. Our Lord is no identikit figure; He is a real man – though of course much more than a man.

Lord Jesus Christ, while I rejoice that You are the central character of Scripture, I am more thankful still that You are the central character in my life. Without You life would not be worth living. Amen.

FURTHER STUDY
Gen. 3:14–15; Isa. 53:1–12; Mal. 3:1–4
1. How do we see Christ in Genesis and Isaiah?
2. How do we see Christ in Malachi?

FOR READING & MEDITATION – LUKE 19:1–10

'For the Son of Man came to seek and to save what was lost.' (v10)

We continue reflecting on the thought which we started to consider yesterday, namely that Jesus is the central character – the star – of God's story. The glory goes not to the ones who are saved but to the one who saves. Some time ago, I watched a television programme featuring the remarkable story of a woman who was saved from drowning on an Australian beach. The man who saved her was not a life-saver – just an ordinary Australian citizen who had been walking along the beach with his dog. He couldn't even swim. However, when he saw the woman was in difficulty he raced to get a lifebelt, waded into the sea as far as he could, and threw it to her. Fortunately she managed to grasp it, and because a rope was attached to the lifebelt he was able to pull her safely to the shore.

A television crew happened to be close by and immediately started filming and interviewing the rescuer. While one cameraman focused on the crowds who had gathered around the man to congratulate him, another zoomed in on the woman who had just been saved – sitting all alone, gathering her breath. No comment was given and no comment was needed. The glory, as I said above, goes not to the ones who are saved but to the one who saves.

People who don't know Christ often wonder why we make so much of Jesus. If only they could know the joy of abundant living, of sins forgiven, and, as the old hymn so beautifully puts it, 'of hell subdued and heaven begun'. A preacher I once heard, declared, 'Jesus is my hero.' At first I was slightly offended by the expression. But the more I thought about it the more I realised he was right. Jesus is not only God's hero; He is my hero and role model too.

Lord Jesus Christ, how can I ever thank You enough for saving me and for being such a wonderful Saviour? I give You all the praise for my salvation – and will do for ever. Amen.

FURTHER STUDY

1 Sam. 8:19–20; 18:6–7

1. What do many people look for?
2. How does Jesus fulfil the role of a true hero?

The Only Saviour

FOR READING & MEDITATION – ACTS 4:1–12

'Salvation is found in no-one else, for there is no other name under heaven… by which we must be saved.' (v12)

Today we meditate further on the fact that Jesus is the hero of God's big story. Other religions hold Jesus in high honour, but they do not regard Him as the centre of God's purposes. Hindus gladly recognise Him as an 'avatar' (incarnation) of Vishnu. Muslims acknowledge Him as one of the great prophets whose virgin birth, sinless life, acts of kindness, miracles, and return one day to this earth are all affirmed in the Qur'an. Jews, who reject Jesus as the Messiah, still write of Him as a man of outstanding character. Karl Marx, who was fiercely critical of religion and regarded it as opium that drugged the oppressed into tolerating the injustices of those in power, nevertheless had a high regard for Jesus.

Some years ago I spoke to a group of non-Christian students on the theme 'The Historic Jesus'. After I had finished, the young chairman got up and called for 'Three cheers for Jesus'. I felt sad that somehow my point had been missed, for it is not 'three cheers' Jesus wants but the homage of our hearts.

Jesus Christ is not one Saviour among others; He is the *only* Saviour. He is not one of Hinduism's 330 million gods or one of the 40 prophets recognised in the Qur'an. He is not even, in the words of John Stott, 'Jesus the Great, as you might say Napoleon the Great or Alexander the Great.' He continues, 'To us He is the only; He is simply Jesus. Nothing could be added to that; He is unique.' In an age when schools teach that all religions have equal value, we should never forget that Christianity is not one faith among many other faiths; it is in a category all by itself. Christianity is not a religion but a relationship. Jesus Christ is not *a* Saviour, He is the *only* Saviour.

Father, save me from being carried along by the pluralism which is so rife in today's society and from losing sight of the fact that Jesus is the only Saviour. Help me be true to Scripture, but without arrogance. In Jesus' name I pray. Amen.

FURTHER STUDY
Acts 17:22–34; 1 Tim. 2:5–6
1. Why were the religious Athenians confused?
2. What makes Jesus unique?

The Star of the Story

FOR READING & MEDITATION – MATTHEW 3:13–17

'And a voice from heaven said, "This is my Son, whom I love..."' (v17)

For one more day we consider the implications of the fact that Jesus is the central character in God's great story. There are some who like to downplay Jesus' role, and who regard Christianity as just an ethical system. They speak about the fine principles of the Sermon on the Mount, the Golden Rule, and so on, forgetting that without Christ's presence in one's life the principles given in the Sermon on the Mount are impossible to keep. As I have said before, when Jesus presented the principles outlined in the Sermon on the Mount He was not saying, 'Live like this and you will become a Christian'; what He was saying was, 'Become a Christian and you will live like this'. You cannot extract Jesus' teaching on morality and present it in isolation.

It makes no sense to talk about the Christian ethic and ignore Christ. You cannot take the words of Jesus and pretend that they came from the lips of any other person. How would it sound if any other man, however great he may be, were to talk about himself in the way Jesus did? Think, for instance, how it would sound if the British prime minister were to say, 'I am the resurrection and the life.' Or if some other good-living world-renowned personality were to claim, 'Before Abraham was born, I am.' That is not their story. Those lines belong to one Person and one Person alone – our Lord Jesus Christ.

Those who regard Christianity as nothing more than moral teaching miss the point. 'Christianity,' said one theologian, 'is Christ.' On Him all the Old Testament truths converge and from Him all the New Testament truths emerge. He is the centre of gravity of the Bible, the hub of the evangel, *the star of God's story.*

Father, with great humility I confess it: Jesus is not only the star of Your story but the star of my story also. Without Him I am nothing. Just as You rejoiced in Your Son so do I rejoice in Him too. Amen.

FURTHER STUDY
John 5:16–18; Rev. 5:1–14
1. Why did the Jews try to kill Jesus?
2. Who is worshipped in heaven?

FOR READING & MEDITATION – JOHN 5:16–30

'Jesus said... "My Father is always at his work... and I, too,
am working."' (v17)

Having recognised the centrality of Jesus Christ in God's big story, we now consider the question: What happens if we fail to grasp the sense of story, which is the pre-eminent theme of Scripture? One thing that will occur is this: we will get caught up in our own story and become preoccupied with self rather than the Saviour. The philosopher Jean-Paul Sartre said that no finite point can adequately serve as its own context. If I take the finite point of my own story, I cannot get meaning without a larger context. God's bigger story puts my own story in context. My finitude is linked to infinity. I must ask myself: Do I see a story that is much bigger than my own personal story or do I simply see myself as the beginning and end of the story?

Another thing that can happen if we fail to grasp the sense of story is that we lose the awareness of being drawn into the action of God. The Almighty is at work in the world. The verse that is our text today makes that quite clear. Notice that the words 'is always at his work' and 'am working' are in the present tense. What work is the Father engaged in? A whole range of things, of course, but part of His work is developing His salvation story – a story in which you and I have a special part.

Every believer is included in God's story, is travelling towards Him, and being drawn closer to Him. Are you not aware of a sense of journeying as you move from day to day – a sense that you are being shaped, moulded, discipled and fitted into His plan? If you do not have this sense of being caught up in the action of God then stop everything right now, get down on your knees, and reflect on what I have been saying over these past few days.

Father, if I am slow to learn the lesson that my life is part of a bigger story, an eternal story, please forgive me. Help me look at this truth not through the eyes of chilling doubt but through the eyes of kindling faith. Amen.

FURTHER STUDY

2 Kgs 5:1–15; Eph. 2:10
1. How was a humble slave girl linked to infinity?
2. What has God planned?

Driven – or Drawn?

FOR READING & MEDITATION – MARK 12:18–27

'Jesus replied, "Are you not in error because you do not
know the Scriptures or the power of God?"' (v24)

Yesterday we mentioned two things that are likely to happen if we fail to grasp a sense of story: we will become preoccupied with our own self, and we will deprive ourselves of the knowledge and thrill of being caught up in the action of God. Yet another thing that will happen is this: we will treat the Bible as an exegetically precise system and miss its real power. Eugene Peterson puts this thought in a compelling way when he says, 'When we fail to develop a sense of story then we start applying the Bible, taking charge of a verse or doctrine or moral with which we intend to fix some fragment of ourselves.'

But isn't that what we are supposed to do with the Bible – apply it? Certainly we should apply biblical teaching and principles, but we miss the essential meaning of the Bible if that is all we do. The ancient Sadducees were studious readers of the Scriptures, but they overlooked their main purpose; they were good at alighting on specific texts but, as our reading today tells us, they failed to understand what was really being said. Many Christians' lives are flawless in terms of morality but yet are flat in terms of passion. They know how to apply particular Bible texts to life's issues but they cannot see beyond the texts of Scripture to the bigger story. They are driven people rather than drawn people.

Christianity first and foremost, as we have already said, is not an ethical system; it is a story. The story is mainly about the Master – who He is, where He came from, what He has done, and what He is still doing. 'The things we Christians do,' says William Kilpatrick, 'we do not so much for ethical reasons but because we are caught up in a story.'

Father, help me examine myself today to see whether I am driven by an inner urge to conform to a code or drawn to live for You because I am caught up in the story You are telling. In Jesus' name I ask this. Amen.

FURTHER STUDY

Mark 16:14–20; 2 Cor. 5:11–15
1. How did the disciples apply the words of Jesus?
2. What drove Paul?

No Sense of Story

FOR READING & MEDITATION – JOSHUA 4:1–24

'No sooner had they set their feet on the dry ground than
the waters of the Jordan returned to their place...' (v18)

I have no hesitation in saying that the Christian life without a sense of story tends to lack vibrancy. What I am about to describe now will be regarded by some as over-imaginative, but others will, I am sure, recognise that it is true.

Christians go to church on Sunday, and for a while the waters of chaos and confusion roll back as they focus on the worship of God. For an hour or two truth clears away the fog that swirls in their minds and, like the Israelites, they prepare to go out to possess the land.

The pastor shakes hands with people as they leave and, as he does so, touches hands that are trembling with anxiety, resentment, guilt, and many other emotions. A mother, perhaps, has just discovered her son is on drugs. An executive is about to be made redundant. A wife has discovered her husband is having an affair. A family is facing the death of a loved one. How many believers find within hours of getting home that the waters are again overflowing the banks, as in the passage we have read today? If Christians have no sense of story – of what one commentator describes as 'knowing that our private histories are grafted into the stock of salvation history' – the waters soon rush back in waves of confusion and distress.

How I wish this message was preached from more pulpits: God is at work, taking everything that goes on in our lives and weaving it into His salvation story. If we do not view the details of our existence as chapters in God's story then we will easily fall prey to gloom and pessimism. I know of nothing that enables us to possess the land of our spiritual inheritance more effectively than the knowledge that our personal stories are being woven into God's own story.

Gracious Father, open my eyes that I might see – really see – that my personal story is congruent with the story of Your salvation. Help me, my Father, for I must get hold of this. In Jesus' name. Amen.

FURTHER STUDY
Isa. 43:1–11; John 9:1–7
1. What is God's promise?
2. What did Jesus explain?

Everyone Has a Part

FOR READING & MEDITATION – RUTH 1:1–14

'There was a famine... a man from Bethlehem... together with his wife and two sons, went to live... in... Moab.' (v1)

Yesterday we commented that one of the saddest things that can happen to a Christian is failing to recognise that our personal story is congruent with the story God is telling. Far too many Christians, when presented with the fact that they are part of God's salvation story, respond by saying something like this: 'I can't believe that my life has any place in the eternal scheme of things. I am too small and insignificant to have any part in God's cosmic purpose.' Their guilt, fears, and inferiority combine to make them feel that a place in God's universal purposes may be right for others but not for them. How do we break free from such a jaundiced outlook?

A helpful suggestion, which we are about to follow, is to dip into the Old Testament story of Ruth. This book, perhaps more than any other, helps us understand that our lives are chapters in the epic of God's salvation history. The interesting thing about the book of Ruth is that there are no outstanding personalities in the narrative – no kings, prophets, judges, or priests. It is a simple, ordinary story about three widows and a farmer whose personal experiences of everyday life are woven into God's universal epic.

The great characters of the Bible, such as Abraham, Isaac, Jacob, Joseph, Solomon, David, and Daniel, can be intimidating to ordinary people. 'Surely,' they say, 'there is no way that I can be included in such a star-studded cast.' The story of Ruth, as we shall see, gives the lie to such a viewpoint. Every detail of every believer's life is part of a universal epic – the story of salvation. And you are as much an integral part of that as are Abraham, Isaac, Jacob, Joseph, Solomon, David, Daniel – and Ruth.

O Father, can it really be true that the details of my life are being tied in to the story of salvation... that I am a part of Your big story? It sounds too good to be true, but then too good not to be true. Show me more, dear Lord. Amen.

FURTHER STUDY

1 Cor. 12:1–14
1. What did Paul want us to know?
2. What is common to us all and what is different?

Three Funerals and a Wedding

FOR READING & MEDITATION – RUTH 1:15–22

'Don't call me Naomi... Call me Mara, because the
Almighty has made my life very bitter.' (v20)

Now we look in closer detail at the lives of some very ordinary people to see how their personal stories were woven into God's universal epic. Over the years I have heard and read many interesting comments on Ruth, but none so wonderful as this: 'Ruth was an inconsequential outsider whose life is essential for telling the complete story of salvation.' A woman who was not born into the Jewish faith – an outsider – became integrated into the larger story of God's people.

Those who think God only weaves into the tapestry of His eternal purposes the big names of the Bible need to study the book of Ruth, for her simple but delightful story is proof to the contrary. It is a story about a famine, three funerals, and a wedding! But let's begin at the beginning.

The story starts with the announcement of a famine in the land of Judah. In the small town of Bethlehem a man by the name of Elimelech takes his wife Naomi and their two sons, and goes to live for a while in the land of Moab. After a period of time Elimelech dies, and his two sons marry Moabite women. Later the two sons also die, leaving Naomi and her daughters-in-law in difficult circumstances. Naomi decides to return to Bethlehem, and Ruth, one of her daughters-in-law, pleads to be allowed to accompany her.

When, after a ten-year absence, Naomi finally arrives back in Bethlehem, her return creates a great stir in the town. Naomi, however, can only respond to their excitement with words of lament: 'I went away full, but the Lord has brought me back empty' (v21). That might sound a very negative thing to say, but her very emptiness is woven into the plot and becomes, as we shall discover, the occasion for God's providence.

Father, I see that negative feelings or even complaints that are voiced do not preclude us from contributing to Your story. You treat our complaints seriously. For that I am deeply grateful. Amen.

FURTHER STUDY

1 Cor. 12:14–31

1. Why is no one insignificant?
2. How is the Church similar to, yet different from, a sports team?

No Editorial Deletion

FOR READING & MEDITATION – JEREMIAH 20:7–18

'O Lord, you deceived me, and I was deceived;
you overpowered me and prevailed.' (v7)

Yesterday we ended with the thought that Naomi's emptiness was woven into God's plot and became the occasion for God's providence. Naomi's complaint, we noted, was taken seriously; it was not deleted from the story, toned down, or spiritualised. The point must not escape us that Naomi's complaint becomes, in fact, part of the story. Complaints are quite common in Scripture. Jeremiah's – the one in our reading today – is probably the best known.

Edward F. Campbell, in the comments on Ruth which he makes in the *Anchor Bible*, says, 'Not only is complaint tolerated by God but it can even be the proper stance of a person who takes God seriously: petulant Jonah, earnest Jeremiah, persistent Job – Naomi stands in the company.' If there had been an editorial deletion of Naomi's complaint – if it had been judged unsuitable for a story about salvation – then the account would not have been an entirely factual one. Though she viewed herself as empty, she was given a symbolic filling when Ruth returned from Boaz with a generous gift of barley for her. 'You can't go back empty-handed to your mother-in-law!' Boaz had told Ruth (3:17, *The Message*).

Later we see that Naomi's emptiness is reversed when, after the birth of Obed, Ruth's first child, the women of Bethlehem cry, 'Naomi has a son!' (4:17). Not Ruth, notice, but Naomi. Notice too that when Naomi first uttered her complaint God did not immediately intervene and give her an explanation of His ways. Instead she found herself, as one commentator describes it, 'in a living, developing set of relationships that extend into the future'. Her negative feelings were not edited out of God's story but integrated into it.

O Father, I am glad that You did not edit Naomi's complaint out of the narrative or judge it unsuitable to be included in a story about salvation. You took it and used it to demonstrate Your providence. How wonderful. Amen.

FURTHER STUDY
Ruth 2:1–23
1. How did God guide Ruth?
2. Why did Boaz admire and bless Ruth?

Speaking Your Own Lines

FOR READING & MEDITATION – RUTH 3:1–18

'Spread the corner of your garment over me,
since you are a kinsman-redeemer.' (v9)

We have seen that Naomi became included in the story of salvation outlined for us in the book of Ruth by way of a complaint. Today we ask: How did Ruth enter the story? *By making clear what she wanted.* By this stage Naomi had informed Ruth that Boaz was a close relative and a kinsman-redeemer. They knew, therefore, that if they handled the situation correctly then they would be rescued from poverty and that Ruth would have a husband. Thus Naomi coaches Ruth: 'Wash and perfume yourself, and put on your best clothes. Then go down to the threshing-floor... When he lies down, note the place where he is lying. Then go and uncover his feet... He will tell you what to do' (vv3–4).

Ruth does exactly what her mother-in-law suggests with one exception. She does not wait for Boaz to tell her what to do; instead, she takes the initiative and tells *him* what to do: 'Spread the corner of your garment over me, since you are a kinsman-redeemer.' This was a symbolic way of saying, 'Will you marry me?' Ruth's intervention may seem somewhat forward, but as one commentator puts it, 'Being in God's story does not mean passively letting things happen to us. It does not mean dumb submission, nor blind obedience.'

There are times when it is right to speak our own lines, not just parrot those that have been given us by others. Be assured of this: you will not be excluded from God's story when you speak the lines that come from your own heart rather than those that are imposed on you by others. Of course, it is right to allow ourselves to be coached by parents, schoolteachers, and others, but there are times when we must be ready to ask for what we want – to speak our own lines.

Father, I see that just as You accept complaint, so You acknowledge creativity also. You do not reject those who make up their own lines. And for that, too, I am again deeply thankful. Amen.

FURTHER STUDY

Mark 10:46–52; John 20:24–29

1. Why was Bartimaeus healed?
2. What was the result of Thomas speaking his mind?

Not a Passive Player

FOR READING & MEDITATION – EZEKIEL 16:1–14

'I spread the corner of my garment over you and covered
your nakedness.' (v8)

You may have thought that a comment I made yesterday – that Ruth's action of asking Boaz to spread the corner of his garment over her was a symbolic way of asking him to marry her – is somewhat far-fetched. But this language is used again in our text for today in connection with God's marriage contract with Israel: 'Later I passed by, and when I looked at you and saw that you were old enough for love, I spread the corner of my garment over you and covered your nakedness.' By her action Ruth was signalling that she was putting herself under the protection of Boaz. The Amplified Bible translates Ruth's request in this way: 'Spread your wing [of protection] over your maidservant, for you are a next of kin.'

Evidence of this custom is given by commentators such as Edward F. Campbell, who refer to the ancient Arabic custom of placing of a garment over a woman as a symbolic claim to marriage. When I visited Bahrain some years ago, I was told that some Arabs still practise this symbolic gesture when selecting a wife.

I make the point once again: for Ruth to be in God's story it did not follow that she had to be a passive player. Even though she is a foreigner (six times in the story she is called a Moabitess), and had been born outside the boundaries of the covenant nation of Israel, she enters the central action of the story when she steps out of the role in which she had been placed by others and, in addition to doing what Naomi had instructed, takes the initiative and speaks her own lines. And the consequences of Ruth's courageous actions are astounding. She takes her place in history as the great-grandmother of King David and an ancestor of Jesus Christ, the Messiah.

O Father, although I am grateful for those who have coached me in spiritual things, help me not to just repeat the statements of others but, whenever necessary, to step out and speak the words I feel compelled to speak. In Jesus' name. Amen.

FURTHER STUDY
1 Sam. 14:1–23
1. How did Jonathan take the initiative?
2. What was the result?

'Mr So and So'

FOR READING & MEDITATION – RUTH 4:1–4

'No-one has the right to do it except you, and I am next in line.' (v4)

Another important player in the narrative we are considering is, of course, Boaz. How did Boaz become part of God's salvation story? By accepting responsibility. Boaz was a wealthy relative of Naomi's husband, and is seen in the story as a perfect gentleman and a man of outstanding character: solid, honest and upright. His name means 'strength' or 'substance', and he is the hero of the story. He agreed to marry Ruth according to the custom of levirate marriage by which the nearest male relative married a man's widow (see Deut. 25:5–10).

There was, however, a kinsman who was more closely related to Ruth – an unnamed character with whom Boaz bargained. Boaz succeeded in persuading this man to give up his right to marry Ruth. Had he wished, Boaz could have avoided marrying Ruth and still kept his good name since there was another man who had a greater responsibility than he had. One commentator says of him, 'Boaz could have kept the letter of the law by referring the matter of Ruth to the nearer kinsman, "Mr So and So". The scene at the city gate in which the redeemer obligations are worked out makes it clear that Boaz, "the man of substance", will live up to his name.'

In the story we see that Boaz had an opportunity to act responsibly and he seized it, not simply because it was expected of him but because he wanted to. He was the kind of man who was not content to live by the letter of the law, but one who sought ways to put his wealth and position to work on behalf of others. This is demonstrated not only by his treatment of Ruth but also by his concern for the welfare of his workers. In Boaz we find a man who lived not by the letter of the law but by the spirit of it.

O Father, save me from seeking to conform to the letter of the law and not going beyond it. Help me to look for creative ways in which I can put all my gifts and abilities to work on behalf of others. In Jesus' name I ask it. Amen.

FURTHER STUDY
Mark 7:1–13; 2 Cor. 3:1–6
1. Why may keeping the letter of the law be wrong?
2. How can we live by the spirit of the law?

That is How it Should Be...

FOR READING & MEDITATION – RUTH 4:5–8

'So the kinsman-redeemer said to Boaz, "Buy it yourself."
And he removed his sandal.' (v8)

We must not overlook the fact that the story of Ruth is set in 'the days when the judges ruled' (1:1), a period of Israel's history when 'Israel had no king; everyone did as he saw fit' (Judg. 21:25). It was a time when 'might was right' – 'an era', says one commentator, 'in which strength became bullying and domineering and people took care of themselves at the expense of the widows and the poor'. How refreshing, therefore, to discover in such turbulent times a man like Boaz who went beyond the letter of the law and sought to use his wealth and position for the good of others who were not so well off.

In Israel, every woman was the responsibility of the man who was her next of kin. According to family law, the nearest relative had certain obligations. These included providing an heir, when a man had died childless, to carry on his name, and buying land to keep it in the family. Boaz was one of those in line to take responsibility for Ruth, as Naomi's comment reveals: 'That man is our close relative; he is one of our kinsman-redeemers' (2:20).

Edward F. Campbell describes the role of a redeemer in this way: 'to function on behalf of persons and their property within the circle of the larger family... to take responsibility for the unfortunate and stand as their supporters and advocates... to care for those who may not have justice done for them'. Because Boaz took on the responsibility that came his way, lived up to his name, and did more than was required of him by the law, he became a leading character in a story that has made his name immortal. The energy that pulsed through his soul was other-centred. That is how it should be with everyone who is part of God's story.

My Father and my God, help me to live out my part in Your story by taking up every responsibility that is presented to me with enthusiasm and a generous spirit. Make me a truly other-centred person. In Jesus' name Amen.

FURTHER STUDY

Gen. 44:1–33; Heb. 7:24–25; 1 John 2:1–2

1. How did Judah assume responsibility for his brother?
2. How does Jesus assume responsibility for us?

My Utmost for His Highest

FOR READING & MEDITATION – RUTH 4:9–12

'I have also acquired Ruth... as my wife, in order to maintain the name of the dead with his property...' (v10)

For one more day we reflect on the role Boaz has in the story of God's salvation as it is narrated in the book of Ruth. Here is a man in whose heart burns a desire not merely to keep to the letter of the law, but to give *all* of himself in the service of others. His concern was not to discover what was the *least* he could do, but what was the *most* he could do. His life motto could have been (to borrow Oswald Chambers' beautiful words) *my utmost for His highest*.

The theme of redemption is highlighted in this story by the fact that Boaz was not only conversant with the details of an old Mosaic law, but had a generous enough heart to go beyond it. The name Boaz, we said, means 'substance' or 'strength'. There are some people who use their strength and substance simply to maintain themselves, possibly at the expense of others. The question each one of us must answer is this: Where is the energy that drives our personalities being directed – towards ourselves or others?

Some Christians regard their wealth as theirs by right and never consider the fact that with rights come responsibilities. I like what one commentator says concerning Boaz: 'When he decided to act in this way [in generosity rather than the mere keeping of the law] God's "wings" (2:12–13) are experienced in the story through the "wings" of Boaz (3:9).' Again I say: more is expected of us than keeping to the letter of the law. We are expected to go the second mile (see Matt. 5:41). And if you will forgive a change of metaphor here: when the Holy Spirit indwells us it is expected that out of our innermost beings will flow not trickles or rivulets but streams of living water (see John 7:38). *Streams!*

Loving heavenly Father, may what You pour into me also flow out from me. You are not niggardly in what You give to me; help me not to be stingy in what I give out to others. In Jesus' name I ask it. Amen.

FURTHER STUDY

Matt. 5:41–42; Acts 20:22–24; 2 Cor. 11:21–33
1. What does the Lord ask of us?
2. What did Paul offer the Lord?

Anyone Can Get In

FOR READING & MEDITATION – RUTH 4:13–17

'And they named him Obed. He was the father of Jesse,
the father of David.' (v17)

There is a very wonderful purpose behind God's direction to include the story of Ruth in the canon of Scripture. This short book shows us so clearly the way in which God takes ordinary people and lifts them out of their ordinariness into the drama of His universal epic. There are, of course, characters other than Naomi, Ruth, and Boaz in the book, and though most of them are unnamed, they are also important: the young man who was foreman of the harvesters, for example, the nearer kinsman in chapter 4, the anonymous women who sang 'Naomi has a son' in 4:17, and so on. They also get into the story. Who knows whether, if the spotlight could be turned on them, they too could tell stories which, though perhaps not as dramatic as Ruth's, nevertheless have significance.

But we must come now to the concluding words of the book, particularly the verse that is our text for today. This verse appears to make a straightforward genealogical statement, but what a wealth of truth lies within it. The words take us by the hand and lead us from a romantic story to an understanding of how ordinary characters became caught up in a larger story. It says in effect, 'See now how God has woven the things that happened to these characters into the story He is telling – the story of salvation. Ruth became the mother of Obed, who was the father of Jesse, who was the father of David... from whose line the Messiah Himself was born.'

The story of Ruth, therefore, though a narrative in its own right, must not be read in isolation. It is a story which leads us into God's epic. And anyone can get into that story – providing they are willing to come in through the door, which is, of course, Jesus Christ.

O Father, how can I ever thank You enough that I have entered through the door and become part of Your salvation story? Anything that happens to me is bearable when I see it as contributing to Your story. Amen.

FURTHER STUDY
Acts 2:36–41; Rom. 10:4–17
1. What did Peter proclaim?
2. What did Paul explain?

God's Great Redemptive Range

FOR READING & MEDITATION – RUTH 4:18–22

'Boaz the father of Obed, Obed the father of Jesse,
and Jesse the father of David.' (vv21–22)

Genealogies in the Bible are regarded by many as rather uninteresting and seemingly irrelevant, but the information they provide reveals some of the most exciting aspects of God's story. We saw yesterday how the simple statement: 'And they named him Obed. He was the father of Jesse, the father of David' (4:17), tells us that Ruth was the great-grandmother of King David, from whose line came our Lord Jesus Christ.

Matthew 1, which we looked at earlier in our studies and which provides the genealogy of Jesus, has a connection with the thoughts that have been occupying us as it mentions the name of Ruth. In fact, Matthew's genealogy is highly unusual because it departs from the normal custom of listing the male line only and includes the names of four women: Tamar, Rahab, Ruth, and Solomon's mother, Bathsheba. Tamar tricked her father-in-law into fathering her child (Gen. 38:18). Rahab was a prostitute who lived in Jericho (Josh. 2). Ruth, as we have seen, is referred to several times as a Moabitess – a foreigner. Bathsheba was the wife of Uriah the Hittite, and had an adulterous affair with King David (2 Sam. 11:4). Commentators have pointed out that each of these women was either foreign, immoral, or undesirable, and yet was included in the Messianic family tree.

This is what Eugene Peterson says concerning this point: 'Redemptive history is inventive and incorporative. It doesn't make any difference who your mother was. Anyone can get into the family. Anyone's personal history can be incorporated into the family history.' Though at first glance genealogical lists may seem tedious, the reality is that they demonstrate most powerfully God's redemptive ways.

Father, I am awestruck when I think about the endless ways You have of redeeming situations. Your skill at turning negatives into positives not only fascinates me but encourages me. Thank You Father. Amen.

FURTHER STUDY

Acts 11:1–18
1. Why was Peter criticised?
2. What was his defence?

Thick With Names

FOR READING & MEDITATION – REVELATION 2:12–17

'I will also give him a white stone with a new name written
on it, known only to him who receives it.' (v17)

Yesterday we saw that the genealogical lists in the Bible, synonymous in so many minds with monotony and irrelevance, become, when we understand their purpose, some of the most exciting parts of Scripture. It has not escaped your attention, I am sure, that there are few nameless people in the Bible. Scripture, as someone has put it, is 'thick with names'. 'The name,' says one writer, 'is the form of speech by which a person is singled out for personal love, particular intimacy, and exact responsibilities.'

That great storyteller of Victorian times, George MacDonald, knew how important a name is. In his exposition of the text before us today he wrote, 'The giving of the white stone with the new name is the communication of what God thinks about the man to the man. The true name is one which expressed the character, the nature, the meaning of the person who bears it... Who can give a man this, his own name? God alone. For no one but God sees what the man is... It is only when the man has become his name that God gives him the stone with his name upon it, for then first can he understand what his name signifies.' One day every believer is going to have a new name – a name that perfectly describes the person to whom it has been given.

What does all this say to us? It says this: God's love extends to details and is a love that delights to minister to us not just corporately but individually. If you find it hard to believe that you will be of consequence in heaven because you feel you are of such little consequence down here on earth then think about this: God has reserved for you a new name which will be given to you because of what you have become.

O Father, the more I see how Your love extends to details, the more my love flows out towards You. I can't wait to receive my new name describing the character You have formed in me. Thank You my Father. Amen.

FURTHER STUDY
Gen. 25:24–26; 32:24–28; Acts 11:19–26
1. Why was Jacob's name changed?
2. What was special about the Antioch Christians?

Christic — God's Alphabet

FOR READING & MEDITATION – REVELATION 1:1–8

'"I am the Alpha and the Omega," says the Lord God...' (v8)

Before we leave the story of Ruth and move on to other aspects of our theme we pause to make this central point once again: lovely as the story of Ruth is, it is not the whole story. The whole story is about the Messiah – the One whom our text for today describes as the 'Alpha and Omega'. Alpha and Omega, as many of you will know, are the first and last letters of the Greek alphabet, and the term 'Alpha and Omega' is used to signify the beginning and the end.

Some time ago I came across this by an anonymous writer: 'Christ is the alphabet out of which God frames every sentence, every paragraph, and every chapter of His salvation story.' When I first read that I remember shouting to myself *He is!* As we acknowledged earlier, every road in the Old Testament converges on Him and every road in the New Testament emerges from Him. Everything in the Bible revolves around Jesus Christ. Little did the women who prayed that Ruth would be 'like Rachel and Leah' (Ruth 4:11) know that the small town of Bethlehem would be set in the mainstream of God's wonderful purposes and become the birthplace of the Saviour Himself. It was one of the roads that led to *Him*.

The story recorded in the book of Ruth leads us ultimately to Jesus Christ. Though Ruth, Naomi, and Boaz were the participants, it is because of their relationship to Jesus Christ that they take on their significance. And it is the same with you and me. Our life stories may in themselves be interesting, even absorbing, but what makes them *significant* is when, through our relationship with Jesus Christ, they are woven into *His* story. Our names are on Christ's family tree – not prior to His coming, of course, but subsequent to it.

Father, I bow before You once again with gratitude in my heart that through Your Son's sacrifice for me on the cross I, an outsider, am now an insider. My name is on the Saviour's family tree. Hallelujah!

FURTHER STUDY
Acts 4:13–22; Eph. 1:11–14; 2:11–13
1. What made ordinary fishermen significant?
2. What makes excluded Gentiles significant?

Accepting the Inevitable

FOR READING & MEDITATION – PSALM 73:1–28

'Surely in vain have I kept my heart pure...' (v13)

Having seen something of the way in which God weaves the details of our lives into His big story we move on now to consider the question: How should we live as participants in God's big story? First, we must accept the inevitabilities of life. A famous psychiatrist, M. Scott-Peck, to whom I have often referred in the past, began his book *The Road Less Travelled* with these words: 'Life is difficult.' Once we face that fact, he points out, 'once we truly know that life is difficult, then life is no longer difficult. Because once it is accepted, the fact that life is difficult no longer matters. Then we can transcend it.'

We have been born into a fallen world, and things inevitably happen that are not to our liking. As Christians we must not expect to be exempted from the consequences of the Fall. It is true that sometimes God overcomes its effects (when, for instance, He mercifully heals our illnesses). But even those who have experienced His healing touch (and I am one of them) know that God does not heal every illness and that eventually every one of us will have to die.

Some Christians still claim that if we live close to Jesus Christ then it is possible to live a life that is free from all troubles and illness – a kind of Garden of Eden experience. But there is no way back into the Garden of Eden because God positioned some angelic bouncers there (Gen. 3:24). Something better than the Garden of Eden awaits us, but it lies up ahead. Meanwhile we wait, and accept life's inevitabilities with fortitude and grace. 'Here,' as a friend of mine puts it, 'there is something wrong with everything; there [speaking of heaven] nothing will be wrong with anything.'

My Father and my God, help me to understand that I live in a fallen world, and that though evil and disease are not part of Your good purposes, I have to live with them. Teach me how to accept the things I cannot change. In Jesus' name. Amen.

FURTHER STUDY

Rom. 8:18–25; 2 Cor. 12:7–10

1. What has Christ's sacrifice not done in the present?
2. Why can we delight in troubles?

Don't Dam the Stream

FOR READING & MEDITATION – JOB 21:1–21

'Who is the Almighty, that we should serve him?' (v15)

Yesterday we said that the first thing we must do in living as a participant in God's big story is to accept the inevitable. If we insist that because we are Christians we should be exempt from the effects of the Fall, our attitude will bring us into conflict with God's purposes for our lives. We can accept whatever happens to us with grace and not with a grudge. God is unable to work the divine alchemy in a heart that harbours resentment.

Take, for instance, the matter of bereavement. Some people suffer a crushing loss but never come to terms with it in their hearts. They accept that they cannot summon the one they loved from the dead, but they still remain bitter. They envy the happiness of others and resent the good health that those whom they regard as undeserving appear to enjoy. In their hearts they are hostile to God. Similarly Job, as we see from the passage we have read today, experienced some moments of antagonism towards God. Later on, however, he came to see the foolishness of his position.

Dr Barnardo, the founder of Barnado's children's homes in Britain, lost his little son from diphtheria when he was nine years of age. Did he accuse heaven of being unfair, and protest to the Almighty? No. He said, 'As my dear little boy lay gasping in my arms and as I gazed into the little pinched face growing cold in death, hundreds of other children's faces appeared to me through his. I resolved afresh that by God's grace I would consecrate myself anew to the blessed task of rescuing helpless little ones from the miseries of a neglected and sinful life.'

Are you harbouring a grudge? Dare to surrender it now. Grace may flow like a river but a grudge will dam the stream.

O God, forgive me if a grudge is damming the stream of Your grace. Help me surrender all my grudges to You right now so that grace might flow uninterrupted through my heart. In Christ's name I pray. Amen.

FURTHER STUDY
Mark 6:17–29; Heb. 12:14–15
1. How may we nurse a grudge like Herodias?
2. What is the antidote to grudges?

The Power of Lament

FOR READING & MEDITATION – PSALM 55:1–23

'My heart is in anguish within me; the terrors of death assail me.' (v4)

Another matter we need to face as participants in God's big story is this: we must be willing to lament. I am aware that this theme is not popular with the majority of Christians today, who seem to think that when a negative feeling arises, it is best to pretend it isn't there. Do you realise that 70 per cent of the psalms are laments? These laments arose from the disappointments, losses, and tragedies the psalmists faced, because they did not avoid these issues or deny that things were as they were.

One commentator says, 'The theology of lament is one of the most under-emphasised aspects of today's Christian culture.' Eugene Peterson, when contrasting the psalms with the secular culture of our day, said, 'We have a style of print and media journalism that reports disaster endlessly. In the wake of whatever has gone wrong or whatever wrong is done, commentators gossip, reporters interview, editors pontificate, pharisees moralise, but there is not one line of lament.' Notice these words: *there is not one line of lament*. Few of today's secular writers are ready to mourn the violation of moral principles. And why? Because generally speaking such things as truth, righteousness, and love are not taken seriously in today's world. What counts is 'news'. People cry out for the facts, and often are not interested in the underlying ethical issues. I tell you, when we trivialise the virtues of truth, righteousness, and love, then our culture is heading for the rocks.

Look again at David's words in Psalm 55. He faces everything, and prays through everything. Eugene Peterson claims that 'the craggy majesty and towering dignity of David's life are a product of David's laments'. I agree.

My Father and my God, help me understand the importance of lament. Save me from trying to get from one place to another too quickly, without giving my soul time to feel the pain. In Jesus' name I pray. Amen.

FURTHER STUDY

Prov. 25:20; Matt. 5:1–12; Rom. 12:15–16

1. How should we relate to those who lament?
2. What does God promise to those who mourn?

The Angry Psalms

FOR READING & MEDITATION – PSALM 64:1–10

'Hear me, O God, as I voice my complaint...' (v1)

Yesterday we noted that the majority of the psalms are laments. One Christian said in connection with the psalms of lament, 'I never read the angry psalms as they make it harder, not easier, for me to trust in God. I feel when I read them that I am doing little more than grumbling against God – something the Bible condemns.'

Dan Allender makes this point: 'Lament is as different from grumbling as a search is from aimless wandering.' A grumbler has already reached a conclusion about life, has shut down all open-mindedness with questions that are barely concealed accusations. In contrast, a person uttering a lament is expressing a desire to understand what is happening. That person is knocking at the door of God's heart and saying, 'Help me comprehend what is going on, what is the purpose behind my predicament.' He or she is not ranting and raving with conclusions they have already reached, but pouring out painful feelings in the hope that some answers might be given. Lament is a cry of agony.

Psalm 80 has several examples. Here is just one of them: 'O Lord God Almighty, how long will your anger smoulder against the prayers of your people?' (v4). Lament, properly understood, is entering the agony of loss, an expression of a desire for understanding.

Notice how often the psalmists, after they have expressed their pain, fall back into the arms of God and say, 'But as for me, I trust in you' (Ps. 55:23). When you lament you are being real with your emotions, being true to how you feel about what has happened to you. But having expressed your feelings, you then fall back on the certainty that God knows exactly what He is doing. There is a place for lament in the lives of all of us and it has great power.

Teach me the power of lament, my Father, so that I might deal with all my soul's needs in a way that contributes to my spiritual health. Save me, I pray, from the kind of idealism that has no realism. In Jesus' name. Amen.

FURTHER STUDY

Ps. 42:1–43:5

1. How was the psalmist real with his emotions?
2. What was the fall-back position?

Knowing God Better

FOR READING & MEDITATION – PSALM 77:1–20

'When I was in distress, I sought the Lord...' (v2)

We must spend another day reflecting on the significance of lament. The reason why the psalms of lament are included in Scripture is because we need to see the importance of being honest and real about our emotions. When loss strikes us or dampening disappointments affect our lives, we must be willing to face the pain and feel it. It is not easy, as a certain Christian once told me, to come to terms with some personal tragedy when you have just read words like these: 'A thousand may fall at your side, ten thousand at your right hand, but it will not come near you' (Ps. 91:7). We struggle at such times, and lament is part of that struggle.

Lament has the potential to change our attitudes because it compels us to strip our hearts of all pretence and forces us to wrestle with God. And out of that wrestling will come a new awareness of God and a new sense of His presence. There is no guarantee that our questions will be answered, but we will know *Him* better.

Many who study the psalms wonder why, as in the psalm before us, one moment the writer can seemingly rail against God, and then the next moment affirm His goodness. This is simply the experience of the soul rising through confusion – even anger – to recognise that, after all, God knows what He is doing and that He is good. And the struggles we go through to reach that conclusion are in themselves strengthening. Lament has been described as making the most of our losses and disappointments without getting bogged down in them. We admit how we are feeling, struggle with it, and then move on to acknowledge the greatness and goodness of our God. Lament is an important way of participating in God's story.

O Father, I see that if I want to be involved in Your story then dealing honestly with the affairs of my soul is part of that process. Lament is a sober subject but a necessary one. Please help me as I seek to understand it more thoroughly. Amen.

FURTHER STUDY

Lam. 3:19–26; Mark 14:32–42

1. What did Jeremiah call to mind in the midst of lament?
2. How did a period of lament affect Jesus?

How Evil Can Become Good

23
OCT

FOR READING & MEDITATION – PSALM 9:1–10

'I will be glad and rejoice in you...' (v2)

Over the past few days we have been saying that to be a participant in God's big story we must be willing to give up our grudges, accept the inevitable, and be ready to lament. But another point is this: we must believe in God's power to change things. Unbelief can hinder (though not outmanoeuvre) even the Almighty. So develop confidence in God's skill at turning life's setbacks into springboards. He can take even the most evil situation and make it work for good.

A curious thing happened in South Africa some years ago. A black woman was found guilty of a minor offence and fined a sum that amounted to the value of a gold coin she had in her possession, which had been bequeathed to her by her mother. When she handed the coin to the clerk of the court, he saw that according to the current gold standard, the coin was now worth much more than its face value. So he gave back to her in change a sum that exceeded what she thought the coin was worth. Knowing nothing about the gold standard, the woman left the court with her mind in a whirl. Back home in her village she asked her friends how she could possibly be condemned for a crime and yet be paid a dividend.

You may have experienced something similar in a different realm of life. Evil is evil, you say, tragedy is tragedy. Nothing can alter that. The death of someone you loved, the loss of an investment, a spouse's infidelity, hateful slander – these are things fit only for condemnation. How can one gain by them? The answer is: accept what happens without bitterness, enter into it with lament for an appropriate length of time, and have faith in God's transforming power. You will find that He can bring good out of everything bad.

Father, I might not live to see some of the transformations You are bringing about, but those who come after me may exclaim with the psalmist, 'The Lord has done this, and it is marvellous in our eyes.' For that I am thankful. Amen.

FURTHER STUDY
Dan. 3:13–30; Acts 8:1–8
1. What good resulted from the king's evil act?
2. What was the result of persecution?

When Sin Recoiled

FOR READING & MEDITATION – COLOSSIANS 2:6–15

'And having disarmed the powers... he made a public spectacle
of them, triumphing over them by the cross.' (v15)

Yesterday we said that God can transform everything that happens and make it work for good – even the worst form of evil. Think of the cross. That is the supreme example. If God could transform what happened there, He can do the same anywhere. At the cross, He took the foulest thing that has ever occurred and made it into the most sublime. The crucifixion is the world's worst sin; it is the world's supreme hope. It is the very essence of evil; it is the highest expression of love.

One writer has said this: "If a friend or a member of your family had died on a gallows you would not walk about with a gold gibbet around your neck. You would seek to hide his shame from every eye. But the manner of Christ's dying we hold up to all the world. The top of a church steeple is not too high for it; the communion table is barely prominent enough. Observe how complete is the transformation. It is His message it bears, not that of the ones who crucified Him.' When the sound of the last hammer stroke fell on the ears of the crowd and the cross was dropped into its socket they might have expected curses, but instead they heard Jesus say, 'Father, forgive them, for they do not know what they are doing' (Luke 23:34). The mystic alchemy had begun. Sin recoiled, was beaten, and became only the dark background of His radiant love.

If God can do that with the cross, what might He not do with the evil that comes into our lives? Will He be beaten by abuse, rampant hatred, crime, loss? No. He will dip His pen in these dark colours and write a story that will transform the evil into good. *God* is telling this story, remember – the greatest story writer in all the universe.

O Father, whenever doubts assail me about Your ability to turn evil to good, help me linger at the cross. There the worst thing that could ever have happened was turned into the best thing that could ever happen. Glory be to Your name. Amen.

FURTHER STUDY
John 12:23–33; Rom. 8:28–34
1. How did Jesus explain?
2. What did Paul affirm?

Entering Into Mystery

OCT

FOR READING & MEDITATION – JOB 42:1–6

'Surely I spoke of things I did not understand,
things too wonderful for me to know.' (v3)

Another thing we must do as participants in God's big story is to enter into mystery and celebrate it. (This is a matter we thought about earlier this edition in the January/February meditations, *The Nature of the Spiritual Journey*.) What do I mean when I say we must enter into mystery? Let me put it like this: most of us, when we are faced with mystery, instead of entering into it and rejoicing that God knows more than we do, attempt to resolve the mystery by reducing it to manageable proportions. Mystery erodes our sense of competence so we struggle to explain it, to rationalise it.

Some of God's 'mysterious' purposes, of course, can be explained. The romantic purpose that we talked about earlier is something that, once explained, can easily be comprehended. However, some things that happen to us cannot be understood, no matter how hard we try to make sense of them, for we are, as C.S. Lewis said, riding 'with our backs to the engine'. We are not able to see what the train driver can see up ahead. So we must enter into the mysteries and celebrate them, trusting that our lives are in safe hands. Mystery challenges us in the area of trust. God allows things to happen to us that have no apparent explanation, and so we accept and deal with whatever God is doing with absolute trust.

In one of his stories C.S. Lewis talks about a girl named Lucy who asks one of the other characters, Mr Beaver, about Aslan the Lion (a symbol of Christ): 'Is he safe?' 'No,' says Mr Beaver, 'he is not safe, but he is good.' The world in which we live is not safe, but God is good. We must go on believing that even in the presence of the deepest of mysteries.

My Father and my God, take my hand and walk with me through every mysterious situation in which I find myself. And help me remember that though sometimes life may be bad, You are always good. In Jesus' name. Amen.

FURTHER STUDY
Ps. 139:1–12; Isa. 40:21–31
1. What could the psalmist not attain?
2. What did Isaiah understand he could not understand?

Rejoice in Mystery

FOR READING & MEDITATION – PSALM 45:1–17

'My heart is stirred by a noble theme as I recite my verses
for the king...' (v1)

You may remember that when we were talking about Naomi's role, I said God did not delete the complaint she made about her situation from the inspired record but kept it and used it to advance His purposes. This statement, which I came across some time ago, intrigued me: 'God does not look kindly on our editorial deletions, but He delights in our poetry.' What does that mean, I wondered.

As I thought about it, this was my conclusion. There is a difference between poetry and prose. In nature and purpose they are totally distinct. Poetry is the product of passion. It has something volcanic about it, surging up in the poet's soul like molten lava and spilling over in strangely moving language. The poet cannot help but write a poem. He or she writes it even if nobody is ever likely to read it. In fact, some poets are not too concerned if no one does read their poems; all they want to do is to give their thoughts verbal expression. Not so prose. Speaking generally, a prose writer first makes up his mind what he wants to say and then says it as plainly as possible.

When the author of the statement quoted above talks about God not looking kindly on our editorial deletions but delighting in our poetry, I believe he is thinking of the different approaches that a poet and a prose writer might have to the mysterious. The prose writer might look at things analytically and say, 'I need more illumination before I can comment.' The poet is more likely to respond by entering into the mystery and composing a poem about it. This is what the psalmist is doing in the psalm we have read today. He doesn't attempt to manage the mystery of God; he simply rejoices in it.

O Father, grant that I may respond to what You are doing in my life with the poetry of thanksgiving and praise. Save me from seeking to make editorial deletions. Instead, may I receive everything with grace and gratitude. Amen.

FURTHER STUDY
Ps. 71:14–24; Phil. 4:4
1. Why would the psalmist praise more and more?
2. What did Paul emphasise?

FOR READING & MEDITATION – ROMANS 11:25–36

'Oh, the depth of the riches of... God! How unsearchable his judgments, and his paths beyond tracing out!' (v33)

We continue thinking about the statement we looked at yesterday: 'God does not look kindly on our editorial deletions, but He delights in our poetry.' G.K. Chesterton, in his book *The Romance of Faith*, said that when you face life honestly you become aware that chess players go mad but poets never do. He is using an hyperbole, of course – exaggeration for the sake of emphasis. A chess player is constantly working on strategy, and tries to find some order in an attempt to understand things. Once, when I was watching my favourite television programme, *Star Trek: The Next Generation*, I heard Commander Data, the Android, say that he preferred chess to poetry because he was more comfortable with order that could be manipulated. But then an Android has no emotion. A poet realises that there is order in life but he doesn't struggle to try and understand it; instead he floats on the waves and enters into the mystery of it through poetry.

When faced with the mystery of God's story in our lives we have two choices: either we respond by trying to figure out God's ways and seek to introduce some 'editorial deletions', or we respond by floating on the waves of His purposes and say, 'Lord, I praise You because Your ways are beyond tracing out', as Paul does in the passage we have just read. Poets recognise mystery and rejoice in it without trying to manage it.

Don't try to make sense of mystery when you find yourself caught up in it. Respond poetically to it. Rejoice in it. The very nature of existence requires that we be poets and not chess players. Blessed are those who allow themselves to be awed by what God is doing in their lives and respond to it with poetic rhythm and praise.

Father, help me respond to life's mysteries in the same way that Paul did – not by attempting to figure things out but by bowing in wonder, love, and praise. Amen.

FURTHER STUDY

Ps. 92:1–5; Eccl. 3:1–14
1. What is good for us?
2. What did Solomon realise?

Don't Sigh – Sing!

FOR READING & MEDITATION – 1 SAMUEL 1:21–2:11

'As surely as you live, my lord, I am the woman who
stood here beside you praying to the Lord.' (1:26)

Surely there can be no greater thrill than knowing that we are caught up in God's big story. Take the case of Hannah. You are probably familiar with the story, but permit me to briefly sketch some of the details.

Hannah was one of Elkanah's two wives, the other being Peninnah. Peninnah, we read, 'had children, but Hannah had none' (1:2). Regularly, Peninnah would scorn Hannah and make fun of her because she was infertile (1:6–7). But though deeply hurt, Hannah appears to have handled the situation with dignity and restraint. In the Temple Hannah pours out her soul to the Lord (1:15), and God hears her prayer. She conceives and gives birth to a child whom she names Samuel. A little while after his birth, Hannah keeps the promise she has made and presents Samuel to the Lord for a lifetime of service in the Temple. As she hands Samuel over to the Lord, she sings a song that is one of the most beautiful in Scripture. But notice *when* she sang her song – not when Samuel was conceived or born, but when she gave him up to the service of the Lord.

Dr Larry Crabb says, 'The deepest and richest songs are sung, not in the moments of blessing, but in those moments when we sense we are being caught up in the movement of God, that we have been lifted into a larger story.' Mary, the mother of Jesus, sang her most sublime song when she realised she was being caught up in a divine movement that would bring salvation to the world (Luke 1:46–55). Are you aware at the moment of something going on in your life that is bigger than your personal agenda – that you are being caught up in a bigger story? Then sing your song! It will be the most significant song you will ever sing.

My Father and my God, whenever I feel called to give something up – to surrender it to You – help me see my action in the context of the bigger story. And instead of sighing, help me sing. In Jesus' name. Amen.

FURTHER STUDY

2 Chr. 20:1–24

1. Who led the army?
2. When did the Lord bring deliverance?

A Transcendent Drama

FOR READING & MEDITATION – ISAIAH 38:9–22

'Surely it was for my benefit that I suffered such anguish.' (v17)

A good part of my life has been spent listening to people's stories. I have discovered that people can tell their story in many different ways. Some tell it as if it is a comedy – they joke about it because to deal with it seriously would reduce them to tears. Others tell it as a tragedy – they see no point in what has happened to them. Then there are those who tell it as an irony – they speak mockingly about the fitness of things. But I have met some – all too few – who talk about their lives in terms of a transcendent drama. They recount the things that have happened to them with the clear awareness that a loving God has allowed them to pass through these things for a purpose.

Whenever I have listened to Joni Eareckson Tada tell her story, for example, I hear nothing that comes anywhere close to tragedy, comedy or irony. There is something inspiring, something of God, about her story. She talks about the events that made her a quadriplegic not in terms of tragedy but in terms of a transcendent drama. One has only to listen to her to be aware of the grace of God that shines out from her personality. She has the attention and admiration of millions because she speaks out of suffering – suffering that has been redeemed. She admits, of course, that there was a time of complaint in her life – a time when she shook her fist in God's face – but she has worked through that now and has come to recognise that in allowing her accident to take place, God had a purpose for her life that has touched the lives of millions.

How would you tell the story of your life if you were asked, I wonder? As a comedy, a tragedy, an irony, or a transcendent drama?

Father, I am on the spot. How would I tell my story? As a comedy, a tragedy, an irony, or a divine drama? Please help me think this matter through today. In Christ's name I pray. Amen.

FURTHER STUDY

2 Cor. 1:3–11; 2 Tim. 4:6–8

1. How was Paul triumphant in adversity?
2. What could he say at the end of his life?

How Do I Get In?

FOR READING & MEDITATION – JOHN 3:1–15

'I tell you the truth, no-one can see the kingdom
of God unless he is born again.' (v3)

One thing I feel I must do as we draw to a close is to invite those who do not know Jesus Christ to become part of His story. In many areas of the world *Every Day with Jesus* is read by people who are interested in Christian things but have not yet committed themselves to Jesus. Today I want to invite those of you who are not yet included in God's salvation story to enter into it. And so, for the benefit of those who do not know Him personally, I pose this question: How do I enter into a relationship with God and become part of His eternal epic?

You enter into a personal relationship with God through His Son Jesus by being what the Bible calls 'born again'. I once preached a series of sermons on the text 'You must be born again' (v7), which were spread over six Sunday evenings. Someone asked me why I took the same text six successive Sunday evenings. I replied, 'Because you must be born again.' The necessity of the new birth is spoken of throughout the New Testament. We divide people into races, sexes, nationalities, the rich and the poor, the educated and the uneducated, but Jesus divided all men and women into only two classes: the once born and the twice born.

If you already know Jesus Christ, if you have been born again, you are in the kingdom of God, and if you are not, then you are not in His kingdom. If you have not been born again I invite you now to open your heart to God and His Son Jesus Christ. Say the following prayer and you will receive the new birth as countless multitudes down the ages have done. You will be born again.

Heavenly Father, I want to be part of Your story. I come to You now to be born again. I surrender everything to You – my whole life, my heart... everything. Accept me and make me Your child. In Jesus' name I pray.

If you have prayed this prayer for the first time, please consider purchasing a copy of our booklet entitled Every Day with Jesus for New Christians.

FURTHER STUDY
John 1:1–13; 3:16–18
1. What is the difference between physical and spiritual birth?
2. Why did God send Jesus?

FOR READING & MEDITATION – COLOSSIANS 1:1–14

'We are asking God that you may see things, as it
were, from his point of view...' (v9, Phillips)

On this our last day of thinking together about God as the divine story writer, I would like to drop into your heart this thought: no matter how insignificant you may feel, if you believe in the Lord Jesus Christ and have been born again, the truth is that you are included in God's big story. Your name is written into His universal epic. One day, when the whole story is unfolded in eternity, you will see what part you have played in the eternal scheme of things. You don't have to spend your time scrupulously trying to figure out in what scene you appear. Trust that the Casting Director has given you a role that highlights not only your special talents and individuality but, more importantly, the way in which divine grace is at work in your life.

Just to be part of God's great epic, to be caught up in the narrative He is telling, is one of the highest privileges afforded any human being. A friend of mine, Phil Greenslade, says, 'I don't mind being just a spear carrier as long as I am part of God's big story.'

I leave you with these lines by Paul Goodman, which he describes as 'a little prayer':

Page after page I have lived Your world
In the narrative manner, Lord,
In my own voice I tell Your story.

In my own voice I tell *Your story*. Powerful words. How different life is when we realise that through all that happens to us a divine story, a bigger story, is being written. Drop your anchor into the depths of this reassuring and encouraging revelation. In the strongest currents of life it will, I promise, help to hold you fast.

My Father and my God, how can I ever sufficiently thank You for the priceless privilege of telling in my own voice Your story? Help me from this day forward to see all things from Your point of view. In Jesus' name. Amen.

FURTHER STUDY

Rom. 12:1–13; Col. 4:5–6; 1 Pet. 3:15
1. What did Paul teach?
2. What do both Paul and Peter tell us to do?

NOV
&
DEC

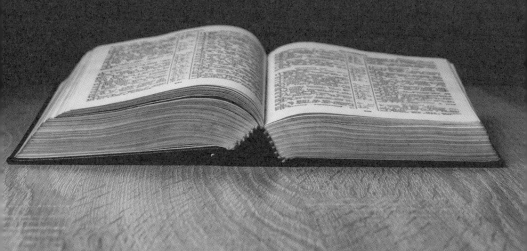

A Deepening Desire

FOR READING & MEDITATION – JOHN 17:1–10

'Now this is eternal life: that they may know you, the only
true God, and Jesus Christ, whom you have sent.' (v3)

At this time when we are surrounded by spiritual darkness, nevertheless there are a number of encouraging signs. One of them is that there is in the hearts of Christians everywhere a deepening desire to know more of God. A man once wrote to me and said, 'Something inside me longs to know more about my Creator. Can you show me how this hunger can be satisfied?' There are, I believe, multitudes of people who share that man's feelings, and this is why, with God's help, I intend over the next two months to steer you through a series of studies designed to increase your knowledge of God through an understanding of His different names.

To know God is the greatest goal a person can have. If sin had not entered the world then men and women would have devoted themselves to the knowledge of God for ever. It is because of lack of knowledge, says the Bible, that God's people are destroyed (Hos. 4:6). So the question must be raised immediately: How can we come to know God more fully? We can know God only through the means by which He chooses to reveal Himself, which are: the material creation, the Scriptures, and through His Son, the Lord Jesus Christ.

The aim of this series of studies is to discover God more fully through the various names He uses in Scripture. A name, when used in the Bible, is not merely a designation; it is a definition. The names of God reveal His characteristics, and reflecting on them should have a bearing on our own lives and character. As we meditate on God's greatness, His grace and His love, every problem we have falls into its proper place. From experience I can tell you that major problems become far less significant when measured against the greatness of an omnipotent God.

Gracious Father, already I sense that over the next two months my hunger for You will be satisfied. But not fully satisfied, for knowing You means that I am satisfied with an unsatisfied satisfaction. Amen.

FURTHER STUDY
Deut. 4:29; John 14:6–11
1. What type of person finds God?
2. How can we know God?

Cosmic Backing

FOR READING & MEDITATION – GENESIS 1:1–13

'In the beginning God created the heavens and the earth.' (v1)

Yesterday we said that one of the most thrilling discoveries we can make in our study of the Bible is to see the way in which God reveals Himself through His different names. The Old Testament, written originally in Hebrew and Aramaic – the languages of the Jews – contains meaning that is sometimes lost in translation, and this is true in connection with the various names of God. When, however, we look at those names in detail and use them as a lens to examine the nature and character of God, we find such majesty and power that to miss the exercise would be very sad indeed.

So right away let us focus our thoughts on the first Hebrew name for God found in the Bible. It occurs in the opening verse of the book of Genesis: 'In the beginning God created the heavens and the earth.' The name for God here is 'Elohim', and points to the One who possesses all the divine powers. What if the Bible did not begin with a picture of an almighty Creator? What if, instead, we read this: 'In the beginning the heavens and the earth came together of their own accord'? That chilling thought would lay a cold hand on all our hopes and endeavours and give us what one able and earnest man once described as 'a sense of cosmic loneliness'.

If there is no Creator behind the universe then I cannot be sure that my life has any cosmic backing. I do not know if I am working with anything significant or just working alone and meaninglessly with no one to back my work or even to care. Life cannot be meaningful unless it has meaningful resources. If there is no Creator then life is, indeed, meaningless. If, however, there is a Creator then all of life takes on a new and wondrous meaning.

O God, I see that when I lose You then everything is lost. I have no basis for my life, no meaning and no purpose. The world just doesn't make sense without You. Amen.

FURTHER STUDY
Gen. 1:26–31; Ps. 148:1–14
1. Why did God create humankind?
2. How should we respond to our Creator?

God's in His Heaven...

FOR READING & MEDITATION – JOB 23:1–17

'If only I knew where to find him; if only I could go to
his dwelling!' (v3)

Yesterday we made the comment that 'life cannot be meaningful unless it has meaningful resources'. If God is not our starting point then creation has no proper framework of reference; we have no star to steer our boat by and, having no star, we cannot reach our harbour. When God is not placed firmly in the centre of the universe – His rightful place – we lose the meaning of life.

If there is no God to give meaning to earthly life and existence then we end up in the condition described by Professor E. Hocking, a Harvard philosopher, who believed that man becomes frustrated because he discovers he needs to be completed by something beyond himself. This was his verdict: 'If there is no God to give worth and meaning to life then human beings are just animated bubbles that rise to the cosmic surface, glisten in the sunlight for a brief space and then burst, leaving a nasty wet spot on the surface of things.' Another person has summed up the matter in this way: 'If there is no God we go through loud days that have no meaning and no end.'

Those who ignore the fact that the universe began through the creative act of a loving God are left with that 'sense of cosmic loneliness' to which we referred yesterday. And those who dismiss God altogether are in an even worse situation for they have no hope of ever coming to terms with a vast universe. As I have mentioned before, an atheist has been described as 'someone with no invisible means of support'. Only as God is given the central place in His universe can the sense of cosmic loneliness be overcome for, to borrow a line from the poet Robert Browning, when 'God's in His heaven then all's right with the world'.

O God, I see that when people lose You then life loses its music. I am so glad that I already know You, and now I yearn to know You more fully. Please help me in my quest. For Jesus' sake. Amen.

FURTHER STUDY
Gen. 28:10–17; Ps. 146:5–10
1. What did Jacob discover?
2. What did the psalmist affirm?

I Wish God Were Back

FOR READING & MEDITATION – PHILIPPIANS 3:1–14

'I want to know Christ and the power of his resurrection...' (v10)

Today we continue meditating on the thought that God is first seen in Scripture in His capacity as Creator of the universe. The fact that the Bible opens in this way teaches us that without a Creator the universe has no proper framework of reference and lacks a cosmic meaning.

Sir Winston Churchill, as skilful with an artist's brush as he was with words, said, 'Whenever I set out to paint a nature scene I first try to get the sky right, for when I get the sky right then I know the picture will come out right.' From what we have been saying over the past few days we should now be aware that if we lose our sky we shall soon lose our earth. However, once we put God where He belongs – at the centre of the cosmos He created – then 'the sky is right' and everything falls into place.

A minister from the West Coast of America, who sadly surrendered his Christian faith to the 'God is dead' theory several years ago, said in an interview with a television reporter, 'Life is hard and contains little sense or meaning... the heavens are like brass... sometimes I wish God were back.' This deluded man was suffering from something termed 'the paralysis of analysis' – he was trying to live on a denial, and it just cannot be done. His case can be likened to that of a man who walks over to a table each day, takes a look at the food, and then turns away in disdain. He could live with this disdainful attitude for a while – but only for a while. In the end the biting pangs of hunger and the weakness he experienced would tell him, even though he refused to eat, that his body was made for food and that to refuse to accept that fact would result in certain death.

Heavenly Father, the conclusion is inescapable – without You my sky is continually overcast. Let the clouds part today and may I see – really see. In Jesus' name. Amen.

FURTHER STUDY
Acts 17:22–31; Eph. 1:15–23
1. How can we paint our spiritual sky right?
2. Why did Paul pray for Christians to know Jesus?

Searching for Me

NOV

FOR READING & MEDITATION – JOB 22:12–30

'When men are brought low and you say, "Lift them up!"
then he will save the downcast.' (v29)

By now it should be clear to all of us that the reason why God reveals Himself to us in the opening pages of the Bible as the Creator of the universe is because He wants us to have a strong framework of reference in which to construct our beliefs. Without the knowledge that the universe came into being by His hand, life has no meaning or purpose. If God goes then everything worthwhile goes with Him – everything lacks permanence, stability, and reality.

Centuries ago the prophet Isaiah summed up the whole matter in these words: 'And then – so the Lord of hosts declares – the peg driven in so firmly shall be wrenched out and give way, till everything that hung upon it shall come down' (Isa. 22:25, Moffatt). When the peg of materialistic philosophy, upon which almost everything is hanging in this generation, is wrenched out by economic calamity – a possibility that is causing much fear now – then our hopes, our plans, our confidence go with it. This generation is hanging its hopes on the wrong peg – materialism. That peg should be God, for as He holds amid the stress of things, everything holds.

Here, in the twenty-first century, we are in the position of being what Sorokin calls a 'sensate society'. It is a society that has exhausted itself against the facts of life. Our age is becoming bankrupt morally, spiritually, and financially. When we decide to take a new centre – God – then life for us will have new meaning and new purpose. A one-time agnostic, who passed from agnosticism to faith in Christ, said this: 'I came to the conclusion that the universe did not make sense without God. I set out to search for Him and found that He was searching for me.'

O God, now I see clearly the framework in which I have to win or lose the battle of life. Help me to give You Your rightful place at the centre of my universe. Then – and only then – will life make sense. Amen.

FURTHER STUDY
Luke 15:11–24; 19:1–10
1. How do we seek God?
2. How does God seek us?

320

FOR READING & MEDITATION – GENESIS 2:1–7

'The Lord God formed the man from the dust of the ground
and breathed into his nostrils the breath of life...' (v7)

As we move from the account of the material creation recorded in Genesis 1 to the detailed story of man's creation in Genesis 2, an interesting development takes place. We find as we read today's text that as the Creator (Elohim) bends down to take the dust of His creation and make out of it a living, breathing man, He introduces Himself by a new name – the Lord God or, in the Hebrew, Jehovah Elohim.

In these studies we shall discover that often, when God introduces a great change in history or responds to a need of His people, the Israelites, He announces Himself under a new name. Here God's personal name is added to that august and majestic name of Elohim as if He wants to soften its solemn title and show Himself not only as a God who can build mountains and create vast seas, but One also who is tender enough and loving enough to enter into a personal relationship with His human creation.

In the New International Version the Hebrew word 'Jehovah' (also translated 'Yahweh') is rendered 'Lord' with an initial capital and small capitals to distinguish it from another Hebrew word, 'Adonai', also translated 'Lord'. The name 'Jehovah' means 'to be actively present' and contains the thought of faithfulness and unchangeableness. Is it not significant that the first time God is seen in His capacity as the Creator of a human being He is seen as a God who is faithful and who keeps His promises? When God introduced Himself by His personal name He did more than expand His titles; He also revealed to the whole world His deep desire to create beings who could and would reciprocate His love. This is not evolution but involution – God involving Himself in His creation in a distinctively personal way.

O Father, I am so grateful for this picture of a God who bends to the lowest point of creation – the dust – that I might rise to the highest intention of the universe and have a relationship with the Deity. Amen.

FURTHER STUDY

Ps. 103:8–18; 104:10–18

1. What does the Lord remember?
2. How does God involve Himself in creation?

Myth – or Reality?

FOR READING & MEDITATION – GENESIS 2:8–17

'Now the Lord God had planted a garden in the east, in
Eden; and there he put the man he had formed.' (v8)

Today we shall explore an issue that is controversial and is troubling a great many people these days: Is man the product of a distinctive act of divine creation or is he the result of an evolutionary process?

As for myself, I believe the Genesis account to be true – that man was created not by an evolutionary process but by a divine act. I am aware, though, that many Christians suggest the account given in Genesis is clothed in the language of myth. There was no literal Adam and Eve, they say; the story of their creation is somewhat like the myth of Santa Claus. All grown-ups know that there is no Santa Claus, but the ideas associated with him – jollity, reward for good behaviour, and a universal kindness of spirit – are valid. We must treat the opening chapters of Genesis in the same way, so they claim.

This approach, in my opinion, violates the integrity of the book of Genesis, for we must ask ourselves: Where does myth end and history begin? If Adam and Eve are myth then so, perhaps, is the story of Cain and Abel. And then what about Noah and the Flood? Maybe that is myth also. It becomes impossible to draw the line between myth and reality. What is more, the whole process can be carried over into the New Testament. Is the virgin birth a myth? And the miracles? And the resurrection?

Jesus accepted the reality of Adam and Eve's creation (Matt. 19:4) and so do I. If evolution (and not a specific creation) provides the explanation of man's origin then there was no Fall. And if no Fall, no need for salvation or redemption. Fundamental issues are at stake here. Let us put our full weight on the Scriptures and submit our intellects to the authority of God's Word.

O God, hold me fast in the turbulence of current thought and give me a certainty of faith that sustains my heart as well as my intellect. In Jesus' name I ask this. Amen.

FURTHER STUDY
Rom. 1:18–32; Heb. 11:1–3
1. What may be the result of thinking the Bible is myth?
2. How are faith and understanding linked?

Choose Life

FOR READING & MEDITATION – DEUTERONOMY 30:15–20

'This day... I have set before you life and death, blessings and curses. Now choose life, so that you and your children may live...' (v19)

Whether we are conscious of it or not, the issues of life are before us. We must vote for or against a view of life that has worth, purpose, and a goal. If we vote that the universe has no meaning and that there is no distinct purpose running through the story of man's creation then we vote that our own lives have no purpose and no meaning. As I said yesterday, fundamental issues are at stake here. We are told by psychologists (and it is a fact which is corroborated by the whole of life) that when life has no distinct meaning and purpose then it goes to pieces. 'Without a strong controlling purpose,' says one famous psychologist, 'the personality disintegrates through its own inner clashes – no purpose, no personality.'

A young university student in a church of which I was the pastor once talked with me until the early hours of the morning about what he described as his 'crisis of faith'. He told me that after listening to lectures at his university on the origin of life, he could no longer believe in a literal interpretation of the events recorded in the book of Genesis. When I asked him how this affected his view of life he responded, 'Well, I must confess that the things taught here in church don't seem as important as they once did.' Two years later that student telephoned me in the middle of the night to say that he was about to commit suicide. Mercifully, he refrained from doing so, and later came to renewed faith in Christ.

Not all react in a similar way, of course, to the theories and philosophies presented by their places of education. Some listen, evaluate, and respect the sincerity of those who teach them, but when called upon to vote – they vote for life.

O God my Father, my vote is for life. I choose life with You as its Creator and Designer, and Your Word, the Bible, as its true exposition. Amen.

FURTHER STUDY
Josh. 24:14–24; John 6:66–69
1. What choice did Joshua present?
2. Why did Peter vote the way he did?

FOR READING & MEDITATION – PSALM 8:1–9

'What is man that you are mindful of him, the son of man
that you care for him?' (v4)

We are seeing that life will work in one way only – God's way. The following statement made centuries ago by Augustine of Hippo is often repeated because it is often corroborated: 'Thou hast made us for Thyself, and our hearts are restless until they find their rest in Thee.' Let that fact be burned into our minds. Let it save us from all preoccupation with triviality and inclination to dodge issues, and bend us to the business of holding God and His Word firmly in the centre of our hearts.

Though we are just nine days into our current theme, it is time to reach a firm conclusion: the ultimate purpose behind our creation is that we might discover and live in God. God is not just Elohim, the august and majestic Creator, but He is Jehovah Elohim – the personal God who condescends to breathe His life into humankind and extend His arms in the offer of a loving relationship.

A question that I was often asked when I was involved in counselling was this: 'Why was I created?' It is a question that haunts the minds of many people. My answer to such a question usually goes along this line: 'Why does a parent create children? Though procreation is the result of a physical act, in the highest reaches of parenthood it is the result of an impulse to love – the impulse that desires an object to whom love and character can be given. Is parenthood different in God? Could God, being love, have done anything other than create objects of that love? And, having created us, will He not give Himself to us? If not, then the whole point and purpose of creation is stultified. As Elohim, God is a mighty Creator but, as Jehovah Elohim, He is also the tender and loving Lord.

O Father, how thrilling it is to be reminded of the divine purpose behind my creation. You made me to know You and live in You. I shall be grateful for all eternity. Amen.

FURTHER STUDY

1 Cor. 1:9; Eph. 5:25–33; Col. 1:24–27
1. What is our heavenly calling?
2. What mystery did Paul reveal about creation?

El Shaddai

FOR READING & MEDITATION – GENESIS 17:1–8

'When Abram was ninety-nine years old, the Lord appeared
to him and said, "I am God Almighty... "' (v1)

Now we move on to consider another name of God – El Shaddai. This name first appears in connection with the patriarch Abram. The occasion was the confirmation of a promise made to him earlier (Gen. 12:2) concerning his becoming the father of a great nation. Abram's wife, Sarai, had by now passed the age of natural child-bearing, and God's promise of a child through her seemed a human impossibility. Nevertheless, God confirms His promise and assures Abram that what He has promised He is well able to perform.

The promise of a child, at such an age, must have been staggering to Abram and Sarai, but with the unfolding of His purposes, God, in keeping with His character, announces Himself under a new name. 'I am,' He says, 'God Almighty' – 'El Shaddai'. The sense of the Hebrew is uncertain but the title appears to mean 'God the Mountain', conveying the thought of His strength in contrast to human frailty.

We have already pointed out that often in the Old Testament God introduced a significant stage of development in the lives of His people by revealing Himself under a new name. And what is more, the name exactly fitted the situation. In the building of the material universe God announces Himself as Elohim, the One who possesses all the divine powers. When breathing His own life into the body of a man, He reveals Himself as the personal God who is faithful – Jehovah Elohim. Now, when the destiny of His people, the children of Israel, is at stake, God steps in, touches the reproductive system in Sarai's body so that she is able to have a child and, at the same time, announces Himself as the great El Shaddai – the strengthener and nourisher of His people.

O God, how reassuring it is to realise that difficulties are the doors through which You impart Your own inner resources to Your people. Your supply so immeasurably exceeds all human demands. For that I am truly grateful. Amen.

FURTHER STUDY

Gen. 35:9–12; 1 Sam. 1:10–20; Gal. 5:22–23
1. What is the purpose of God's nourishment?
2. What part do we play in becoming fruitful?

FOR READING & MEDITATION – PSALM 145:1–16

'You open your hand and satisfy the desires of every
living thing.' (v16)

At present we are seeing that difficulties and problems, to a God who is infinite and loving, serve only to bring out a characteristic which, previously hidden and unknown, He delights to reveal. When confronted by Sarai's physical inability to produce a child, God steps in, takes charge of the situation, breathes fresh vitality into her whole being and, at the same time, takes the opportunity to reveal Himself under a new name – El Shaddai (Gen. 17:1).

The traditional interpretation of the Hebrew name *El Shaddai* is this: 'God who is sufficient' or 'God the Enough'. What a beautiful word picture this presents of the infinite resources of an Almighty God. There are many things in this world of which people think they do not have enough. Some nations, for instance, claim they do not have enough money, oil, mineral resources, and power. And it is generally assumed that if only it were possible to have a sufficiency of the things we feel we lack then satisfaction would immediately result. That assumption, however, is a false one. The problem is not so much that people do not have enough of these things but rather that the things themselves are not enough. There is only one way the human heart can have enough. Dr Henry Van Dyke expressed the truth in this way: 'There is absolutely nothing that man cannot do without – except God.'

Perhaps at this very moment you are caught in a situation that to all human intents and purposes seems hopeless. You do not know where to turn. Though you may not always realise it, difficulties and problems are the dark backdrop against which God paints, in vibrant and illuminating colours, the beauty of His infinite care and love.

O God my Father, I bow in adoration as You speak to my need today. Forgive me for not always recognising that Your resources so infinitely exceed all my requirements. Amen.

FURTHER STUDY

Ps. 104:21–28; 107:1–9

1. How can we be satisfied?
2. Are there conditions for God's provision?

How Great is Our God

FOR READING & MEDITATION – ISAIAH 40:18–31

'The Lord is the everlasting God, the Creator of the ends
of the earth. He will not grow tired or weary...' (v28)

Yesterday we said that the traditional translation of the name El Shaddai is 'God the Enough'. Isn't it positively reassuring to know that God's eternal sufficiency so immeasurably surpasses every demand that we may make upon it? In an age when the world has to consider the possibility of running out of many of its natural resources, we have the comfort of being able to fix our gaze upon the God who created and designed the universe – the God who is *Enough*.

Isaiah's prescription for Israel's despondency and despair, in the passage we have read today, was to draw their attention to the might and power of the everlasting God. He did what a good doctor would do when walking into a sickroom where the blinds were drawn and the windows closed – he pulled back the curtains, opened the windows and allowed the sun to stream through. If only we could learn to set all our problems against the vastness and greatness of an almighty God. Listen again to these comforting words: 'Do you not know? Have you not heard? The Lord is the everlasting God, the Creator of the ends of the earth. He will not grow tired or weary, and his understanding no-one can fathom' (v28).

Dr Luccock, a writer who was greatly concerned about the increasing amount of traffic on the roads, once said, 'If I die on the streets you can put on my tombstone, "Died of looking the wrong way".' Life is bound to hit you if you look to earth rather than to heaven. Many of us are dying spiritually because we are looking the wrong way. We look at earth's ruin instead of heaven's resources. We see the gloom instead of the glory. Our gaze must be focused continually on God – God the great El Shaddai, God the Enough.

O God my Father, help me not to depend any more upon Your creatures but only on You, the Creator. You alone have the answers that really resolve matters and do not let me down. And for that I am deeply thankful. Amen.

FURTHER STUDY

Ps. 34:1–7; 123:1–4; Dan. 4:28–37
1. How, exactly, do we look to God?
2. When was the king restored?

'Him-Possible'

FOR READING & MEDITATION – GENESIS 17:15–22

'God also said to Abraham, "As for Sarai your wife, you are no longer to call her Sarai; her name will be Sarah."' (v15)

Now and again, in a world that is coming apart at the seams, we need to stop what we are doing and look at the resources available to us. This is what we have been attempting to do over the past few days. We have been gazing at El Shaddai – God the Enough – and have seen that He is the only being in the universe who has the resources and power to meet our every need. And we must keep our gaze continually fixed on Him, for if we gaze too long at our problems we will become obsessed by them; they will dominate us and it will not be long before we become a problem to ourselves and to others.

After God promised Abram that he would be 'the father of many nations' (v4), Abram and Sarai considered their physical limitations and found the idea of being a father and mother utterly incredible. But their age was no obstacle to the God who is the nourisher and strengthener of His people, and what He had promised He would bring about. The interesting thing about the story of Abram and Sarai is that at this point not only did God change His own name, but also He changed Abram's and Sarai's, too. Abram's name became *Abraham* and Sarai's name became *Sarah*. What really was the difference? This: God put an aspirate in their names – the sound of 'h'. The Almighty breathed His supernatural breath into them and to signify this He added an aspirate to their names. The letter 'h' cannot be pronounced without using breath. Try it and see.

The great El Shaddai is always ready to breathe into situations and circumstances where a miracle is required. When He does then the word impossible becomes *Him-possible*. What is not possible to us is indeed gloriously possible to Him.

Gracious God and heavenly Father, breathe into me today so that instead of being weak I shall be strong; instead of faithless, believing; instead of uncertain, confident; instead of a servant, a son. In Jesus' name I ask it. Amen.

FURTHER STUDY

Isa. 62:1–4; Acts 7:59–8:1; 11:25–26; 13:9

1. How does a new name signify a new life?
2. What is your new name and how does it inspire faith?

FOR READING & MEDITATION – GENESIS 22:1–14

'So Abraham called that place The Lord Will Provide.' (v14)

We come now to a series of names beginning with the word Jehovah, most of which are introduced at specific moments in the history of the children of Israel, when God is presented as meeting new and unusual aspects of human need. The first of these titles is the name Jehovah Jireh. The occasion when this name was given is one of the most moving in the whole of the Word of God. It was the last great crisis in Abraham's life.

One day God appears to him with the astonishing command to offer up his son Isaac as a human sacrifice. Abraham, unaware that this is a test of his faith, grimly sets out with Isaac for Mount Moriah, and once there he prepares to sacrifice his son. At the last moment, however, just as the gleaming blade is about to be plunged into Isaac's body, God intervenes and calls a halt to the proceedings. Out of that great crisis of faith and the clear word that 'God himself will provide the lamb' (v8) comes a new vision of God. Abraham called the name of the place where God intervened Jehovah Jireh – 'The Lord Will Provide'.

We must be careful not to miss the significance of this thrilling revelation. God provides very many things for the people He has created. He provides the food we eat, the air we breathe and the light by which we see. But what is His greatest provision? It is atonement for our sin. The term Jehovah Jireh carries with it clear intimations of the sacrificial death at Calvary of Jesus, 'the Lamb of God, who takes away the sin of the world' (John 1:29). It is a signpost directing us to the cross. Abraham, at this moment, looked into the very heart of reality. Only through the cross can we see fully into the heart of God.

Gracious God and loving heavenly Father, help me to realise that if I miss seeing Your provision for my salvation through that great act of love at Calvary, then I miss everything. Give me eyes that see, for I long to see everything. Amen.

FURTHER STUDY
John 1:29; Heb. 9:11–10:4
1. Contrast the blood of animals and the blood of Jesus.
2. What does forgiveness require?

FOR READING & MEDITATION – PSALM 22:22–31

'They will proclaim his righteousness to a people yet unborn
– for he has done it.' (v31)

Of all the different names of God we have considered so far, the name Jehovah Jireh, in my opinion, reveals the most about His character. And why? Because it gives clear intimations of Christ's death for us at Calvary. Nothing unveils the nature and character of God so effectively as does the cross. This is why we said yesterday that when Abraham saw that God was Jehovah Jireh – the Lord who provides – he looked, at that moment, into the heart of reality. At Calvary the highest revelation of God was given; it is the one place in the universe where His love can be truly measured and His character truly unfolded. We can learn much about God, but we can never fully know Him until we look into the inner depths of His being and see Him as bleeding and suffering love.

Let us travel back through the centuries for a moment and stand at the foot of the cross. Who was it on that first Good Friday who saw clearly into the heart of God? Was it Peter? No. Was it any of the other disciples? No. It was the dying thief (see Luke 23:40–43). Out of the great crowd who had gathered around the cross, he alone saw into the very heart of reality. And the moment he did so he passed from perdition to paradise. He knew little about God, but when he saw the self-giving love of Christ being poured out on those timbers of torture he knew everything. Through the cross he saw God's heart. Then, by a leap of faith, he took hold of God's provision. One moment hell yawned beneath his feet. Another moment and heaven shone before his eyes. The cross threw back the curtains, letting him see the heart of God. And the result? A robber and the Saviour walked hand in hand into paradise.

O God, I tremble to think that though I may know much about You, unless I have met You at the cross I can never truly know You. I bow before Your cross today in sincere acknowledgement that You really are my Lord and my God. Amen.

FURTHER STUDY
Luke 23:32–43; Rom. 6:3–11
1. Contrast the two thieves.
2. In what sense have we already died?

Why Was Man Made Free?

FOR READING & MEDITATION – ROMANS 5:6–17

'But God demonstrates his own love for us in this:
While we were still sinners, Christ died for us.' (v8)

At the moment we are meditating on the fact that, of the names of God used so far in the book of Genesis, the most revealing, so I believe, is that of Jehovah Jireh – the Lord will provide. In the title Jehovah Elohim we saw God giving Himself to His human creation by breathing into Adam the breath of life. Here, however, in the title Jehovah Jireh, and the circumstances out of which the name arose, the implication is this: God is willing to do more than give Himself *to* His creation – He is prepared to give Himself *for* it. Quietly but purposefully God is revealing through His names that He is not just interested in giving gifts to His people; He is prepared to go to the utmost lengths when necessary and give *Himself*.

Out of this fact comes a hint as to why man was created in the first place. I have often wondered, and doubtless you have, too, why God dared to create man and to create him free. To make man free meant that God had to somewhat limit Himself. He had to step back and allow a free human will to operate. He could not coerce it for if He did then the will would not be free. Suppose that will would go wrong – it would break the human heart and God's heart, too, for God would have to live alongside that rebellious, straying human will and still love.

But God took the risk on one condition. Anything that fell on man would fall on Him. Speaking of Christ, Paul tells us, 'God made him who had no sin to be sin for us' (2 Cor. 5:21). All love has the desire to make the sins and sorrows of the one it loves its very own. And here, in the unfolding of the name Jehovah Jireh, that most incredible and most glorious truth is beginning to be revealed.

O God my Father, as I consider the love that went into the making of man, my heart overflows with gratitude. The love that would take such risks and carry its purpose through must inevitably face a cross. Such love has won me for ever. Amen.

FURTHER STUDY
John 3:14–18; 2 Cor. 5:17–21
1. Outline God's plan of salvation.
2. List the characteristics of God revealed in this plan.

Not a Needle – A Nail

FOR READING & MEDITATION – ISAIAH 53:1–12

'But he was pierced for our transgressions, he
was crushed for our iniquities...' (v5)

Yesterday we said that God, being love, was bound by His very nature to create man and to create him free. Some then argue, 'God, by making man free, must also accept the responsibility for man's sin.' Well, He did. He accepted that responsibility and discharged it upon the cross.

An Italian painter has painted a picture of the cross in which the nails go through the wood into the hands of God, who stands behind it in the shadows. Every time I look at this picture I feel a tremendous sense of awe. An elderly Chinese scholar, hearing for the first time the story of a redeeming God, ran his fingers through his hair, turned to his neighbours, and said, 'Didn't I tell you there ought to be a God like that?'

Amy Carmichael was a well-known missionary to India who in 1901 began rescuing children, many of them girls who had been forced into prostitution. Eventually she cared for over 1,000 children. One girl, who resisted the spirit of the home founded at Dohnavur in southern India, caused Amy Carmichael great concern, and she did everything she could to persuade the girl to change. One day she took the girl aside, bared her own arm, took a needle and said, 'This is what your rebelliousness is doing to me.' Then she plunged the needle into her arm so that the blood spurted out. As the girl saw the blood she threw her arms around Amy Carmichael's neck and wept as if her heart would break. 'I didn't know that you loved me like that,' she cried, and from that moment she was completely changed.

Deep down on the inside we all know that our sin has hurt God, but we did not see it clearly until we saw it at the cross. And it was not a needle that our sin drove into God's heart. It was a nail.

O Father, now I see what my sin cost You. It cost a cross. As I gaze again at the cross my heart responds, as did that girl's in India many years ago, and I cry out, 'I didn't know You loved me like that.' Thank You, Father. Amen.

FURTHER STUDY

Col. 2:13–16; Heb. 12:1–14
1. What was nailed to the cross?
2. Why did Jesus not avoid the cross?

Jehovah Rophe

FOR READING & MEDITATION – EXODUS 15:22–26

'I am the Lord, who heals you.' (v26)

Now we come to another of God's titles, Jehovah Rophe, which means 'The Lord who heals'. It is the second of the compound names of Jehovah and gives us a further insight into the way God progressively reveals Himself through His names. An intriguing fact about this revelation, as we have said, is that God often made Himself known through a new and different name when His Old Testament people met with some emergency or problem that they had not encountered before. Difficulties and problems served only to bring out in God a characteristic that hitherto had remained hidden from His people and had not been revealed.

The name Jehovah Rophe was given during one of the children of Israel's earliest experiences in the wilderness. Downcast and discouraged by the bitter disappointment they experienced when they found the waters of Marah too bitter to drink, they discover a new and comforting characteristic of God as He says to them, 'I am the Lord, who heals you.'

Next to sin, nothing has taken a greater toll on human happiness than illness and disease. It may be, as you read these words now, that your body is racked with pain or you are weighed down with some physical complaint. Cast your gaze once again on the words at the top of this page and let them sink into your spirit until they become part and parcel of your personality. We can be grateful for all that medical science contributes to our physical health, but when medical science fails there is still God. Indeed, I can testify to the direct healing God gave me when medical help proved ineffectual. Here, in the twenty-first century, over 3,000 years since the words of our text were first uttered, God is still Jehovah Rophe.

O Father, how I need this revelation of Your ability to heal. While I am grateful for medical expertise, may I never take my eyes off You. Let Your health and vitality flow through every part of my being now, I pray. In Jesus' name. Amen.

FURTHER STUDY
Exod. 23:25; Deut. 7:11–15; Ps. 103:1–5
1. What were the conditions for Israel to know divine healing?
2. How relevant are these for us today?

FOR READING & MEDITATION – MATTHEW 8:5–17

'This was to fulfil what was spoken through the prophet Isaiah:
"He took up our infirmities and carried our diseases."' (v17)

We continue examining the Hebrew name for God, Jehovah Rophe, which means, 'The Lord who heals'. The subject of divine healing presents more problems that any other subject I know. A greater number of letters have been sent to me about this topic than any other issue. This is why we must explore together a biblically-based philosophy of healing that can help us cope with this problem in the future.

Disease, sickness, and physical disharmony come from two main sources: (1) actual structural disease brought about by, for example, heredity, accident, contagion, ignorance, abuse, poverty, and unbalanced nutrition, and (2) functional disease (which may pass into structural disease) brought about by incorrect mental, moral, and spiritual attitudes. There are those who claim that all disease has a physical origin. There are others who say that all disease has a spiritual or mental origin. Both are wrong. Many people have died repeating the slogan 'Disease is simply in the mind' when a doctor could have applied a relatively simple remedy and helped them to regain their health. On the other hand, many people fail to find health because the sickness is not structural but functional, that is, it is not so much in their bodies as in their attitudes – in their minds.

My own view is that about 75 per cent of our illnesses and maladies are functional, and about 25 per cent are due to structural faults or damage. Even those who regard Christianity as being merely one of the great faiths have to admit that this is so. True Christianity takes both types of illness seriously. Christianity is founded on the truth of the incarnation: 'The Word became *flesh* and made his dwelling among us' (John 1:14).

O Father, You are the God of body as well as soul. You have made me for health and rhythm. Make this body of mine the finest instrument of Your purposes. For Jesus' sake. Amen.

FURTHER STUDY
Ps. 32:1–7; 1 Thess. 5:23; 1 Pet. 2:24
1. Why was David sick and when was he healed?
2. What is God's will for our bodies?

Not the Will of God

FOR READING & MEDITATION – JOHN 10:1–10

'I have come that they may have life, and have it to the full.' (v10)

Yesterday, in attempting to identify the two main sources of disease, sickness, and disharmony, you might have noticed that I did not mention the will of God. God does not *will* disease. It is true that God often turns what is bad into something good, but we must not fall into the trap of believing that because He does so He actually willed the sickness in the first place.

Some argue that certain forms of illness arise from breaking the laws that God has written into the constitution of things and thus He wills these illnesses. But that is taking matters too far. We break God's laws and they break us. That makes *us*, and not God, the author of that disease or sickness. Doctors tell us that the human frame is designed for health and that if we co-operate with nature, nature will produce health. Health, then, is written into the constitution of things. God wills it.

If we do not have good health it is possible that some law has been broken somewhere by our ancestors, by ourselves, by society, or by factors in our environment. What is important is that if we are sick we should endeavour to discover whether the illness has come about from a purely structural breakdown or from incorrect or functional attitudes. Most sicknesses by far stem from our negative attitudes to life and are rooted in our emotions. So make time to go over your mental and spiritual attitudes and consider this question: Do these attitudes contribute to physical health? If they do not then in all probability they contribute to sickness and disease. Change those attitudes. Give up resentment, bitterness, worry, anxiety, fear, and hate. Believe me, your body will record the difference.

O God, help me to purge from my mind all fear, worry, bitterness, resentment, and anxiety so that my body will not be beset by the problems these attitudes create. I long to be strong for You. Make me the best I can be. In Jesus' name. Amen.

FURTHER STUDY

Ps. 38:1–22
1. What was the cause of the psalmist's sickness?
2. What did he do to stop his troubles?

How to Handle Sickness

FOR READING & MEDITATION – 2 CORINTHIANS 12:1–10

'Three times I pleaded with the Lord to take it away from me.' (v8)

Today we come to a question that troubles many people in relation to this subject of health and healing, namely: If my sickness is purely physical and does not stem from wrong mental attitudes – what then?

If the sickness is serious you should consult a doctor. You may consider that this is not a very 'spiritual' step to take, but remember it was God who planted in nature physical remedies for physical disease. And do not think that because you take something that has been medically prescribed God is going to be offended and say, 'I will only heal you when you stop taking medication and start trusting Me.'

As God wills health, approach the matter positively and also ask Him to heal you. Pray for your own healing and then, if nothing happens, invite others to join you in prayer. Keep in mind the command in James 5:14: 'Is any one of you sick? He should call the elders of the church to pray over him and anoint him with oil in the name of the Lord.' This course of action is non-optional. God instructs you to follow it.

If after prayer and medical help the sickness persists then ask God for His peace and understanding. Remember that He is with us in all our troubles and difficulties, and with His strengthening and help we can make chronic ill health contribute to His ends. God's chief way of developing qualities in our lives is through exposure to His Word, the Bible. But if we neglect His Word or fail to observe its teaching even though we read it then He will sometimes delay healing a sickness and use it to develop in us the qualities He desires for us. If the illness goes then all is well. If it remains, we can use it to help develop inward qualities. So either way we win.

O God, make me, I pray, a vital person – one who sees in everything a purpose. I am so glad that when I view life through Your eyes I never lose but always win. Thank You, Father. Amen.

FURTHER STUDY

Rom. 5:3–5; Jas 5:13–18

1. How can sickness be used to develop our spiritual lives?
2. What is the Christian attitude to sickness?

FOR READING & MEDITATION – EXODUS 17:8–16

'Moses built an altar and called it The Lord is my Banner.' (v15)

Today we are introduced to another new name for God – Jehovah Nissi. Those familiar with Old Testament history will know the details of the great battle at Rephidim between the Israelites and the Amalekites – a nomadic tribe descended from Esau. Joshua, acting under the instructions of Moses, led the people into battle while Moses climbed to the top of a nearby hill with Aaron and Hur to watch and pray.

As he surveyed the battle Moses held in his hand the staff which had played such a major part in the deliverance of Israel from the land of Egypt. When Moses held the staff aloft the battle went in favour of the Israelites but when, through weariness, he lowered it the battle went in favour of the Amalekites. The problem was solved when Aaron and Hur held Moses' hands up until the battle was over and won.

Following this incident another new revelation of God's ability to meet the needs of His people is unfolded. An altar is built by Moses and a new name of God is connected to it – Jehovah Nissi, meaning 'The Lord is my Banner'. A banner in ancient biblical times was not necessarily a flag such as we use nowadays. The word is translated variously as pole, ensign or standard. It was this staff, the banner of God, which brought the victory. What was the significance of the Amalekites' success when it was lowered and Israel's success when it was raised? This happened in order to impress upon Israel's warring soldiers that only under God's raised banner was victory assured. No matter what the odds, then, 'Five of you shall chase a hundred, and a hundred of you shall put ten thousand to flight; your enemies shall fall by the sword before you' (Lev. 26:8, NKJV).

O God, how thankful I am that beneath the banner of the cross every spiritual foe can be routed, every enemy discomforted, and every adversary overcome. Help me to stay beneath Your banner. In Jesus' name. Amen.

FURTHER STUDY

Ps. 20:1–9; 60:4; John 12:32

1. What is the purpose of a banner?
2. How can we lift up a banner today?

There's a War On!

FOR READING & MEDITATION – EXODUS 17:1–7

'Then Moses cried out to the Lord, "What am I to do with these people? They are almost ready to stone me."' (v4)

As the children of Israel made their way through the desert they were confronted on several occasions with serious dangers and difficulties. They discovered, however, that God was present in each crisis and that sometimes He took advantage of a difficulty to reveal to His people a new characteristic of Himself.

A few days ago we read how God turned the bitter, undrinkable waters of Marah into sweetness and, at the same time, revealed Himself as Jehovah Rophe, the Lord who heals (Exod. 15:22–26). Here, at Rephidim, the situation is different; it is not that the waters are bitter but that there is no water at all. The discovery of this fact led to a great deal of discontent and anger directed against Moses. The problem was resolved only when God worked a miracle for the Israelites by providing them with water from out of the solid rock.

But lack of water was not their greatest problem. As we saw yesterday, they were soon attacked by a fierce and warring people who were about to prove themselves to be implacable human foes. These foes were the Amalekites, descendants of Esau (Gen. 36:12). Though they were defeated at Rephidim they were to become persistent enemies of Israel (Num. 14:43,45; Judg. 3:13; 7:12).

This ongoing struggle against the hostile Amalekites is an analogy of the spiritual warfare in which we, God's people, are continually and steadfastly engaged. When men and women take their Christian faith seriously, they can expect spiritual opposition. I am deeply convinced that we will understand life better when we view it as the Bible views it. The Bible says that for every believer there is a war on. But keep in mind that in this war the outcome is already decided: we win.

Gracious Father, Your every revelation is an encouragement. I see today that in the midst of this spiritual warfare in which I am engaged You are truly my Jehovah Nissi. Your very character is behind those words. And I am so thankful. Amen.

FURTHER STUDY

2 Sam. 5:17–25; 2 Tim. 2:1–7

1. What were the keys to David's victories?
2. What are the characteristics of a Christian soldier?

Peaceful Co-Existence

24

NOVNOV

FOR READING & MEDITATION – EPHESIANS 6:10–18

'For our struggle is… against the rulers, against the
authorities, against the powers of this dark world…' (v12)

Yesterday we said that the experience of the children of Israel at
Rephidim, where they were attacked by the hostile Amalekites, is an
analogy of the spiritual warfare in which we, God's people, find ourselves
constantly engaged as we move ahead in our Christian lives.

Consider for a moment the striking contrast between what happened
at the Red Sea and what happened at Rephidim. At the Red Sea, when
the Israelites were delivered from Egypt's bondage, God's command was,
'Stand firm and you will see the deliverance the Lord will bring you today'
(Exod. 14:13). This illustrates beautifully God's work in our salvation. In
bringing us into the Christian life God alone is the agent. The Israelites could
do nothing to secure their salvation at the Red Sea – God did it for them.
But having been delivered from Pharaoh and introduced to a new life, they
soon discovered that there was a warfare in which they had to engage.

All Scripture has a purpose; it is inspired by God to teach and instruct
us in the art of effective Christian living (2 Tim. 3:16). The experience of
the Israelites at Rephidim, described in Exodus 17, serves to remind us that
once we come into the Christian life we must recognise that we are thrust
right into the middle of a spiritual battle between the Church and Satan
and his forces. For too long many Christians have neglected this fact and
have been enjoying a peaceful coexistence pact with the archenemy, the
devil. We have adopted this attitude towards Satan: 'Don't bother me and
I won't bother you.' The war between Satan and ourselves is not a 'cold
war' but a hand-to-hand combat, waged in the power of the Spirit. We
should never forget that.

**Father, You have put Your finger on a major problem in the Church. We have
been so busy fighting each other that we have been diverted from fighting
our real enemy – the devil. Forgive us we pray. Amen.**

FURTHER STUDY
2 Cor. 10:3–5; 1 Pet. 5:8–9; Rev. 12:9–11
1. What are the tactics of the enemy?
2. How do we overcome Satan?

339

The Finger of God

FOR READING & MEDITATION – LUKE 11:14–23

'But if I drive out demons by the finger of God, then
the kingdom of God has come to you.' (v20)

Does this talk about the devil and spiritual warfare, which has been the focus of our attention over these past few days, make you feel somewhat apprehensive and afraid? If so, then don't worry because this is not unusual; the majority of Christians feel a degree of trepidation when the subject of Satan and his forces is raised.

'This fear of the devil,' said Corrie Ten Boom, 'is most likely from the devil himself.' Satan will do everything in his power to prevent you from seeing your true authority in Christ. He will try to keep you away from every book, every sermon and every situation in which you might discover that although he is a cunning and tremendously influential foe, yet, because of what Jesus Christ did for us when He died on Calvary, he is a defeated foe. 'The reason the Son of God appeared was to destroy the devil's work' (1 John 3:8).

Now listen to me carefully and please do not misunderstand what I say. If you could only see the power that is available to you in Jesus Christ and would reach out to possess it then, instead of you being afraid of the devil, the devil would be afraid of you. Some Christians view the devil as great and powerful while they view God as relatively small and insignificant. If you want to see how much greater God and Christ are than the devil then consider the passage before us right now. Jesus seems to be saying, 'You wonder how I cast out devils? Well, such is the supremacy of My Father that I do not need to use God's arm, or even God's hand – I simply use His finger.' Praise God there is more power in God's little finger, so to speak, than in all the might and energy of Satan and his forces put together.

O God, as I prepare to go into battle against Satan and his forces, keep ever before me the thrilling truth that there is more power in one of Your fingers than in the whole of Satan's kingdom. This I ask in Jesus' name. Amen.

FURTHER STUDY
Exod. 8:1–19; Luke 10:17
1. How was Moses an extension of God's finger?
2. How much power do Christ's disciples have?

FOR READING & MEDITATION – LEVITICUS 20:1–8

'Keep my decrees and follow them. I am the Lord, who makes you holy.' (v8)

We come now to the next of the Jehovah titles – Jehovah Qadesh. Although the words do not appear in this form in the translated Scriptures, the phrase 'I am the Lord, who makes you holy', as used in our text for today, is in Hebrew 'Jehovah Qadesh' and means 'The Lord who sanctifies'. Its appearance in the book of Leviticus is most appropriate. Indeed, all the revelations of a divine name or title occur at such strategic times and with such striking meaning that even the most casual observer cannot help but conclude that behind them there is a divine plan at work.

Genesis, the book of beginnings, reveals the beginning of sin. Exodus, the second book of the Bible, reveals the way by which sin can be redeemed through the shedding of blood. Leviticus, however, is the book of life and deals with the matter of how a people already redeemed should conduct their walk before God and their worship of Him. Leviticus could not be written until Exodus was completed, just as in Christian experience sanctification cannot be achieved until we have experienced the power of salvation.

The very first mention in the Bible of God sanctifying anything is in connection with the Sabbath day. 'God,' we are told, 'blessed the seventh day and made it holy, because on it he rested from all the work of creating that he had done' (Gen. 2:3). That day's rest, however, was broken by the entrance of man's sin into the universe. The word 'sanctify' does not appear again until Exodus 13:1–2, and, from here on, it is found over and over again in both Old and New Testament Scriptures. The word 'sanctify' means 'to set apart'. A holy God longs for holiness to be found in His people – in you and in me.

O God, I cannot walk in this light unless You take my hand. I realise that my likeness to You depends on how much I am willing to give myself to You. So here I am, Lord. Take me, cleanse me, and make me holy. In Jesus' name. Amen.

FURTHER STUDY

Exod. 31:12–17; Lev. 21:5–15
1. How were the Israelites set apart?
2. Why did priests have special rules?

FOR READING & MEDITATION – LEVITICUS 20:22–26

'You are to be holy to me because I, the Lord, am holy...' (v26)

Earlier in our studies we said that God's dealings with Israel in Old Testament times typify the way in which He works with His Church in New Testament times. Once the Israelites had been delivered from Egypt's bondage, God's next concern was that they should learn how to walk before Him in holiness. This concern for their moral and spiritual purity is seen in the fact that this title of God, Jehovah Qadesh, is repeated six times in the two chapters that follow its first appearance.

We must never forget that God desires our holiness today just as much as He did in Old Testament times. Sometimes I think we are in danger of overlooking this fact. At a time when things that once would have offended or upset us are ignored or even accepted, we must hold continually before us, as God's redeemed people, the truth that He requires us to walk in holiness before Him and to be not only His redeemed but also His sanctified people.

The word 'sanctification' means, as we said yesterday, to set something apart, and it is used in four ways in the Old Testament. In Genesis 2:3 it signifies *separation*. In Exodus 13:12 it means to dedicate something to God's use – *dedication*. In Exodus 19:10 it means to cleanse – *purification*. In Exodus 28:41 it means to use something – *ministration*. A Welsh preacher once defined sanctification as 'the action which God takes in order to make His people clean enough to be used by Him'. Perhaps one of the reasons why some of us are not being used by God to the extent that we should is that we have not taken steps to rid ourselves of uncleanness. God does not wait until we are sinless before He uses us but He does expect us to break with all known sin.

O God, forgive me if I hinder Your purposes by my lack of holiness. I come to You for cleansing – for deliverance from all uncleanness and sin. Make me pure, dear Lord. In Jesus' name. Amen.

FURTHER STUDY

Lev. 8:10–30; 1 Pet. 1:13–17; 2:11–12

1. What can we learn from Aaron's dedication?
2. How can we be separate yet lead others to Christ?

'You Clean It – I'll Use It'

FOR READING & MEDITATION – JOHN 17:13–23

'Sanctify them by the truth; your word is truth.' (v17)

Today we continue discussing this important subject of sanctification. Yesterday we were introduced to a definition of sanctification given by a Welsh preacher, who said that it is 'the action which God takes in order to make His people clean enough to be used by Him'.

A certain group of Christian young people I knew became concerned about the souls of the other young people in their community, and arranged the screening of a series of evangelistic films in their church. As they met together for prayer before the showings, one of the group became deeply concerned about the need to clear the unused gallery of junk so that more adequate seating could be provided. When he expressed this concern to the rest of the group they said, 'But we haven't used the gallery for years. Even when the church was at its best the gallery was never used. Let's not waste our time on something that will not be needed.' They continued to pray, but as they did God seemed to speak to them individually regarding the need to clean out the gallery and prepare it for use. The Spirit appeared to be saying, 'You clean it – I'll use it.' So they decided to spend a whole Saturday cleaning, painting, and preparing the gallery for occupation. They threw away clutter, repaired the cracks in the seating and made sure it was in tip-top condition.

On the first night of the evangelistic film showings they held their breath as they saw the church fill up; first the ground floor and then the gallery! Many turned to Christ that night and, as they watched a number come down from the gallery and walk forward in an act of commitment, they remembered the Spirit's instruction: 'You clean it – I'll use it!'

O Father, at one stroke You break down the barriers between me and Yourself. And You do so out of love. I confess my need of inner cleansing. Please cleanse me so that I can be fully used. In Jesus' name. Amen.

FURTHER STUDY

Ps. 119:9–11; 2 Cor. 6:14–7:1; 2 Tim. 2:19–22
1. What part does God take in our sanctification?
2. What part do we take?

An Act or a Process?

FOR READING & MEDITATION – EPHESIANS 5:15–27

'Christ loved the church and gave himself up for her
to make her holy...' (vv25–26)

Now we come to the real heart of this matter of sanctification and ask: Is sanctification instantaneous or is it a process? There are those who say God sanctifies in a single act, and those who say that sanctification is a process that goes on in our lives day by day. In many ways both views are correct. Day by day, as we open our lives to the gentle, convicting power of the Holy Spirit, He points out our wrong attitudes or wrong behaviour and, as we respond, He applies His cleansing and sanctifying power to our hearts. This is the process of sanctification.

Without laying aside the necessity of a daily sanctifying process, it is also true that sanctification can be linked, for some, to a definite moment in time. Commissioner S.L. Brengle of the Salvation Army, speaking of the great experience when, as he put it, 'God sanctified my soul', said, 'On January 9th, 1895, at about nine o'clock in the morning, God sanctified me. He gave me such a blessing as I never dreamed a man could have this side of heaven.' As one reads the biographies of great Christian men and women one finds that many, such as John Wesley, Hudson Taylor and Frances Ridley Havergal, testified to receiving sanctification as a gift from God.

However we view the matter, one thing is sure: God wants us to be clean, pure, and holy. Christ is waiting to deliver us from inbred evil, the stubbornness of self-will, and the self-centred attitudes that leave a dark stain upon our spirits. Let us invite Him to cleanse our inner being from every sin and stain. 'God paints in many colours,' says Gilbert Chesterton, 'but He never paints so gorgeously as when He paints in white.'

Lord Jesus Christ, You purify me as I breathe the air of Your new creation. But I want not just to be cleansed but to be kept clean. Help me, Lord. In Jesus' name. Amen.

FURTHER STUDY
John 13:5–10; 15:3; 1 Thess. 4:1–7; 1 John 5:6
1. What parts do blood and water play in holiness?
2. Define holiness.

Jehovah Shalom

FOR READING & MEDITATION – JUDGES 6:11–24

'So Gideon built an altar to the Lord there and called it
The Lord is Peace.' (v24)

The next divine title we find as we make our way through the Old Testament is Jehovah Shalom, which means 'The Lord is Peace'. It was now more than a hundred years since God had revealed Himself to His people as Jehovah Qadesh. Joshua had long since died. The land of Canaan had been conquered and divided among the tribes of Israel but, nevertheless, it was a period when 'everyone did as he saw fit' (Judg. 21:25).

After Joshua's death, the people had forgotten all about the miraculous deliverance from slavery in Egypt, the supernatural experiences in the wilderness and their providential entry into the promised land. Now they were worshipping the gods of the nations that surrounded them. In this way Israel lost its power, its purity and its peace.

At this time of great need the angel of the Lord appeared to a man named Gideon and outlined to him God's plan for the deliverance of His people. Gideon, encouraged by this revelation, then built an altar and called it 'Jehovah is Peace'. As in the book of Leviticus God was appropriately seen to be 'The Lord who sanctifies', so in this turbulent period of Israel's history, as depicted in the book of Judges, God reveals Himself as the 'God of peace'. After the conquest of the land of Canaan the Israelites should have entered into a period of rest but instead they experienced a great deal of restlessness. And why? Because they failed to appropriate God's promises of security and relied on their own energy and understanding.

Perhaps right now you, too, are restless, nervous, apprehensive, and full of fear. Take heart. The God of this majestic creation is also Jehovah Shalom – the God of peace.

O God, how glad I am that in the hour of my deepest need You find a way to speak directly to my heart. You are truly Jehovah Shalom. You are my peace. And I am so thankful. Amen.

FURTHER STUDY
Ps. 119:165; Rom. 16:20; 2 Cor. 13:11–14
1. How can we know God's peace?
2. Define peace.

Peace of Mind

FOR READING & MEDITATION – PHILIPPIANS 4:1–13

'And the peace of God, which transcends all understanding,
will guard your hearts and your minds in Christ Jesus.' (v7)

We continue meditating on the fact that God reveals Himself through His names and that these names – Elohim, El Shaddai, Jehovah Jireh, Jehovah Rophe, Jehovah Nissi, Jehovah Qadesh – reveal some different facet of His character. At the moment we are considering the occasion when, during a period of Israel's history in which there was great restlessness and fear, God appeared to one of His discouraged servants, Gideon, as the One who dispenses perfect peace.

Before we look further into this matter of peace, let us get one thing straight; it is important to settle whether we are looking for perfect peace or just rest. More and more in these troubled days people are looking to various religious rituals as a means of obtaining peace of mind. In fact, the very phrase 'peace of mind' reveals the flaw in that kind of thinking. You cannot have peace of mind until you have something deeper than peace of mind. When you have peace in the depths of your spirit then peace of mind is an outcome of that deeper peace. In other words, you cannot experience the peace *of* God until you have experienced peace *with* God. No one can experience real peace if there is a conflict in the spirit. We must first experience the joy of sins forgiven and then, and only then, can we know the peace that Paul, in today's text, describes as 'the peace... which transcends all understanding'. And, for that matter, all misunderstanding also.

Those who attempt to find peace by different techniques of mental adjustment are doomed to disappointment. As a result of these techniques they may experience a little peace of mind. But it will not last. A crisis quickly dispels it.

O Father, help me to experience, day by day, the peace that transcends all understanding – peace that I do not merely possess but a peace that possesses me. In Jesus' name I ask it. Amen.

FURTHER STUDY

Isa. 26:1–4; 27:5; Rom. 5:1–2

1. How do we experience the peace of God?
2. How do we experience peace with God?

Lift the Latch

FOR READING & MEDITATION – JOHN 14:25–31

'Peace I leave with you; my peace I give you. I do
not give to you as the world gives.' (v27)

At present we are studying the difference between perfect peace, the peace that comes from God, and imperfect peace, the peace that comes from mental tricks. Any peace resulting from mental exercises will inevitably let you down. The peace that comes from God, however, holds up because it has the God of the universe behind it. It is unshakable peace. It is the kind of peace of which Jesus spoke in the text before us today: 'Peace I leave to you, my peace I give to you; I give it not as the world gives its "Peace!" Let not your hearts be disquieted or timid' (Moffatt).

Some years ago at one of the seminars held at Waverley Abbey, I met a man who was in a wheelchair. When I asked him how long he had been unable to walk he replied, 'Ever since I was a boy of fifteen years.' Sensing that he felt no bitterness about his condition I asked him what was the first thing he would do when he got to heaven. He responded, 'Well, after gazing at the face of Jesus for the first few billion years, I am then going to run all over God's heaven.' This was peace, perfect peace, in the face of trials, troubles, and difficult life circumstances. Calmly this man looked out at life and said, 'Do your worst or your best. Inside I have peace, perfect peace, sufficient peace to deal with anything that comes.'

God's peace can stand anything that challenges it. Since it is possible in this restless age to experience the peace of God, do not let anything prevent you allowing peace to invade you. Peace is knocking at the door. Lift the latch and let it come in. Make it your life affirmation to say: the peace of God helps me; the peace of God holds me; the peace of God protects me.

O God, help me to live in You, to abide in You, for I know that when I am in You and You are in me then I can meet anything that comes. For this I am so grateful. Amen.

FURTHER STUDY

Mark 5:1–15; John 14:1; Acts 10:36

1. Contrast how Jesus and others tried to bring the man peace.
2. How does Jesus' peace differ from the world's peace?

His Rest

FOR READING & MEDITATION – COLOSSIANS 3:12–25

'Let the peace of Christ rule in your hearts, since as
members of one body you were called to peace.' (v15)

Today we ask ourselves: Is God's peace an attainment – something we strive to achieve – or is it an obtainment – something He gives us as a free gift? I believe it to be an obtainment. This puts the latch low enough for it to be within the reach of the least and most humble.

One minister cried out to the Lord in an impetuous moment, 'Lord, I'd give my right arm to get this.' In response the Lord seemed to say, 'I don't want your right arm. Just give me your hand and I'll lead you into it – free.' The minister admitted that this revelation of God's willingness to lead him into something he genuinely longed to receive changed his whole perspective on life. From then on, he said, 'The universe became a place of open and infinite possibilities for my power to receive was infinite.' Remember that God's peace is obtained not by the shedding of your blood but by the shedding of His!

In the book of Hebrews there is a rest which is spoken of as 'his rest' (4:1). After the conquest of Canaan the Israelites should have entered into 'his rest' – a rest foreshadowing that referred to in Hebrews 4:1. But because of disobedience they failed to gain that rest. How sad it is that millions of Christians, who have been freed from bondage through the shed blood of God's Paschal Lamb, His Son Jesus Christ (see 1 Pet. 1:18–19), fail to enter into the rest provided for them by Jehovah Shalom. In Hebrews 4:4 this rest is spoken of as a Sabbath rest because the Sabbath was a day when work and struggle ceased; for us it is a day to accept the gifts of God, to be quiet and receptive. Don't struggle to gain peace by attainment; all you need to do is to empty your hands and take the gift.

O Father, You know how all my striving to gain peace leaves me utterly defeated and exhausted. Breathe upon me Your best gift – the gift of the Holy Spirit who provides me with adequate power and perfect peace. In Christ's name. Amen.

FURTHER STUDY

Matt. 11:28–30; Heb. 3:12–4:11

1. What are the conditions to know Jesus' peace?
2. What prevented the Israelites knowing God's rest?

Jehovah Rohe

FOR READING & MEDITATION – PSALM 23:1–6

'The Lord is my shepherd, I shall not be in want.' (v1)

Today we come to yet another name of God – Jehovah my Shepherd, or, as it is in Hebrew, Jehovah Rohe. Some commentators hold that it should not be included along with the other Jehovah titles that we are looking at because it is a metaphor, but it deserves our attention nevertheless. It is not an exaggeration to say that no description of Jehovah has brought more comfort to the heart or sounded sweeter to the ears of the saints of both Old and New Testaments than this beautiful expression. One writer says of it, 'The phrase, "the Lord is my shepherd", forms the mould into which the faith of countless saints has been poured.'

Before looking at the expression in more detail let us allow our gaze to sweep across the whole psalm, for we shall find in it a glorious summary of Jehovah's names and attributes. He is, of course, first Jehovah Rohe, the Good Shepherd. The words 'I shall not be in want' lead us to think of Him as Jehovah Jireh, the Lord who will provide. The second verse of this psalm is a perfect picture of Jehovah Shalom – the Lord who is peace. Then the words, 'He restores my soul' (v3) cause us to think of Jehovah Rophe, the Lord who heals. As He leads us in the paths of righteousness (v3) He becomes our Jehovah Tsidkenu, the Lord our Righteousness.

Even in 'the valley of the shadow of death' (v4) we are not alone for there He becomes Jehovah Shammah, the Lord who is always there. The preparation of the table (v5) indicates He is Jehovah Nissi, the Lord our Banner. And the anointing of our heads with oil (v5) reminds us that He is Jehovah Qadesh, the Lord who sanctifies. What a glorious gathering together of the mighty attributes of our God.

O Father, how can I sufficiently thank You for the revelation of Your love contained in this matchless psalm? At every level of my need You present some different facet of Your character. And for that I am eternally grateful. Amen.

FURTHER STUDY

Isa. 40:10–11; Ezek. 34:11–24

1. Why does God portray Himself as a shepherd?
2. What are the responsibilities of a shepherd?

The Good Shepherd

DEC

FOR READING & MEDITATION – PSALM 23:1–6

'Surely goodness and love will follow me all the days
of my life...' (v6)

It is right, I believe, to spend another day thinking about this deeply moving psalm. In the revelation of Himself as Jehovah Rohe, God is seeking to show us that everything a good shepherd is to his sheep God is to His people. We should keep in mind also that Jehovah Rohe is not only the shepherd of His people, He is *my* shepherd, the shepherd of each one of His people.

This psalm was written by David and has running through it the stamp of a mature faith. As David surveys his past life, he recalls his early experiences as a young shepherd boy in the hills around Bethlehem. Many times he had put his life on the line to rescue a sheep from a lion or a bear, and God had delivered him (see 1 Sam. 17:34–37). He appears to think also of the stormy, troubled years when he was outlawed and hunted as a fugitive by King Saul. As he reflects on the guiding hand of God in all his affairs, he can find no more beautiful and fitting analogy of Jehovah's relationship to himself than that of a shepherd to his sheep. No other name for God has such a tender and intimate tone as Jehovah Rohe. None of the titles we have dealt with so far can mean quite the same to His people as this precious name.

It is difficult for those of us who live in the West to understand the loving and tender relationship that an Eastern shepherd has with his sheep. Such a shepherd lives with his sheep night and day, cares for them as if they were his children, and calls each one of them by name. Again I say that everything a good shepherd is to his sheep Jehovah is to His people. If such a tender intimacy can exist between a shepherd and his sheep, how much more so between Jehovah and His redeemed children.

O God, You are the Good Shepherd, but more, You are my shepherd. Help me to live out this day and every day with confidence knowing that each step of the way Your guiding hand is over my life. In Jesus' name. Amen.

FURTHER STUDY

John 10:1–15, 27; 1 Pet. 2:25
1. Contrast a thief, hired hand, and good shepherd.
2. What is required of sheep?

Ways in Which God Guides

FOR READING & MEDITATION – PSALM 31:1–15

'Since you are my rock and my fortress, for the sake
of your name lead and guide me.' (v3)

We continue meditating on the fact that God is Jehovah Rohe – the Lord my Shepherd. This means that in the life of every one of us the Good Shepherd is guarding, guiding, and governing with the most tender and loving care. On their earthly pilgrimage God guides His sheep by suiting His guidance to their individual need. Sometimes He guides us through circumstances. Perhaps a door opens before us unexpectedly, and as we walk through it we find that this has been God's way of directing us. Or He may close a door in front of us, and the closure of that door proves to be His preventative guidance. But, remember, God shuts lesser doors so that He may open bigger ones.

Our Divine Shepherd guides us not only through circumstances but also through those with whom He brings us in contact. Way back in the 1960s an American evangelist telephoned me from a hotel in central London and said, 'I was in the airport in Tokyo about to get on a plane for the USA when God spoke to me and told me to come to London.' He went on to explain that he had a message for me from the Lord. The special message that this servant of God travelled so far to bring me had a great effect upon me and set my life in a completely new direction.

Another way in which the Good Shepherd guides us is through the group of believers with whom we have Christian fellowship. More and more I believe that God is speaking to this generation through groups. The play of mind upon mind, attitude upon attitude, method upon method, generates a body of ideas and conclusions that point the way into the future. The correction and support given by a fellowship helps to keep the individual from going astray.

O God, I thank You for those You have brought into my life who have helped me with a kindly word and their deep insight. May I this day be the agent of Your mind to some other person. In Jesus' name. Amen.

FURTHER STUDY

Gen. 24:1–4,10–27; Acts 13:1–4
1. How did God guide Abraham's servant?
2. How did God guide Paul?

FOR READING & MEDITATION – PSALM 25:1–14

'He guides the humble in what is right and teaches them
his way.' (v9)

At present we are looking at ways in which our Good Shepherd guides His sheep. So far we have seen that He guides through circumstances, through other individuals, and through the group of believers with whom we have close Christian fellowship. God guides also through our own spiritually developed reason and discernment. Any scheme of guidance that neglects the mind is not helpful. God wants us to love Him with the whole of our being – including the mind. Guidance will flow into our mental processes if we are inwardly honest with ourselves and accept all the facts, and He will enable us to think things through to the right conclusions without overriding our personalities. He guides, remember, not overrides.

Another way God guides us is through the inner witness of His Spirit to our hearts. Some call it the 'Inner Voice'. For instance, Peter heard it when the Spirit said to him, 'Simon, three men are looking for you. So get up and go downstairs. Do not hesitate to go with them' (Acts 10:19–20). Sometimes we need a special word for a special situation. Then the Inner Voice speaks. And when God speaks, believe me, you will know it, for the message is self-authenticating.

Finally, however, we must always remember that God's chief way of directing us is through the Scriptures. In fact, all guidance, however it comes, must be checked against the Bible. Jesus said, 'You are in error because you do not know the Scriptures' (Matt. 22:29). The way to keep from erring is to know the Scriptures. If you ever receive any 'guidance' that is contrary to the Scriptures then think again because God never guides in opposition to His Word. Somewhere you have got your wires crossed.

O God, You who guide me in so many loving ways, help me to check everything against the Scriptures. Then, and only then, can I be sure that my guidance is truly from You. Amen.

FURTHER STUDY

Acts 9:10–17; 15:5–20
1. How did the Spirit guide the Early Church?
2. How did Scripture and reason guide the Early Church?

FOR READING & MEDITATION – ISAIAH 6:1–13

'In the year that King Uzziah died, I saw the Lord
seated on a throne, high and exalted...' (v1)

Over the next few days we shall divert our attention from the Jehovah titles and instead examine another name for God – Adonai. The Hebrew name Adonai is translated in the New International Version as 'Lord', using only an initial capital letter, the rest being in lower case letters. This is to distinguish it, as we said earlier, (see 6 Nov), from the Hebrew name 'Jehovah', which is also translated 'Lord' but using an initial capital and small capitals – 'Lord' (see Gen. 2:7). Although the first appearance of this word Adonai is used in connection with the patriarch Abraham, when he pleaded with God to spare Sodom (see Gen. 18:27), I have not dealt with it before as I consider its meaning comes over with fuller force when seen in the context of the beautiful and moving chapter we have just read – Isaiah 6.

The literal meaning of Adonai is 'Lord and Master', and the word contains the thought of ownership, lordship, and divine authority. Following the death of the godly King Uzziah in 740 BC after a long and prosperous reign, a period of national darkness settled upon Judah. In the midst of the crisis, however, Isaiah is given a vision of an eternal throne on which sits the Lord and Master of the universe. It is as if the Almighty is saying, 'The throne of Judah may be empty and its occupant dead but such is the nature of Adonai's throne that it is never unoccupied and never unattended.'

From this vision of the holy, sovereign God who rules from His throne in heaven, Isaiah draws a good deal of comfort and courage, and moves forward into a powerful, prophetic ministry. How true it is that sometimes we do not see God as Adonai until an earthly power has let us down.

O God my Father, I see more clearly every day that my only true security is found in You. Help me to say, as did the psalmist, 'I seek you with all my heart; do not let me stray from your commands' (Ps. 119:10). Amen.

FURTHER STUDY

Isa. 33:17–24; Heb. 12:1–4

1. How do we change when we see God?
2. Where should we focus our attention?

The Everlasting Arms

FOR READING & MEDITATION – DEUTERONOMY 33:20–29

'The eternal God is your refuge, and underneath are the everlasting arms.' (v27)

It is necessary for us to spend another day examining in more detail the statement made by Isaiah: 'In the year that King Uzziah died, I saw the Lord' (Isa. 6:1). Was the fact that Isaiah's vision occurred soon after Uzziah's death a mere coincidence? I think not. Some commentators believe that Isaiah, along with many others in Judah at that time, had unconsciously allowed his hopes and expectations to become so entwined around the godly King Uzziah that when he was removed those hopes toppled and his expectations died. If this is true then it is reasonable to assume that God could not appear to Isaiah until first the object on which his hopes and expectations were pinned had been removed. Perhaps it was not until he came to recognise the impotence of the one who lay in a tomb that he was prepared to lift his eyes to gaze at the One who sits on the eternal throne.

I wonder, am I talking to someone today who over the past few weeks and months has been experiencing a removal of the props that support their life? Perhaps you can no longer depend on the situations, circumstances, and people you have relied on in the past; the things you have stood on for many years have been removed. Inside you are deeply hurt and from within your soul comes the cry, 'Why is God doing this to me? Does He no longer care? Is He indifferent to my great needs?'

No, my dear friend, God is not indifferent to your needs. Sometimes, though, it's when the props fall away from under our feet that we then rest our weight fully upon Him. We may need to be willing to see our earthly securities buried before we can see the glory of the heavenly King who sits upon the throne.

O God, I see so clearly now that You allow the support to give way beneath my feet in order that I might know the greater security of Your everlasting arms. Thank You for this revelation. In Jesus' name. Amen.

FURTHER STUDY
Ps. 71:1–3; 91:1–16
1. Why can we stand firm in trouble?
2. How can we 'dwell in the shelter of the Most High'?

Let Us Be Grateful

FOR READING & MEDITATION – ISAIAH 12:1–6

'Surely God is my salvation; I will trust and not be afraid.' (v2)

We are acknowledging that when we lose the things we have depended on and which have acted as props under our feet, we then truly discover that God alone is our true security – one that is sure and certain. Apart from Him all other securities have upon them the stamp of death and decay. If we do not learn this lesson, and learn it soon, then life will be filled with many dampening disappointments.

Some time ago when the world's news headlines carried reports of an oil crisis, I turned to my Bible to see what God had to say to me. I came across some words that have become exceedingly precious to me over the past few years: 'Since we are receiving a kingdom that cannot be shaken, let us be thankful... ' (Heb. 12:28). The message seemed so personal, so appropriate, and so to the point.

All around us at the moment there is a great shaking of earthly values and earthly kingdoms. This is the time, I believe, that God wants us to look up and see that He is still Adonai – the Lord of the universe and Master of every situation. He is allowing kingdoms to be shaken so that men and women might discover the one kingdom that is unshakable – the kingdom of our God and of His Son, the Lord Jesus Christ. The kingdom of materialism is shakeable. To survive it has to be held together by force. Relax the force and, as we have seen, it goes to pieces. The kingdom of finances is shakeable. The stock market goes up and down with the events of the day. The kingdom of health is shakeable. The doctor announces, 'You've got an incurable illness.' Shakeable. But in a world of flux and change, be assured of this: God is an unchanging Person and dwells in an unshakeable kingdom.

O Father, what comfort it gives me to realise that I belong to an unchanging Person and an unshakeable kingdom. And for that reason passing events cannot shake me. I am eternally grateful. Amen.

FURTHER STUDY
Matt. 7:24–27; Heb. 12:25–29
1. How can we become unshakeable people?
2. Why does God allow us to be shaken?

In This Year

FOR READING & MEDITATION – ISAIAH 43:8–21

'See, I am doing a new thing! Now it springs up; do you not perceive it?' (v19)

The thought we have been focusing on over the past few days has been this: sometimes God allows the props beneath our feet to fall away in order that we rest our full weight upon Him and depend on Him rather than earthly securities. This is as true for nations as it is for individuals. Today we are in the midst of a great shaking ideologically and outwardly – perhaps the greatest shaking our planet has ever seen. Someone has called it 'the great cosmic sifting hour'. Every alternative to God's programme for the world is failing and breaking down. Materialism is failing. Humanism and political ideologies are failing. Capitalism is failing. Democracy is failing. Where is all this leading us?

It is my conviction that what is shakeable will crumble to dust and the one thing that will survive the ages is the everlasting kingdom of our Lord and our God. Believe me, the day is coming when wealth and material things will become meaningless. Earth's inhabitants will begin to see that their one and only hope is in Adonai – the Lord of glory and the Master of every situation.

Taking a more personal perspective for a moment, I wonder, as you look back over the past twelve months, what kind of a year it has been for you. Has there been an upheaval resulting in the loss of many of the things on which your security was based? Have you experienced, as Isaiah did, an end to your hopes, your expectations, and your ambitions? Then take heart, for a new vision of God is about to break upon you. You will be able to say, as did the great prophet, 'In the year that my hopes vanished, my security was destroyed and my expectations came to nothing, in that year... *I saw the Lord*'' (Isa. 6:1).

O God, I know You allow nothing to happen to me unless it accords with Your perfect purpose. Help me, before this year ends, to see a new vision of Yourself – a vision that will send me singing into the future. This I ask in Christ's name. Amen.

FURTHER STUDY
Ezek. 36:25–27; Lam. 3:17–26
1. How did the prophet find new hope?
2. What new thing has God promised?

Jehovah Tsidkenu

FOR READING & MEDITATION – JEREMIAH 23:1–8

'This is the name by which he will be called:
The Lord Our Righteousness.' (v6)

Having spent the past few days looking at the title Adonai, we now continue examining the Jehovah titles, and today we come to the penultimate of these – Jehovah Tsidkenu. This title is revealed for the first time in one of Jeremiah's stirring prophecies – a prophecy given when the kingdom of Judah was hastening towards its conquest by the Babylonians and the exile of its people. Conditions in Judah had reached an all-time low – morally, materially, and spiritually. Forsaking Jehovah Shalom (the Lord is Peace), the nation was torn by dissension and internal strife.

Against this background the word of Jeremiah comes with a strong message of hope. He foresees a time when the people would no longer struggle to find God under leaders and shepherds who hardly knew Him themselves and who failed to care for those entrusted to them. Instead they would be visited by none other than the Messiah Himself. Here, amid this dark, sombre setting of Judah's sin and failure, a new name for God shines out: Jehovah Tsidkenu – the Lord our Righteousness.

The word *tsidkenu* is derived from the Hebrew word *tsedek*, which means 'to be straight', and there is no more significant word in the whole of the Old Testament. Pious Jews wanted more than anything to be righteous, but their righteousness often turned into self-righteousness; the Pharisee was the end product. The righteousness of the Jews destroyed itself because it became a legal righteousness intent on obeying laws instead of a life righteousness eagerly obeying principles. The promise is given, however, that One will come who will make men and women righteous according to His righteousness – a righteousness that blends with life.

O God, save me from the righteousness of the Pharisees that is nothing more than legal enslavement. Give me, I pray, the righteousness that follows Your own life principles. For Jesus' sake. Amen.

FURTHER STUDY
Heb. 2:9–18; 4:14–15; 1 John 2:1–2
1. How can righteousness blend with life?
2. What did John reveal about Jesus?

God's Handwriting

FOR READING & MEDITATION – EXODUS 20:1–17; 31:18

'When the Lord finished speaking to Moses on Mount Sinai, he gave him... the tablets of stone inscribed by the finger of God.' (31:18)

We continue meditating on the fact that God is righteous. Throughout the Old Testament, both by implication and by direct statement, God is portrayed as being righteous in all His ways. Today we turn our attention to the righteousness that underlies God's own handwriting.

As you are no doubt aware, there are two different times in the Old Testament when mention is made of God's handwriting. The first time God wrote to men and women was when He wrote the Ten Commandments on the top of Mount Sinai. Then, as our text for today tells us, God inscribed with His own finger the words of the Ten Commandments on tablets of solid stone.

Graphologists claim it is possible to determine something of a person's character by studying their handwriting. If it is small and cramped, so they say, the person is probably shy and nervous. If it is large and showy the person is likely to exhibit a degree of conceit, perhaps even arrogance. It is impossible for us to know what God's handwriting looked like because it has long since disappeared. In fact, Moses shattered the first pair of stone tablets when he saw the Israelites worshipping the golden calf made by Aaron (Exod. 32:19), and God rewrote the words (Exod. 34:28). But even though we cannot see the style of God's handwriting, what He wrote reveals His character in the clearest of ways. His writing at Sinai says this: God is holy.

Other nations knew that God was powerful. They saw Him in the thunder and in the lightning and concluded that He was the personification of powerful unseen forces. But it was the Hebrews who grasped the sublime truth that the greatest thing about God is not His might but His moral character.

O God, since the greatest thing about You is Your moral character, may I possess this same quality, too. In Jesus' name I ask it. Amen.

FURTHER STUDY

Deut. 6:20–25; John 8:1–11

1. How do the commandments reveal God's righteousness?
2. What happened when Jesus wrote?

Belshazzar's Feast

FOR READING & MEDITATION – DANIEL 5:1–9

'Suddenly the fingers of a human hand appeared
and wrote on the plaster of the wall...' (v5)

Yesterday we examined the writing of God as seen in the giving of the Ten Commandments and concluded that if God's penmanship reveals His personality then He is indeed a holy God. Today we examine the second occasion recorded in the Old Testament when God communicated with mankind in His own handwriting.

The time is 539 BC, and the Jews are still in exile in Babylon. Ungodly King Belshazzar, ruler of Babylon, decides to hold a magnificent banquet to which he invites a thousand of his nobles. During the banquet the king orders the gold and silver goblets which had been taken from the Temple in Jerusalem to be brought to the banqueting hall so that, in the words of Scripture, 'the king and his nobles, his wives and his concubines might drink from them' (v2). As the king and his guests drink from the sacred vessels and praise 'the gods of gold and silver, of bronze, iron, wood and stone' (v4), suddenly there appears 'near the lampstand' the fingers of a hand writing upon the wall. The message cannot be understood but Daniel, one of God's servants, interprets it as meaning, 'You have been weighed on the scales and found wanting' (v27).

Once again the truth comes over clearly in the handwriting on Belshazzar's palace wall – God is righteous. Now if God is righteous it follows that those who approach Him and seek to gain His favour must themselves become righteous. Yet how can human beings, tainted as they are by sin, obtain a righteousness that will satisfy the demands of a holy God? It is precisely at this point that Jeremiah's promise, which we discussed two days ago, brings a ray of hope. The righteousness He demands of us He, Himself, provides. Hallelujah!

O God, without the righteousness that comes to me through Jesus, Your Son, I would be filled with a nameless dread. But as Your Son has made me free I am indeed free. Thank You, Father. Amen.

FURTHER STUDY

Isa. 64:6; Gal. 3:10–14,19–29
1. Compare God's righteousness with our own.
2. How can we obtain righteousness?

God Obeys His Own Laws

FOR READING & MEDITATION – JEREMIAH 33:15–26

'In those days Judah will be saved... This is the name by which it will be called: The Lord Our Righteousness.' (v16)

Over the past three days we have been thinking about Jehovah Tsidkenu – the Lord our Righteousness – and seeing that God's righteousness is an essential part of His character. This means that morality is rooted not in the will of God but in the nature of God. Many people think that God arbitrarily decides certain things to be right and certain things to be wrong, and issues commands accordingly. They argue that since God's commands are based on His arbitrary will they are not to be questioned but simply obeyed. This, however, is not the Christian position.

In giving the promise of One who would come whose righteousness would cover the nakedness of the human condition, God does everything that He commands us to do. He obeys His own laws of right and wrong. He commands us to obey them because He Himself does so – obeys them because they are inherently right. The Almighty is not a cosmic signpost pointing the way; He is a shepherd who goes before His sheep and leads them. He initiates nothing that He does not illustrate.

When, in the winter of 1776, General George Washington found that his troops at Trenton had no shelter except cold tents, he made the decision to join his men and live in the same condition as his soldiers. No wonder they loved and followed a man like that. You and I could not be followers of an immoral God. As I read Jeremiah's promise, first given in 23:6 and repeated in today's text, of a Messiah who will come and wear my flesh, measure its frailty and provide me with a righteousness that will satisfy the highest demands of a holy God then I simply run out of words. That kind of God has my wholehearted allegiance and gratitude for ever.

O Father, what delight it gives me as I look into the face of Jesus to see there a consistent God. Since morality is rooted in You it shall be rooted in me. Amen.

FURTHER STUDY

Matt. 3:15; 1 Cor. 1:30; 2 Cor. 5:17–21

1. How and why did Jesus fulfil all righteousness?
2. What was the result?

FOR READING & MEDITATION – EZEKIEL 48:30–35

'And the name of the city from that time on will be:
the Lord is there.' (v35)

Now we reach the last of the Jehovah titles – Jehovah Shammah – which means 'The Lord is there'. As we study the context in which this name of God is revealed, we will discover that it is a most fitting name with which to conclude the Old Testament revelation of God.

It is not without some significance that the name Jehovah Shammah is found in the last verse of the last chapter of the book of Ezekiel. Ezekiel was called to be a prophet at a time when the people of Israel, in captivity in Babylon, were at their lowest ebb (Ezek. 1:2–3), and he prophesied in Babylon for at least another twenty-two years (Ezek. 29:17). The sun of Israel's strength had long since set and the night was closing in. Israel's spirit was broken. It appeared to the Israelites that they had been delivered from bondage in Egypt only to be sent into captivity in Babylon. By the rivers of Babylon, the psalmist tells us, the exiles sat and wept as they remembered Zion (Ps. 137:1). Now that enthusiasm for Zion was beginning to wane.

At this point God breaks into the situation and, speaking through His prophet Ezekiel, He assures the exiled Jews that a day will come when the full glory of Israel will be revealed. The nation would experience a revival and a restoration in a measure far beyond anything it had experienced in the past or could have ever imagined. It is as if God is telling His people that whatever lay ahead of them, whatever circumstance or situation they would meet, they should never forget that the God who brought them out of Egypt is also Jehovah Shammah – always there. He would be with His people for ever.

Are you about to face a difficult day? Then take heart. Remember, the Lord will be there.

O God, how I praise You for the unutterable peace that possesses me when I realise that, no matter what lies ahead, You will always be there. Life's consequences are safe because You are safe. I am so thankful. Amen.

FURTHER STUDY
Gen. 28:10–17; Deut. 20:1–4
1. How aware are we of God's presence?
2. What happens when God is with us?

FOR READING & MEDITATION – ROMANS 8:31–39

'Neither the present nor the future... will be able to separate us from the love of God that is in Christ Jesus our Lord.' (vv38–39)

We continue considering the wonderful truth that no matter what may lie ahead of us in this life, God, by virtue of the fact that He is Jehovah Shammah, will always be there.

One of the most arresting reads of recent decades is a book written by the sociologist and futurologist Alvin Toffler, *Future Shock*, published in 1970. This book went on to become a bestseller. In it Toffler argued that changes take place so rapidly that it is psychologically difficult for people to adapt to them. He claimed that people in the new millennium would face what he called 'a collision with the future'. 'It is going to be impossible,' he said, 'for people to keep up with the incessant demand for change that characterises our time. For many the future will arrive too soon.' What implications does this have for us? Does it mean that 'the roaring current of change' that is continuing to gather speed in this new millennium will overturn such an institution as the Christian Church? Will this cultural shockwave push Christianity to one side? The answer is: No. Although society may undergo enormous change, Jesus remains 'the same yesterday and today and for ever' (Heb. 13:8).

An Athenian orator writing in the second century to the Emperor Hadrian said, 'These Christians who know and trust their God are prepared for anything that comes their way for they believe that no matter what happens to them in the future, their God will always be there.' Notice the words *their God will always be there*. What a thought with which to face the future! Followers of Jesus Christ in every age have clung to a simple truth that, though oft repeated, still carries a powerful message: we may not know what the future holds but we know who holds the future.

Gracious heavenly Father, I see that You are wanting to free me from the paralysis of wondering what tomorrow holds and to give me instead the power to live one day at a time. I take that power now – in and through Your precious name. Amen.

FURTHER STUDY

Ps. 139:1–18; Rom. 14:7–8
1. List the places where the Lord would be with the psalmist.
2. Why should Christians adapt more easily to change?

One Grain of Sand

FOR READING & MEDITATION – MATTHEW 6:24–34

'Therefore do not worry about tomorrow, for
tomorrow will worry about itself.' (v34)

Today we ask ourselves: How can the truth, revealed by the prophet Ezekiel, that God is Jehovah Shammah – the Lord who is there – be related to our daily living? All belief must affect our behaviour, so what practical application can we make of this? We need to see clearly that being concerned about what may happen tomorrow will make us unable to rise and meet today with confidence and joy. On one occasion a Christian said to me, 'I can get through today all right but what I am afraid of is that I will not be able to get through tomorrow.' All of us at some time or another feel like that.

In my teens I was extremely apprehensive of the days that lay ahead. But then a man took me aside and gave me this advice: 'Think of your life as an hour glass. There are thousands of grains of sand in the top of the glass and they all pass slowly and evenly through the narrow neck without impairing the glass in any way. Take life a grain at a time and let the grains pass through the day slowly and evenly. If you do not take them one at a time then you will impair your own physical and mental structure.' That guidance had a profound effect upon me and completely changed my life. And I have practised that simple philosophy ever since: 'One grain of sand at a time.'

If you are fettered by the fear of what will happen tomorrow and you are living on what someone termed 'a diet of fingernails rather than a diet of faith', then surrender tomorrow into the hands of Jehovah Shammah, the God who is there, and go out to live joyously, effectively, and abundantly today. And you will find that tomorrow will blossom with joy because you have lived – really lived – today.

Gracious God, my Jehovah Shammah, I commit into Your hands all my tomorrows. Let me live today a relaxed and eager life so that I can be alive to everything You want for me tomorrow and not be numbed by my fears or apprehension. Amen.

FURTHER STUDY
Luke 12:22–31; 1 Pet. 5:7
1. What is the Christian attitude to tomorrow's problems?
2. What should we do with all our problems?

What He Was He Is

FOR READING & MEDITATION – ISAIAH 43:1–7

'When you pass through the waters, I will be with
you... For I am the Lord, your God...' (vv2–3)

Yesterday we said that a Christian who fails to see that God is Jehovah Shammah, the God who is there, will tend to live on a 'diet of fingernails rather than a diet of faith'. Biting your nails because you are worried about tomorrow is not nourishing; it gets you into the raw. Sir William Osler, a great Canadian physician, said, 'The twenty-one words from Carlyle helped to free me from a life of continued worry.' And what were those words? Here they are: 'Our main business is not to see what lies dimly at a distance but to do what lies clearly at hand.' If you are to live today effectively then you must shut off the future as tightly as the past.

Some will object to this and say, 'But what about insurance? What about my old age?' There is nothing wrong with preparing for the future. By all means take thought for tomorrow – careful thought and careful planning. But there must be no anxiety concerning the future or else life will fall apart. The God who promised Ezekiel that the nation of Israel would be restored and revived – has He not kept His word? The Bible assures us over and over again that God keeps His promises. Joshua said of God's promises, 'You know with all your heart and soul that not one of all the good promises the Lord your God gave you has failed. Every promise has been fulfilled; not one has failed' (Josh. 23:14). God is always there – Jehovah Shammah – ready to fulfil His eternal promises.

If you are afraid of the future and wonder whether or not God will be there in the days, weeks, months, and years that lie ahead then take courage from the fact that what He is, He was, and what He was, He is, and what He was and is, He ever will be – world without end.

Gracious God and Father, burn upon my heart the fact that because You are Jehovah Shammah the future can hold no fear for me if we travel together. My hand is in Yours – now and for ever. Amen.

FURTHER STUDY
Deut. 31:1–8; Matt. 28:20; Heb. 13:5–8
1. Differentiate between careful thought and anxiety.
2. What is our confidence?

The Name of Jesus

FOR READING & MEDITATION – MATTHEW 1:18–25

'You are to give him the name Jesus, because he
will save his people from their sins.' (v21)

Having examined over the past seven weeks the revelation of God through His different names, it has become increasingly obvious that the divine titles, although giving us clear indications of His character and teaching us much about Him and His dealings with His people, fail to fully reveal God as He really is. Something more was needed for us to see right into the heart of the Deity.

What, then, was needed for a perfect revelation of God? A life had to come among us – a divine life – in order to put a new content into the words used to describe God, and illustrate them in ways that we cannot fail to understand. This is what happened in the incarnation. God came into the world in the Person of His Son, who took on a human life and proceeded to live out that life in a way that fully revealed His Father's heart.

Through an angel God made known to Joseph the fact that the name He had arranged for His Son to receive when He arrived here upon earth was 'Jesus'. The literal meaning of the name is 'Jehovah saves'. It gathers up in itself the attributes of God's character and presents them in a name that is at once warm, endearing, and human. Through the name 'Jesus' the character of God is presented in a way that does not overpower human thought. In the Old Testament men suffered from overstrain, trying to define God and describe the character of the Almighty. Even though the divine titles revealed Him to a certain extent, there were still dark shadows surrounding the face of the Deity. 'Jesus,' someone once remarked, 'puts a face on God.' He does, and when we look at God through Jesus we see Him not only as a great Creator, but more – a great Saviour.

Lord Jesus, how can I ever thank You sufficiently for putting a face on God and for showing me that the greatest characteristic of the Deity is not the power to create but the power to save? Praise be to Your name. Amen.

FURTHER STUDY
John 4:39–42; Acts 4:1–12
1. What does the name of Jesus reveal about God?
2. Why is the name of Jesus so important?

God As He Really Is

FOR READING & MEDITATION – JOHN 1:1–5

'In the beginning was the Word, and the Word was
with God, and the Word was God.' (v1)

The Old Testament revelation of God begins with words of great majesty and power: 'In the beginning God created the heavens and the earth' (Gen. 1:1). The New Testament revelation of God begins much more quietly: 'The Word became flesh and made his dwelling among us' (John 1:14). Professor William Barclay said of this verse, 'It might well be that this is the greatest verse in the whole New Testament.' Without the great fact of the incarnation we would still be left wondering what God is really like.

Why, we ask ourselves, does John refer to Jesus Christ as the *Word*? Well, words are the expression of a hidden thought. If you stood in front of an audience without saying a word but just hoping that the people present would get your thought instinctively then the issue would end in futility. Only as the hidden thought is put into word is the thought communicated. Those who say, 'I can know God intuitively in my heart without the necessity of knowing Christ', are deceiving themselves. If our heart becomes the medium of communication then, due to cross-currents of sin and self-centredness, it becomes a very unsafe vehicle for the revelation of God.

Down the ages God has revealed Himself in different ways. He has revealed Himself through nature (Acts 14:17; Rom. 1:19–20). But not perfectly. He has revealed Himself through prophets and teachers (2 Kings 17:13; Ps. 103:7). But not perfectly. In both cases the medium of revelation was imperfect. When He revealed Himself through His Son – 'the Word become flesh' – then for the first time God found a perfect vehicle of communication. In Jesus we see God as He really is.

O Father, I realise today that as I take hold of Your Word, I take hold of Your highest thought. And that highest thought is love. I am deeply thankful. Amen.

FURTHER STUDY

Ps. 19:1–4; Heb. 1:1–9; 1 John 1:1–4

1. Compare the ways God speaks for us.
2. How can we have complete joy?

He Made His Dwelling Among Us

FOR READING & MEDITATION – TITUS 2:1–15

'For the grace of God that brings salvation has appeared
to all men.' (v11)

Over the past two days we have been driven to the conclusion that the only way for God to fully reveal Himself was for the Word to become flesh. So the Scripture reads, 'The Word became flesh and made his dwelling among us. We have seen his glory, the glory of the One and Only, who came from the Father, full of grace and truth' (John 1:14).

Let us consider for a moment the words 'and made his dwelling among us'. This revelation of God was not like the momentary disclosures of the Old Testament, when God unfolded some facet of His character through a divine title or name. This was no sudden rift in the clouds that surrounded the Deity – a swift insight into what God is like, a fleeting vision. No. He made His dwelling among us! Some people wonder why it is that Jesus lived on the earth for the short span of thirty-three years only. Well, it was long enough for Him to reveal God's character in operation in the surroundings where your character and mine are developed.

I love the verse that says, 'Praise be to the Lord, the God of Israel, because he has come and has redeemed his people' (Luke 1:68). The only way God could redeem His people was to come to them. Did He choose to save us by sitting on a cloud and uttering commands or by picking us up and transferring us to heaven in the grip of celestial tongs, thus not soiling His fingers with the messy business of human living? No. Jesus made His dwelling among us – amid our poverty, our misery, our temptations, our problems, our choices, our opposition, and our disappointments. He lived among us, wore our flesh, felt our pains, and showed us by a sustained, day-by-day revelation what God is really like.

Gracious Saviour, You came to where I was in order to take me to where You are. You came to show life in the midst of life. And, now I know what life is like, I am set on fire to know more. Thank You, Lord Jesus. Amen.

FURTHER STUDY

Luke 4:2; 9:58; 22:61; John 4:6; Heb. 5:1–10

1. What common experiences did Jesus share with us?
2. Why did Jesus endure these experiences?

He Has Been Made Known

FOR READING & MEDITATION – JOHN 1:1–18

'God the One and Only, who is at the Father's
side, has made him known.' (v18)

Dr E. Stanley Jones, a famous missionary and evangelist, and a man to whom I owe so much, once said, 'Apart from Jesus we know little about God and what we do know is mostly wrong.' In other words, if we do not see God in the face of Jesus Christ, we just do not see Him. We may, of course, have a vague idea in our imagination of what He is like but that is only our idea of God – it is not what He is really like. The Word was made known in Old Testament days through words – a verbal revelation – but when the Word became flesh then the revelation was no longer verbal but vital. Jesus made God known in the only way He could be made known – by life.

Isn't this the point today's text is making? 'No-one has ever seen God, but God the One and Only, who is at the Father's side, has made him known.' The New King James Version says, 'The only begotten Son, who is in the bosom of the Father, He has declared Him.' But 'declared him' is not as powerful as 'has made him known'. You cannot describe God, or even define Him, but He can be shown. And Jesus did just that. He made Him known in the only way He can be known – by revealing His innermost character. What is the central thing about God? Is it not His character?

The words 'in the bosom of the Father' found in the New King James Version suggest that Jesus has made God's heart known to us. Jesus is not depicted here in the arms of the Father – that would reveal only His omnipotence. He is not spoken of as in the mind of the Father – that would reveal His omniscience. He is 'in the bosom of the Father' and, because of this, He is able to reveal the innermost heart of the Deity. And that heart is a heart of love.

O God, I am thankful that I find in You the love I so desperately need. I would never have found it unless I had been shown it – shown it in Your Son. In Him I see, not merely hear. And this seeing is believing. So I believe. Amen.

FURTHER STUDY

Luke 7:20–23; John 17:20–26
1. How did Jesus make God known?
2. To whom does Jesus make God known?

Father and Mother

FOR READING & MEDITATION – JOHN 1:6–14

'We have seen his glory, the glory of the One and Only, who came from the Father, full of grace and truth.' (v14)

Some years ago a theologian claimed that the revelation of God in Jesus Christ is partial and incomplete. He said, 'Jesus presented God as a Father but not as a Mother – therefore His unfolding of the Deity lacks universality.' What nonsense! When we examine the different characteristics of fatherly love and motherly love, we see that the two are blended together perfectly in Jesus Christ.

The nature of fatherly love is that it makes demands, establishes clear rules or laws, and takes a firm grip on the one it loves. Motherly love is somewhat different; at its highest level it is unconditional, nurturing, all-protective, and all-enveloping. Our text tells us that in Christ both of these are to be found. He is 'grace' and He is 'truth'. Grace is the motherly characteristic and truth is the fatherly characteristic. In Jesus, the Son, the motherly quality of grace and the fatherly quality of truth come together and are one. When He said, 'O Jerusalem, Jerusalem, you who kill the prophets and stone those sent to you, how often I have longed to gather your children together, as a hen gathers her chicks under her wings' (Matt. 23:37), that was the motherly side of God. When He continued, 'but you were not willing. Look, your house is left to you desolate' (Matt. 23:37–38), that was the fatherly side of God.

Love and law meet and combine perfectly in Christ for all love is law and all law is love. Our Lord is at one and the same time both tender and terrible, strict and saving, demanding and delivering. A careful examination of the nature of our Lord leads us to the firm conclusion that in the incarnate Son we see both the Fatherhood and the Motherhood of God.

O God my Father, as I look at You through Jesus, Your Son, I see You as strict yet saving, terrible yet tender, and I am grateful for both. Amen.

FURTHER STUDY

Matt. 21:12–14; Luke 7:36–50; Col. 1:19

1. How did Jesus show grace and truth?
2. Why can we be sure Jesus truly represented God?

FOR READING & MEDITATION – LUKE 2:1–17

'Today in the town of David a Saviour has been
born to you; he is Christ the Lord.' (v11)

Once again we come to Christmas Day – a day when we joyfully celebrate the coming of our Lord Jesus Christ to this earth. The message of Christmas is this: there is only one way that God can be found and that is through Jesus, the Babe of Bethlehem.

Some try to find God through nature – the nature worshippers. Some attempt to find Him within themselves – the 'ego' worshippers. Still others attempt to find Him through teachers and gurus – the men worshippers. But if you want to find God – to really find Him – then you must come face to face with His Son, Jesus Christ. Jesus is God approachable, God available, God lovable. A little boy, when asked what he was doing, answered, 'I'm drawing a picture of God.' 'But no one knows what God is like,' responded his mother. 'They will when I'm finished,' said the boy with an air of finality. All attempts to draw or tell what God is like are childish. Except one – the revelation made by Jesus. As we saw yesterday, 'No-one has ever seen God, but God the One and Only... has made him known' (John 1:18).

A woman I knew in Wales who had gone from one psychiatric unit to another, and had experienced several bouts of severe depression, stood one Christmas morning in a hospital ward and looked at the Nativity scene which had been created by the nurses. As she gazed at it the Holy Spirit spoke directly to her heart and brought home to her the real meaning of Christmas. Later she testified, 'I looked into the face of Jesus and I found a joy that cannot be put into words.' Today she is a radiant Christian and has led many others to know her Saviour. If you have never found God then you can do so today. Look into the face of Jesus and live.

Gracious God, just as I cannot say the word 'Christmas' without first saying 'Christ', so I accept that I cannot really understand any of the great words such as peace, love, and joy until I first spell out that name – Jesus' indefinably precious name. Amen.

FURTHER STUDY
John 3:13–18; 6:40
1. What did God reveal about Himself in Jesus?
2. What is the Father's will?

Jesus – The Only Way

FOR READING & MEDITATION – JOHN 14:1–14

'Jesus answered, "I am the way and the truth and the life.
No-one comes to the Father except through me."' (v6)

'Jesus,' said a well-known Bible commentator, 'is God's other name.' He meant, of course, that all the majesty, beauty and wonder of God's Person is caught up and focalised in His Son, Jesus Christ, so that when we gaze at Him we see what God is really like.

Apart from Jesus, 'the Word become flesh', people despair of finding reality. The search ends in disillusionment. There have been two great attempts to find God apart from Christ – they are the attempts of philosophy and moralising. The Greeks tried to find Him through philosophy and the Jews tried to find Him through moralism or through the law. Both failed in their quest. The Greeks produced the philosophers who declared that God was reality but that He could not be found by men. The Jews, in an attempt to find God through the law, produced the Pharisee who stood in his pride and said, 'God, I thank you that I am not like other men...' (Luke 18:11). Jesus pronounced His verdict on this attempt to find God when He said, 'I tell you that unless your righteousness surpasses that of the Pharisees and the teachers of the law, you will certainly not enter the kingdom of heaven' (Matt. 5:20). Neither the Greeks nor the Jews could gain entry into the kingdom of heaven by their own efforts.

Into a world troubled by these doubts and difficulties, Jesus came and announced, 'I am the way and the truth and the life. No-one comes to the Father except through me.' The philosophers and the moralists could not find the way for there is no way created by words. The only way is 'the Word become flesh'. A missionary being helped through the African bush by a local guide asked, 'Is this the way?' 'No,' replied the guide, 'I am the way.'

O Father, how simple and yet profound is the message of the gospel. I follow You as the way, the way directs me to the truth, and the truth leads to life – life eternal. Thank You, dear Lord. Amen.

FURTHER STUDY
Heb. 10:8–25; 1 John 2:6
1. How is Jesus the way for non-Christians?
2. How is Jesus the way for Christians?

I Am The Gate

FOR READING & MEDITATION – JOHN 10:1–14

'I am the gate; whoever enters through me will be saved.' (v9)

To understand the full significance of these words of Jesus we must cast our minds back to that famous incident in the Old Testament when God met with His servant Moses at the burning bush and called him to free His people from slavery in Egypt. In that encounter Moses asked God to reveal His name, and this He did. However, the name, when given, appeared to be vague and confusing. God said, 'I am who I am' (Exod. 3:14). The name seemed to go out like a boomerang and double back on itself: 'I am... who I am.' This great name of God never seemed to have a clear definition. The nearest we can get to interpreting it is in the words 'The ever-present One'.

Now, here in the passage before us today, we find Jesus taking that name of God, which seemed so nebulous, and linking it to simple objects such as a gate. 'I am the gate,' He says. It might not have been possible for the Old Testament saints to fully understand the meaning of the august title God revealed to Moses, 'I am who I am,' but now all that is changed. Jesus takes that vague name of God and gives it clear identity by stating that He is a 'gate', a 'shepherd', a 'light', and so forth. 'I am the good shepherd,' He says (v11). 'I am the light of the world' (8:12). 'I am the way and the truth and the life' (14:6).

Through Jesus the great name of God, 'I am,' no longer swings back upon itself but opens out into the most wonderful, the most exciting of all revelations – that He is the only way by which men and women can know and understand God. Christ took the most complicated name of God in the Old Testament and linked it to the most ordinary objects of life. And by so doing, He showed us what God is really like.

Lord Jesus Christ, You have clarified our understanding of God by taking His great name and linking it to objects that I can clearly comprehend. You are the Word for which I have always waited. I offer You all the gratitude and appreciation of my heart. Amen.

FURTHER STUDY
John 6:35; 9:5; 11:25; 15:1–7
1. List the 'I ams' of Christ.
2. How do these show what God is really like?

A Word Become Word

FOR READING & MEDITATION – 1 TIMOTHY 3:16–4:9

'He appeared in a body, was vindicated by the Spirit... was believed on in the world, was taken up in glory.' (3:16)

Dr E. Stanley Jones, the famous missionary to whom I referred earlier, recounts in one of his books his first experiences when confronted by the religions of the East. He tells of reading the Sermon on the Mount to a Muslim who listened intently and then commented, 'That is beautiful but we have something similar in the Qur'an.' Later he met a Hindu and read to him Jesus' teaching about turning the other cheek and going the second mile (Matt. 5:39–41). The Hindu responded, 'Our sacred books tell us that also. We are to be like the sandalwood tree which, when smitten by the axe, pours its perfume upon the axe that smites it.'

At this stage the missionary became somewhat non-plussed and wondered to himself, 'How can I demonstrate the uniqueness of the Christian faith?' The thought occurred to him that the Hindu would have nothing to compare in his religion with the story of the cross, so he read for him the account of the crucifixion. 'This, too, is beautiful,' said the Hindu. 'Again our sacred books tell us that our gods did not hesitate to sacrifice themselves for others.' Everything the missionary talked about had its parallel.

Then it dawned upon him that all that had been said by the Muslim and the Hindu was simply a word become word. The story of the sandalwood tree was an illustration, not an exhibition. The other stories, too, were illustrations, not reality. The difference between the Christian faith and other religions is that other religions are a word become word, whereas the Christian faith is a Word become flesh. This makes the Christian faith not just a little better than other faiths; it sets it on a level where no comparisons are possible.

Lord Jesus Christ, the fact that You became flesh astounds me. You have gone further than I dreamed possible. And now, because of that, I'm going further than I could ever have dreamed. Thank You, dear Lord. Amen.

FURTHER STUDY

Rom. 7:22–8:11; Gal. 4:4–5
1. What are the words of the law unable to achieve?
2. Why is the Christian faith incomparable?

Not Just Better – Different

FOR READING & MEDITATION – PHILIPPIANS 2:1–11

'Who, being in very nature God... made himself nothing, taking the very nature of a servant, being made in human likeness.' (vv6–7)

During these last few days of the year we are meditating on the significance of the Word becoming flesh. Yesterday we saw how Dr E. Stanley Jones, when confronted by Eastern religions, came to the conclusion that the Christian faith is unique because it has at its heart the incarnation. In other religions it is always a matter of the word becoming word – a philosophy; in Jesus the Word became flesh – a fact. This is the touchstone by which all other religions should be evaluated.

In some of the liberal theological seminaries, during the study of comparative religions, students are shown the various parallels between the Christian faith and other faiths. Although the Christian faith is acknowledged to be a little higher than other religions, and possibly more moral, it is not presented as being unique. The result is that those who leave such places enter the Christian ministry with few or no convictions and nothing unique to preach. Many (not all) are preaching the Word become word – moralism – hence the barrenness in so many churches.

The Christian faith is not just better than every other faith – a little more moral, a little more lofty in its concepts – it is completely different. All other religions tell of man's search for God; Christianity tells of God's search for man – of the One who 'came to seek and to save what was lost' (Luke 19:10). This is why though there are many religions there is only one gospel. The world's religions tell of the word become word; the gospel is the Word become flesh. In the face of all rivals our gospel quietly affirms, 'The Word became flesh and made his dwelling among us. We have seen his glory...' (John 1:14).

O God my Father, my heart is filled with unutterable joy as I realise that my salvation came not because of my knocking on the door of heaven but because You knocked at the door of my heart. What grace. What humility. What love. Amen.

FURTHER STUDY

Mark 10:42–45; John 13:1–7; Gal. 6:2

1. How did Jesus make Himself nothing?
2. How can we follow His example?

Christ – The Perfect Revelation

FOR READING & MEDITATION – MATTHEW 13:1–17

'But blessed are your eyes because they see,
and your ears because they hear.' (v16)

For a further day we meditate on the reason why the divine Word had to become flesh and dwell among us. Suppose God had decided against an incarnation and instead had given us a book similar to the Bible as His highest revelation – what would be the result? We would attempt to read into those words our highest interpretation but nevertheless we would be greatly limited.

Take, for example, the word 'purity'. If I read into that word my highest experience of purity, which, because of sin and human failure, must be partial and incomplete, I would still emerge with an impoverished understanding of the word. But what if I can see that word exemplified in a divine illustration? Now the word 'purity' is elucidated by a Person who shares my temptations, minus my failures, and the word takes on a new and precise meaning.

The same would happen with other words. Take the word 'God'. Were it not for the incarnation I would interpret the word in the light of my imagination, but now, because Christ has come, I look up through Jesus, the Son of God, and I know without any shadow of doubt what God is like. The apostle Paul reminds us that Jesus 'is the image of the invisible God, the firstborn over all creation' (Col. 1:15). 'Jesus,' said a little boy, 'is the best photograph God ever took.' He is.

A lecturer in the Bible college I attended used to say something which startled me every time I heard it, until I pondered it and came to see that it was true. He said, 'If God isn't like Jesus I am not interested in Him.' But we need not worry – God is like Jesus. Our Saviour has confirmed it. 'Anyone who has seen me has seen the Father,' He assures us (John 14:9).

Blessed Jesus, I am so thankful to You for showing me the Father. I would never have known what He is like had I not looked into Your face. But seeing Him in Your face stirs me to be like You. Lord Jesus, You have my deepest gratitude. Amen.

FURTHER STUDY
Matt. 5:8; 2 Cor. 3:12–4:6
1. How might we see God?
2. What happens when we see the Lord?

His Name – Our Name

FOR READING & MEDITATION – REVELATION 22:1–7

'They will see his face, and his name will be on their foreheads.' (v4)

We come now to the last day of our studies on the theme of God's revelation of Himself through His names, and also to the last day of another year. What a tremendous note on which to end our studies: 'They will see his face, and his name will be on their foreheads.'

Over the last weeks we have seen how God's names reveal certain facets of His character, which are disclosed only when His people reach a significant new stage of development in their lives or enter an area of special need. God revealed Himself in the first verse of the Scriptures as Elohim – a name that is full of awe-inspiring majesty. Then, when He made man in His own image, He introduced Himself by a new name: Jehovah Elohim. This took some of the awesomeness out of the name of Elohim and gave a picture of a personal God who longed to link Himself with man. During Old Testament times God continued to reveal Himself through His various names until, of course, we come to the final unfolding of Himself through Jesus – the name by which we fully know God.

Now, as a climax to our theme, the Holy Spirit directs our attention in the last chapter of the Bible to a breathtaking and vibrant truth: *one day God's name is to become our name!* Just think of it. At this moment all the privileges of His name are ours – salvation, healing, cleansing, sanctification. But in eternity all these characteristics, instead of being available to us, will become an integral part of us because when we see God we shall be like Him (1 John 3:2). Then His virtue will become ours, His victory will become ours, His nature will become ours and, what is more, His name will become ours. For ever and ever. Amen.

O Father, this is more than I could ever dare hope for. To be given Your name in eternity and to carry it in my own personality is a truth that staggers my imagination. All I can say is thank You, Father. Thank You. Amen.

FURTHER STUDY

Exod. 28:36–38; Acts 11:26; Rev. 3:12; 14:1

1. Compare Aaron's forehead with the foreheads of Christians.
2. How do we bear Christ's new name now?